Hong Kong Cantopop

Hong Kong Cantopop

A Concise History

Yiu-Wai Chu

Hong Kong University Press
The University of Hong Kong
Pokfulam Road
Hong Kong
www.hkupress.org

© 2017 Hong Kong University Press

ISBN 978-988-8390-57-1 (*Hardback*)
ISBN 978-988-8390-58-8 (*Paperback*)

British Library Cataloguing-in-Publication Data
A catalogue record for this book is available from the British Library.

10 9 8 7 6 5 4 3 2 1

Printed and bound by Hang Tai Printing Co., Ltd. in Hong Kong, China

For Nancy, Sebastian, Nathaniel, and our beloved family members

Contents

Acknowledgments

If my life had a theme song, it would definitely be a Cantopop. I grew up listening to Cantopop, without which I cannot imagine how my life would have been like. Having witnessed and experienced the rise and decline of Cantopop in the past four decades or so, I feel obliged to do something for the genre that sings my joy and sorrow. Cantopop has long been marginalized in not only the academia in general but also popular music studies in particular. Over the past twenty years, numerous works on Cantopop, especially its lyrics, in Chinese have been published. In the English-speaking academic world, however, there are only academic essays scattered across journals in different fields. A comprehensive introduction to this distinctive voice of Hong Kong to the audience in the English-speaking world is still to be in order. I have been hoping that someone who is familiar with the different aspects of this genre would take up the task. Sadly, years after years the song remains unsung. Perhaps John Keats is right in the poetic world: "Heard melodies are sweet, but those unheard are sweeter." In reality, however, being unheard in the academic world would not do justice to such a unique melody. Without the generous support of many people, I could not make up my mind to take the liberty of writing this book. It is not possible to name them all, but I must express my sincere gratitude to Chi-Wah Wong—mentor, collaborator, and friend. I started reading his popular music columns when I was in high school. Thanks to his ground-breaking efforts over the years, Cantopop gradually developed into a topic that attracted attention in the cultural arena. My first research project on Cantopop lyrics could not have been completed without his selfless offering of guidance and reference materials. Throughout these years, he has been giving me untiring support. He also kindly lent me his chronology of major events in the Cantopop industry originally written in Chinese, on which I developed the appendix of this book. In preparing the manuscript, I have been greatly inspired by the helpful comments and suggestions of the anonymous reviewers.

My thanks also go to Chris Munn and Eric Mok; without their professional advice at various stages, this book would not have materialized. As always, I would conclude by recording my love for Nancy, Sebastian, Nathaniel, and our family members.

Yiu-Wai Chu
April, 2016
Hong Kong

A Note on Romanization

Chinese names are generally romanized according to the style commonly used in Hong Kong, with English first names followed by Chinese surname (e.g., James Wong). For the sake of consistency, those without English first names are also romanized in the same way (e.g., Chi-Wah Wong), except those commonly known by pinyin (such as Lin Xi) or internationally known by other formats (such as Tsui Hark).

1 | Introduction

"Every generation has its own voice," claimed James Wong 黃霑, the late god-father of Cantopop, in his doctoral thesis on the development of Cantopop.[1] The English term "Cantopop"—Cantonese popular songs—did not come into existence until the 1970s, when *Billboard* correspondent Hans Ebert used it "to describe the locally produced popular music in Hong Kong" in 1978.[2] Per James Wong's remark—which was adapted from the well-known saying of the Qing dynasty master of Chinese culture, Wang Guowei 王國維: "Every dynasty has its own representative form of literature"[3] —Cantopop is a musical form from and the voice of contemporary Hong Kong. As the saying of the legendary John Lennon goes, "music reflects the state that [a] society is in,"[4] so, hailed as an "outlier" in Hong Kong culture by James Wong, Cantopop witnessed and reflected the rise and decline of Hong Kong culture over the past fifty years. A unique genre, with lyrics written in standard modern Chinese

---

1. Jum-Sum Wong 黃湛森 (a.k.a. James Wong), "The Rise and Decline of Cantopop: A Study of Hong Kong Popular Music (1949–1997)" 〈粵語流行曲的發展與興衰：香港流行音樂研究 1949–1997〉 (in Chinese) (Hong Kong: PhD thesis, University of Hong Kong, 2003), 182. I would like to begin with a note about Chinese sources. I decided to cite a sizable number of Chinese publications on the topic throughout the book because most of them are very important materials not previously available in English, and thus I think it is essential to address them (I have reorganized them according to the emphases of different sections). For readers conversant with Chinese references, there may seem to be too many details. But since I hope that this book may be of interest to general readers who cannot read Chinese, it is necessary at times to offer an elaborated account of what may seem obvious to some. For this I would like to ask for the indulgence of all readers.
2. According to Joanna Lee, Ebert first coined the term "Cantorock" in 1974 in an essay in *Billboard*. However, as noted by Helan Yang 楊漢倫 and Siu-Wah Yu 余少華, the term cannot be found in any *Billboard* essays published in 1974. See Joanna C. Y. Lee, "Songs on Emigration from Hong Kong," *Yearbook for Traditional Music* 24 (1992): 14–23, and Helan Yang and Siu-Wah Yu, *Reading Cantonese Songs: The Voice of Hong Kong through Vicissitudes* 《粵語歌曲解讀：蛻變中的香港聲音》 (in Chinese) (Hong Kong: Infolink, 2013), 2.
3. Wang Guowei, "Preface," in *History of Drama during the Song and Yuan Dynasties* 《宋元戲曲史》 (in Chinese) (Taipei: Taiwan Commercial Press, 1964), page number missing.
4. Quoted from an interview with John Lennon in 1971. Available at: https://rhinospike.com/script_requests/j8lila/681/; retrieved on March 15, 2016.

but pronounced in Cantonese, Cantopop was once very popular not only in Hong Kong but also in neighboring regions.

Hong Kong was a British colony for 156 years before sovereignty over the territory was handed to China in 1997. In all colonies there are distinctly drawn social lines. In Hong Kong, the lower stratum of society was understandably composed of Chinese. According to John Carroll in his study of Hong Kong history, this is clearly reflected in government-enforced racial divides: "Despite their status and wealth, the members of the Chinese bourgeois, like all Chinese in Hong Kong, continued to face racial discrimination at every turn."[5] The racial and class divides in a society have profound impacts on the cultures of a colony. For instance, colonial culture defined the taste of Hong Kong; in other words, grassroots Chinese culture was inferior to British culture, which was considered classy by local Hong Kong people. As convincingly argued by the cultural sociologist Pierre Bourdieu, "systems of domination find expression in virtually all areas of cultural practice and symbolic exchange, including such things as preferences in dress, sports, food, music, literature, art, and so on, or, in a more general sense, in taste."[6] Since Cantonese was, and arguably still is, considered an inferior dialect that is not formal enough to be used in standard Chinese writing, Cantopop has long been considered nothing more than a grassroots pastime limited to the lower class of Hong Kong people. In other words, Cantonese, spoken by more than 90 percent of the population, "was and continues to be treated as an inferior or inauthentic version of Chinese."[7] Moreover,

> [t]o *write* in simple prose, the Hong Kong school-child must memorize not only the composition of the written characters (which exists in an order independent of speech), but also the way things are *said* in standard written Chinese (the grammar of which corresponds to speech in Mandarin/ Putonghua rather than to speech in Cantonese). (original emphases)[8]

When compared to English as the auxiliary "high" language, Cantopop served as an everyday "low" language in Hong Kong during its colonial years.[9] After its reversion to China the situation got worse; Cantonese became further marginalized, and now it is generally considered inferior to Putonghua. Despite this situation, language—that is, Cantonese—is considered one of the most

---

5. John Carroll, *A Concise History of Hong Kong* (Lanham: Rowman & Littlefield, 2007), 74.
6. Randal Johnson, "Editor's Introduction," in Pierre Bourdieu, *The Field of Cultural Production: Essays on Art and Literature* (New York: Columbia University Press, 1993), 2.
7. Rey Chow, *Not Like a Native Speaker: On Languaging as a Postcolonial Experience* (New York: Columbia University Press, 2014), 13.
8. Chow, *Not Like a Native Speaker*, 45.
9. Martha Pennington, *Forces Shaping a Dual Code Society: An Interpretive Review of the Literature on Language Use and Language Attitudes in Hong Kong* (Hong Kong: City Polytechnic of Hong Kong, 1994).

important markers of the Hong Kong identity.[10] Hong Kong musicians and lyricists have been successful in creatively developing Cantopop into a unique hybrid—Chinese and Western music styles with lyrics written in Cantonese and standard Chinese.[11] Cantopop has also given a style and an accompanying lifestyle to several generations of Hong Kong people.

"Popular music" is often believed to defy a precise definition, but according to Roy Shuker, various attempts at providing a definition can be identified, one of which is based on its commercial nature.[12] In this book I would follow his definition, equating it "with the main commercially produced and marketed musical genres."[13] While Shuker's emphasis is on traditional "rock" and "pop" forms, the latter has been playing a central role in the Hong Kong context. It is commonly believed in the popular music industry that "popular" has to be defined by sales and profits.[14] "Popular" may also mean "of or relating to the people." Richard Middleton has identified two definitional synthesis related to "popular music" in his *Studying Popular Music*: positivist and essentialist. In short, while the former measures "not 'popularity' but sales," the latter places an emphasis on "quality" rather than "quantity"—either the organizing principle as "manipulation" and "standardization" from above or "authenticity," "spontaneity," and "grassroots" from below.[15] As Tony Bennett put it,

> "the people" refers neither to everyone nor to a single group within society but to a variety of social groups which, although differing from one another in other respects (their class position or the particular struggles

---

10. According to Gordon Mathews, "[a]ffluence and the freedom that money can provide are one perceived mark of difference between Hong Kong and Chinese identities; another key marker is that of language . . . A third mark of Hong Kong identity . . . involves political ideals such as democracy, human rights, and the rule of law." Gordon Mathews, "Heunggongyahn: On the Past, Present, and Future of Hong Kong Identity," *Bulletin of Concerned Asian Scholars* 29, no. 3 (July–September 1997): 10–11.

11. Wong, "The Rise and Decline of Cantopop," 132–34.

12. Roy Shuker, *Popular Music: The Key Concepts*, second edition (London and New York: Routledge, 2005), 203–4; see also Roy Shuker, *Understanding Popular Music Culture*, third edition (London and New York: Routledge, 2008), 5–7.

13. Shuker, *Popular Music: The Key Concepts*, xiii.

14. Deanna Robinson et al., *Music at the Margins: Popular Music and Global Cultural Diversity* (Newbury Park, London, and Delhi: Sage, 1991), 10. It has to be noted that nonmainstream genres "can develop and become part of the musical 'mainstream', usually through 'crossing over into the pop and rock mainstream and charts." Shuker, *Understanding Popular Music Culture*, 128. It is noteworthy to mention Lawrence Grossberg's point here: "[T]oo much of cultural studies has continued to locate popular culture within two binary normative economies: on the one hand, the popular (as poaching, fragmented, contradictory, bodily, carnivalesque, pleasurable) versus the legitimate (as reified, hierarchical, intellectual, etc.), and on the other hand, the popular (as stylized, artificial, disruptive, marginal resisting) versus the mainstream (as naturalized, commonsensical, incorporated, etc.)." Lawrence Grossberg, *Dancing In Spite Of Myself: Essays on Popular Culture* (Durham and London: Duke University Press, 1997), 2–3. What is more important is the articulation of the in-betweenness.

15. Richard Middleton, *Studying Popular Music* (Buckingham: Open University Press, 1990), 5–6.

in which they are more immediately engaged) are distinguished from the economically, politically and culturally powerful groups within society and are hence *potentially* capable of being united.[16]

Over the past forty years or so, Cantopop has proved that it was not only a commercial success but also capable of uniting a variety of social groups. This typical hybridized genre has provided the people of Hong Kong with a strange sense of belonging over the past fifty years or so, articulating, together with other media such as film and television, a distinctive kind of Hong Kong cultural identity.[17] Having said this, it would be beneficial to readers who are not familiar with Hong Kong and Cantopop to have a brief account of terms such as "pop" and "rock" in the context of Hong Kong here. In most places, popular music was overwhelmingly concerned with love and romance, but, as argued by David Hesmondalgh, "pop and rock each articulated, reflected, and shaped two conflicting ethics of love and sex."[18] In a slightly different vein but with a slightly different emphasis, Shuker made the following remark: "The terms 'pop' and 'rock' are often used as shorthand for 'popular music,' at the same time as there is a tendency to contrast and polarize the two styles."[19] The relationship between pop and rock is different in Hong Kong. In the Anglophone world, the mainstream popular music genres are pop and rock.[20] Although the two are not synonymous, scholarly literature in English tends to equate "pop-rock" with "popular music."[21] While rock in most other societies is considered mainstream, it is not so in Hong Kong. The usual approach to defining musical genres is "to follow the distinctions made by the music industry, which, in turn

---

16. Tony Bennett, "The Politics of the 'Popular'," in *Popular Culture and Social Relations*, ed. Tony Bennett et al. (Milton Keynes: Open University Press, 1986), 20; original emphasis.

17. The "genre" here can be defined as "systems of orientations, expectations and conventions that bind together industry, performers, critics, and fans in making what they identify as a distortive sort of music." Jennifer Lena, *Banding Together: How Communities Create Genres in Popular Music* (Princeton: Princeton University Press, 2012), 6.

18. David Hesmondalgh, *Why Music Matters* (Chichester: Wiley Blackwell, 2013), 62. Although "pop" and "popular" may have different meanings in popular music studies, especially in traditional musicological studies, for the sake of brevity I have no intention to distinguish the two in this book. "Pop" is an inherently dismissive term in older cultural studies tradition, whereas "popular" embodies the voice and values of the people; see Simon Frith, "The Popuar Music Industry," in *The Cambridge Companion to Pop and Rock*, ed. Simon Frith, Will Straw, and John Street (Cambridge: Cambridge University Press, 2001), 26–52. Chris Rojek has also offered a full-length discussion on their differences; see Chris Rojek, *Pop Music, Pop Culture* (Cambridge and Malden: Polity, 2011), 1–8.

19. Shuker, *Understanding Popular Music Culture*, 122.

20. Hesmondalgh, *Why Music Matters*, 7.

21. Motti Regev, "Notes on Sociological Theory and Popular Music Studies," in *The SAGE Handbook of Popular Music*, ed. Andy Bennett and Steve Waksman (Los Angeles, London, New Delhi, Singapore and Washington DC: Sage, 2015), 35. For a detailed discussion of the difference or similarity between rock, pop, and popular music, see Motti Regev, *Pop-Rock Music: Aesthetic Cosmopolitanism in Late Modernity* (Cambridge and Malden: Polity, 2013), 17–22.

reflect both musical history and marketing categories."[22] During the forty-some years before the handover, because of the absence of political autonomy in Hong Kong as a colony of Britain and as a Special Administrative Region of China, Hong Kong people have come to accept a so-called "compensatory logic" as argued by Rey Chow, i.e., "because the people in Hong Kong are lacking in something essential—political power—that they have to turn their energy elsewhere, economics."[23] Due to this compensatory logic and its consequent economism, Hong Kong has been shaped as a port city that places commerce and trade on the top of its priority list. The music industry in Hong Kong has been accordingly led to direct most of its resources to mainstream pop, which can be musically defined by "its general accessibility, its commercial orientation, an emphasis on memorable hooks, or choruses, and a lyrical preoccupation with romantic love as theme," and it is "increasingly identified with the wider culture of celebrity."[24] The definition borrowed from the Anglophone world can aptly describe the characteristics of Cantopop.

In a popular music market overwhelmingly dominated by pop, rock is customarily taken to be alternative music in Hong Kong, and so concepts such as "mainstream," "oppositional," and "underground" had to be understood differently. Alternative music refers to "a loose genre/style, which has been used since the late 1960s for popular music seen as less commercial and mainstream, and more authentic and 'uncompromising'."[25] In a Western context, "[a]lternative music is frequently associated with local music scenes," and "[f]or many participants in alternative local scenes, the perceived dualities associated with indie and major record labels are central to their commitment to the local."[26] In Hong Kong this has to be understood differently. Hong Kong music critic Lai-Chi Fung 馮禮慈 used the umbrella term "alternative" to cover underground, nonmainstream, independent music, and genres beyond the mainstream popular music industry.[27] To borrow Shuker's point that the term "indie" actually "denotes not just a type of economic entity, but a musical attitude,"[28] "alternative music" refers to those musics that uphold values

---

22. Simon Frith, "Toward an Aesthetic of Popular Music," in *Music and Society*, ed. Richard Leppert and Susan McClary (Cambridge: Cambridge University Press, 1987), 133.
23. Rey Chow, *Ethics after Idealism: Theory—Culture—Ethnicity—Reading* (Indianapolis and Bloomington: Indiana University Press, 1998), 171.
24. Shuker, *Understanding Popular Music Culture*, 123–24.
25. Shuker, *Popular Music: The Key Concepts*, 8. "At the historical heart of alternative music was its rejection of the commercial music industry, and the emphasis it placed on rock music as art or expression rather than as a product for sale for economic profit."
26. Shuker, *Popular Music: The Key Concepts*, 9–10. "Local" refers to "college/university towns or large cities that are somehow 'alternative'."
27. Lai-Chi Fung, *On the Small Path: The Steps of Hong Kong Alternative Music*《小路上：香港另類音樂的腳步》(in Chinese) (Hong Kong: Music Communication, 1996). Meanwhile, Fung reminded us that the quality of alternative music could be lower than that of mainstream pop.
28. Shuker, *Understanding Popular Music Culture*, 21.

opposed to a stereotyped mainstream. The 1980s saw the surge of Hong Kong's independent music scene,[29] followed by a wave of bands in the mid to late 1980s (refer to Chapter Four for details). In the 1980s, Hong Kong bands, including rock bands such as Beyond and electronic duo such as Tat Ming Pair 達明一派, were considered alternative despite the fact they signed with major labels. Their songs—commonly known as band songs in Chinese—were generally considered to be voicing values significantly different from those of the mainstream. However, it is difficult, if at all possible, to draw a precise boundary between "alternative" and "mainstream." Take the legendary rock band Beyond as an example: as their debut cassette *Goodbye My Dreams* 《再見理想》 was self-financed (the production cost of cassette tapes being much lower than that of vinyl discs), they were seen by their fans as "independent" and/or "underground." When they signed with Kinn's Music Ltd. and later a big label Cinepoly, some of their fans thought they betrayed alternative music. But history proved that they sailed on to become a rock legend after they entered the mainstream, and were seen by several generations of Hong Kong fans as an antiestablishment symbol. "Like rock, however, alternative soon became a marketing category: in the 1990s, major record retail outlets usually feature[d] an 'alternative' section [in the West]."[30] As warned by Hesmondalgh, alternative became "a questionable term in an era where indie and alternative rock [were] big-ish business."[31] In the mid-1990s, there was also a wave of "alternative music" in Hong Kong. Major record companies launched diffusion labels (such as PolyGram's "Musician" 「非池中」) to produce "alternative" music, but the craze died out very soon. Having said this, it has to be noted that although rock music has not been mainstream in Hong Kong, it has exerted a profound influence on Hong Kong bands and hence its music industry (this will be further discussed in Chapter Two).[32] For example, the Cantopop legend Samuel Hui 許冠傑 was the mainstay of the band Lotus in the 1960s.

29. "At that time, people called all forms of music that were different from the mainstream as 'underground music'. Later, the label 'alternative music' was also used. However, many musicians either resisted or rejected labelling their music as 'underground' or 'alternative'. While the term 'indie music' seemed more neutral, it has been commonly used locally since the 1990s. The history of the Hong Kong indie music – known locally as 'underground music' at the time – began in the mid-1980s, the era of vinyl records and cassette tapes. Unlike the vibrant foreign music scene where various independent record labels flourished, when Hong Kong's indie bands in the 80s wanted to record and release their works, they never expected any support from major recording companies. Since there were no independent recording labels for indie bands, they would rather choose to produce, publish and release their music at their own expense." Jockey Club Music Series, "Definition of Independent Music," http://hkstreetmusic.com/educator-toolkit/indie-music-hong-kong; retrieved on March 15, 2016.
30. Shuker, *Popular Music: The Key Concepts*, 9.
31. Hesmondalgh, *Why Music Matters*, 68.
32. The term "rock music" used here refers to its roots in "rock and roll" in the United States in the 1950s. Since the 1960s, largely due to the "British Invasion" and other factors, it has incorporated different genres, such as blues and jazz, and has become more diversified.

Rock/pop, as argued by Fabian Holt in his in-depth study of popular music genres, has become "a cultural mainstream" in recent decades, and "increasingly functions as a discourse for articulating public memory of peoples and nations at major official events."[33] Although rock may not be a cultural mainstream in Hong Kong's popular music industry, it does carry the function as a discourse for articulating public memory of peoples and nations at major official events in Hong Kong. In terms of market share, the role of rock in the territory may be less significant than pop, but as evident from the impact of band songs, such as those of Beyond, over the past three to four decades, rock music did exert significant influence on the Hong Kong society per se.

The following chapters will show that Cantopop remained at the margins, albeit being quite popular in the Hong Kong society per se, in the 1950s and 1960s. The precursor of Cantopop can be traced to songs produced in the 1930s and 1940s. However, its production remained small-scale and it did not gain popularity among audiences. The question whether there was a Hong Kong culture in the 1950s or 1960s is a vexing one. Ping-Kwan Leung's 梁秉鈞 large-scale research into Hong Kong literature and culture in the 1950s, which reexamines the momentum and vitality of Hong Kong literature and movies in the 1950s, has demonstrated that a Hong Kong culture appeared in the 1950s.[34] As I will discuss in the next chapter, Cantopop has begun to hybridize different music styles to become a popular genre in the 1950s. Notwithstanding this, Cantopop was seen as inferior to Euro-American songs in the 1950s and the 1960s, and the market of popular songs in Hong Kong during that period was dominated by songs produced in the US and Europe, including those of the Beatles and Elvis Presley. It was not surprising because Hong Kong people were dominated by a kind of refugee mentality during the 1950s and 1960s, as the British colony was not considered a permanent home by many newcomers who had fled Mainland China for political and other reasons. The generation that was born and raised in Hong Kong gradually changed this mentality. "According to the official statistics of the 1961 Census, less than half (47.7 percent) of the population was born in Hong Kong. But that figure went up to 53.8 percent in the 1966 by-census, indicating the emergence of a locally born generation in a migrant society."[35] Hugh Baker stated that "[i]n over 30 years they have perforce begun to look on Hong Kong as their permanent home, and a whole generation has grown up knowing nothing

33. Fabian Holt, *Genre in Popular Music* (Chicago and London: University of Chicago Press, 2007), 1.
34. See among others Ping-Kwan Leung (a.k.a. Ye Si 也斯), *Ye Si's 1950s: Essays on Hong Kong Literature and Culture* 《也斯的五〇年代：香港文學與文化論集》 (in Chinese) (Hong Kong: Chung Hwa, 2014).
35. Gordon Mathews, Eric Ma, and Tai-Lok Lui, *Hong Kong, China: Learning to Belong to a Nation* (Abingdon and New York: Routledge, 2008), 29.

else."[36] Subsequently, a sense of local identity was emerging: "By the late 1960s and 1970s, however, a postwar generation, which had only known Hong Kong as a home, reached adulthood, and a sense of Hong Kongese as an autonomous cultural identity began to emerge."[37]

It was not until the early 1970s that, because of considerable social and demographic changes and transformation of Hong Kong's local media and society, Cantopop gradually acquired its long overdue status as the dominant genre of Hong Kong popular music. The year 1974 is generally agreed to be the watershed of the development of Cantopop, when the biased impression toward Cantopop was rectified by the unprecedented success of songs and singers such as Sam Hui, later known as the God of Cantopop. This generation of Hong Kong people, at long last, found its own voice in a musical genre sung in its mother tongue. The swift development of other forms of Cantonese popular culture contributed an unprecedented synergy, which in turn contributed to the increasing popularity of Cantopop: "As Hong Kong society developed in its own direction, so did its popular culture. A distinct Hong Kong local culture came into being in the mid-1970s."[38] In the television sector, the localization of free-to-air television programs nurtured a new collective sensibility in the newly emergent indigenous culture of Hong Kong.[39] Meanwhile, Hong Kong cinema also witnessed the emergence of a new Cantonese cinema after a brief domination by Mandarin movies in the early 1970s. In 1973, after a year in which no Cantonese films were produced, Shaw Brothers, which was still regarded as the king of Mandarin film studios, took the lead in the revival of Cantonese films by making and releasing *The House of 72 Tenants* 《七十二家房客》. The film, a remake of a 1963 movie of the same title, was inspired by TVB television programs. This was the only Cantonese production out of the 94 Hong Kong movies released in 1973. An extremely pleasant surprise for Cantonese popular culture, the movie unexpectedly broke the box office record set by Bruce Lee's *Way of the Dragon* 《猛龍過江》 (1972), and subsequently it successfully brought Cantonese movies back to the Hong Kong film

36. Hugh Baker, "Life in the Cities: The Emergence of Hong Kong Man," *The China Quarterly* 95 (September 1983): 478.
37. "Since the 1960s, the contextual factors, which became the material base of a new cultural identity, can be summarized under four general rubrics: 1. Anglicized educational system; 2. Social preconditions (e.g. government-subsidized housing, transportation); 3. Economic opportunities; 4. Influx of new Chinese immigrants. Hong Kong people, perhaps for the first time in the post-war decades, saw themselves as locals." Refer to Eric Ma, *Culture, Politics and Television in Hong Kong* (London: Routledge, 1999), 25.
38. Mathews, Ma, and Lui, *Hong Kong, China*, 36–37.
39. "Due to the deficiency of the Hong Kong polity as a representative structure, and also because of other social factors . . . television culture plays a central role in identity formation in post-war Hong Kong. Before the mid-1980s, the newly emergent indigenous culture of Hong Kong was closely related to the development of the local television industry." Ma, *Culture, Politics and Television in Hong Kong*, 18.

industry. In 1974, out of 101 Hong Kong movies, 21 were Cantonese productions. The highest-grossing films were Cantonese productions, including the monumental *Games Gamblers Play* 《鬼馬雙星》 (1974) by the Hui brothers. Based on these vigorous Cantonese popular cultures, the dialect was revived "as a younger generation came onto the scene, aware of its own identity as Hong Kong filmmakers. Cantonese would be recognized throughout the 1980s as the *lingua franca* of Hong Kong cinema."[40]

The growth of Cantopop in the early 1980s continued with a fresh impetus from transnational music production companies. Throughout the 1980s and up until the mid-1990s, Cantopop was the leader in the pan-Chinese popular music industry, having developed into a multibillion-dollar pop industry—"the Chinese cool"[41]—that attracted those who did not speak Cantonese. Cantopop was the trendsetter in Asian music industries for almost two decades, exerting a profound influence on popular music made locally in East Asian Chinese-speaking counterparts such as Taiwan, Singapore, and Mainland China. It was also very popular in Chinese diasporic communities. According to the *Baseline Study on Hong Kong's Creative Industries* conducted by the University of Hong Kong for the Central Policy Unit of the Government of Hong Kong Special Administrative Region,

> [t]he music industry in Hong Kong is dominated by Cantopop in production and sales. It constitutes a major part of the entertainment business of the territory in terms of employment and contribution to GDP. It is also a major part of the popular cultural phenomenon of Hong Kong, which has significant influence in the region and also a large market in every community overseas.[42]

This was true until the mid-1990s. For Cantopop, the 1990s were considered "the best of times" as well as "the worst of times"—borrowing Charles Dickens's often cited words from his *A Tale of Two Cities*. By the late 1990s, however, due to piracy and other factors, Cantopop had begun to decline in terms of its market share as well as popularity. According to statistics of the International Federation of Phonographic Industry (Hong Kong Group), Cantopop sales dropped by more than half, from HK$1.853 billion in 1995 to HK$0.916 billion in 1998.[43] This prompted James Wong to use 1997 as the end boundary for the timeline of Cantopop in his doctoral thesis entitled "The Rise and

---

40. Stephen Teo, "The 1970s: Movement and Transition," in *The Cinema of Hong Kong: History, Arts, Identity*, ed. Poshek Fu and David Desser (Cambridge: Cambridge University Press, 2000), 108.
41. Geoff Burpee, "As Sun Sets on British Empire in Hong Kong, Industry Gears for Return to China," *Billboard* 108, no. 43 (October 26, 1996): APQ-1.
42. Cultural Policy Studies Centre of the University of Hong Kong, *Baseline Study on Hong Kong's Creative Industries* (Hong Kong: Central Policy Unit, the Government of Hong Kong Special Administrative Region, 2003), 114.
43. Wong, "The Rise and Decline of Cantopop," 169.

Decline of Cantopop." In the new millennium, the transformation of the global mediascape brought about a change that forced Cantopop into a vicious circle. Cantopop was gradually taken over by Mandapop (Mandarin popular songs), while Hong Kong's regional competitors, including Taiwan, Singapore, and South Korea, aggressively invested in and pursued cultural policies to develop their music industries. Worse still, the passing away of Cantopop superstars Leslie Cheung 張國榮 and Anita Mui 梅艷芳 and lyrics masters James Wong and Richard Lam 林振強 seemed to symbolize the end of the era of Cantopop. When sales dropped, vehement criticisms of Cantopop surfaced: "People are getting tired of mainstream Cantopop because it rehashes the formula of big ballads and cheesy dance tunes year in, year out."[44] Notwithstanding this, Cantopop, once very popular across Chinese communities, must have been doing something right. Before I go into the historical development of Cantopop from the margin in the 1950s and 1960s to its heyday from the mid-1970s to the mid-1990s, and its decline in the new millennium, related studies on Cantopop will be introduced.

While it focuses on Cantopop, this book also positions itself in the wider field of popular music studies, a field that is heavily slanted toward Western popular music.[45] Thanks to the stellar rise of the cultural and creative industries in East Asia (such as the wave of K-Pop), studies of Asian popular music has found itself in the limelight. Allen Chun, Ned Rossiter, and Brian Shoesmith's *Refashioning Pop Music in Asia* is an example of focusing attention on Asian popular music, and in 2013, *Popular Music* devoted a special issue to East Asian popular music, with many articles shedding light on the mapping of a new mediascape in the Asian popular music industry.[46] In this special context, Chinese popular music studies have been receiving more critical attention. Academic work on Chinese popular music, however, shows a bias toward rock music from Beijing rather than pop music from either Hong Kong or Taiwan. Cantopop studies, thus, has been doubly marginalized: popular music studies tend to ignore music outside the West, and Chinese popular music studies lean toward Mandarin pop and rock. This book could be seen as an intervention

---

44. Samuel Lee, "East Asia Is Crazy over Taiwanese Pop Stars Such as Jay Chou as Cantopop Fades Away," *The Strait Times* (September 20, 2002): 8.

45. It has to be stressed that this book is first and foremost intended to be a concise introduction to the genre of Cantopop. My major objective is not to have a critical intervention into popular music studies. Given the scope of this book, this would be very difficult if not impossible at all. For a succinct account of the development of popular music studies, see Andy Bennett and Steve Waksman, "Introduction," in *The SAGE Handbook of Popular Music*, ed. Andy Bennett and Steve Waksman (Los Angeles, London, New Delhi, Singapore, and Washington DC: Sage, 2015), 1–10.

46. Allen Chun, Ned Rossiter, and Brian Shoesmith, eds., *Refashioning Pop Music in Asia: Cosmopolitan Flows, Political Tempos, and Aesthetic Industries* (London and New York: Routledge, 2004); Hyunjoon Shin, Yoshitaka Mōri, and Tunghung Ho, eds., "Special Issue: East Asian Popular Music and Its (Dis)contents," *Popular Music* 32, no. 1 (2013).

into the wider field of Chinese popular music studies, in which Cantopop is too often neglected owing to the stereotype of it being "cheesy love songs." To this end, it would be helpful to underscore the significance of the topic by positioning it in the context of the field of Chinese popular music studies. Earlier works on contemporary Chinese popular music discuss such important issues, among others, as nationalism, and ideology and genre.[47] Mainland China's popular music industry took shape much later than Hong Kong's, but with Cantopop having been overtaken by Mandopop in recent years, more research on Chinese popular music has appeared in the past few years. The alleged rise of China's cultural industries and soft power since the late 1990s has also drawn the attention of many academics to Chinese popular music, and the bias toward Chinese, especially Beijing, rock in popular music studies has become even more pronounced in this context. In the new millennium, there have been numerous studies on Chinese rock and pop, including, among others, Andrew Jones' *Yellow Music: Media Culture and Colonial Modernity in the Chinese Jazz Age*, Nimrod Baranovitch's *China's New Voices: Popular Music, Ethnicity, Gender, and Politics, 1978–1997*, Matthew Niederhauser's *Sound Kapital*, Jeroen de Kloet's *China with a Cut: Globalisation, Urban Youth and Popular Music*, Jeroen Groenewegen's *Tongue: Making Sense of Underground Rock, Beijing 1997–2004*, Jonathan Campbell's *Red Rock: The Long, Strange March of Chinese Rock & Roll*, and Andreas Steen's *Between Entertainment and Revolution: Gramophones, Records and the Beginning of Shanghai Music Industry, 1878–1937*.[48]

Rock and roll, given its rebellious nature, is often seen as incongruent with contemporary Chinese society. Therefore, Chinese rock, especially Beijing rock, has attracted attention to explore the reception and cultural translations of this Western import in a country with its own unique characteristics. Campbell's general account of the "long, strange march" of Chinese rock music

---

47. For examples, Andrew Jones, *Like a Knife: Ideology and Genre in Contemporary Chinese Popular Music* (Ithaca: Cornell University East Asia Program, 1992) and Gregory Lee, *Troubadours, Trumpeters, Troubled Makers: Lyricism, Nationalism, and Hybridity in China and Its Others* (Durham: Duke University Press, 1996).

48. Andrew Jones, *Yellow Music: Media Culture and Colonial Modernity in the Chinese Jazz Age* (Durham: Duke University Press, 2001), Nimrod Baranovitch, *China's New Voices: Popular Music, Ethnicity, Gender, and Politics, 1978–1997* (Berkeley and Los Angeles: University of California Press, 2003), Matthew Niederhauser, *Sound Kapital: Beijing's Music Underground* (New York: powerHouse Books, 2009), Jeroen de Kloet, *China with a Cut: Globalisation, Urban Youth and Popular Music* (Amsterdam: Amsterdam University Press, 2010), Jeroen Groenewegen, *Tongue: Making Sense of Underground Rock, Beijing 1997–2004* (New York: Lambert Academic Publishing, 2011), Jonathan Campbell, *Red Rock: The Long, Strange March of Chinese Rock & Roll* (Hong Kong: Earnshaw Books, 2011), Andreas Steen, *Between Entertainment and Revolution: Gramophones, Records and the Beginning of Shanghai Music Industry, 1878–1937*《在娛樂與革命之間：留聲機唱片和上海音樂工業的初期，1878–1937》(in Chinese) (Shanghai: Shanghai Lexicographical Publishing House, 2015).

in *Red Rock* surveys the development of rock and roll in China from the Mao years to the new millennium. Through interviews with musicians, journalists, and industry experts, the author examines how the music rocks China. Groenewegen's *Tongue* also focuses on Beijing's underground rock, showing that musicians have been using politics to engage audiences in postsocialist China. Niederhauser's *Sound Kapital* zooms in on revolutionary Beijing nightclubs, such as D-22 and MAO Livehouse, to investigate the underground scene in Beijing, exploring the (im)possibility to push the boundaries of independent thought and musical expression. Also focusing on Beijing, Baranovitch's *China's New Voices* offers a more comprehensive study of the popular music scene in the period between 1978 and 1997, touching on the ethnicity, gender, and politics of new Chinese popular music. The book argues how rock and pop became a medium through which the underprivileged could acquire a new public voice not dependent of the state. From a different angle, De Kloet's *China with a Cut* offers an inspiring account of the impact of Western music on China through illegally imported compact discs, detailing how it influenced the younger generation in the age of globalization. Based on extensive fieldwork in Beijing, Shanghai, and Hong Kong, places of Chinese popular music in the context of globalization, this book examines how illegally imported compact discs in the 1990s inspired the young generation in China to strive to break free from the Maoist past by experimenting with new sounds and new lifestyles. Unlike previous studies with their main focus on politics and/or institutions, *Yellow Music* and *Between Entertainment and Revolution* are both historical accounts of Chinese popular music; the former studies the emergence of Chinese popular music in early twentieth century China, whereas the latter traces the development of Shanghai music industry from 1878 to 1937. While both adopt an interdisciplinary (history, sociology, media studies) and cross-cultural (China-West, colonial modernity) approach, they focus on early Chinese popular music. As convincingly noted by Marc Moskowitz in the introduction of his *Cries of Joy, Songs of Sorrow: Chinese Pop Music and Its Cultural Connotations*:

> There is already some excellent academic work on Chinese popular music, yet most of this scholarship concentrates on Beijing rock and for the most part excludes Mandopop [Mandapop] produced in Taiwan. This focus has more to do with the People's Republic of China economic and political might, and perhaps with western academics' musical preferences, than with actual Chinese musical tastes, however.[49]

---

49. Marc Moskowitz, *Cries of Joy, Songs of Sorrow: Chinese Pop Music and Its Cultural Connotations* (Honolulu: University of Hawai'i Press, 2010), 1–2.

To fill this lacuna, *Cries of Joy, Songs of Sorrow* offers a full-length study of contemporary Mandapop with particular emphasis on Taiwan. Although the book focuses more on the construction of male and female identities in Mandapop, it does provide a rare account of the historical background necessary to understand the contemporary Mandapop scene. The citation above, especially the second sentence, can well be applied to the studies of Cantopop. Till today there is no comprehensive historical account of the genre of Cantopop, despite its strong cultural influence over the past decades. In popular music studies in Western academies, Cantopop is often not distinguished from Chinese popular songs, and thus it is "poorly served in surveys of non-Western music."[50] While academic interest has shifted to Mainland China, Yiu-Fai Chow and Jeroen de Kloet's *Sonic Multiplicities: Hong Kong Pop and the Global Circulation of Sound and Image* is an exceptional attempt at understanding and studying Hong Kong popular music despite its shift. As stressed by the authors, they wanted to sustain Hong Kong and its popular culture "in the research agenda of scholars concerned with Hong Kong, Chinese, Asian and global popular culture."[51] I would emphasize that it is necessary to distinguish Cantopop from Chinese pop. Too often the two are conflated, but clearly they are not the same. Despite its not being considered seriously by scholars outside Hong Kong, Cantopop once received great attention from audiences around the world. I do not deny that possible interactions among different popular songs can generate an energetic music culture for a cosmopolitan city like Hong Kong, but the point of concern is that this special genre sung in the Cantonese dialect has its own inherent hybridity that is not available elsewhere.[52]

As I have discussed elsewhere, the widely used discourse of hybridity constitutes a disputed terrain of cultural theory and criticism.[53] One of the most disputed terms that has dominated conceptual discussions of mixed identities in postcolonial studies, it is commonly defined as "the creation of new transcultural forms within the contact zone produced by colonization."[54] According to Homi Bhabha, the vocal theoretician to advocate hybridity as a kind of tactic to subvert hegemonic discourse, holds that hybridity can point toward a new cosmopolitanism that can engage different possibilities of cultural agency.[55]

50. Lawrence Witzleben, "Cantopop and Mandapop in Pre-post-colonial Hong Kong: Identity Negotiation in the Performances of Anita Mui," *Popular Music* 18, no. 2 (1999): 242–43.

51. Yiu-Fai Chow and Jeroen de Kloet, *Sonic Multiplicities: Hong Kong Pop and the Global Circulation of Sound and Image* (Bristol and Chicago: Intellect Books, 2013), 154.

52. Yiu-Wai Chu, *Lost in Transition: Hong Kong Culture in the Age of China* (Albany: SUNY Press, 2013), 135.

53. Yiu-Wai Chu, "Introduction," *Contemporary Asian Modernities: Transnationality, Interculturality and Hybridity*, ed. Yiu-Wai Chu and Eva K. W. Man (Bern: Peter Lang, 2010), 22–23.

54. Bill Ashcroft, Gareth Griffiths, and Helen Tiffin, *Key Concepts in Post-Colonial Studies* (London: Routledge, 1998), 118.

55. Homi Bhabha, *The Location of Culture* (New York and London: Routledge, 1994).

While Néstor García Canclini celebrates hybridity in his *Hybrid Cultures,* he still worries that hybridization might also reinforce the already existing asymmetrical relationships of domination and subordination.[56] Meanwhile, different challenges to the concept of hybridity can also be found. "The importance of hybridity is that it problematizes boundaries," but hybridity is "inauthentic" and "multiculturalism lite" according to anti-hybridity arguments.[57] This brings us to the potential problem resulting from the uncritical celebration of hybridity. In short, the interaction of different cultures seems to have provided chances for them to hybridize, but whether it is merely a mixture or true hybridity is not easy to tell. For my present purpose I would just concentrate on Bhabha's differentiation of diversity and hybridity: "it is insufficient to record signifiers of cultural diversity which merely acknowledge a range of separate and distinct systems of behavior, attitudes and values."[58] Cultural diversity may sound exotic to many ears, but what matters is "the inscription and articulation of culture's *hybridity*" but not "the *diversity* of cultures."[59] In the context of this book, diversity refers in a more neutral sense to the existence of different genres, styles, subject matters, and the like in the Cantopop industry, whereas "hybridity" articulates the theoretical possibilities of engendering new conceptions. Meanwhile, media scholars have employed the notion of hybridity to investigate cultural mixture in the age of globalization.[60] K-Pop, among others, is considered "hybrid music," which is "a careful negotiation of Korean and Japanese traits, under the influence of Western music trends."[61] The important point to note is that the hybridization of Korean, Japanese, and Western musics has generated a new form of K-Pop, which is not just a mixture of these elements.

Cantopop, once the leading pop genre of Chinese popular music across the world, has a history that needs to be written, which is especially important for the present and the future of Hong Kong, a city whose citizens have been witnessing the decline of not only its popular cultures but also core values. This book aims to show how the rise of Cantopop is related to an upsurge of Hong Kong culture in general, and how its decline since the 1990s is connected to changes in the music industry as well as, and more importantly, geopolitical

---

56. Néstor García Canclini, *Hybrid Cultures: Strategies for Entering and Leaving Modernity* (Minneapolis: University of Minneapolis Press, 1995).
57. Jan Nederveen Pieterse, "Hybridity, So What? The Anti-Hybridity Backlash and the Riddles of Recognition," *Theory, Culture & Society* 18, nos. 2–3 (2001): 219–45.
58. Ashcroft, Griffiths, and Tiffin, *Key Concepts in Post-Colonial Studies*, 60.
59. Bhabha, *The Location of Culture*, 38.
60. Marwan Kraidy, *Hybridity, or the Cultural Logic of Globalization* (Philadelphia: Temple University Press, 2005).
61. Ju Oak Kim, "Despite Not Being Johnny's: The Cultural Impact of TVXQ in the Japanese Music Industry," in *K-Pop: The International Rise of the Korean Music Industry*, ed. JungBong Choi and Roald Maliangkay (Abingdon, Oxon: Routledge, 2015), 76.

changes. As such, this book is not only a concise history of Cantopop but also of Hong Kong culture. It could also be read as "a story about localization and how a group of urban youth successfully created a culture that was grounded in the social, cultural and political reality defined by institutionalized colonialism."[62] I also hope that this book, against the backdrop of Hong Kong's reversion to China, would be meaningful by bringing awareness to the field of Hong Kong studies. Despite the important role of Cantopop in Hong Kong culture and society, academic Cantopop research is a relatively new but important field of scholarship. Cantopop, compared to film and other genres of popular culture, has received very little critical attention from academia. When Cantopop enthralled Chinese audiences across the globe in the 1980s, its discussions remained akin to *bricolage*, as it was scattered in newspaper columns, music magazines, and periodicals published by organizations such as the Composers and Authors Society of Hong Kong (CASH) and the Amateur Lyric Writers' Association of Hong Kong. Although some studies on Hong Kong popular culture in general did touch upon Cantopop,[63] Cantopop was treated merely as a subtopic of the studies on Hong Kong popular culture in general. The situation did not change much with the rise of cultural studies in Hong Kong in the late 1980s. In the beginning, the growing interest in Hong Kong popular culture did not stimulate extensive research on Hong Kong popular songs. The study of Cantopop per se did not gather momentum until the mid-1990s. The *bricolage* situation of Cantopop studies began to change when a renowned Hong Kong music critic, Chi-Wah Wong 黃志華, published his historical survey of Cantopop in 1990.[64] The book, titled *Forty Years of Cantopop* 《粵語流行曲四十年》, is a collection of Wong's Chinese columns published in *Wen Wei Po* in the 1980s. These columns, unlike other columns of impressionist talks on Hong Kong popular songs in general, systematically sketched the development of Cantopop and offered a detailed analysis of Cantopop lyricists. However, due to market considerations, the original manuscript was significantly short-ened and some very important materials were left out. The book thus lost some

---

62. I am indebted to an anonymnous reviewer for this point.
63. Examples include the following: Wah-Shan Chau 周華山, *Consumer Culture: Images, Words, Music* 《消費文化：影像、文字、音樂》 (in Chinese) (Hong Kong: Youth Bookstore, 1990); Ping-Kwan Leung 梁秉鈞, ed., *Hong Kong Popular Culture* 《香港的流行文化》 (in Chinese) (Hong Kong: Joint Publishing, 1993); Lok Fung (a.k.a. Natalia Sui-Hung Chan) 洛楓, *Fin de Siècle City: Hong Kong Popular Culture* 《世紀末城市：香港的流行文化》 (in Chinese) (Hong Kong: Oxford University Press, 1995); Elizabeth Sinn 冼玉儀, ed., *Hong Kong Culture and Society* 《香港文化與社會》 (in Chinese) (Hong Kong: Centre of Asian Studies, the University of Hong Kong, 1995); and Rey Chow, *Writing Diaspora: Tactics of Intervention in Contemporary Cultural Studies* (Indianapolis and Bloomington: Indiana University Press, 1993).
64. Chi-Wah Wong, *Forty Years of Cantopop* (in Chinese) (Hong Kong: Joint Publishing, 1990). Kei-Chi Wong 黃奇智 published a book entitled *On Popular Songs* 《時代曲綜論》 (in Chinese) in 1979 (Hong Kong: School of Continuing Studies, the Chinese University of Hong Kong, 1979), but it focuses mainly on Mandarin popular songs.

of the impact it could have made. Chi-Wah Wong published another book in 2000 to complete his survey of Cantopop. In that book, he traced the development of Cantopop from the 1950s to the mid-1970s, providing rare and valuable information about early Cantopop in Hong Kong.[65] Chi-Wah Wong also provided insightful analyses and detailed reference materials related to Hong Kong lyricists, but only up to the mid-1990s.[66] Sharing the view that although the legitimation of cultural products involves complex discursive and organizational practices and the basic first step must be to produce serious intellectual and critical writing on the products,[67] Yiu-Wai Chu 朱耀偉 started to research Cantopop lyrics in the mid-1990s, trying to defend the artistic value of Cantopop lyrics in a comprehensive review of historical studies.[68] The study of Cantopop lyrics could be considered a first step toward the institutionalization of the study of Cantopop per se.

Since the mid-1990s, there have been more studies on Cantopop, but most of them are either historical or cultural studies. In the 1990s, there were some books on popular music published in Mainland China, Taiwan, and Hong Kong, thanks to the rise of cultural studies. They used mostly the cultural studies approach, analyzing, for instance, gender politics or the center-margin dialectic in popular music, and they considered popular lyrics a product of the culture industry. There have also been attempts to study Cantopop from a sociological and communication studies point of view. For instance, Hong Kong Policy Viewers offered a statistical survey and content analysis of Hong Kong Gold Songs from 1984 to 1993.[69] Only a few (such as Stephen C. K. Chan 陳清僑, ed., *The Practice of Affect: A Study of Hong Kong Popular Lyrics* 《情感的實踐：香港流行歌詞研究》), however, placed a sole emphasis on Hong Kong Cantopop, giving attention to the politics of cultural production and reception, the relation of affect to the meaning of music, and the study of cultural issues (e.g., identity politics and gender issues) through the textual and contextual study of song lyrics.[70] For example, the content analysis of song lyrics has been carried out with consideration of how cultures are received and circulated.

---

65. Chi-Wah Wong, *Early Hong Kong Cantopop* 《早期香港粵語流行曲》 (in Chinese) (Hong Kong: Joint Publishing, 2000).

66. Chi-Wah Wong, *Hong Kong Lyricists and Lyric Talks* 《香港詞人詞話》 (in Chinese) (Hong Kong: Joint Publishing, 2003).

67. Priscilla Ferguson, "A Cultural Field in the Making: Gastronomy in the 19th Century France," *American Journal of Sociology* 104, no. 3 (1998): 597–641.

68. Yiu-Wai Chu, *A Study of Hong Kong Popular Lyrics: From the Mid 70s to the Mid 90s* 《香港流行歌詞研究：七十年代中期到九十年代中期》 (in Chinese) (Hong Kong: Joint Publishing, 1998).

69. Hong Kong Policy Viewers, *Popular Culture under Hegemony: A Study of Hong Kong "Gold" Songs* 《霸權主義下的流行文化：剖析中文金曲的內容及意義研究》 (in Chinese) (Hong Kong: Policy Viewers, 1994).

70. Stephen C. K. Chan, ed., *The Practice of Affect: A Study of Hong Kong Popular Lyrics* 《情感的實踐：香港流行歌詞研究》 (in Chinese) (Hong Kong: Oxford University Press, 1997).

Yiu-Wai Chu's *Age of Glory: A Study of Hong Kong Popular Bands/Groups 1985–1990*《光輝歲月：香港流行樂隊／組合研究》adopted a similar approach, but Chu shifted the target of analysis to Hong Kong popular bands and groups from 1985 to 1990.[71] Bands and groups in the 1980s made a significant impact on local Hong Kong Cantopop in terms of both music and lyrics. While Chu's book regards content analysis of lyrics as an integral part of the study, it also examines the politics of the music industry, the larger political and social backdrop of pop music, and how pop music is circulated and received. Chu also studied the relationship between cultural policy and the development of local Cantopop through the "Chinese Songs Campaign" and the "Original Songs Campaign" launched by Hong Kong Commercial Radio in 1988 and 1995, respectively.[72] Some used cultural studies as a theoretical framework to analyze popular idols.[73] While there has been an increasing determination to move toward cross-disciplinary among these intellectual endeavors, more studies have been focused on Cantopop per se. Anthony Fung 馮應謙, among others, edited a volume entitled *Riding a Melodic Tide: The Development of Cantopop in Hong Kong*《歌潮・汐韻・香港粵語流行曲發展》based on a conference and exhibition hosted by the Hong Kong Heritage Museum.[74] Fung also coauthored a book on the development of the Hong Kong music industry entitled *Melodic Memories*.[75] Elvin Wong's 黃志淙 *Flowing Melody*《流聲》was another attempt at examining Hong Kong popular music from the industry's perspective.[76] While Chi-Wah Wong and Yiu-Wai Chu continued to focus on Cantopop lyrics in their works,[77] Helan Yang and Siu-Wah Yu

71. Yiu-Wai Chu, *Age of Glory: A Study of Hong Kong Popular Bands/Groups 1985–1990*《光輝歲月：香港流行樂隊／組合研究》(in Chinese) (Hong Kong: Infolink, 2000).

72. Yiu-Wai Chu, *A Study of the "Chinese Songs Campaign" in Hong Kong*《音樂敢言：香港「中文歌運動」研究》(in Chinese) (Hong Kong: Infolink, 2001); Yiu-Wai Chu, "Developing Local Popular Songs in Hong Kong: A Study of the 'All Cantonese Pop Music Station' Format," *Media International Australia Incorporating Culture & Policy* 105 (November 2002): 147–62; Yiu-Wai Chu, *A Study of the "Original Songs Campaign" in Hong Kong*《音樂敢言之二：香港「原創歌運動」研究》(in Chinese) (Hong Kong: Bestever, 2004).

73. Anthony Fung, *Hong Kong Popular Music Culture: A Reader in Cultural Studies*《香港流行音樂文化：文化研究讀本》(in Chinese) (Hong Kong: Wheatear, 2004).

74. Anthony Fung, *Riding a Melodic Tide: The Development of Cantopop in Hong Kong*《歌潮・汐韻・香港粵語流行曲的發展》(in Chinese) (Hong Kong: Subculture Press, 2009).

75. Anthony Fung and Shen Si, *Melodic Memories: History of the Development of Hong Kong Music Industry*《悠揚・憶記：香港音樂工業發展史》(in Chinese) (Hong Kong: Subculture Press, 2012).

76. Elvin Wong, *Flowing Melody*《流聲》(in Chinese) (Hong Kong: Civil Affairs Bureau, 2007).

77. Here are some examples: Chi-Wah Wong and Yiu-Wai Chu, *Guided Interpretation of Hong Kong Popular Lyrics*《香港流行歌詞導賞》(in Chinese) (Hong Kong: Infolink, 2009); Chi-Wah Wong and Yiu-Wai Chu, *Eighty Talks on Hong Kong Popular Lyrics*《香港歌詞八十談》(in Chinese) (Hong Kong: Infolink, 2011); Chi-Wah Wong, Yiu-Wai Chu, and Wai-Sze Leung, *The Way of Hong Kong Lyricists: Interviews with 16 Hong Kong Lyricists*《詞家有道：香港16詞人訪談錄》(in Chinese) (Hong Kong: Infolink, 2010); Yiu-Wai Chu and Wai-Sze Leung, *A Study of Post-1997 Cantopop Lyrics*《後九七香港流行歌詞研究》(in Chinese) (Hong Kong: Enlighten & Fish, 2011); Chi-Wah Wong, *Forgotten Treasures: The Chinese-Style Melodies in Hong Kong Popular Songs*《被遺忘的瑰寶：香港流行曲裡的中國風格旋律》(in Chinese) (Hong Kong: Jim and Hall Publication,

broke new ground in their *Reading Cantonese Songs: The Voice of Hong Kong through Vicissitudes* by introducing a musicologist approach to the study of Cantopop.[78] Music historian Ching-Chih Liu 劉靖之 also included Cantopop in his *A History of Hong Kong Music* 《香港音樂史論》.[79] Sociologist Chun-Hung Ng 吳俊雄 published a book on Sam Hui and launched a website on James Wong.[80] To sum up, critical studies on popular music in Hong Kong have mainly focused on discussions in roughly three notable directions: (1) textual and contextual studies; (2) sociological and communication studies; and (3) music history, musicology, and cultural studies. Besides books published in Chinese, which cater mainly to the Chinese audience, there have also been essays published in international journals, which has sparked the possibility of cross-cultural inquiries. These include: Eric Ma's "Emotional Energies and Subcultural Politics: Alternative Bands in Post-97 Hong Kong," Wai-Chung Ho's "Between Globalisation and Localisation: A Study of Hong Kong Popular Music," Yiu-Wai Chu's "The Transformation of Local Identity in Hong Kong Cantopop," and Yiu-Wai Chu and Eve Leung's "Remapping Hong Kong Popular Music: Covers, Localisation and the Waning Hybridity of Cantopop."[81]

The incomplete list above has already spoken adequate volumes for the growing importance of Cantopop studies. These research projects have developed the study of Cantopop into a recognized, albeit still marginal, area in the study of Hong Kong culture in academia. However, without a historical introduction, the gap between argumentation and data cannot be bridged. In their study of popular music in Asia, Allen Chun, Ned Rossiter, and Brian Shoesmith make this inspiring remark:

2005); Chi-Wah Wong, *Master of Melodies and Lyrics: A Study of the Works of Wu Man Sam* 《曲詞雙絕：胡文森作品研究》 (in Chinese) (Hong Kong: Joint Publishing, 2008); Chi-Wah Wong, *Wen-Cheng Lu, Cantonese Opera and Cantopop* 《呂文成與粵曲、粵語流行曲》 (in Chinese) (Hong Kong: Joint Publishing, 2012); Chi-Wah Wong, *Pioneers: Popular Songs Composed by Cantonese Opera Writers* 《原創先鋒：粵曲人的流行曲調創作》 (in Chinese) (Hong Kong: Joint Publishing, 2014); and Chi-Wah Wong, *Selected Lyric Criticisms by Jimmy Lo* 《盧國沾詞評選》 (in Chinese) (Hong Kong: Joint Publishing, 2015).

78. Yang and Yu, *Reading Cantonese Songs*.

79. Ching-Chih Liu, *History of Hong Kong Music* 《香港音樂史論》 (in Chinese) (Hong Kong: Commercial Press, 2014).

80. Chun-Hung Ng, *Here and Now: Sam Hui* 《此時此處許冠傑》 (in Chinese) (Hong Kong: Enrich Publishing, 2007); "James Wong's Study." Available at: http://www.hkmemory.org/jameswong/wjs/web/; retrieved on March 15, 2016.

81. Eric Ma, "Emotional Energies and Subcultural Politics: Alternative Bands in Post-97 Hong Kong," *Inter-Asia Cultural Studies* 3, no. 2 (2002): 187–200; Wai-Chung Ho, "Between Globalisation and Localisation: A Study of Hong Kong Popular Music," *Popular Music* 22, no. 2 (2003): 143–57; Yiu-Wai Chu, "The Transformation of Local Identity in Hong Kong Cantopop," *Perfect Beat: The Pacific Journal of Research into Contemporary Music and Popular Culture* 7, no. 4 (January 2006): 32–51; Yiu-Wai Chu and Eve Leung, "Remapping Hong Kong Popular Music: Covers, Localisation and the Waning Hybridity of Cantopop," *Popular Music* 32, no. 1 (2013): 65–78.

[I]t is the local context which imbues special meanings for different audiences, in turn allowing a creative synthesis that makes pop music a unique channel through which cultural identity, political resistance, social expression and personal desire can be experienced. Popular musical expression in Asia – its meaning and its practice – cannot be reduced to the state, market, tradition or to a simple appropriation of western forms.[82]

As a general introduction to the topic, this book will hopefully pave the way for future research by contributing important empirical, local data not available in recent studies. A critical account of Cantopop can be conceptualized from different persepctives, such as its music, lyrics, industry, and/or audience. As this is the first introduction to the genre in English, it would be more effective for this "ground-laying" endeavor to cater to a wider readership by offering a balanced and chronological account, which would be easier for readers to comprehend the genre and its development. I do understand that the development of any musical genre has to rely on the interrelationships between producers and consumers and all those involved in the creative process. This book would be greatly enriched by incorporating information collected from sources such as singers' voices, audience reception, radio logs, concerts, and statistics from media broadcasts, but given the scope and objective of this book, they cannot be dealt with in adequate depth. Besides, the use of personal accounts is a common practice in pop music study methodology. Owing to my academic training and the primary purpose of this book, I have decided not to adopt these approaches. As a book about a musical genre, it would be necessary to discuss music. I will touch on renowned composers in this book, but since my objective is to offer a balanced account, I would not offer an elaborate account of one particular aspect. I have been researching lyrics for two decades, but in this book I have decided to refrain from going into details of lyrics/lyricists. If you have chosen this book for such information, you may find other sources more useful. In short, this book is desgined to provide information about the genre and fill a vacuum by offering non-Chinese readers a useful resource about the topic. If a reader could have the abovementioned theoretical reflections on the topic after reading this book, it has already fulfilled its primary purpose.

Having said that, I would conclude by stressing that this book focuses on Cantopop (and hence the potential danger of parochialism seeping through it) because it aims primarily to fill a unique niche in academic studies and cater to those who are interested in the topic. As will be argued later in this book, the rise of Cantopop could be accounted for by its diversities and hybridities, which can be seen as a result of cultural translations between different music genres and/or regions. It was exactly due to its refusal to be parochial that

82. Allen Chun, Ned Rossiter, and Brian Shoesmith, "Refashioning Pop Music in Asia," in *Refashioning Pop Music in Asia*, ii.

Cantopop became the most popular music genre in Chinese communities across the world. When the market of Cantopop began to shrink in the mid-1990s, the problem of a lack of diversity surfaced and was subsequently aggravated. Because of its promotional packaging in recent years, as warned by music critics, the audience base of Hong Kong Cantopop has shrunk significantly and the problem of homogenization and standardization (the mass reproduction of "cheesy love songs") has become more serious. Cantopop has thus become trapped in a vicious circle. When the market reduces in size, the space for diversity as well as hybridity shrinks, which in turn conjures up a myth: Cantopop as mass-produced, stereotypical love ballads. However, Cantopop, once very popular across Chinese communities, must have been doing something right. By tracing the trajectory of Cantopop over the past sixty years or so, this book aims to deconstruct this myth. Let me end this introduction by citing David Brackett's words in the "Preface" of his *Interpreting Popular Music*:

> Finally, I may write a thousand new prefaces, but I will not arrest the play of meaning in which these words participate, nor would I, despite appearances, choose to do so even if it were an option. Readers will continue to find what they want to here, and I am grateful to them for that.[83]

---

83. David Brackett, *Interpreting Popular Music* (Berkeley, Los Angeles and London: University of California Press, 2000), xiv.

2 | Days of Being Marginalized
The 1950s to the Early 1970s

Introduction

The English term "Cantopop" did not come into existence until the 1970s, when *Billboard* correspondent Hans Ebert used it "to describe the locally produced popular music in Hong Kong" in 1978.[1] It was perhaps not a coincidence that 1974 was widely considered to have marked the rise of Cantopop. As noted in a historical account of Hong Kong, "[t]he year 1974 saw the creation of Cantopop, sentimental love songs with Cantonese lyrics backed by Western-style pop music."[2] The beautiful misunderstanding had probably been caused by the fact that before 1974 Cantopop was generally marginalized in Hong Kong, a city where 90 percent of the population spoke Cantonese.[3] In fact, Cantopop had not only existed but been quite popular among the local people long before 1974. However, it had generally been considered a working-class pastime until the theme song of the Television Broadcasting Company (TVB) drama *Romance between Tears and Smiles* 《啼笑因緣》 became popular in 1974 and changed Hong Kong people's impression about Cantopop. As noted in the

---

1. According to Joanna Lee, Ebert first coined the term "Cantorock" in 1974 in an essay in *Billboard*. But, as noted by Helan Yang and Siu-Wah Yu, the term cannot be found in any *Billboard* essay published in 1974. See Joanna C. Y. Lee, "Songs on Emigration from Hong Kong," *Yearbook for Traditional Music* 24 (1992): 14–23, and Helan Yang and Siu-Wah Yu, *Reading Cantonese Songs: The Voice of Hong Kong through Vicissitudes* 《粵語歌曲解讀：蛻變中的香港聲音》 (in Chinese) (Hong Kong: Infolink, 2013), 2.

2. John Carroll, *A Concise History of Hong Kong* (Plymouth: Rowman & Littlefield, 2007), 168.

3. According to Hong Kong government figures in July 2013, 89.2 percent of the population (7.15 million) are Cantonese speakers. See "Hong Kong—the Facts," http://www.gov.hk/en/about/abouthk/facts.htm; retrieved on March 15, 2016. "The perception and description of experience as 'marginal' is a consequence of the binaristic structure of various kinds of dominant discourses, such as patriarchy, imperialism and ethno-centrism, which imply that certain forms of experience are peripheral." Bill Ashcroft, Gareth Griffiths, and Helen Tiffin, *Key Concepts in Post-Colonial Studies* (London: Routledge, 1998), 110. The term "marginalized" is being used with care in the Hong Kong context because of shifting political alliances and social hierarchy. Earlier Cantonese urban songs were mostly for low-class audience but were nevertheless popular and not marginalized by the grassroots community.

doctoral thesis of the late "Godfather of Cantopop," James Wong, the song "Romance between Tears and Smiles" 〈啼笑姻緣〉 (melody by Joseph Koo 顧嘉煇, lyrics by Siu-Tak Yip 葉紹德, and sung by Sandra Lang 仙杜拉) marked the dawn of an era in which Cantopop became the dominant genre of popular lyrics in Hong Kong.[4]

The origin of Cantopop remains an unresolved issue. The first albums (consisting of eights songs in four albums) that were packaged with the term "Cantopop" in Chinese, according to renowned local music critic Chi-Wah Wong, were not released until August 26, 1952.[5] Long before this time Cantopop had already existed, but the concept was not yet distinct enough to be recognized as a genre. A song entitled "Shauzai Goes Dating" 〈壽仔去拍拖〉 can be found on an album published by the New Crescent Record Company in 1930.[6] The first popular Cantopop was arguably "Lullaby" 〈兒安眠〉, a song from the movie *Lifeline* 《生命線》 (1935). According to Lu Jin 魯金, renowned expert in Hong Kong anecdotes and history, this song, sung by Yee-Nin Lee 李綺年, was so popular that it marked the birth of Cantopop.[7] It should be noted that although Cantopop was used as film songs in Hong Kong cinema, the mainstream genre then was Cantonese opera. The theme song of *Lifeline*, "Can't Bear to Look at My Old Battle Robe Again" 〈不堪重睹舊征袍〉, sung by the "Movie King of South China" Cho-Fan Ng 吳楚帆, was actually a Cantonese opera that proved to be very popular according to the singer himself. As it remains controversial whether the song was really popular, Chi-Wah Wong argued that it would be safe to say that there were Cantopop hits once in a while back in the 1930s and 1940s, but it is not possible to trace the exact origin of Cantopop.[8] To avoid confusion and discrepancy between the different understandings of the term, it would be better to adopt Chi-Wah Wong's point to define the timeline; in other words, the concept of Cantopop (in Chinese) did not take shape until 1952.

---

4. James Wong, "The Rise and Decline of Cantopop: A Study of Hong Kong Popular Music (1949–1997)" 《粵語流行曲的發展與興衰：香港流行音樂研究 1949–1997》 (in Chinese) (Hong Kong: PhD thesis, the University of Hong Kong, 2003), 92.

5. Chi-Wah Wong, "The First Cantonese Popular Songs in the History of Hong Kong" 〈香港史上首批粵語時代曲唱片〉 (in Chinese), *Opera View* 《戲曲品味》 138 (May 2012).

6. Helan Yang and Siu-Wah Yu, *Reading Cantonese Songs*, 2–3. The tunes and lyrics of the song can be found in Andrew Jones, *Yellow Music: Media Culture and Colonial Modernity in the Chinese Jazz Age* (Durham: Duke University Press, 2001), 63.

7. Lu Jin, "Yee-Nin Lee's 'Lullaby': The Forerunner of Cantopop" 〈粵語流行曲鼻祖是李綺年唱的《兒安眠》〉 (in Chinese), *Ming Pao* (April 15, 1991); cited from Chi-Wah Wong, *Early Hong Kong Cantopop* 《早期香港粵語流行曲》 (in Chinese) (Hong Kong: Joint Publishing, 2000), 3.

8. Wong, *Early Hong Kong Cantopop*, 5–11. Wong later supplemented in his personal blog that there was still no such notion as "Cantopop," and the song was merely promoted by the record company as "a new kind of song." http://blog.chinaunix.net/uid-20375883-id-1958904.html?page=2; retrieved on March 15, 2016.

Early popular Cantopop included two very well-known anti-Japanese invasion songs—"Triumph Song" 〈凱旋歌〉 (theme song of *Stories on Canton 3 Days Massacre in 1650* 《廣州三日屠城記》; 1937) and "Anti-Japanese Invasion Song" 〈抗日歌〉 (theme song of *Stage Lights* 《舞台春色》; 1938).[9] According to Chi-Wah Wong's research on early Cantonese popular songs, there were at least six songs in *Stage Lights*, all written by Tit-Hung Siu 邵鐵鴻. He also pointed out a very interesting detail from the advertisement of the film:

> In the special issue of *Stage Lights*, there was a line reading "don't miss these six works of 'Cantonese opera'" [in Chinese identical to Cantonese songs]. The Cantonese opera actually means Cantonese popular songs. It is thus apparent that people did not differentiate Cantonese popular songs from Cantonese opera back then.[10]

That the audience did not differentiate Cantopop from Cantonese opera remained true up to the early 1950s, as evident from the popular Cantonese ditty "Blooming Beauty by the Silver Pond" 〈銀塘吐艷〉 (a.k.a. "Fragrant Water Lily" 〈荷花香〉; melody by Yuet-Sang Wong 王粵生 and lyrics by the Cantonese opera master Tik-Sang Tong 唐滌生) in the Cantonese opera movie *Hongling's Blood* (Alias: *Mysterious Murder*) 《紅菱血》 (1951). During the three years and eight months of Japanese occupation, a special genre of "New Songs of Illusion" 幻景新歌 was popular in Hong Kong. Although the style of these songs was not significantly different from Cantonese opera, some critics argued that they were the prototypes of Cantopop.[11] This type of urban Cantonese songs, which was based on Cantonese opera, was marginalized by the upper class, which preferred Western music and culture, but it was nonetheless popular among the general public. These songs, albeit seen as inferior to Euro-American popular songs, had their own market and audience support. Moreover, the music basis of these songs, which had close affinity to Cantonese opera, was significantly different from those imported from the West. This tradition element still played an important role in later Cantopop; for example, it was "modernized" and "hybridized" with Western elements by composers such as Joseph Koo and Sam Hui in the 1970s, which contributed to the stellar rise of Cantopop to become the dominant popular music genre in Hong Kong.

Meanwhile, in the first Cantonese movie after the Japanese occupation in August 1945, *Never Too Late to Come Home* (Alias: *My Love Comes too Late*) 《郎歸晚》 (1947), there was also a very popular Cantonese song. In fact, the

9. Chi-Wah Wong, *Pioneers: Popular Songs Composed by Cantonese Opera Writers* 《原創先鋒：粵曲人的流行曲調創作》 (in Chinese) (Hong Kong: Joint Publishing, 2014), 32–34.
10. Wong, *Pioneers*, 35.
11. Wong, *Pioneers*, 49; see also Sai-Shing Yung 容世誠, *Sounds of Cantonese Tunes: Record Industry and the Art of Cantonese Songs 1903–1953* 《粵韻留聲：唱片工業與廣東曲藝 1903–1953》 (in Chinese) (Hong Kong: Cosmos Books, 2006), 245.

title of the movie was borrowed from a song (the traditional Cantonese tune "Flowing Water Floating Clouds" 〈流水行雲〉 composed by Tit-Hung Siu, with new lyrics written by Luk-Ping Chan 陳綠萍). As the movie also used it as its theme song, it became very well received among Hong Kong audiences. Chi-Wah Wong also noted that in the first color production in the history of Hong Kong cinema, *Madame Butterfly* 《蝴蝶夫人》 (1948), there were four theme songs. Among them, "Sing and Dance" 〈載歌載舞〉 (melody by Man-Sum Wu 胡文森 and lyrics by Yat-Siu Ng 吳一嘯) was later rewritten and became the Cantopop classic "Sigh of Bettors" 〈賭仔自嘆〉 (the most popular version was sung by Kwan-Min Cheng 鄭君綿, circa 1961; lyricists unknown).[12] All of these songs spoke volumes for the synergy between popular songs and movies in Hong Kong, which continued to contribute to the development of Cantopop in the next fifty years or so (as will be discussed in the following chapters).

The Age of Mandapop

Even though there were Cantopop hits in the 1930s and the 1940s, the local music scene in Hong Kong was dominated by Cantonese opera. It was not until Shanghainese music workers came to Hong Kong that the popular music industry took root in Hong Kong. Before the Communists took over leadership, Shanghai was the center of Chinese popular music production, not only in China but also in Southeast Asia. Popular music was widely believed to have been brought to China by the songwriter Li Jinhui 黎錦輝, revered as the "Father of Chinese popular music," in the 1920s.[13] "At the time, Hong Kong did not have its own record production facilities, but Mandarin and Cantonese songs were composed and recorded locally, then sent to Shanghai for production and distribution."[14] The change of regime in the Mainland had an immense impact on the popular music industry, which was seen as capitalist and thus banned. The Shanghai popular music industry subsequently fled the Mainland and resumed their business in Hong Kong. These immigrants, including businessmen, singers, and musicians, brought capital as well as expertise to Hong Kong. After EMI started its new Hong Kong office in 1952, the then British colony took Shanghai's place and became the center of production of Chinese popular songs. It was thus understandable that *shidaiqu* (songs of the era) sung in Mandarin (hereafter abbreviated as "Mandapop"), which was immensely popular in the Mainland before 1949, became the mainstream

---

12. See http://blog.chinaunix.net/uid-20375883-id-1959392.html; retrieved on March 15, 2016.
13. Nimrod Baranovitch, *China's New Voices: Popular Music, Ethnicity, Gender and Politics, 1978–1997* (Berkeley: University of California Press, 2003), 14.
14. Cited from the Centre for Popular Culture in the Humanities, "Hong Kong Pop History," http://home.ied.edu.hk/~hkpop/music/hkpophistory.html; retrieved on March 15, 2016.

genre in Hong Kong at that time.[15] While Cantopop was not widely considered the voice of the city, newly arrived Mandapop stars such as Zhou Xuan 周璇 enthralled the Hong Kong audience with increased popularity. The famous Shanghainese singer Jao Li and her twin brother composer Jao Min moved to Hong Kong in 1950. Their now monumental "The Spring Breeze Kisses My Face" 〈春風吻上我的臉〉 (from the movie *Who Isn't Romantic?* 《那個不多情》, which premiered in 1956), among others, became a golden hit. This is the reason James Wong called this period (1949–1959) "The Era of 'Night Jasmine'" in his doctoral thesis—"Night Jasmine" 〈夜來香〉 is an all-time Shanghainese Mandapop classic originally sung by the legendary Li Xianglan 李香蘭 in 1945.[16] While it is correct to call this the age of Mandapop, it is also worth noting that not all music industry workers from Shanghai focused on Mandapop. The Cantonese musician Lu Wencheng 呂文成 transplanted his Shanghai music production experiences in Hong Kong. As "one of the most notable Cantonese musicians who spent the first half of his life in Shanghai and moved to Hong Kong in the late 1930s," he composed a large number of Cantonese pop songs, and thus "[i]t is not overstated to suggest that his pioneering efforts laid the foundation for the emergence of Cantonese pop songs in the 1970s."[17]

That Cantopop was considered inferior to Mandapop can also be attributed to its image. Mandapop was widely used as theme songs in trendy musical films, whereas early Hong Kong Cantopop was derived from Cantonese opera. Thanks to its cosmopolitan Shanghainese style, the former overshadowed the latter, making it look utterly outmoded among the younger generation. Back in the 1930s and 1940s, the main genre of entertainment of Hong Kong people was Cantonese opera. Parts of popular Cantonese operas would be extracted to form a shorter version known as a "ditty" 小曲 ("small song" in Chinese). Typically, songs in a Cantonese opera were 30 to 45 minutes long; even the shorter ones were more than 15 minutes and much longer than a popular

---

15. For a detailed account of *shidaiqu*, see Kei-Chi Wong, *The Age of Shanghainese Pops* (Hong Kong: Joint Publishing, 2001), 1–4. "Between 1920 and 1949, popular music of China was referred to as *shidaiqu* which was founded by Li Jinhui in Shanghai. *Shidaiqu* was influenced by American jazz music brought by Buck Clayton, an American jazz trumpet player influenced by Louis Armstrong, as Li Jinhui worked closely with Buck Clayton in Shanghai. The new music genre spread primarily in nightclubs and dancehalls during the 1920s and started to become popular through the media such as radio between the 1920s and the 1950s. The Shanghai popular music of the 1930s was spread through radio, movies and recordings, with the French-owned EMI-Pathé label playing the leading role." Cited from Centre for Popular Culture in the Humanities, "HK Pop History."

16. Wong, "The Rise and Decline of Cantopop," 11; Li Xianglan, also known as Yoshiko Yamaguchi, was a prominent movie star and singer from the late 1930s to the 1950s. She was very popular among Chinese fans until she was put on trial for spying for Japan after the Second World War.

17. May-Bo Ching, "Where Guangdong Meets Shanghai: Hong Kong Culture in a Trans-regional Context," in *Hong Kong Mobile: Making a Global Population*, ed. Helen Siu and Agnes Ku, (Hong Kong: Hong Kong University Press, 2009), 48, 61.

song. In addition, the habit of listening to a popular song is arguably different from that of a Cantonese opera, so Cantonese operas did not appeal to the general public outside the opera house. Producers, therefore, would extract certain parts of a Cantonese opera to make a ditty, which could be considered an early version of Cantopop. Famous examples include "Autumn Moon over the Han Palace" 〈漢宮秋月〉 and "Autumn Moon over a Calm Lake" 〈平湖秋月〉. According to veteran Cantopop lyricist Kwok-Kong Cheng 鄭國江, some ditties such as "Thunder in a Drought" 〈旱天雷〉 did not have lyrics, but eventually lyrics were composed according to the tunes. At that time, there was still no concept of Cantopop (not even in Chinese; as mentioned above, the first albums packaged with the term "Cantopop" were released on August 26, 1952), and these ditties were considered derivatives of Cantonese opera. Given the fact that it was popular mainly among the working class and the older generation, Cantopop in the 1950s was either social satire that poked fun at everyday life, or love songs inherited from the Cantonese opera tradition.

Years of Shaping the Future

In the 1950s and the 1960s, Cantopop was not considered mainstream in Hong Kong, despite the fact that Cantonese was spoken by over 90 percent of the people. At that time Euro-American and Mandarin popular songs were the dominant genres. Cantopop could be said to be popular among the Hong Kong audience, but most people considered it inferior to mainstream Mandarin and English popular songs. In the 1960s, Cantopop, albeit gradually gaining popularity in terms of market share, was still very much marginalized. It was not until the mid-1970s that Cantopop finally came to the fore. Having said this, it is also necessary to note that the 1950s and 1960s were very important periods during which Cantopop gradually built up its character. The late renowned poet and critic Ping-Kwan Leung (a.k.a. Ye Si) conducted a large-scale research project on Hong Kong literature and culture in the 1950s shortly before he passed away in 2013. In the "Preface" to "Hong Kong Literature and Culture in the 1950s" 《一九五〇年代香港文學與文化》, part of the Chinese book series he edited for Chung Hwa Book Co., he made it very clear why he chose the 1950s as the theme of his research:

> Before and after 1949, lots of literati fled the Mainland and moved to Hong Kong. Coming from different parts of the country, most of them were Shanghai and Guangzhou immigrants. They brought with them various cultural impact[s] and blending from different regions. Meanwhile, these cultural workers came from very different backgrounds, from writers, editors, philosophers, film directors and script-writers, actors, painters and musicians, etc. Some of them even [had] multiple talents . . . They inherited

traditional cultures on the one hand, and developed diasporic experience as well as assimilated/transformed Western literature and arts on the other. Their visions gradually turned to the future of Hong Kong, advancing a new, pluralistic direction for local culture.[18]

The special context of the 1950s—the assimilation of Cantonese culture and the urban cultures of Shanghai and other regions of the Mainland, the industrialization and commercialization of society, the growth of the postwar generation, etc.[19]—made Hong Kong a very good place for the generation of a unique, hybridized urban culture. The cultural industries, owing to their highly commercial operational logic, developed their local consciousness a bit more slowly than Hong Kong literature. While "Hong Kong already had a flourishing Cantonese dialect film industry with an annual output of some 150 films" in the 1950s, "Cantonese films produced at that time suggest a curious exclusion of local social reality."[20] This could be attributed to the prevailing refugee mentality and commercial consideration—"localism was to be avoided because these films exported to markets outside Hong Kong."[21] Despite this situation, these works became more hybridized in terms of styles, and Cantopop experienced a similar situation. After the first batch of albums packaged with the term "Cantopop" was released in 1952, the 1950s witnessed a proliferation of styles of Cantopop, which gradually distinguished it from Cantonese opera. Here are some examples of different styles of Cantopop: the use of Western musical arrangements (such as "Belle of Penang" 〈檳城艷〉, 1954); the hybridized genre of dance Cantonese opera 跳舞粵曲 (such as "A Wisp of Tender Love" 〈一縷柔情〉, 1956); Cantonese cover versions such as "View on the Sea" 〈海上風光〉 (1956) (the Cantonese version of a Filipino folk song) and "Teddy Boy in the Gutter" 〈飛哥跌落坑渠〉 (1958) (the Cantonese version of "Three Coins in the Fountain"); and the highly popular song-and-dance Cantonese movie songs, such as Patricia Lam's 林鳳 "Young Rock" 〈青春樂〉 (1959) and "The Fragrance of Durians" 〈榴槤飄香〉 (1959).[22] Although the younger generation still saw English and Mandarin popular songs as the dominant popular music genres, Cantopop was gathering momentum by the end of the 1950s and was beginning to broaden its fan base in the 1960s.

---

18. Ping-Kwan Leung and Mary Wong 黃淑嫻, "Preface" to "Hong Kong Literature and Culture in the 1950s" Series, in Ping-Kwan Leung, *Ye Si's 1950s: Essays on Hong Kong Literature and Culture* (Hong Kong: Chung Hwa, 2013), i.
19. Leung, *Ye Si's 1950s*, 9–10.
20. Eric Kit-Wai Ma, *Culture, Politics and Television in Hong Kong* (London: Routledge, 1999), 23. Song-and-dance movies, such as *Songs of the Peach Blossom River* 《桃花江》 (1956), would be an example of a popular genre of Hong Kong cinema at that time.
21. Ma, *Culture, Politics and Television in Hong Kong*, 23.
22. For more details, see Wong, *Pioneers*.

The 1960s in Hong Kong was a period of radical social and cultural changes. If Hong Kong was still dominated by its refugee mentality in the 1950s, it saw a rise of local awareness in the 1960s, thanks to changing demographics: "According to the official statistics of the 1961 Census, less than half (47.7 percent) of the population was born in Hong Kong. But that figure went up to 53.8 percent in the 1966 by-census, indicating the emergence of a locally born generation in a migrant society."[23] "It was the gradual emergence of the first post-war generation that shaped changes in the social horizons and popular consciousness of Hong Kong society."[24] By the late 1960s, "a postwar generation, which had only known Hong Kong as a home, reached adulthood, and a sense of Hong Kongese as an autonomous cultural identity began to emerge."[25] According to Eric Ma, there were four general rubrics under which the material base of a new cultural identity could be summarized: "1. Anglicized educational system; 2. Social preconditions (e.g., government-subsidized housing, transportation); 3. Economic opportunities; 4. Influx of new Chinese immigrants."[26] The new contextual factor brought forth Hong Kong's own local lifestyles, which "began to diverge sharply from those of Taiwan or the Communist Mainland," thus the 1960s could be seen as "a brutal weaning of Hong Kong from China as well as from Britain."[27] Interestingly enough, as noted by Matthew Turner, "'Life-style' here presents itself as a site of resistance for local identity. It is perhaps all the better for being unarticulated, yet at the heart of the Joint Declaration, for life-style can be expressed, but it cannot easily be censored."[28] Although Cantopop was still considered inferior to English and Mandarin popular songs in the 1960s, the local awareness of the Hong Kong people was growing gradually, which enhanced the development of local lifestyles, as well as paved the way for the later rise of Cantonese popular culture in the 1970s.

The Media Effect

The swift development of radio broadcasting in the 1950s exerted a significant impact on the music scene in Hong Kong. The government broadcaster

23. Gordon Mathews, Eric Kit-Wai Ma, and Tai-Lok Lui, *Hong Kong, China: Learning to Belong to a Nation* (Abingdon and New York: Routledge, 2008), 29.
24. Mathews, Ma, and Lui, *Hong Kong, China*, 31.
25. Gordon Mathews, "Heunggongyahn: On the Past, Present, and Future of Hong Kong Identity," *Bulletin of Concerned Asian Scholars* 29, no. 3 (July–September 1997): 7.
26. Ma, *Culture, Politics and Television in Hong Kong*, 25.
27. Hugh Baker, "Life in the Cities: The Emergence of Hong Kong Man," *The China Quarterly* 95 (September 1983): 469–79.
28. Matthew Turner, "Hong Kong Sixties/Nineties: Dissolving the People," in *Hong Kong Sixties: Designing Identity*, ed. Matthew Turner and Irene Ngan (Hong Kong: Hong Kong Arts Centre, 1995), 34.

"GOW," later renamed "Radio Hong Kong" in 1948, began broadcasting in 1928. Music was not an important element in its programs, but the broadcasting scene witnessed a drastic change in the 1950s. Founded in Hong Kong in 1949, Radio Rediffusion featured the wired distribution of the highly successful Rediffusion radio channels comprising one in the English language and one in Chinese, and another Chinese channel was added in 1956.[29] In the beginning, radio was not very popular due to its high price. With the popularization of radio among grassroots families, the music scene underwent a radical transformation and popular music became an important part of radio programming in the 1950s. One of the significant impacts was made by Chung Chow 周聰, a famous host of music radio programs for both Radio Hong Kong (RHK, Hong Kong's sole public broadcaster, which became Radio Television Hong Kong [RTHK] in 1970) and Rediffusion, and was later known as the "King of Broadcasting." He began broadcasting a variety of popular songs on air in 1954. As most of the population in Hong Kong at that time spoke Cantonese and grassroots Hong Kong people constituted a large portion of the audience of radio programs, there was a strong demand for local Cantopop. Chung Chow was interested in Cantopop himself, so he later tried writing new Cantopop or Cantonese lyrics according to the tunes of English and Mandarin popular songs (e.g., "Wishing for You Every Night" 〈夜夜寄相思〉 sung by Hing-Hing Hui 許卿卿 in 1959—the Cantonese version of "Wishing for the Moon Far Away" 〈明月千里寄相思〉 (originally sung by the Shanghainese superstar Wu Yingyin 吳鶯音).

According to Chung Chow, RHK's program featured both Mandapop and Cantopop, whereas Rediffusion focused on Cantopop.[30] Having Redifussion as the main medium of its dissemination, Cantopop became more popular among the general public, but it was still considered inferior to Mandapop and English popular songs. As per a mini-survey conducted by Chi-Wah Wong on the evening radio programs on April 6, 1958 (prime time on a Sunday) in Hong Kong, the airtime was dominated by Mandapop and English popular songs.[31] In 1959, Commercial Radio also began its first broadcasts, and Chung Chow was among the first cohort of radio hosts. Not only did Chung Chow write a large number of Cantonese lyrics, he also sang some of the songs himself. Thus, it was not surprising that he was hailed by James Wong as the "Father of Cantopop."[32]

---

29. "On 29 May 1957, a subscription Television Service was introduced using the same HF wired distribution technique as in the UK. The service was predominantly English but a Chinese service was introduced in 1963. By 1967 RTV had over 60,000 subscribers." Cited from the website of Rediffusion, http://www.rediffusion.info/hk.html; retrieved on March 15, 2016.
30. Cited from Wong, *Early Hong Kong Cantopop*, 59–60.
31. Wong, *Early Hong Kong Cantopop*, 60–61.
32. James Wong, "The Only Voice of the Age" 〈那時代唯一聲音〉 (in Chinese), *Hong Kong Economic Journal* (January 16, 1991).

Although Cantopop became more and more popular on the radio, Mandapop was still the dominant genre of Chinese popular songs. A famous example was the theme song of the Commercial Radio drama *Love of Rose*《薔薇之戀》sung by Kitty Lam 林潔 in 1962. The radio drama was broadcasted in Cantonese, but the theme song (melody by Tin-Pui Kwong 鄺天培 and lyrics by Chung Chow) was, ironically enough, in Mandarin. Moreover, in the 1950s and 1960s, Chung Chow sang a number of popular Cantopop with Lu Hung 呂紅, daughter of Lu Wencheng (e.g., "Happy Partners"〈快樂伴侶〉), but, as recalled by James Wong, the focus of Lu Hung's record company was not Cantopop but rather Mandapop.[33] It is worthwhile to note that the style of Cantopop at the time was dichotomized. On the one hand, some Cantopop inherited the style of Cantonese opera, with lyrics written in elegant, even at times archaic, language; on the other hand, given the fact that the target audience was mainly the working class, some Cantopop lyricists focused on social satire written with local Cantonese slangs. Such a dichotomy restricted the spread of Cantopop among the younger generation, who found it either outdated or in bad taste (e.g., "to line up at the toilet" in "Pretend to have a Belly Ache"〈詐肚痛〉sung by Kee-Chan Tang 鄧寄塵 and Pik-Ying Cheng 鄭碧影, 1961).

Television would prove to be a very effective platform to disseminate popular songs. When Rediffusion Television started cable television operations in Hong Kong in 1957, "[t]he high prices and the exclusively English-language programming meant that it never caught on among the local public."[34] TVB, the first free television network in Hong Kong, made a great impact on the development of Hong Kong popular music. As English and Mandarin popular songs were considered superior to Cantopop, TVB focused on them after it started broadcasting in 1967. The flagship multientertainment program then, *Enjoy Yourself Tonight*《歡樂今宵》, featured mostly Mandapop and English popular songs from the 1960s. The main cast of *Enjoy Yourself Tonight* (*EYT*) consisted of Cantonese movie stars (such as Sing-Por Leung 梁醒波 and Lydia Shum 沈殿霞), but they did not take the opportunity to promote Cantopop. Mandapop was the indispensable element of *EYT* in the 1960s. Sau-Lan Hai 奚秀蘭 was the mainstay, and renowned Mandapop songstresses like Rebecca Poon 潘迪華 and Mona Fong 方逸華 performed one to two times a week. Mandapop was further popularized as there were more than 900,000 households that could watch TVB free of charge. Meanwhile,

---

33. James Wong, "[Cantopop] Discriminated for Decades"〈受歧視數十年〉(in Chinese), *Eastweek* 65 (November 24, 2004): 174.

34. "Subscribers had to pay an installation fee of $25, a television set rental fee of $45 and an additional $36 for the license." Cited from Hong Kong Heritage Museum, *Hong Kong's Popular Entertainment* (Hong Kong: Hong Kong Heritage Museum, 2006), 20.

with an eye toward the younger generation as the target audience of its music programs (such as *The Star Show* and *Soundbeat*), TVB focused on English popular songs. Sam Hui, the mainstay of the band Lotus and who later became one of the most important figures in the history of Cantopop, was the host of the *The Star Show*, which aired five times a week and was immensely popular among teenagers. Together with the English popular song programs on radio and promotion by newspaper columns in *The Star* and *China Mail*, a tidal wave of English popular songs in the 1960s emerged in Hong Kong.

The British Invasion

In the 1950s, when Hong Kong was a British colony without a strong sense of local consciousness, it was expected that the local music scene would be dominated by Euro-American popular songs. RHK and Rediffusion aired many Western popular songs, and Elvis Presley, Pat Boone, Connie Francis, and Cliff Richard, among others, were the idols of Hong Kong music fans. In the early 1960s, when Elvis Presley and the Beatles were enjoying worldwide popularity, Euro-American popular songs continued to be the preferred music genre. "The early 1960s were the golden years of Hong Kong's night life scene, with the upper end nightclubs and ballrooms presenting dance bands and cabaret singers for adult audiences and a host of smaller venues presenting 'combos' to younger audiences."[35] Both English popular songs and Mandapop were popular in high-end nightclubs. The English side at that time was dominated by Filipino musicians. In the early 1960s, there was an unprecedented "British Invasion" that became an important milestone in the development of popular music in Hong Kong.

Around late 1963 and early 1964, Mersey Beat band music, including the Beatles, Gerry and the Pacemakers, and Searchers, was introduced to local audiences by radio stations in Hong Kong, but the impact was rather restricted. The Beatles visited Hong Kong in June 1964, exerting a profound influence on the local music scene. Subsequently, Beatlemania generated a rock band wave in Hong Kong, in the midst of which there were many band shows and contests, and rock band music became the vogue of the time. Band music was heard in night clubs and pubs, which offered lots of space for local bands to perform their music. Most importantly, this first wave of band music in Hong Kong allowed the younger generation to rebel with a cause. With the advent of rock music in the mid 1950s, "rock, its aesthetic and its associated culture did more to shape the political and social events of the times than vice-versa."[36] This

---

35. Centre for Popular Culture in the Humanities, "Hong Kong Pop History."
36. Richard Peterson, "Why 1955? Explaining the Advent of Rock Music," *Popular Music* 9, no. 1 (1990): 97.

was exactly the situation in Hong Kong in the 1960s. Veteran Hong Kong disc jockey Anders Nelsson explained in an interview that his generation of youngsters was enthralled by the "breakthrough" spirit of the Beatles.[37] Local music critic Ka-Ho Wong 黃嘉豪 highlighted a very important point regarding this wave of band music: "Different walks of life had the possibility to participate . . . the younger generation began to understand the importance of the right to participate."[38]

English popular songs, in particular band songs, were further disseminated by nightclubs and bars. While the main customers of nightclubs were adults, band music was very popular at "tea dances"—trendy weekend gatherings for youngsters.[39] In the midst of this band wave, a local record company called Diamond Music issued many albums promoting band music. Local bands such as Lotus, Teddy Robin and the Playboys, Joe Junior and the Side Effects, Anders Nelsson & The Inspiration, Mystics, D'Topnotes, and Kontinentals came onto the scene, and some of their members (such as Sam Hui and Teddy Robin) later became mainstays of the Cantopop industry in the 1970s and 1980s. Band music remained all the rage until the late 1960s. By the end of the 1960s, the rising popularity of Taiwanese popular songs in Hong Kong contributed, at least in part, to the recession of the first wave of band music. By the early 1970s, many popular bands had broken up, and members later continued their music careers as musicians in Chinese night clubs and hotels. There were still repercussions of band music, such as Wynners and New Topnotes. In the mid-1970s, the age of Cantopop arrived, bringing a paradigm shift to Hong Kong popular music. Arguably, the disbanding of The Wynners formally brought the curtain down on band music in Hong Kong. While there were scattered efforts by nonmainstream bands, many former band members turned to Cantopop in the late 1970s (such as Alan Tam 譚詠麟 of Wynners, George Lam 林子祥 of Jade, and Elisa Chan 陳潔靈 of New Topnotes). By the end of the 1970s, Cantopop had engulfed the music industry in Hong Kong, and it later dominated not only local but also overseas Chinese popular music markets. Despite its waning influence, band music exerted a very important impact on Cantopop in the 1970s when band members turned to the Cantopop

---

37. "Two Renowned Musicians in Love with the Rebellious Beatles" 〈兩大音樂人獨愛不規矩披頭四〉 (in Chinese), *Sing Tao Daily* (December 9, 2009).
38. Cited from Carmen, "Conference on 'Social Trends and Rock Music'" 〈社會趨勢與搖滾音樂〉 (in Chinese), *100 Marks Music Magazine* (October 14, 1989).
39. According to Joe Junior, the lead singer of Zoundcrackers and the Side Effects, "[d]uring the weekend afternoon, the night club will be temporarily changed into a party/dance venue, with bands like us playing live on stage. The young people, as long as they paid the entry ticket fee, they could enter and enjoy a screaming afternoon with drinks or snacks." Cited from an interview with Joe Junior, http://60spunk.m78.com/hongkong.html; retrieved on March 15, 2016.

industry for greener pastures, among whom was the legendary Sam Hui who later signed on to the Polydor label and became a Cantopop legend.[40]

Cantonese Movies Sing

Popular songs were often used in Hong Kong movies back in the 1940s and 1950s. "The transplantation of Shanghai *shidaiqu* to Hong Kong naturally accompanied the songstresses in Hong Kong feature films."[41] In this sense the popular songs in movies mirrored the popular music scene, with Mandapop assuming the superior position. In the 1960s, a new synergy was generated between Hong Kong cinema and popular music. Both Mandarin and Cantonese movies included popular songs, and at times there were win-win situations. *Love Without End* 《不了情》 (1961) is a prime example.[42] The title tune of this Shaw Brothers Mandarin classic love story, starring the four-time Asian Movie Queen Lin Dai 林黛, was awarded the Best Theme Song at the Ninth Asia and Pacific Film Festival. The perennial favorite "Love without End" was written by Fook-Ling Wong 王福齡 and sung by Mei Koo 顧媚, elder sister of the Hong Kong composer Joseph Koo, who was the mainstay of the Cantopop industry in the 1970s and 1980s. Wong Fook Ling was born in Shanghai and developed his music career in Hong Kong after he moved to the then British

---

40. "Hong Kong had never quite taken to rock'n'roll in the way it took to pop, so it was not until the sixties that Hong Kong discovered the teenager through the tea dance, Diamond 45's, band competitions and concerts at Mongkok Stadium and the newly built City Hall, radio shows such as 'Lucky Dip' and Sam Hui's TV 'Star Show'. The band scene also signaled a decisive shift from Mandarin to English, and from female to male lead singers. But with a much smaller fan base, the Hong Kong band scene turned out to be more fragile than its counterparts overseas. Many of the more popular bands traced their origins to elite schools and, as their members grew older, they could often find more lucrative employment in business, the law, government and, in some cases, the commercial music industry. In 1960s' Hong Kong, as it is today, band music was more of an adventure than a career. By the end of the decade many of the bands had broken up. Teddy Robin 泰迪羅賓 left Hong Kong to pursue musical interests in the US, while Norman Cheng 鄭東漢 and William Kwan 關維麟 of the now-defunct Playboys joined the international label Polydor, on the business side, after it had acquired Diamond Records in 1970. Sam Hui was signed up as one of Polydor's first artists and a new chapter in the history of Hong Kong pop had begun." http://www.ied.edu.hk/cpch/view.php?secid=3440; retrieved on March 15, 2016.

41. Jennifer Feeley, "Mandarin Pop Meets Tokyo Jazz: Gender and Popular Youth Culture in Late-1960s Hong Kong Musicals," in *Sinophone Cinemas*, ed. Audrey Yu and Olivia Khoo (New York: Palgrave Macmillan, 2014).

42. It should be noted that although Mandapop dominated the scene, different kinds of popular music crossed over in the context of Hong Kong. As Ping-Kwan Leung notes in his perceptive account of Derek Yee's *C'est la vie, Mon Cheri*, a 1993 remake of *Love Without End* (the Chinese title literally means "new love without end"), "the trends have shifted from the vulgar Cantonese songs and elegant Cantonese operas to Mandarin songs from Taiwan, to various kinds of western music from the United States and Great Britain . . . [and] these musical cultures from different urban spaces in the film are not necessarily isolated or compartmentalized." Ping-Kwan Leung, "Urban Cinema and Cultural Identity," *The Cinema of Hong Kong: History, Arts, Identity*, ed. Poshek Fu and David Desser (Cambridge: Cambridge University Press, 2000), 247.

colony in 1952. At that time Hong Kong had overtaken Shanghai to become the center of Mandapop production, and most Hong Kong people were attracted to Mandapop. Eyeing the big market for Mandapop, film companies began to produce musical films. Tao Qin's 陶秦 *Calendar Girl* 《龍翔鳳舞》 (1959), produced by Motion Picture and General Investment Co. Ltd., was the first Hollywood-style musical in Hong Kong. Trying to beat its major competitor, the Shaw Brothers Company bankrolled a handsome budget for musical films and produced, among others, *Les Belles* 《千嬌百媚》 (1961, also directed by Tao Qin). Being the first Eastman color production shot in CinemaScope, this film was partly shot in Tokyo and became a huge success in Hong Kong. While Tao Qing's subsequent *Love Parade* 《花團錦簇》 (1963) and *The Dancing Millionairess* 《萬花迎春》 (1964) might be considered "poor knock-offs" of Hollywood musicals,[43] the melodies became hits as the audience was captured by the extravagant sets and costumes. The genre was further developed when Shaw Brothers invited Japanese director Inoue Umetsugu 井上梅次 to make *Hong Kong Nocturne* 《香江花月夜》 (1967), *Hong Kong Rhapsody* 《花月良宵》 (1968), and *The Millionaire Chase* 《釣金龜》 (1969), signaling a "horizontal transplant between Hong Kong and Japan."[44] Thanks to their big budgets, these Mandarin musical films successfully hit the fancy of Hong Kong movie fans.

While the musical films in the late 1950s and the 1960s were dominated by Mandarin productions, the rise of a new generation of Cantonese movie stars, such as Connie Chan 陳寶珠 and Josephine Siao 蕭芳芳, gradually changed the scene. Back in the 1940s and 1950s, the songs used in Cantonese movies were basically Cantonese opera. Even when the setting was modern, the actors sang in the Cantonese opera style in a rather awkward manner. The song "Smoking a Big Cigar" in *A Bachelor's Love Affair* 《光棍姻緣》 (1952), sung by Sing-Por Leung, was a famous example. Later there were different kinds of Cantopop theme songs, but the genre had to wait for Connie Chan and Josephine Siao to turn the situation around. Meanwhile, the market leader Shaw Brothers had been focusing on Mandarin productions. Its short-term Cantonese Division (1958–1963) did bring fame to actresses such as Patricia Lam, but the songs in these productions could not be put on a par with the songs in Mandarin films in terms of budget and quality. In the 1960s, the popular music market steadily expanded as a result of the developing economy. Moreover, it was in 1966 that for the first time more than half

43. Emilie Yueh-Yu Yeh, "China," in *The International Film Musical*, ed. Corey Creekmur and Linda Mokdad (Edinburgh: Edinburgh University Press), 183.
44. Feeley, "Mandarin Pop Meets Tokyo Jazz"; see also Kinnia Shuk-Ting Yau, *Japanese and Hong Kong Film Industries: Understanding the Origins of East Asian Film Networks* (New York: Routledge, 2010).

of the population of Hong Kong was born locally, and the younger generation all spoke Cantonese. As noted in an interview with Josephine Siao, there was a trend of youth culture sweeping across the globe in the 1960s.[45] The Cantonese cinema "became in this decade a social discourse in which the processes of capitalist modernization and the questions of youth culture and generation gaps were projected and debated," creating a big demand for youth movies in Hong Kong.[46]

Young Hong Kong movie fans throughout the 1960s were divided into the Connie Chan and Josephine Siao camps. Connie Chan, a child star born in a Cantonese opera family, captured the hearts of the new generation of "factory girls" (young women working in factories) in the 1960s and was crowned the "Princess of Movie Fans." She noted in an interview that her most popular song was "Long Live Factory Girls" 〈工廠妹萬歲〉 from the movie *Her Tender Love* (a.k.a. *Court Attendant Like Spring Day Wind*)《郎如春日風》(1969).[47] Meanwhile, Josephine Siao, born in a middle-class family in Shanghai, was also a child star who became a superstar after she grew up, epitomizing the spirit of youth together with Connie Chan, but her fans were mainly college students. Moreover, "youth" was arguably a magic word in Hong Kong cinema in the 1960s, and the teen musical *Colorful Youth*《彩色青春》, starring Connie Chan and Josephine Siao, was the trendsetter of the decade. It broke box office records when it premiered in 1966, and the Cantopop songs in the movie, such as "The Young Generation" 〈年青的一代〉, "Precious Youth" 〈莫負青春〉, and "Happy Together" 〈及時行樂〉, were well received by their fans. The soundtrack albums of Connie Chan and Josephine Siao's movies sold tremendously well, popularizing Cantopop among the younger generation. Despite their popularity, the quality of these songs was much lower than their Mandarin counterparts owing to their low budget. As the record companies were paying peanuts, they ended up getting monkeys. However, the fans were so attracted to Connie Chan and Josephine Siao that they were willing to purchase those albums, regardless of their lackluster quality.

James Wong cited an interview with Chung Chow to support his claim that the quality of mass-produced Cantopop was very low compared with Mandapop and English popular songs: "In order to save production cost, we could not have high expectation of the music and singing. Even if there were

---

45. See "Song and Dance through the Century," *Dream Factory Revisited* (DVD) (Hong Kong: RTHK, 2007).

46. Poshek Fu, "The 1960s: Modernity, Youth Culture and Hong Kong Cantonese Cinema," in *The Cinema of Hong Kong*, ed. Fu and Desser (Cambridge: Cambridge University Press, 2000), 71–72.

47. Victor Chau, "Legendary Movie Star, Connie Chan Po-chu," *Hong Kong Magazine* 19 (January 2006); http://hk-magazine.com/article/inside-hk/interviews/5035/legendary-movie-star-connie-chan-po-chu; retrieved on March 15, 2016.

errors, we had to go on releasing the song if they are not very conspicuous."[48] And to lower the cost, most of these songs were cover versions (e.g., in the film *Opposite Love* 《玉女痴情》 [1968], Connie Chan's "Another Three Years of Waiting" 〈春風秋雨三年〉 was a Cantonese version of the Mandapop classic "Three Years" 〈三年〉, and "An All-Consuming Love" 〈長相思〉 was a cover of "The End of the World."). James Wong also started writing Cantopop lyrics around 1968, being involved in "making music for several Cantonese films, occasionally creating tunes and lyrics for their theme songs . . . Among these songs, there was one entitled 'A Rose that Does not Fade' 〈不褪色的玫瑰〉, which came from the film *The Forsaken Love* 《青春玫瑰》, starring Connie Chan." The quality of the song, however, was not promising: "pleasing enough, but rather timid in style and substance."[49] As argued by Chi-Wah Wong, notwithstanding the fact that these movie songs sold well, they did not promote a positive image for Cantopop: "From 1963 to 1969, Connie Chan released a total of seventy albums, in which more than 95% of movie songs . . . but this had not had much to contribute to the status of Cantopop."[50] James Wong and Chi-Wah Wong concurred on the point that the title tune of the movie *The Story between Hong Kong and Macao* (literally, *World of Water Apart*) 〈一水隔天涯〉 (1966) was an exception. The lyrics, written by Zuo Ji 左几, basically inherited the style of Cantonese ditties, but the melody, composed by Lun Yu 于粦, and the performance of Winnie Sau-Han Wei 韋秀嫻 generated a special effect of modernity.[51]

Before the Dawn of a New Era

During the heyday of Cantonese movies in the 1960s, Cantopop was popular but still very much marginalized owing to its image as well as its quality. When Cantonese movies began to decline in late 1980s, the situation worsened. In the early 1970s, almost all Chinese movies that premiered in Hong Kong were in Mandarin. The production of Cantonese movies eventually ceased in March 1971 until the unexpected box office success of *Seventy-Two Tenants*, which premiered in September 1973, cauing Hong Kong to slant heavily toward Mandarin popular culture. As mentioned above, Mandapop was a major

---

48. Wong, "The Rise and Decline of Cantopop," 63, 78. Interview cited from Sau Yan Chan 陳守仁 and Sai-Shing Yung 容世誠, "Hong Kong Cantopop in the 1950s and the 1960s" 〈五、六十年代香港的粵語流行曲〉 (in Chinese), *Wide Angle Monthly* (February 1990): 74.
49. Cited from "James Wong's Study," Hong Kong Memory Project, http://www.hkmemory.org/james-wong/wjs/web/wjsmusic.php?page=%E7%BF%92%E4%BD%9C%E9%BB%83%E9%9C%91&musicId=126&locale=en_US; retrieved on March 15, 2016.
50. Wong, *Early Hong Kong Cantopop*, 227.
51. Wong, "The Rise and Decline of Cantopop," 78; Chi-Wah Wong, *Early Hong Kong Cantopop*, 72.

selling point in the early stage of TVB's flagship entertainment program *EYT*. In 1970, in order to boost declining ratings, the producers of *EYT* invited a group of Taiwanese singers to perform new Taiwanese Mandapop (different from the previous Mandapop oldies). This was so popular that "cabarets" featuring Mandapop, albeit short-lived, sprang up like mushrooms.[52] Among these singers Yao Surong 姚蘇蓉 was arguably the most popular, generating a heated wave by her golden hit "I'm Not Going Home Today"〈今天不回家〉. It is interesting to note that the wave of Mandapop in the late 1960s was generated across the strait in Taiwan. While the music scene in Hong Kong was captivated by English popular songs and band songs in the 1960s, the production of Mandapop gradually moved to Taiwan. After the Kuomintang relocated to Taiwan after 1949, Mandarin became the official language there. As the government marginalized local dialects, Mandapop had a hold over Taiwanese popular songs. At first Mandapop was imported from Hong Kong through the channel of the Taiwan Television Enterprise music program *Star Club*《群星會》. Not long after, Taiwan began to develop its Mandapop industry, which exported its Taiwanese-style Mandapop in the late 1960s. Taiwanese singers such as Qing Shan 青山 and Yao Surong generated a wave of Taiwanese Mandapop in Hong Kong. Due to the tense political situation in Taiwan, many Mandapop songs were censored. For example, the huge hit "I'm Not Going Home Today" by Yao Surong was banned in Taiwan, but enthralled audiences not only in Hong Kong but also in Asia. The Taiwanese wave continued into the 1970s when the theme songs of Chiung Yao's 瓊瑤 style of *wenyi pian* (romantic melodrama) hit Hong Kong. You Ya 尤雅, Feng Fei Fei 鳳飛飛, Jenny Tseng 甄妮, and the legendary Teresa Teng 鄧麗君 gained popularity in Hong Kong. Similar to the band wave mentioned in the precious section, the impact exerted by the Taiwanese wave on Cantopop was twofold. First, its attractiveness to the Hong Kong audience suppressed the development of Cantopop, keeping it within the periphery in the field of popular music. However, later it contributed a new impetus to Cantopop: cover versions and Mandapop created Cantopop singers such as Jenny Tseng, who later became the most popular female singer in Hong Kong in the early 1980s.

In the 1970s, there was a boom in the Hong Kong economy, but its local culture was still marginalized. Initially, Hong Kong Cantopop represented Hong Kong in a way similar to the Cantopop of the 1950s and 1960s, which was still perceived in the music industry as subordinate to English and Mandarin popular songs. As per the introduction in *Ten Years of Golden Hits* published by RTHK in commemoration of its flagship music program *Top Ten Chinese Gold Songs*, which was written by veteran disc jockey Ping-Long Ngai 倪秉郎,

---

52. Suet-Lo Lee, "In Memoriam of James Wong," *Hong Kong Economic Journal* (August 24, 2011).

[i]n the early 1970s, Taiwanese Mandapop swept its neighboring region—Hong Kong with irresistible force . . . At that time Hong Kong people almost forgot their dialect—Cantonese . . . It was until 1974 when the two ground-breaking albums *Romance between Tears and Laughter* and *Games Gamblers Play* changed the scene, occupying a place for Cantopop in a music industry dominated by Mandapop.[53]

This situation gave the impression that Cantopop was not born until *Romance between Tears and Laughter* and *Games Gamblers Play* broke the ice. It is worthwhile to note the viewpoint of Chi-Wah Wong, which differed from the common belief that the history of Cantopop did not really begin until 1974. In the midst of the heated wave of Taiwanese Mandapop there were very popular Cantopop, such as "Sound of the Bell at the Zen Temple" 〈禪院鍾聲〉 and "Tears of Love" 〈相思淚〉 by Singaporean singers Kam-Cheong Cheng (Kim-Chong Tay) 鄭錦昌 and Lisa Wong 麗莎. The myth that Cantopop was not born until 1974 can be attributed to the fact that these songs were devalued by local Hong Kong people as a dying pastime at the grassroots level. Chi-Wah Wong cited the convincing example of "My Lover Got Married" 〈愛人結婚了〉 by Adam Cheng 鄭少秋, released in 1971, to argue that Cantopop albums were actually quite well received. Some songs on this album, such as the title song "My Lover Got Married" and "Autumn Winds Blighted the Spring Blossoms" 〈秋風吹謝了春紅〉 (lyrics by the famous veteran lyricist Yung So 蘇翁; the latter song was later renamed "Autumn Winds of Sorrow" 〈悲秋風〉), were so popular that Adam Cheng published two more Cantopop albums in the next couple of years.[54] Chi-Wah Wong continued by pointing out that the music industry had already paid attention to the growing market of Cantopop in 1973. Paula Tsui 徐小鳳, one of the superstars during the later heyday of Cantopop, included some Cantopop oldies (theme songs of the radio dramas of Commercial Radio in the 1960s) such as "Strong Grass Fragile Flower" 〈勁草嬌花〉 and "Pink Tears" 〈癡情淚〉. Another big hit from that year was "Departed Swallows" 〈分飛燕〉 by Sau-Yee Yan 甄秀儀 and Ho-Tak Chan 陳浩德. First collected on Sau-Yee Yan's album *Everything Is Wonderful* 《一切太美妙》, with the original title "Please Treasure My Soft Reminders" 〈囑咐話兒莫厭煩〉, this duet became an all-time Cantopop classic, still well-liked in karaokes after forty years. The problem was that the style of "Departed Swallows," "Sound of the Bell at the Zen Temple," and "Tears of Love" still resembled the Cantopop from the 1960s inherited from Cantonese opera, which failed to become chic among the younger generation. In short, although

53. Ping-Long Ngai, "Introduction," *Ten Years of Golden Hits* (Hong Kong: Radio Television Hong Kong), cited from Chi-Wah Wong, "Reminiscences of Cantopop in the Early 1970s" 〈回顧七十年代初香港粵語歌〉 (in Chinese), *Tai Kung Pao* (February 17, 2013): B11.
54. Wong, "Reminiscences of Cantopop in the Early 1970s."

it is generally agreed that Cantopop did not emerge as a dominant genre until the mid-1970s,[55] the earlier type of urban Cantonese songs based on Cantonese opera is important and popular among the general public. Cantopop of the 1950s and 1960s was a hybridized genre that embodied the creative impulse of songwriters in basing their music on a variety of music such as Cantonese opera, Nanyan culture, and popular music of the English-speaking world. An elaborate account of the influence of these Cantonese songs on later Cantopop would require an in-depth study of Cantopop in the 1950s and 1960s, which has extended beyond the scope of this book. The account of the 1950s and 1960s in this chapter serves mainly as an introduction to the background of the rise of Cantopop.

The 1970s was arguably the time that Hong Kong developed most quickly in terms of its economy and popular culture. In the early 1970s, the living standards of Hong Kong were on the rise, and the capitalist mode of living began to mature, but local culture was still very much in an embryonic state. Initially, Hong Kong Cantopop represented Hong Kong in a way similar to the Cantopop of the 1950s and 1960s, which was perceived in the music industry as subordinate to English and Mandarin popular songs. While Cantopop was still marginalized, it began to gather momentum with the rise of local consciousness among a new generation of Hong Kong people. Although TVB was founded in the 1960s, its localization procedure did not finish until the mid-1970s. Free television service provided Hong Kong people with common leisure, and it united the taste of Hong Kong people by offering a common ground for the "Hong Kong" consciousness to develop. The swift development of television broadcasting not only led to the revitalization of Cantonese films but also the development of the Cantopop market.[56] In the midst of this new mediascape, Cantopop was about to start a new chapter in the history of Hong Kong popular music.

---

55. For example, James Wong's "The Rise and Decline of Cantopop," Ching-Chih Liu's *A History of Hong Kong Music*, Elvin Wong's *Flowing Melody*, and Yiu-Wai Chu's *A Study of Hong Kong Popular Lyrics* use 1974 as the timeline to chronicle the rise of Cantopop.

56. For a detailed discussion of the influence of television on the film industry in the 1970s, see James Kung and Zhang Yueai, "Hong Kong Cinema and Television in the 1970s: A Perspective," in *A Study of Hong Kong Cinema in the Seventies*, ed. The Eighth Hong Kong International Film Festival (Hong Kong: Urban Council of Hong Kong, 1984), 14–17.

3 The Rise of Cantopop
The Mid- to Late 1970s

Introduction

As a British colony before sovereignty over the territory was handed to China in 1997, Hong Kong had been seen as a transient shelter rather than a permanent home. Local identity was arguably absent owing to its colonial history: "The Chinese community of Hong Kong did not have an identity of its own before the Second World War, and the non-Chinese community was essentially an expatriate one."[1] It was not until the late 1960s that the local consciousness of the Hong Kong people took shape. Although

> a sense of local identity had in fact emerged by the late 1800s when many wealthy Chinese in Hong Kong came to see themselves as permanent residents and as a special kind of Chinese . . . it was during the 1960s and the 1970s that other parts of the population also began to identify more closely with Hong Kong.[2]

By the late 1960s, as noted by Gordon Mathews in his account of the history of Hong Kong identity, "a post-war-generation, which had known Hong Kong as a home, reached adulthood, and a sense [of] Hongkongese as an autonomous cultural identity began to emerge."[3] This was at least partly due to the change in governance policy of the United Kingdom after the 1967 riots. Briefly, as a repercussion of the riots over fare hikes on the Star Ferry in 1966, the 1967 riots began with a labor dispute in April 1967. It later turned into large-scale demonstrations with waves of bombing against British colonial rule. "The colonial government reacted to the riots by enhancing young people's social

---

1. Steve Tsang, "The Rise of a Hong Kong Identity," in *China Today: Economic Reforms, Social Cohesion and National Identities*, ed. Taciana Fisac and Leila Fernandez-Stembridge (London and New York: Routledge Curzon, 2003), 222.
2. John Carroll, *A Concise History of Hong Kong* (Lanham: Rowman & Littlefield, 2007), 167.
3. Gordon Mathews, "Heunggongyahn: On the Past, Present, and Future of Hong Kong Identity," in *Narrating Hong Kong Culture and Identity*, ed. Ngai Pun and Lai-Man Yee (Hong Kong: Oxford University Press, 2003), 58–59.

integration and directing their energy into formal channels such as participation in government-sponsored social services."[4] In the aftermath of the riots, the Hong Kong government also designed a series of programs, such as Hong Kong Week and the Hong Kong Festival, with the aim of constructing a kind of local consciousness in order to curb the national and/or anticolonial sentiments of the post-1967 society. Concepts such as "civil identity" and "society" were widely disseminated in Hong Kong after the 1967 riots, and "a distinct Hong Kong identity first emerged in the 1970s."[5] Before that time, Hong Kong people were not self-conscious about their own identity, and they even looked down upon their own culture.

The 1970s was a decade of "legendary" adventure for Hong Kong.[6] The radical transformation of Hong Kong's sociopolitical background and the swift development of local mass media in the 1970s also provided a historical juncture in which a "Hong Kong consciousness" at long last came into being. "Demographically, while before the 1970s Hong Kong was largely regarded as a refugee society, the 1970s saw the coming of age of a new class of educated youth, who were born or brought up in Hong Kong, having a better sense of belonging to Hong Kong."[7] This historical juncture provided Hong Kong popular culture with an excellent opportunity to develop. The rise of a Hong Kong identity among this generation created an unprecedented demand for local culture. "The people of Hong Kong had come to recognize themselves reflected in vernacular pop songs, newspapers and comics, new expressions of identity in English-medium school textbooks and in images purveyed by advertising, popular photography and television."[8] Thanks to the emergence of new media platforms, especially television,[9] Hong Kong people had many more chances to "see" the world. Not only did they "see" Hong Kong "for the first time through the daily broadcast of television news,"[10] they also had new platforms on which to hybridize new Western ideas with local genres.

4. Tai-Lok Lui, "The Malling of Hong Kong," in *Consuming Hong Kong*, ed. Gordon Mathews and Tai-Lok Lui (Hong Kong: Hong Kong University Press, 2001), 33.
5. Matthew Turner, "Hong Kong Sixties/Nineties: Dissolving the People," in *Hong Kong Sixties: Designing Identities*, ed. Matthew Turner and Irene Ngan (Hong Kong: Hong Kong Art Center, 1994), 13–19; Gordon Mathews, Eric Kit-Wai Ma, and Tai-Lok Lui, *Hong Kong, China: Learning to Belong to a Nation* (London and New York: Routledge, 2008), 34.
6. Tai-Lok Lui, *Hong Kong's 1970s* 《那似曾相識的七十年代》 (in Chinese) (Hong Kong: Chung Hwa, 2012), 6; this book offers a very perceptive account of social changes in Hong Kong in the 1970s.
7. Ngok Ma, "Social Movements and State-Society Relationship in Hong Kong," in *Social Movements in China and Hong Kong: The Expansion of Protest Space*, ed. Khun Eng Kuah and Gilles Guiheux (Amsterdam: Amsterdam University Press, 2009), 47.
8. Turner, "Hong Kong Sixties/Nineties: Dissolving the People," 16.
9. "Newly fashionable, television took the lead in bringing in the world's latest trend." Cited from "e-wave: The TV films of Patrick Tam," Hong Kong Film Archive (September 19–October 12, 2008). Available at: http://www.movingimagesource.us/events/e-wave-the-tv-films-of-patrick-20080919; retrieved on March 15, 2016.
10. Ma, *Culture, Politics and Television in Hong Kong*, 30.

"If the Hong Kong Chinese up to the 1970s were Chinese sojourners in Hong Kong, the generation of the 1970s [was] Hong Kong people of Chinese descent."[11] The "refugee mentality" of Hong Kong in the 1950s and 1960s was replaced by a new "market mentality" in the 1970s. While "the emergence of Hong Kong identity was partly a result of demographic change," as argued by Gordon Mathews, Eric Ma, and Tai-Lok Lui, "in a larger sense, a local identity developed in the context of growing affluence in the colony."[12] Meanwhile, the late 1970s also witnessed a new China after the launching of economic reforms. There were more interactions between Hong Kong and the Mainland, thanks to the restoration of the Guangzhou-Kowloon Through Train in 1979, and Hong Kong people began seeing a sharp distinction between "we" (the locals) and "them" (the new immigrants) with "a new sense of pride and superiority."[13] By the end of the 1970s, the Cantonese cultural industries had developed into the trendsetter of Chinese pop culture across the globe. Hong Kong people took great pride in their pop culture, which was an important source of their identity. In short, the rise of Cantopop can be attributed to the huge growth in local audiences in Hong Kong in the early 1970s, when local Cantonese popular cultural industries became a profitable business.

The Localization of Popular Media

The localization of free television programs significantly expanded the discursive space for local Hong Kong culture. Although the Television Broadcasting Company (TVB) launched free-to-air television in 1967, its localization procedure was not completed until the mid-1970s. During its early years, TVB relied heavily on foreign-purchased dramas. Besides news, weather reports, music programs, and the famous *EYT*, there were only a handful of domestic productions, such as *Love Story* 《夢斷情天》 (1968) and *The Net of Justice* 《法網難逃》 (1969). Considering the increasing demand for local programs, TVB began to place more emphasis on domestic productions, including, among others, *The Hui Brothers Show* 《雙星報喜》 (1971) and the situation comedy *Seventy-Three* 《七十三》 (1973). Meanwhile, the series entitled *Television Theatre* 《電視劇場》 launched in 1970 was well received among audiences, and domestic dramas began to gather momentum in the early 1970s. "[F]or TVB Jade, the Cantonese channel which virtually monopolized viewership throughout the 1970s and the 1980s, the share of home-made programs rose

---

11. David Faure, "Reflections on Being Chinese in Hong Kong," in *Hong Kong's Transitions, 1942–1997*, ed. Judith M. Brown and Rosemary Foot (Basingstoke: Macmillan Press, 1997), 103–4.
12. Mathews, Ma, and Lui, *Hong Kong, China*, 35.
13. Ibid., 38.

from under 30 per cent in 1972 to over 60 per cent in 1982."[14] By 1974, more than 780,000 out of 850,000 households in Hong Kong had a television set.[15] Free television service provided Hong Kong people with common leisure, and it united the taste of Hong Kong people by offering a common ground for the "Hong Kong" consciousness to develop. "The identity of the local generation was fostered in the relatively autonomous television culture in the 1970s."[16] Local television programs were so popular that the TVB-inspired movie *The House of 72 Tenants* (1973), a remake of a 1963 movie of the same title, unexpectedly broke the box office record set by Bruce Lee's *Way of the Dragon* (1972). This was the only Cantonese production out of the 94 Hong Kong movies released in 1973. It was a pleasant surprise for Cantonese popular culture, which successfully brought Cantonese movies back to the Hong Kong film industry. In 1974, out of a total of 101 Hong Kong movies, 21 were Cantonese productions. Moreover, the highest-grossing films were Cantonese productions, including the monumental *Games Gamblers Play* (1974) by the Hui brothers.[17] Thereafter, Hong Kong experienced a swiftly increased demand for local productions, including movies, television programs, and popular songs. Ackbar Abbas's famous "doom and boom" notion can be used here to account for the development of popular culture in Hong Kong in the mid-1970s. Abbas argued that "the more frustrated or blocked the aspirations to democracy are, the more the market booms."[18] In other words, the more frustrated or blocked the aspirations to the economy are, the more the cultural industries boom. This seems applicable to Hong Kong, at least in the 1970s and the 1980s (refer to the next chapter). Dealt a heavy blow by the oil crisis between 1973 and 1974, the real GDP growth of Hong Kong slowed drastically from 12.3 percent in 1973 to 2.3 percent in 1974 and further to 0.4 percent in 1975.[19] The Hang Seng Index fell from its peak of nearly 1,800 in 1973 to 200 and bottomed out at about 150 by December 1974. Despite this decline in growth, Hong Kong cultural industries developed swiftly after 1974, and

---

14. Po-King Choi, "Popular Culture," in *The Other Hong Kong Report 1990*, ed. Richard Y. C. Wong and Joseph Y. S. Cheng (Hong Kong: Chinese University Press, 1990), 540.

15. Ho Ng 吳昊, *Talks on the History of Hong Kong Television* 《香港電視史話》 (in Chinese) (Hong Kong: Subculture Press, 2003), 7.

16. Eric Kit-Wai Ma, *Culture, Politics and Television in Hong Kong* (London: Routledge, 1999), 31; "The television of Hong Kong, at least during its early stages, did not initially appear to be the ideological apparatus of either the colonial government or of the capitalist economy."

17. See Pak-Tong Cheuk, *Hong Kong New Wave Cinema (1978–2000)* (Chicago: Intellect Books, 2008), 41.

18. Ackbar Abbas, *Hong Kong: Culture and the Politics of Disappearance* (Hong Kong: Hong Kong University Press, 1997), 5.

19. Cited from "Oil Shocks in the 1970s and How They Had Impacted on Hong Kong Economy," Hong Kong Economy, Hong Kong Special Administration Region Government, www.hkeconomy. gov.hk/en/pdf/box-05q4-1-2.pdf; retrieved on March 15, 2016.

the local consciousness of the Hong Kong people was enhanced by the rise of Cantonese popular culture. As Cantonese television and cinema became central to the then colony's cultural industries, they provided a new source of Cantonese-speaking stars, as did the Hong Kong–based Cantopop industry.

While the localization of free television programs and *The House of 72 Tenants* changed the operational logic of Hong Kong cultural industries in the early 1970s, Cantopop, which remained at the margin at that time, did not have to wait long for an opportunity to change the game. It was generally agreed by Hong Kong music critics that the year 1974 was the turning point for the development of Cantopop.[20] The first Cantopop television theme song, bearing the same title as the drama *Romance in the Rain* 《煙雨濛濛》, was released in 1973. The twenty-episode *Romance in the Rain*, the very first TVB color drama, premiered in March 1973 as the first hit in the drama series entitled *Jade Theatre* 《翡翠劇場》. According to producer Tin Leung 梁天, the theme song was proposed by him, and it was approved by TVB on the condition that no extra budget would be provided.[21] The song (melody by Joseph Koo and lyrics by Yung So 蘇翁) was sung by the drama's male lead, Adam Cheng. Chi-Wah Wong argued that in terms of the melody, "Romance in the Rain" is much more modern/Western than "A Love Tale between Tears and Smiles." Both songs were composed by Joseph Koo, but since at that time Cantopop was still seen as old-fashioned, and the former song was not broadly aired on the radio, it was not well received among the local audience.[22]

A Love Tale between Tears and Smiles: The Turning Point

In 1974, the drama *A Love Tale between Tears and Smiles* premiered in the series entitled *Chinese Folklores* 《民間傳奇》 on the Jade Channel, the most popular channel in Hong Kong. TVB drama had already attracted a solid fan base by then, and the 25-episode *A Love Tale between Tears and Smiles* became a huge hit. Veteran lyricist Jimmy Lo 盧國沾 noted in an interview that Wong Tin Lam, an established film director who later joined TVB, adopted the style of film production in the making of the television drama. One of the most remarkable measures was the use of theme songs.[23] Joseph Koo, the composer of the theme song "A Love Tale between Tears and Smiles," wrote

20. James Wong, "The Rise and Decline of Cantopop: A Study of Hong Kong Popular Music (1949–1997)" 《粵語流行曲的發展與興衰：香港流行音樂研究 1949–1997》 (in Chinese) (Hong Kong: PhD thesis, the University of Hong Kong, 2003), 92.
21. Cited from Chi-Wah Wong, "Hong Kong Cantopop in the Early 1970s" 〈七十年代早期香港粵語流行曲〉 (in Chinese), *Ta Kung Pao* (February 17, 2013): B11.
22. Wong, "Hong Kong Cantopop in the Early 1970s."
23. Cited from Yiu-Wai Chu, *Songs of Your Life: Talks on Hong Kong Cantopop* 《歲月如歌：詞話香港粵語流行曲》 (in Chinese) (Hong Kong: Joint Publishing, 2009), 32–33.

this first TVB Mandapop theme song for the drama *Star River* 《星河》 in 1972. Koo noted in an interview that he wanted to do something different: "TVB asked me to write a Mandapop, but I think why not Cantopop? And the producer Wong Tin Lam concurred with me. . . . The record company had grave concerns, and I agreed to share the production cost."[24] Since the drama was set in the early twentieth century, the song adopted a typical traditional Chinese folk style. The song, bearing the same title as the drama, sparked a TV theme song craze across the territory. Owing to its immense popularity, the song is often mistaken as the first television theme song.

The difference between "Romance in the Rain" and "A Love Tale between Tears and Smiles" can be examined in light of the rising trend of local Cantonese culture mentioned above. In terms of lyrics, both "Romance in the Rain" and "A Love Tale between Tears and Smiles" (written by Cantonese opera lyrics writer Siu-Tak Yip) still adopted the typical style of Cantopop from the 1960s, which was inherited from Cantopop opera ditties. The impacts exerted by the two songs, however, were extremely different. "Romance in the Rain" came out at a time when Cantonese popular culture was just emerging, and it was not until the end of 1973, after the success of *The House of 72 Tenants*, that Cantonese popular culture became a trend in the mainstream. By the time "A Love Tale between Tears and Smiles" was heard by Hong Kong audiences, Cantonese popular culture had already picked up speed. More importantly, the producers were able to think outside the box and invited Sandra Lang, a mixed singer who used to sing English pop songs, to perform the theme song. It was a big experiment and in the end they were willing to take the risk to use a Westernized singer to sing this traditional Chinese tune. According to Joseph Koo, "We chose Sandra Lang because she has been singing Mandarin and English popular songs, so that the song would not sound old-fashioned to the audience. Actually we were not very confident at that time."[25]

Early television theme songs were usually tailor-made, and thus their styles matched very well with their respective dramas. The lyrics of "A Love Tale between Tears and Smiles," a traditional Chinese tune, adopted the literary if not archaic style of Cantonese opera, which was a perfect match for the Early Republican China setting of the drama. For instance, in the line "Albeit thousand miles apart, lovers are connected by a red thread tied around their ankles" （赤絲千里早已繫足裡）, the lyricist used the literary allusion of the red thread, which is supposedly used by the matchmaker god to connect destined

24. Cited from "Like a Beautiful Sunset: An Interview with Joseph Koo" 〈似夕陽在散餘煇：顧嘉煇〉 (in Chinese), *Sudden Weekly* 587 (November 2006); http://hk.sudden.nextmedia.com/article/587/6449729; retrieved on March 15, 2016

25. Cited from James Wong, "Cantopop Discriminated for Decades" 〈廣東歌受歧視數十年〉 (in Chinese), *Eastweek* 65 (November 24, 2004): 174.

lovers. This kind of literary allusion, a common device in Cantonese opera and Cantopop in the 1960s, was one of the reasons behind the archaic image of Cantopop among the younger generation. (It is ironic to note that similar styles were used by Taiwanese lyricist Vincent Fang 方文山, who generated a trend of "China Wind" in the new millennium with the songs of Jay Chou 周杰倫. While Fang's works were hailed by the young audience as trendy, Cantopop was seen as outdated.)

The use of Sandra Lang, an established songstress in the late 1960s and early 1970s, to sing the song was an effective way of changing this impression. The audience found it quite new to have the songstress from the duo "Chopsticks Sisters," who used to perform Western songs, sing this song. The "Chopsticks Sisters" were signed with Crown Records Limited, a company focused on Cantonese opera in the 1960s. The album *A Love Tale between Tears and Smiles* was published by Crown, which had a close working relationship with TVB in the late 1970s. Crown produced many popular TVB theme songs by Cantopop stars like Adam Cheng and Liza Wang 汪明荃. The tremendous success of the song, which can be attributed in part to the chemistry between the Westernized songstress and the traditional Chinese style of the song, marked a watershed in the history of Cantopop. Although it must be stressed that there were popular Cantopop songs in the early 1970s, it was not until "A Love Tale between Tears and Smiles" that the common perception of Cantopop changed at long last. It began to take on a new look when the prejudice of the general audience was deconstructed by the fact that an established English pop songstress would sing Cantopop. The disharmony between the songstress and the song—both in the melody and in the lyrics—contributed a strange hybridization of different cultural and musical elements, which later proved to be one of the most important factors behind the rise of local Hong Kong popular culture in the 1970s. In the end the experiment by Joseph Koo and Tin-Lam Wong 王天林 was an enormous success, creating a win-win synergy between television programs and popular songs. It was arguably a planned strategy to use Cantopop to promote the television drama, but it was a rather unexpected outcome that the song would open a new chapter in Cantopop's history.

After the success of "A Love Tale between Tears and Smiles," TVB shifted its emphasis from Mandapop to Cantopop. According to Chi-Wah Wong, the music program *Sing & Dance* 《載歌載舞》 featured a Cantopop special episode entitled "Singing at Dusk in Guangzhou" 《羊城晚唱》; in the meantime, Rediffusion, which introduced free-to-air television in April 1973, also promoted Cantopop in their music programs. For example, in *The Sound of Sau Lan* 《秀蘭歌聲處處聞》, the hostess Sau-Lan Hai, who used to sing Mandapop, started singing Cantopop hits such as "Fragrant Water Lily" 〈荷花香〉. Another signal of the rise of Cantopop in the music industry was

Pancy Lau 劉鳳屏, a popular songstress who used to sing Mandapop and who released two Cantopop albums, *How to Settle the Bill of Love/The Bright Moon Speaks Softly Love* 《怎了相思帳／明月訴情》 and *I Am True to Him/ Departed Sparrows* 《我對他真心／分飛燕》, with Life Records in 1974.[26]

The mid-1970s was a time of transformation. English popular songs were still quite popular while Cantopop was emerging.

> When Polydor entered the market in 1970, merging with Phillips to form PolyGram in 1972, it was mainly to market imported and local English language music—a strategy later adopted by EMI and its Columbia subsidiary around the same time. Sam Hui, for example, who would later produce the three best-selling albums of the 1970s for PolyGram in Cantonese, was signed on the strength of his reputation as a singer of English songs.[27]

In 1974, Sam Hui was still focusing on English popular songs in his *The Morning After*, and in the same year, the band The Wynners released several chart-topping English albums, including *Sha-La-La-La-La* and *Listen to The Wynners*. The Wynners, the idol of countless teenage Hong Kong fans, finally released their first Cantopop album *Let's Rock* 《大家樂》 in 1975. Another good example showing that English and Mandarin popular songs were still popular is the Hong Kong Popular Song Contest organized by TVB. In 1974, Joseph Koo won the title in the first contest with his "Shau Ha Ha" 〈笑哈哈〉 (sung by Sandra Lang in English and Mandarin), and the runner-up was "L-O-V-E Love" (sung by The Wynners; melody and lyrics by James Wong). In 1975, the winner of the contest was Chelsia Chan's 陳秋霞 English song "Dark Side of Your Mind," and most other entries were English pop songs as well.[28] Cantopop gradually picked up momentum in the mid-1970s. In 1975, Radio Television Hong Kong (RTHK) launched a new program entitled *New World* 《新天地》 to broadcast Cantonese songs on Channel 2, the popular music channel, which in the following year was renamed *Chinese Pop Chart* 中文歌曲龍虎榜, a weekly top chart for Chinese (*de facto* Cantonese) songs. All of these changes were signs of an emerging trend of a new popular song genre. However, it is also necessary to remark that without the rising star Sam Hui, the tidal wave of Cantopop might not have swept Hong Kong and the neighboring region with such magnitude.

---

26. Wong, "Hong Kong Cantopop in the Early 1970s."
27. Centre for Popular Culture in the Humanities, Hong Kong Institute of Education, Hong Kong Pop Music. Available at: http://www.ied.edu.hk/cpch/view.php?secid=3440#19701; retrieved on March 15, 2016.
28. For a detailed account of other examples showing the dominant status of English popular songs in the mid-1970s, see Wong, *Pioneers*, 134–37.

The God of Cantopop: Sam Hui

Had it just been the unexpected success of "A Love Tale between Tears and Smiles," a Cantopop tidal wave would not have been generated across the territory in the mid-1970s. James Wong, hailed as the Godfather of Cantopop, underlined in his doctoral thesis the importance of Sam Hui in the rise of Cantopop. He was certainly right to claim that any historical account of Cantopop should begin with Sam Hui, who was later revered as the "God of Cantopop."[29] As the mainstay of Lotus, a local band which performed English songs in the 1960s, Sam Hui started singing Cantopop in the 1970s, and thanks to his own background he was able to transform the perceived grass-roots image of Cantopop of the 1960s. Sam Hui's first Cantopop hit, "Eiffel Tower above the Clouds" 〈鐵塔凌雲〉 (original title: "Here and Now" 〈就此模樣〉) was performed on the TVB program *The Hui Brothers Show*, which he cohosted with his brother Michael Hui, in April 1972. Born in China and having relocated with his family to Hong Kong when he was two years old, Sam Hui was a typical example of the first postwar generation that grew up in Hong Kong. He came from a traditional Chinese family and was well educated, exemplifying the new-generation Hong Konger as a hybrid of local and Western cultures. His music was developed amidst the influence of Euro-American music, including the music of Elvis Presley.

When Sam Hui, with a university and middle-class background, started singing Cantopop in the 1970s, he was able to produce a very positive image of the genre. "Eiffel Tower above the Clouds," with lyrics written by Michael Hui and melody by Sam Hui himself, was later included on the album *Games Gamblers Play* released in 1974. This monumental TV program was very popular at that time, and the film *Games Gamblers Play*, which broke Hong Kong box office records, was developed from it. After a round-the-world trip, Michael Hui wrote an English poem, which was later translated into Chinese and used by Sam Hui to compose the tune that became "Eiffel Tower above the Clouds."[30] The 1967 riots created a mass of Hong Kong emigrants looking for a new home elsewhere in the late 1960s and the early 1970s. It was exactly on this occasion that Sam Hui's now legendary "Eiffel Tower above the Clouds" was written as a footnote to the Hong Kong diaspora. The theme of the song embodies a kind of local Hong Kong consciousness in a premature form: "How can the dots of silvery lights on the beaches of Hawaii, /

29. Wong, "The Rise and Decline of Cantopop," 115.
30. Chun-Hung Ng, *Here and Now: Sam Hui* 《此時此處：許冠傑》 (in Chinese) (Hong Kong: Enrich Publishing, 2007), 63.

Be compared to the fish-boat lamps at the other end of the earth?"[31] At the time of its release, the song signaled Hong Kongers' feelings about being at home in Hong Kong despite the turmoil of 1967. The gist of the song is that the protagonist, after traveling around the world, discovers that Hong Kong, the best place to live in the world, is his true homeland. His focus on the present elicited an unprecedented sense of feeling at home in Hong Kong. In the song, Hong Kong is no longer the midway station of a diasporic odyssey, but a here and now that Hong Kong people should treasure. This song can be said to have marked the dawning of a kind of Hong Kong consciousness in Cantopop in the 1970s.[32]

"Eiffel Tower above the Clouds" is now generally agreed to be the pioneering work that paved the way for the later development of the Cantopop music industry in the 1970s. It had to wait a little while, however, before the theme song for *Games Gamblers Play* directly triggered the first wave of Cantopop in a new mediascape reshaped by the success of "A Love Tale between Tears and Smiles" in 1974. Sam Hui started his film career with Gold Harvest in 1972, starring in the Mandarin martial arts comedy *Back Alley Princess* 《馬路小英雄》. In the next two years, he took part in *The Tattooed Dragon* 《龍虎金剛》 (1973), *Back Alley Princess in Chinatown* 《小英雄大鬧唐人街》 (1974), and *Naughty! Naughty!* 《綽頭狀元》 (1974). As mentioned above, the Hong Kong film industry was dominated by Mandarin movies in the early 1970s,[33] but perhaps owing to the popularity of *The Hui Brothers Show* and "Eiffel Tower above the Clouds," Sam Hui had the opportunity in *Naughty! Naughty!* to sing a medley including Cantonese, Mandarin, and English songs—the Cantonese part was the mimicry version of the 1960s Cantopop classic "World of Water Apart," with new lyrics written by James Wong. Hui very much liked his own performance, and, as noted by Chi-Wah Wong, it was perhaps due to the positive response of the audience that the Hui brothers decided to introduce Cantopop into their *Games Gamblers Play*, which was released in 1974.[34]

At first Golden Harvest wanted to market Sam Hui as a martial arts comedy star, but *Games Gamblers Play* changed not only Sam Hui's own film career but also the history of Cantopop. The comedy premiered in October 1974

---

31. Unless otherwise stated, all translations from Cantonese lyrics are mine. The translations are deliberately literal, with an eye to conveying meaning more than structure or rhyme, and thus the translations might not sound lyrical in English.

32. This part is drawn from Yiu-Wai Chu, *Lost in Transition: Hong Kong Culture in the Age of China* (Albany: SUNY Press, 2013), 125–26.

33. Between *Super Boxer* (February 4, 1971) and *The House of 72 Tenants* (September 22, 1973), all Hong Kong movies were Mandarin productions; see Wai-Man Chu 朱偉文, "Filmography" 〈七十年代香港電影片目〉 (in Chinese), *A Study of Hong Kong Cinema in the Seventies*, ed. The Eighth Hong Kong International Film Festival (Hong Kong: Urban Council of Hong Kong, 1984), 165–69.

34. Wong, "Hong Kong Cantopop in the Early 1970s."

and took in more than HK$6.25 million, breaking the box office record of *The House of 72 Tenants*. *Games Gamblers Play* set a Cantopop formula for the Hui brothers' productions: using theme songs with different styles for plot development, as well as promotional strategy. In the film there were the songs "Games Gamblers Play" and "Double Star Love Song" 〈雙星情歌〉—the former had a Western-style melody and colloquial Cantonese lyrics, whereas the latter was Chinese-styled (but inspired by Presley's "Summer Kisses Winter Tears") with literary Chinese lyrics. Notwithstanding the fact that the lyrics of the two songs, written by Sam Hui, inherited the two distinct styles of Cantopop lyrics from the 1960s, the creative hybridization of music styles and lyrics unveiled a new breed of Cantopop. The traditional Chinese (Sam Hui's father was a big fan of Cantonese opera) and Western band music (Hui was the mainstay of the rock band Lotus) backgrounds hybridized songs that broke new ground for Cantopop. The immense popularity of Sam Hui's Cantopop, a result of the synergy between his movies, television programs, and popular songs, could also be attributed to his personal characteristics. Sam Hui became the idol of the younger generation, and his educational background (few if any Hong Kong entertainers were university graduates at that time) and handsome looks also contributed to his magical charisma in creating a new image for Cantopop.

As noted by Norman Cheng, who took part in the production of the album and later became president of PolyGram Far East, Polydor Records did not have a long-term marketing strategy when they released *Games Gamblers Play*. Interestingly enough, not unlike the theme of the movie, the album was a big gamble. According to Ricky Hui 許冠英, Sam's elder brother who took an active part in the production of the album, "[a]t that time we had to gamble . . . we needed to have a facelift for Cantopop, giving it a brand new image."[35] The enormous success of *Games Gamblers Play*, which sold more than 150,000 copies, prompted Sam Hui and his record company to shift their emphasis to Cantopop. Although the subsequent Hui brothers' movie *The Last Message* 《天才與白痴》 (literally *Genius and Idiot* in Chinese) (1975) failed to break the record set by *Games Gamblers Play*, its theme songs were equally popular among local music fans. Sam Hui increased the number of theme songs, covering, besides colloquial social satire and the elegant love song, a new topic on the philosophy of life in "Dream of a Genius-Idiot" 〈天才白痴夢〉. This introduced a new dimension to Cantopop, which was later further developed by James Wong in his TVB soap opera theme songs. *The Private Eyes* 《半斤八兩》 (literally *Half Catty Eight Taels* in Chinese) (1976), which achieved a new box office record of HK$8.53 million, brought Sam Hui's career to new

---

35. Cited from Ng, *Here and Now: Sam Hui*, 93, 101–2.

heights. The title song of the movie, "Half Catty Eight Taels" 〈半斤八兩〉, voiced the discontent of the working class in an age of growing inequalities: "We're just a group of working stiffs, slaves for money all our lives." The song was so popular that it was later translated into Japanese. Similar to "Dream of a Genius-Idiot," "From the Heart of a Loafer" 〈浪子心聲〉 was written as chicken soup for the soul, appeasing the working class with its "Whatever Will Be, Will Be" kind of philosophy. A new superstar in the expanding Hong Kong cultural industries, Sam Hui did not need long to become a trendsetter in not only Hong Kong but also other Chinese communities.

Sam Hui was able to attract different kinds of audiences, from teenagers to adults and from white-collar workers to blue-collar workers. His unique charm originated from the hybridization of his grassroots sensibility and rock star stage performances. Sam Hui claimed in an interview that Elvis Presley was his idol since he was a student, and he tried emulating Presley's hairstyle, fashion sense, ways of speaking, singing, and even walking. Since his voice was significantly different from Presley's, Sam Hui focused his effort on adapting his music style and stage performance.[36] As mentioned above, the chords of "Double Star Love Song" were inspired by Presley's "Summer Kisses Winter Tears." As Chi-Wah Wong has pointed out, Cantopop audiences generally preferred themes such as "inflation, hardships of living, economic problems and other social problems that could reflect the dark side of society" in the 1970s[37] Another commonly held impression of Sam Hui's songs was their ability to represent the *vox populi*. Most of his songs emphasized social problems caused by the uneven distribution of wealth in society, serving as a kind of populist catharsis for the grassroots community. He successfully demonstrated how social parodies might also be a topic in mainstream popular songs.

Songs by Sam Hui and a number of other singers dealt with a whole range of social problems, such as the satiric "Hong Kong Traffic Song" 〈香港交通歌〉 and "Ode to Doctors" 〈醫生頌〉. The various social problems presented in these songs contributed a more comprehensive picture of contemporary Hong Kong life. While local Hong Kong culture witnessed a significant transformation in the mid-1970s, the repercussions of the oil crisis, the unsolved problem of public housing, and a high crime rate were making real life miserable for the general public. One of the important achievements of Sam Hui was that he was able to address these issues in his works. In spite of its social significance, this kind of Cantopop succeeded in representing local popular

---

36. Chu, *Songs of Your Life*, 22.
37. Chi-Wah Wong, "A Kind of Cultural Prejudice? On the Social Significance and Artistic Value of the Cantopop Parodies" 〈一種文化的偏好？論粵語流行曲中的諷刺寫實作品的社會意義與藝術價值〉 (in Chinese), in *Hong Kong Culture and Society*, ed. Elizabeth Sinn (Hong Kong: Centre of Asian Studies, the University of Hong Kong, 1995), 182.

lifestyles more than contributing to any self-conscious construction of local consciousness. In other words, the most important contribution of these songs was less in developing local consciousness than in transforming Cantopop social parodies into a mainstream genre (this genre, probably due to its extensive use of slang, was regarded as being in bad taste in the 1950s and 1960s). Sam Hui successfully demonstrated how social parodies might also be a topic of mainstream popular songs.

Sam Hui's social parodies were gaining rapid audience appeal, thanks to his witty use of local Cantonese slang and his keen sensibility of grassroots problems. In this regard, the contributions of lyricist Peter Lai 黎彼得 should not be overlooked. Peter Lai closely collaborated with Sam Hui, and most of the lyrics of Sam Hui's songs in the late 1970s were cowritten with Peter Lai. The nephew of Cantonese opera master Chi-Pat Lan 靓次伯, Peter Lai grew up in a working-class family and had a number of jobs before he worked with Sam Hui. Owing to his extensive experience in different social sectors, Peter Lai had sharp insights into the everyday life problems of Hong Kong people. At the same time, he had been deeply influenced by Chi-Pat Lan since his early childhood, having the opportunity to be exposed to the literary style of Cantopop opera lyrics. His background matched perfectly with the two styles of Sam Hui's lyrics, and thus they became great collaborators in the late 1970s. Peter Lai said they were a "Beggar and Prince" duo, with his grassroots experience supplementing the works of the superstar.[38] For example, Sam Hui did not know how to play mahjong, one of the most popular games in Hong Kong, but with the help of Peter Lai, he wrote two well-known songs about mahjong, "Mahjong Heroes" 〈打雀英雄傳〉 and "Funs of Mahjong" 〈麻雀耍樂〉. Besides "Half Catty Eight Taels," their "Inflation Craze" 〈加價熱潮〉 (a cover version of Bill Haley's "Rock around the Clock"), which critiqued the impact of inflation on the lives of the common people, became an all-time classic. Both the music career and the local consciousness of Sam Hui continued to develop in the 1980s, which will be further discussed in the next chapter.

Jade Theatre and Its Raging Tide

When Sam Hui popularized Cantopop in the mid-1970s, TVB continued to develop its local programs using Cantopop as their theme songs after the out-of-the-blue success of "A Love Tale between Tears and Smiles." A great variety of TVB dramas started using Cantopop as its theme songs, ranging from the Chinese folklore drama *The Purple Hairpin* 《紫釵恨》 (1975) and the

---

38. Chu, *Songs of Your Life*, 26.

teen drama *Move On* 《乘風破浪》 (1975) to purchased Japanese dramas *Get out on a Journey* 《前程錦繡》 (俺たちの旅 in Japanese, 1975) and *G-Men 1975* 《猛龍特警隊》 (1975). The biggest impact came a bit later from *Jade Theatre*, a long drama series on TVB's Jade Channel, which generated a wave of Cantopop theme songs. As mentioned above, *Romance in the Rain* was the first drama in the *Jade Theatre* series, but it was not until *The Hotel* 《狂潮》 (a.k.a. *Raging Tide*, 1976) that TVB dramas and their theme songs left a mark on the history of Hong Kong popular culture. *The Hotel*, with more than 120 episodes, was arguably the most popular television program at that time. The theme song became very popular as a result of it being aired at least twice per episode during prime time every weekday evening. As convincingly noted by Eric Ma in his study on Hong Kong television, "Hong Kong melodramatic serials quickly gained the cultural prestige that was difficult to acquire in the Western countries where television in general, and soap operas in particular, were rejected as degrading cultural forms."[39]

Although *Jade Theatre* featured only soap operas, their theme songs managed to contribute a new dimension to Cantopop. On the one hand, the composer Joseph Koo could make the most of his modern/Western style as the setting was modern Hong Kong; on the other hand, the lyricist James Wong was very successful in injecting life philosophy into these songs. Later Koo and Wong entered the Hall of Fame of not only Cantopop but also Hong Kong culture per se,[40] and these theme songs eventually generated a wave of Cantopop in the mid- to the late 1970s. Although the arrangement of "A Love Tale between Tears and Smiles" was hybridized,[41] its tune and lyrics still followed the tradition of Cantopop in the 1950s and 1960s. A genuine paradigm shift emerged when *The Hotel* premiered in 1976. The theme song "Raging Tide" (melody by Joseph Koo, lyrics by James Wong, and sung by Susanna Kwan 關菊英) pioneered a new style of Cantopop. As noted by James Wong, "high-quality modern Cantopop lyrics did not appear until 1975." The use of language was "modern" in the sense that lyricists replaced archaic terms like *ge* 哥 and *mei* 妹 with modern expressions like *ni* "you" 你 and *wo* "me" 我. (For instance, James Wong's "Raging Tide" started with the line "It's him, and it's also you and me.")[42] This is the reason James Wong called this period (1974–1983)

---

39. Ma, *Culture, Politics and Television in Hong Kong*, 30.
40. They won many awards over the years. Joseph Koo was presented, among others, the "Life Achievement Award" at the Hong Kong Arts Development Awards in 2010 by the Hong Kong Arts Development Council. He also won the "Highest Honor Award" presented by RTHK in 1981. James Wong received the Golden Needle Award from RTHK in 1990 and the Hall of Fame Award from the Composers and Authors Society of Hong Kong (CASH) in 2000, both of which are considered the most prestigious awards in honor of lifetime achievement in the music industry.
41. Wong, "The Rise and Decline of Cantopop," 99; Joseph Koo's hybridization of Chinese and Western styles can be seen in his handling of "total sound."
42. Wong, "The Rise and Decline of Cantopop," 133.

"I Am Myself," a famous line quoted from his own Cantopop called "Ask Me" 〈問我〉 (melody by Michael Lai 黎小田 and sung by Grace Chan 陳麗思) released in 1975.[43] He understood very well that it was time to "modernize" Cantopop lyrics, but it was also very difficult, if not impossible, to use 100 percent Cantonese in writing his lyrics because Cantonese was and arguably still is considered to be unofficial, if not vulgar. Because of this characteristic, James Wong decided to adopt a hybrid of Cantonese, modern Chinese and classical Chinese in his Cantopop lyrics (his "Below the Lion Rock" 〈獅子山下〉 is a classic example; see below). From the mid- to the late 1970s, James Wong and his contemporaries Jimmy Lo and Kwok-Kong Cheng established a new poetics of hybridity by making ends meet.

The Joseph Koo and James Wong duo was arguably the key to Cantopop's success in the 1970s. Joseph Koo won the melody composition contest with the movie *Love without End* 《不了情》 and its theme song "Dream" 〈夢〉 in 1962. Focusing on film scores during the early stage of his career, he won the Best Music Award with *The Dancing Millionairess* 《萬花迎春》 at the Third Golden Horse Awards in 1965. Having worked for the Shaw Brothers and Golden Harvest movie studios, Joseph Koo joined TVB as its music director in 1967. In the early 1970s, when Cantopop was still at the margin of the music industry, Koo focused his attention on film scores such as Bruce Lee's classics, *Fist of Fury* 《精武門》 (1972) and *Way of the Dragon* 《猛龍過江》 (1972), which were some of his signature works. Although one of his most well-known pieces of work might be the ending song "Good Night Song" 〈晚安曲〉 (1967) from TVB's classic *Enjoy Yourself Tonight* 《歡樂今宵》, his music talent was not fully realized until he had the chance to compose Cantopop theme songs for TVB in the 1970s. His first theme song (in Mandarin) for the TVB drama *Star River* 《星河》 in 1972 failed to make noise, but his "A Love Tale between Tears and Smiles" was indisputably the turning point in the history of Hong Kong popular music. His songs were so well received that they were adopted by the Education Bureau of Hong Kong as teaching materials. In the volume *The Characteristics of Joseph Koo's Music* 《顧嘉煇的音樂特色》, commissioned by the Education Bureau and written by Kwong-Chiu Mui 梅廣昭, his music was praised as "epoch-making." As Kwong-Chiu Mui noted, "His melodies are beautiful with opulent orchestration, being able to hybridize Chinese and Western music elements."[44] His works were so influential that he was awarded the Highest Honor Award, the first of its kind, by RTHK in 1981, and he became the first Hong Kong composer to receive an MBE (Member of the Order of the British Empire) in 1982.

---

43. Ibid., 91.
44. Kwong-Chiu Mui 梅廣昭, *The Characteristics of Joseph Koo's Music* 《顧嘉煇的音樂特色》.

While Joseph Koo specialized in melody, James Wong had expertise in both melody and lyrics. His lyrics arguably brought a brand new style to Cantopop in the mid-1970s (this will be described further in a following section). The first time Joseph Koo teamed up with James Wong was to compose "If Loving You Means Hurting You" 〈愛你變成害你〉, a Mandarin song sung by Rebecca Poon 潘迪華 in her pioneering project *Madame White Snake* 《白娘娘》 (1972). They became a Cantopop dream team at TVB, producing a series of big hits, including Jade Theatre theme songs such as "Raging Tide" 〈狂潮〉 and "A House Is Not a Home" 〈家變〉. Famously known as "Fai and Wong" (meaning "grand" in Cantonese; "Fai" is the Chinese name of Joseph Koo), they collaborated on countless Cantopop classics in the 1970s and 1980s. Similar to Joseph Koo, James Wong was able to master both traditional and modern elements in his lyrics, from the traditional Chinese style in songs like "Time to Forget in the Misty Rain" 〈倆忘煙水裡〉 to modern expressions in songs like "Bright Star" 〈明星〉. Furthermore, James Wong, who had participated in almost all sectors of the music industry, completed a doctoral thesis on the development of Cantopop, which has become a must-read for anyone who is interested in not only Hong Kong Cantopop in particular but also Hong Kong culture in general. Deservedly hailed as the Godfather of Cantopop, he was among the few who were willing to legitimize the study of Cantopop in the academia.

"A House Is Not a Home" (1977), sung by Roman Tam 羅文 with melody by Joseph Koo and lyrics by James Wong, took the craze of TV songs one step further. Roman Tam, who moved from Guangzhou to Hong Kong in the early 1960s, started his singing career as one of the playback singers in the Shaw Brothers movie *The Shepherd Girl* 《山歌戀》 (1964). In the late 1960s, he performed English popular songs in pubs in the Wan Chai District, and at the same time he was the singer of Mandapop movie theme songs, such as "The Singing Thief" 〈大盜歌王〉 (1969). In the early 1970s, he partnered with renowned comedienne Lydia Shum 沈殿霞 in concert tours. But it was not until the TVB theme songs of the mid-1970s that he became a Cantopop superstar. This can be attributed to the new media of television, which had acquired the magical power to create local Cantonese-speaking stars. Most of the TVB Cantopop singers at that time had their roots in the 1960s, but they had to wait until this particular juncture to fully develop their entertainment careers. Similar to Roman Tam, Adam Cheng and Liza Wang, the two popular Cantopop singers who were also leading television actors in Hong Kong, were also in one way or another related to the 1960s. Adam Cheng started his entertainment career with Kin Shing Film Co. in 1966 when he became an actor in Cantonese films. He made his debut leading role alongside the highly celebrated Connie Chan in *The Black Killer* 《黑煞星》 in 1967, but due to the decline of Cantonese movies during the late 1960s, he did not have the chance to advance his career until he signed with TVB in 1970. In 1971, he released his first Cantopop album, *Lover Already Married* 《愛人結婚了》, in which the main plug, bearing the same title, was quite popular. But as previously noted, Cantopop was considered an inferior music genre at that time. He gradually built up a fan base through television dramas and theme songs (such as the first theme song of the TVB drama "Romance in the Rain"). After *The Book and the Sword* 《書劍恩仇錄》 (1976; see below), he eventually became a superstar in both the television and popular music industries. Meanwhile, Liza Wang also began working as a television actress for Rediffusion Television Limited (RTV) in 1967. Since RTV was not a free-to-air broadcaster at that time, she was not as well-known as other TVB entertainers in the 1960s. She released her debut album *Love and Gold* 《黃金與愛情》 (in Mandarin) in 1969, but, like Adam Cheng, she did not have the chance to let her talents shine until she joined TVB in 1971. In 1974, she sang some of the songs in the TVB drama *Autumn Begonia* 《秋海棠》 (included in a Cantopop album bearing the same title), among which "Gold Canary" 〈金絲雀〉 hit the fancy of the audience. Subsequently, she produced three very popular Cantopop albums in 1975, *Broken Dream in a Qing Dynasty Palace* 《清宮殘夢》, *Daiyu Burying Fallen Flowers* 《黛玉葬花》, and *The Legend of the Purple Hairpin* 《紫釵記》, which made her one of the rising Cantopop stars. A point to note is that Adam Cheng and Liza Wang were immensely popular at that time, but regarding Cantopop, their target audiences were mainly restricted to family audiences. It was not until the late 1970s that young Cantopop idols developed a new teenage market for the swiftly growing Cantopop industry.

James Wong offered in his doctoral thesis a detailed analysis of the melody of "A House Is Not a Home," arguing that it was not until this song that a new Westernized style of Hong Kong melody, completely different from other songs produced in Hong Kong, was born:

> If 'A Love Tale between Tears and Smiles' marked the rise of Hong Kong Cantopop, it was [not] until 'A House Is Not a Home' that a new style of Hong Kong melody was established. 'A Love Tale between Tears and Smiles' was still profoundly influenced by Cantonese opera, but it could break away from that tradition in terms of melody, lyrics, singing style and arrangements.[45]

The success of "A House Is Not a Home" was followed by a series of *Jade Theatre* theme songs: "Vanity Fair" 〈大亨〉 (1978), "The Giant" 〈強人〉 (1978), "Conflict" 〈奮鬥〉 (1978), "Over the Rainbow" 〈天虹〉 (1979), "The Passenger" 〈抉擇〉 (1979), and "The Good, The Bad and The Ugly" 〈網中

---

45. Ibid., 141–42.

人〉 (1979). All but "The Good, The Bad and The Ugly" (melody by Joseph Koo and lyrics by Tang Wai Hung 鄧偉雄) were written by Joseph Koo and James Wong, making them a perfect combo almost synonymous with Cantopop in the 1970s. These theme songs were performed by big Cantopop stars and almost all became golden hits that enthralled hundreds of thousands of Hong Kongers in the late 1970s. "The Passenger," sung by George Lam, was a good example of the popularity of Cantopop. Returning from the United States, George Lam was once the lead singer of the local band Jade. He later produced his first English album *Lam* in 1976 before turning to Cantopop. At that time many singers who used to sing English and Mandarin songs turned to Cantopop. As *Jade Theatre* dramas of nearly 100 episodes were all the rage, the theme songs were also able to capture a large audience when they were heard every weekday evening during prime time for four to five months. Only big Cantopop stars had the opportunity to sing these theme songs, and their rising popularity, in turn, significantly expanded the market of Cantopop.

Meanwhile, James Wong was very successful in his creative use of philosophical reflections to package love, hate, and obsession—the banal themes of the soap operas. The signature line "Change alone is eternal" from "A House Is Not a Home," among others, had become a pet phrase of Hong Kong people. James Wong's use of simple modern language to express his philosophy of life not only changed the style of Cantopop lyrics but also expanded its discursive space by stimulating reflections on the meaning of life. The following line from renowned lyricist Lin Xi 林夕 (a.k.a. Albert Leung) "Jade Theatre" 〈翡翠劇場〉, sung by Anthony Yiu-Ming Wong 黃耀明, spoke volumes for the importance of the serics and its theme songs in the lives of Hong Kong people in the late 1970s: "Unbeatable melodies served with our dinners, soap operas as the main courses." The audience had dinner while watching these *Jade Theatre* soap operas, so to speak. "Starting from the 1970s, television stations started showing their television dramas at prime time in the evening, a time when most people were having their dinners. This cultivated the habit of the whole family eating and watching television at the same time."[46] A new craze hitting Hong Kong, the *Jade Theatre* soap operas galvanized the popularity of theme songs of other television programs. Different kinds of dramas also used Cantopop as theme songs, from melodramas such as *Heart with Thousands of Knots* 《心有千千結》 (1976) and stories of first love such as *Fig* (in Chinese *Fruit without Flowers*) 《無花果》 (1976) to costume sword-playing dramas. The album *Raging Tide*, released in 1977, was a prime example of how television dramas contributed to the diversification of the topics of Cantopop. The album included eleven theme songs (excluding different versions of the same

---

46. See Hong Kong Heritage Museum, "Hong Kong's Popular Entertainment" (Hong Kong: Hong Kong Heritage Museum, 2006), 21.

song) of TVB dramas, and besides "Raging Tide," the topics covered romantic ballads like "Heart with Thousands of Knots" and "Fruit without Flowers" and a great variety of other topics from the theme songs of the homemade teen drama *Move On* 《乘風破浪》, the Japanese detective series *G-Men 75* 《猛龍特警隊》, and the Japanese sci-fi series *Rainbow Man* 《彩虹化身俠》. Theme songs from different types of dramas broadened the subject matter of Cantopop, but it was the latter that exerted a deep impact comparable to that of the *Jade Theatre* songs.

In 1975, Commercial Television (CTV), the third free-to-air television station in Hong Kong, was founded. As a newcomer to the market, CTV decided to try something new. They succeeded in stealing market share by pioneering the *wuxia* (martial hero) drama *The Legend of the Condor Heroes* 《射鵰英雄傳》, adapted from the famous novel by Jin Yong 金庸 (a.k.a. Louis Cha). To counterattack, TVB spent a handsome budget on *The Book and the Sword* 《書劍恩仇錄》 (1976), also adapted from Jin Yong's novel, to raise the curtain on *wuxia* dramas. All three of the free-to-air broadcasters, TVB, CTV, and Rediffusion Television (RTV), made many *wuxia* dramas in the late 1970s, and the theme songs for these dramas added a new dimension to the subject matter of Cantopop. "The Book and the Sword," the theme song of the drama bearing the same title, had two versions, one sung by Adam Cheng and the other by Roman Tam. Both Cheng and Tam were already superstars at that time, showing that TVB placed great emphasis on this genre.

Joseph Koo and James Wong were able to make perfect use of the opportunity to give a series of master classes to show how to creatively use the subject to broaden the horizon of Cantopop. "The Heaven Sword and Dragon Saber" 〈倚天屠龍記〉, one of their representative *wuxia* theme songs, can be used to illustrate the typical style of the Koo and Wong *wuxia* Cantopop. Joseph Koo hybridized elements of Western music with a traditional Chinese tune, matching the setting of the period drama without any old-fashioned feelings. James Wong cleverly used the theme of the novel to highlight the paradox of a sensitive hero caught in a paradox between love and hatred: love is so hopelessly mixed with hatred that not even the Heaven Sword and the Dragon Saber can sever them. "Chu Liuxiang" 〈楚留香〉 (1979), another *wuxia* theme song by Joseph Koo and James Wong (lyrics cowritten with Tang Wai Hung), also presented a new imaginary of *wuxia* heroes. The melody was a creative hybridization of traditional Chinese and modern Western elements.[47]

James Wong and Tang Wai Hung presented the cool image of a knight-errant who later swept the entertainment industries in Taiwan in the 1980s. However, it is also necessary to note that these *wuxia* theme songs were not

---

47. Helan Yang and Siu-Wah Yu, *Reading Cantonese Songs: The Voice of Hong Kong through Vicissitudes* 《粵語歌曲解讀：蛻變中的香港聲音》 (in Chinese) (Hong Kong: Infolink, 2013), 94–96.

simply standardized mass productions. Different lyricists had different styles when they presented their heroes. Unlike James Wong, Jimmy Lo focused more on the helplessness of the protagonists, giving his songs a mood of desolation and despair, as exemplified in his "Little Li's Flying Dagger" 〈小李飛刀〉 (1978) sung by Roman Tam: "With all these unbeatable capabilities, I still cannot break the barrier of love!" The catchphrase "Why always me?" in the song became one of the best quotes in Cantopop lyrics. In his "Shooting Star, Butterfly, Sword" 〈流星蝴蝶劍〉, the theme song of a CTV *wuxia* drama, Jimmy Lo zoomed in on another dimension of a *wuxia* hero—his fame was simply "as fleeting as [a] shooting star"—which later became one of his signature styles.[48] These songs proved that Cantopop, though highly commercialized, was not necessarily standardized.

The impact of television theme songs was reflected in the results of the first full-scale Hong Kong popular songs award program, *Top Ten Chinese Gold Songs Awards*, hosted by RTHK in 1978. Out of the ten Gold Songs, six were television program theme songs: "Little Li's Flying Dagger," "The Heaven Sword and Dragon Saber," "Pledge to Enter the Mountain of Swords" 〈誓要入刀山〉, "Wish You Would Remember" 〈願君心記取〉, "Tomorrow Today" 〈明日話今天〉, and "Crocodile Tears" 〈鱷魚淚〉. As evident from these six Gold Songs, the subject matter of Cantopop was quite diversified, ranging from *wuxia* heroes and romances to the life philosophy of the modern man ("Tomorrow Today") and a critique of the vanity fair ("Crocodile Tears"). The unofficial "regional anthem" of Hong Kong, "Below the Lion Rock," sung by Roman Tam (melody by Joseph Koo and lyrics by James Wong), was also the theme song of a television drama series produced by RTHK. *Below the Lion Rock* premiered in 1972 and was seen as being able to evoke the spirit of the "Hong Kong story"—as the famous lyrics go, "Of one mind in pursuit of our dream / All discord set aside / With one heart on the same bright quest / Fearless and valiant inside / Hand in hand to the ends of the earth / Rough terrain no respite / Side by side we overcome ills / As the Hong Kong story we write."[49] Unlike mainstream television soap operas, which presented a vanity fair–styled world of affluence, *Below the Lion Rock* presented an alternative view of grassroots life in a resettlement estate in Wang Tau Hom, a district at the foot of the Lion Rock. Before the theme song was first released in 1979, the program

---

48. Jimmy Lo further developed his *wuxia* songs in the 1980s when he moved to RTV (later renamed Asian Television [ATV]); this will be further discussed in the next chapter.

49. Translation cited from "The 2002–03 Budget: Speech by the Financial Secretary, The Hon Antony Leung Moving the Second Reading of the Appropriation Bill 2002" (March 6, 2002), http://www.budget.gov.hk/2002/eframe2.htm; retrieved on March 15, 2016. According to RTHK, "*Below the Lion Rock* witnesses the growth of Hong Kong. It represents the spirit of the people, riding through many ups and downs together to face the challenges." Cited from http://www.rthk.org.hk/downloads/lionrock/eng/; retrieved on March 15, 2016.

used a piece of traditional Chinese music, "Be Lofty Step by Step" 〈步步高〉, as the theme music. In the midst of the wave of television theme songs, RTHK decided to adopt a theme song for the series, which became the signature Cantopop of Hong Kong. This song, later considered by many Hong Kong people to be the regional anthem, can be seen as a prelude to the development of Hong Kong local consciousness in the 1980s. In short, thanks to various types of TV dramas, the subject matter and styles of Cantopop became more and more diversified.

Cross-Media Synergy

As Cantopop became more popular, other media such as film and radio programs also used it as part of their promotional strategies. Hong Kong cinema had a close relationship with Cantopop since Sam Hui, but the impact was somewhat restricted. The New Wave Cinema, which had its roots in the television sector, magnified the impact made when these movies used Cantopop as theme songs in a way similar to television programs. In the mid-1970s, a group of young directors who graduated from film schools in the West came back to Hong Kong where the markets of the television and movie industries were swiftly expanding. Before finding their right career path in the film industry, they had a chance to make noise in television dramas. Most of the New Wave directors, such as Hark Tsui 徐克 and Ann Hui 許鞍華, started their career with TVB, and perhaps owing to this, when they shifted to the movie sector, they also adopted Cantopop theme songs as part of their creative projects. In fact, as early as *Jumping Ash* 《跳灰》 (1976) directed by Po-Chih Leong 梁普智, generally considered a pioneering work setting the scene for the later New Wave Cinema, there were two very popular Cantopop songs, "A Real Man" 〈大丈夫〉 (melody by Liu Jiachang 劉家昌, lyrics by James Wong, and sung by Michael Kwan 關正傑) and "Ask Me." Although "Ask Me" later became one of the classics of James Wong, it was not closely related to the plot.

In later New Wave works, the theme songs contributed important elements to highlight the theme and/or to advance the plot. Hong Kong New Wave Cinema was famous for its experimental styles, and one of the remarkable features was the diversification of themes. The founding Hong Kong New Wave film, Ho Yim's 嚴浩 *The Extra* 《茄喱啡》 (1978),[50] was a groundbreaking work focusing on the role of extras in movies, as well as in real life. The theme song "An Extra in Life" 〈人生小配角〉 written by Joseph Koo and James Wong (sung by Michael Kwan) was another ingenious endeavor in which James Wong tried mixing Cantonese with English expressions (e.g., "movie

---

50. Cheuk, *Hong Kong New Wave Cinema*, 22.

star" and "camera") in his lyrics. Subsequent New Wave films experimented with new genres, including, among others, Tsui Hark's *wuxia* sci-fi crossover *Butterfly Murderers* 《蝶變》 (1979) and Alex Cheung's 章國明 genre-bending crime and gangster film *Cops and Robbers* 《點指兵兵》 (1979). The theme song "Butterfly Murderers," for instance, was an innovative hybrid of the traditional image of the *wuxia* genre and the modern Western style of the singer George Lam, which matched very well with the genre-crossing of the film itself.

The use of Cantopop as theme songs continued in 1980 (e.g., Priscilla Chan's 陳美玲 "The Happenings" 〈夜車〉, Adam Cheng's "The Sword" 〈名劍〉, Michael Kwan's "The Savior" 〈救世者〉, and Danny Chan's 陳百強 "Encore" 〈喝采〉), paving the way for the up-and-coming crossover of movie and popular songs in the 1980s (this will be further discussed in the next chapter). The crossover effect could also be seen in the theme songs of radio programs. Radio stations had long been major platforms for the dissemination of popular songs. As Cantopop became more and more popular in the late 1970s, in addition to music programs, they also used Cantopop as the theme songs of their radio dramas. In the end this was a win-win situation, as the well-received Cantopop theme songs helped rejuvenate radio dramas. Radio drama songs snatched two awards at the 1979 RTHK Top 10 Gold Songs, Teresa Cheung's 張德蘭 "Endless Road" 〈茫茫路〉 (melody by Joseph Koo and lyrics by Jimmy Lo) and Albert Au's "Return through the Field" 〈陌上歸人〉 (melody by Ricky Fung 馮添枝 and lyrics by Cheng Kwok Kong), evincing the cross-media potential of Cantopop. At first these songs were mostly performed by mainstream singers, but later radio stations realized that it would be an effective way to let their own disc jockeys sing the songs, which would offer a good opportunity for them to become an icon. Disc jockeys such as Ken Choi 蔡楓華 and Blanche Tang 鄧藹霖 later became teen idols, lifting the cross-media synergy to new heights.

This strategy was also adopted by television companies. Market leader TVB used its own actors and actresses to sing the theme songs, such as Bill Chan's 石修 "Heart with Thousands of Knots" and Lawrence Ng's 伍衛國 "Countryside Dream in Spring" 〈田園春夢〉 (1975). Not all of these endeavors fared well in the end, but Adam Cheng and Liza Wang were successful cases showing that a new Cantopop star system was taking shape. Adam Cheng and Liza Wang were the most popular TVB actor and actress from the mid- to the late 1970s. Adam Cheng was an actor and Cantopop singer but was not very popular before his TVB dramas, in particular *The Book and the Sword* and *The Heaven Sword and Dragon Saber*, which sparked a new *wuxia* craze in Hong Kong. The unsung hero finally got a moment to shine in the music industry. Meanwhile, besides her leading role in *wuxia* dramas, Liza Wang's *A House Is Not a Home* was also a big hit across Chinese communities. Besides being the most popular female lead in TVB, Wang was also the singer of many TVB theme songs, including, among others, the *Jade Theatre* theme song "Over the Rainbow." Adam Cheng and Liza Wang's rise to fame in both the television and the pop music industries played an important role in the development of a star system in the entertainment business in the late 1970s.

In addition to having its own actors and actresses, TVB also signed many mainstream singers, such as Roman Tam, George Lam 林子祥, Paula Tsui 徐小鳳, and Jenny Tseng 甄妮, who later became superstars, leading Cantopop into a new era by the end of the late 1970s. These singers were given the opportunity to sing *Jade Theatre* theme songs, such as Paula Tsui's "Vanity Fair," Roman Tam's "The Giant," Jenny Tseng's "Conflict," and George Lam's "The Passenger," which were almost guaranteed to be popular at that time. Paula Tsui and Jenny Tseng were established Mandapop singers before they turned to Cantopop, and George Lam focused on English popular songs. Paula Tsui, the winner of the "Hong Kong Nightingale Singing Contest" in 1965, had been performing Mandapop in nightclubs for many years before she released in 1969 three Mandapop EPs entitled *The Wall* 《牆》, *Autumn Night* 《秋夜》, and *Flames of Love* 《戀之火》. She had built a big fan base but it was the turn to Cantopop that enabled her singing career to soar to new heights in the late 1970s. Similar to Paula Tsui, Jenny Tseng was also a Mandapop singer before she turned to Cantopop. Starting her singing career in Taiwan in the early 1970s, Jenny Tseng was the singer of many Taiwanese movie theme songs. She married Hong Kong movie star Alexander Fu 傅聲 in 1976 and moved her base to Hong Kong. Jenny Tseng became the Cantopop queen in the late 1970s and the early 1980s, winning many popular female singer awards before she was overtaken by the legendary Anita Mui 梅艷芳. Unlike the two Cantopop divas, George Lam, after the release of his first English album *Lam* in 1976, became a television and movie actor. His first Cantopop album came out in 1978, and the title song happened to be the theme song of the movie *Money Trip* 《各師各法》, in which he was the male lead. In short, these singers represented very good examples of an emerging industry in the late 1970s, a time when many singers focusing on English and Mandarin popular songs decided to turn to Cantopop for greener pastures.

Cantopop Industry, Stardom, and Popular Song Awards

As mentioned above, despite the fact that "A Love Tale between Tears and Smiles" and "Games Gamblers Play" were extremely popular, the record companies did not have a long-term marketing strategy when they released the albums. At that time Cantopop was still far from an important genre in the music industry. The situation remained unchanged until "Raging Tide." Although it was the theme song of one of TVB's big-budget *Jade Theatre* dramas, the song was collected on an album of mixed TVB theme songs one year later in 1977, but the singer Susanna Kwan was not highlighted on that album. The Cantopop star system was yet to take shape, so to speak. By the time the next theme song of the *Jade Theatre* soap opera *A House Is Not a Home* was released, it was packaged as a major hit on Roman Tam's album, bearing the same title as the drama. The local Cantopop star system began to develop, and "the emergence and longevity of indigenous stars in Hong Kong were closely related to their crossmedia existence in television, cinema and pop music."[51] Moreover, "[b]etween the mid and late 1970s, international record companies such as Polygram and WEA began to set up affiliates in Hong Kong in order to better exploit the growing record market here."[52]

Roman Tam, together with Adam Cheng, Liza Wang, Jenny Tseng, Paula Tsui, and George Lam, among others, emerged as superstars. More and more singers who were focusing on Mandarin and English popular songs turned to the Cantopop industry for a more promising career. Some of the well-known examples include former band stars Elisa Chan, Johnny Yip 葉振棠, Kenny Bee 鍾鎮濤, and, most importantly, Alan Tam, who later became a megastar in the 1980s. Elisa Chan and Johnny Yip were members of the local band Jade, while Kenny Bee and Alan Tam were members of The Wynners, and these former band members represented the paradigm shift of the Hong Kong pop industry in the mid-1970s. The Wynners began as an English pop band and was once a popular teen idol group, arguably the most popular local Hong Kong band in the 1970s. In response to the rising trend, they turned to Cantopop in the mid-1970s, hosting the TVB show *The Wynners Special* 《溫拿狂想曲》 and starring in the film *Let's Rock* 《大家樂》 (1975) directed by James Wong. Although they continued to fare reasonably well and made two more movies, *Gonna Get You* 《溫拿與教授》 (1976) and *Making It* 《追趕跑跳碰》 (1978), they decided to disband—unofficially—in 1978, and members started pursuing their solo careers. The rise of The Wynners could be seen, in hindsight, as a continutation of the band boom in the 1960s. However, the transformation of the soundscape in the 1970s soon brought this band boom to an end.[53]

---

51. "The interlocking relationships between these media in the 1970s and 1980s capitalized on the mass audiences' familiarity with television as the main source of multi-media stardom and the means to build the stars' subsequent popularity in films and popular music." Wing-Fai Leung, "Multi-Media Stardom, Performance and Theme Songs in Hong Kong Cinema," *Canadian Journal of Film Studies* 20, no. 1 (May 2011): 41.

52. Choi, "Popular Culture," 540.

53. Masashi Ogawa, "Japanese Popular Music in Hong Kong: Analysis of Global/Local Cultural Relations," in *Globalizing Japan: Ethnography of the Japanese Presence in Asia, Europe, and America*, ed. Harumi Befu and Sylvie Guichard-Anguis (London and New York: Routledge, 2001), 122.

It is necessary to note that the use of cover versions was very common at that time, which played an important role in the development of Cantopop in the 1970s and 1980s. The melodies of "cover music" were composed outside Hong Kong, mainly imported from Japan, Korea, Taiwan, or Euro-American countries. The lyrics of these songs were rewritten locally, and music arrangements were kept as original or were rearranged by music companies. One of the reasons for using cover music in the rapidly growing music industry in Hong Kong was the hunger for the success formula of those megahits with proven popularity. Cover music was also used to fill in the gaps in the production process, when local record companies found it hard to cope with the speed of producing megahits. Record companies used cover music as a quick and easy way to produce profit-making popular music. Another important factor was that production costs could be kept to a minimum; Hong Kong music companies only had to pay the copyright fee to the original composer/music company and the cost of rewriting the lyrics. The Hong Kong lyricists, however, only received a fixed amount of compensation but not the future royalties generated by the cover versions. When compared to the music production fees of a song locally composed, using cover music was cheaper, and it was also quicker to produce and publicize the song. Cover versions not only diversified Cantopop in terms of musical cultures but also allowed newcomers a chance at bringing their typical styles to Cantopop. In short, the music industry used cover versions primarily for effective productions and bigger profits in the expanding market in the 1970s. Hybridity was an unforeseen side product of the operation of the music industry, but in the end it was the key element of Cantopop's success in its heyday.[54] In the meantime, record companies found that they had an exceptional opportunity to test the swiftly expanding market for new rising stars. Teenage idols Danny Chan and the legendary Leslie Cheung were among the successful examples of a rising generation of Cantopop stars. Danny Chan, having won first prize at the Hong Kong Yamaha Electone Festival in 1977, was headhunted by EMI and released his debut album *First Love/Tears for You* 《初戀／眼淚為你流》 in 1979. The song "Tears for You" 〈眼淚為你流〉 topped pop charts and jumpstarted his career as a teenage idol. Meanwhile, Leslie Cheung attained first runner-up at the Asian Music Contest held by RTV in 1976. Developing his profession as an RTV television actor-cum-singer, he released his debut English album *I Like Dreamin'* in 1977, and later turned to Cantopop in 1979 with *Lover's Arrow* 《情人箭》, with the main plug a theme song of an RTV *wuxia* drama. These endeavors failed to make a big

---

54. The account of cover versions is drawn from Yiu-Wai Chu and Eve Leung, "Remapping Hong Kong Popular Music: Covers, Localisation and the Waning Hybridity of Cantopop," *Popular Music* 32, no. 1 (January 2013): 65–78.

impact, but Cheung still needed a chance—which finally came in the 1980s—to showcase his talents and his potential of becoming a megastar. As stars are central to the experience of popular music, a new configuration of Cantopop stardom would help further expand its market.

The rapid development of Cantopop stardom was supplemented by the establishment of popular music awards. The International Federation of Phonographic Industry Hong Kong (IFPIHK) introduced the first Gold Disc Award Presentation in 1977. One year later, RTHK organized the first Top Ten Chinese Gold Songs Award. As per the introduction of the IFPIHK, the Award "provides artists the official recognition and measure of success under a common standard of sales and audit supported by the industry."[55] A total of sixteen local Gold Discs (selling more than 15,000 units) were presented at the first Gold Disc Award Presentation, as shown in Table 3.1:

Table 3.1
Local gold discs, First Hong Kong Gold Disc Award Presentation, 1977

Artist	Album Title	Record Company
Teresa Carpio	*You've Got Me for Company*	EMI
Teresa Carpio	*Songs for You*	EMI
Teresa Carpio	*Teresa Carpio*	EMI
Chelsia Chan	*Dark Side of Your Mind*	Polydor
The Wynners	*Same Kind of Magic*	Polydor
Various Artists	*Gold into '76*	Polydor
Teresa Teng	*Island Love Songs Vol. 2*	Polydor
Polystar	*Local & International Artists*	Polydor
Sam Hui	*The Private Eyes*	Polydor
The Wynners	*Special TV Hits*	Polydor
Original Soundtrack	*Jumping Ash*	Bang Bang
Paula Tsui	*Plum Blossoms*	Wing Hang
Paula Tsui	*G-Men 75*	Wing Hang
Rowena Cortes	*Rowena Cortes*	Prod'n Hse
Rowena Cortes	*Not a Baby Any More*	Prod'n Hse
Adam Cheng and Liza Wang	*Happy Every Year*	Fung Hang

As apparent from the table, English popular songs were still the mainstream in 1976. Two big transnational labels, Polydor and EMI, were the market leaders at that time, and they focused mainly on English popular songs. Local record companies like Wing Hang and Fung Hang were much smaller in scale, and they targeted the Cantopop audience. Out of the sixteen Gold Discs, only *The Private Eyes*, *Jumping Ash*, *G-Men 75*, and *Happy Every Year* were Cantopop

---

55. Cited from the IFPIHK website, http://www.ifpihk.org/content-page/award; retrieved on March 15, 2016.

albums. While *Island Love Songs Vol. 2* and *Plum Blossoms* were Mandapop albums, the other ten Gold Discs were composed of English popular songs. The Second Gold Disc Award Presentation in 1978 told a very different story, as can be seen in Tables 3.2 and 3.3:

Table 3.2
Local platinum discs, Second Hong Kong Gold Disc Award Presentation, 1978

Artist	Album Title	Record Company
Chelsia Chan	*Dark Side of Your Mind*	Polydor
Roman Tam	*Little Li's Flying Saber*	Crown Records
Sam Hui	*The Private Eyes*	Polydor
Sam Hui	*Here Comes the God of Wealth*	Polydor
Paula Tsui	*Plum Blossoms*	Wing Hang
Paula Tsui	*G-Men 75*	Wing Hang

Table 3.3
Local gold discs, Second Hong Kong Gold Disc Award Presentation, 1978

Artist	Album Title	Record Company
Al Cheung	*Big AL*	Bang Bang
Roman Tam	*A House Is Not a Home*	Crown Records
Various Artists	*Best of Hit Sounds*	EMI
New Topnotes	*Best of New Topnotes*	EMI
Gracie Rivera	*Gracie Rivera*	EMI
Grace Wong	*Feelings*	EMI
Teresa Carpio	*Greatest Hits*	EMI
Various Artists	*16 Motion Picture Greats for You*	EMI
Various Artists	*Gold Into '77*	Polydor
Sam Hui	*Came Travelling*	Polydor
Various Artists	*Many Many Polydors*	Polydor
Grace Chan	*Grace Chan*	Polydor
Teresa Teng	*Special Collections*	Polydor
Sam Hui	*Special Collections*	Polydor
Chelsia Chan	*Chelsia My Love*	Polydor
Teresa Teng	*Island Love Songs Vol. 3*	Polydor
Paula Tsui	*The Magic Phoenix*	Wing Hang
Fanny and James Fung	*When Changes Occur*	Wing Hang
Adam Cheng	*Luk Siu Fung*	Crown Records

On the one hand, as shown in the number of Platinum Discs (selling more than 30,000 units) and Gold Discs, the market had expanded significantly within a year. On the other hand, among the six Platinum Discs, there were four Cantonese albums, one Mandarin album, and one English album. The number of Cantopop Gold Discs had also increased to eight (including *Many*

Many Polydors comprising ten Cantopop and two English songs). Big labels like Polydor and EMI started shifting their emphases to the Cantopop market. Popular Cantopop singers like Sam Hui, Adam Cheng, Liza Wang, Roman Tam, Jenny Tseng, and Paula Tsui were all well-established stars, and Cantopop had become an unstoppable force in the music industry at long last.

Another sign of the growing industry was the founding of the Composers and Authors Society of Hong Kong Limited (CASH) in 1977. The Performing Rights Society (PRS) of the United Kingdom set up an agency in Hong Kong in 1946 to protect music copyrights. Considering the swiftly expanding market of Cantopop since the mid-1970s, it coordinated with a group of local Hong Kong composers to establish CASH as the agency to perform royalty collections.

> CASH was incorporated in Hong Kong on 23 September 1977 under the Companies Ordinance, being a Company limited by guarantee and not having a share capital. It started operating on 1 October 1977 and a press conference was held at the Mandarin Hotel to mark the establishment of CASH on 20 October 1977.[56]

The establishment of CASH showed that Cantopop had become a lucrative new market with both its sales and profits flourishing in the late 1970s.

Afterword

Since the mid-1970s, Hong Kong popular music has been very much identified with Cantopop. The radical transformation of Hong Kong's sociopolitical background and the swift development of mass media in the 1970s provided a historical juncture in which local consciousness came into being at long last. In this special context, local popular culture had an unprecedented opportunity to develop almost as quickly as its economy. The rapid economic development from the early 1970s to the 1980s in Hong Kong "led to the rise of a local popular culture expressed in film, music and television shows," and "[m]any local people became proud of Hong Kong's hybrid status."[57] In the 1970s, Hong Kong people worked very hard, sharing a common goal of improving their standard of living. In the face of incessant social changes, they were on the one hand discontent with social inequalities, but were on the other hand proud of their own accomplishments in terms of economic growth. In the meantime, the absence of political autonomy as a British colony led the Hong Kong people to come to accept the "compensatory logic" to turn their energy to economics (refer to Chapter One). Hong Kong was thus shaped as a commercial city that

---

56. Cited from the CASH website, http://www.cash.org.hk/en/index.php?main=0&id; retrieved on March 15, 2016.
57. Carroll, *A Concise History of Hong Kong*, 168–69.

placed economic development at the top of its priority list. One may complain that the populist resistance to Cantopop (e.g., Sam Hui's social parodies) reflected a limited form of local consciousness, but the rise of local cultural industries did offer Cantopop singers various platforms to express their paradoxical feelings in an age of innocence. More importantly, together with other emerging cultural industries such as cinema and television, Cantopop gave a sense of self-esteem to the Hong Kong people. As noted by David Faure, "[b]y the late 1970s, the Chinese people in Hong Kong were feeling surer of themselves," and they had become "Hong Kong people of Chinese descent," but not Chinese sojourners in Hong Kong.[58] In a nutshell, the 1970s was a decade in which the Hong Kong society witnessed a significant development of local culture and consciousness.[59]

The rise of Cantopop in the 1970s was also a result of its increased hybridity. The new experiments included, among others, the use of cover versions (English, Japanese, and other popular songs), the hybridization of Chinese and Western elements, the coexistence of Cantonese, classical, and modern Chinese in its lyrics, and the crossover of genres, which changed its soundscape. Moreover, the 1970s in Hong Kong was "an age of hybridity":

> Localization was just about to begin in the 1970s, and the so-called 'local identity' was not yet exclusionary. Hybridized and pluralistic cultures could coexist, and Chinese-Western hybridization had not turned into a cliché of "Chinese-meets-West" . . . At the time Hong Kong was in search of a brand and position—this was an age of genuine hybridity before "hybridity" itself became a brand of Hong Kong.[60]

Thanks to its thriving vitality, the changing mediascape, and the developing economy, Cantopop had grown into a highly profitable business with a quickly expanding market by the end of the 1970s.

---

58. David Faure, "Reflections on Being Chinese in Hong Kong," in *Hong Kong's Transitions, 1942–1997*, ed. Judith Brown and Rosemary Foot (London: Macmillan Press, 1997), 103–4.
59. See, for instance, Tai-Lok Lui, *Hong Kong's 1970*, 32.
60. Kwai-Cheung Lo 羅貴祥 and Eva Man 文潔華, eds., *An Age of Hybridity: Cultural Identity, Gender, Everyday Life Practice and Hong Kong Cinema of the 1970s* 《雜嘜時代：文化身份、性別、日常生活實踐與香港電影1970s》 (Hong Kong: Oxford University Press, 2005), 2.

4 | An Age of Glory
The 1980s

Introduction

The 1980s marked a paramount stage of transformation in local Hong Kong culture. Having experienced some ten years of rapid economic growth, Hong Kong people began to enjoy a considerably higher standard of living. Although the Hong Kong economic myth had fabricated a kind of complacent Hong Kong-ness, Hong Kong people were also led to believe that they had to develop their own local culture in order to supplement their lack of political and cultural significance. The 1980s was a time in which, at least owing in part to the Sino-British negotiations over the future of Hong Kong, there were renewed interests in finding out what Hong Kong culture was. Shortly before the end of the 1970s, Crawford Murray MacLehose, then Hong Kong governor, visited China officially on March 29, 1979 to discuss the future of Hong Kong after 1997. He suggested to the Central People's Government (CPG) that the land grants in the New Territories be approved for a term beyond June 30, 1997, which was shot down by Deng Xiaoping, then chairman of the People's Republic of China (PRC). Deng made it very clear that Hong Kong had to revert to China under his famous "One Country, Two Systems" framework. On September 22, 1982, then British prime minister Margaret Thatcher went to Beijing to discuss the future of Hong Kong with Chinese leaders, after which they jointly declared that "for the common purpose of maintaining Hong Kong's prosperity and stability, the two sides agreed to continue the negotiations through diplomatic channels," and "[t]his signaled the beginning of negotiations on Hong Kong's future."[1] When Lady Thatcher slipped on the stairs in front of the Great Hall of the People in Beijing during her visit in 1982, Hong Kong's economy also fell sharply. Hong Kong people began to realize that their future was hopelessly intertwined with the Sino-British negotiations.

---

1. Cited from *Sino-British Negotiations and the Sino-British Joint Declaration*, 12, http://www.basiclaw. gov.hk/en/publications/book/15anniversary_reunification_ch1_2.pdf; retrieved on March 15, 2016.

Hong Kong's future could not be guaranteed simply by its economic myth, and its reunion with China was inevitable.

In the two years before the Sino-British Joint Declaration was initialed on September 26, 1984 at the Great Hall of the People in Beijing, Hong Kong experienced another crisis of confidence. The confidence of the Hong Kong people at that time was on the line, and there was a new wave of exodus: "In the early 1980s, according to Donald Tsang, the Hong Kong government's point man on the emigration issue, about 20,000 people a year left the territory; in 1987 the number rose to 30,000, and in 1988 and 1989 to more than 40,000."[2] A collective panic resulted among Hong Kong people to such an extent that when taxi drivers went on strike, or even when the soccer team South China was relegated to Division Two, there were subsequent riots. The early 1980s was in a sense not too different from 1967. Since then the China factor has dominated Hong Kong. As discussed in the previous chapter, the more frustrated or blocked the aspirations to the economy are, the more the cultural industries boom. The collective anxiety of the Hong Kong people was effectively channeled by the catharsis provided by popular culture after 1974. History repeated itself in the 1980s. Due to the impasse between China and Britain during handover talks, the Hang Seng Index fell sharply in 1982 and hit bottom at 676 in December before it bounced back. But despite this, Hong Kong cultural industries continued to grow.

Cantopop, thanks to its synergy with Hong Kong cinema and television, had grown into a highly profitable business with a quickly expanding market by the end of the 1970s. Later it developed further into a multimedia industry, becoming so popular that it attracted those who did not speak Cantonese. In the early 1980s, "Cantopop became firmly established as a cultural product for the consumption of the majority of the listening and viewing public."[3] More importantly, Cantopop and related cultural industries were indispensable elements of Hong Kong's lifestyle in the 1980s, which, as lucidly noted by Hugh Baker, led to the emergence of a *sui generis* "Hong Kong Man."[4] Throughout the 1980s, superstars such as Leslie Cheung, Alan Tam, and Anita Mui surpassed their predecessors by developing Cantopop into a multimedia business that also straddled the borders with neighboring regions. These superstars staged hundreds of concerts in the newly built Hong Kong Coliseum, with a seating capacity of more than 10,000; concerts thus became a highly profitable business. By the end of the 1980s, Cantopop successfully helped

2. Cait Murphy, "Hong Kong: A Culture of Emigration," *The Atlantic Monthly* 267, no. 4 (April 1991): 20.
3. Po-King Choi, "Popular Culture," in *The Other Hong Kong Report 1990*, ed. Richard Y. C. Wong and Joseph Y. S. Cheng (Hong Kong: Chinese University Press, 1990), 541.
4. Hugh Baker, "Life in the Cities: The Emergence of Hong Kong Man," *The China Quarterly* 95 (September 1983): 478–79.

Hong Kong establish its leading role in the multibillion dollar idol business of popular culture.

Theme Songs and Cross-Media Synergy

The impact of television theme songs continued with the ongoing localization of television programs. The distribution of the sources of programs for TVB Jade, the most popular television channel, had changed greatly since the early 1970s, as shown in the table below:

Table 4.1
Distribution of the sources of programs for TVB Jade

Year	TVB	RTHK	Western	Japan	Taiwan	Others*	Total
1972	29	0	41	8	2	20	100
1976	41	0	10	5	20	23	99
1982	62	2	11	8	6	11	100
1987	66	5	7	4	4	14	100

*Others include ready-made Cantonese and Mandarin films, programs from the PRC, and those of unknown sources.[5]

As market leader, TVB continued to produce many great television hits in the early 1980s. The theme song of Chow Yun Fat's all-time classic *The Bund*, among others, became one of the most successful cases in the history of Cantopop. The song "The Bund" 〈上海灘〉, sung by Frances Yip 葉麗儀 (melody by Joseph Koo and lyrics by James Wong), generated a huge wave across Chinese communities, including the Mainland which had just adopted the Open Door Policy. The song captivated even non-Cantonese speakers, and it was so popular that it had Mandarin and even Thai renditions. The fact that the theme song of the 2006 Mainland remake of *The Bund* was sung by Frances Yip, and the first two phrases of the original version remained in Cantonese, further attesting to its popularity in the Mainland.

A quick glance at the chart RTHK Top Ten Gold Songs shows the prevailing role of television theme songs in the Cantopop industry. Out of the ten Gold Songs, seven were television theme songs: besides "The Bund," there was Liza Wang's "Yesterday's Glitter" 〈京華春夢〉, Adam Cheng's "Five Easy Pieces" 〈輪流轉〉, Roman Tam's "The Brothers" 〈親情〉, Michael Kwan and Annabelle Lui's 雷安娜 "Tear Drops on the Journey" 〈人在旅途灑淚時〉, Michael Kwan's "Decrepit Dream" 〈殘夢〉, and Johnny Yip's "Drama of Life" 〈戲劇人生〉. One interesting point to note is that while the former

---

5. To-Man Chan, "Competition Would Promote Localization for Cable Television," *Hong Kong Economic Journal* (March 3, 1989); cited from Po-King Choi, "Popular Culture," 540.

four were TVB theme songs, the latter three belonged to RTV. Although Commercial Television had closed down in 1978, the early 1980s witnessed a rare competition in the history of the Hong Kong television industry. TVB was a comfortable market leader in the 1970s, but in 1980 it suffered a shocking defeat. In September 1980, RTV launched a new campaign entitled "Raising a Thousand Sails," challenging the leading role of TVB. RTV released three dramas during prime time: *Fatherland* 《大地恩情》 at 7 p.m., *Tears in a Sandstorm* 《風塵淚》 at 8 p.m., and *Love Story* 《驟雨中的陽光》 at 9 p.m. TVB was showing *Five Easy Pieces* 《輪流傳》 at 7 p.m., but *Fatherland* snatched an unanticipated rating of 40 percent, which was totally unacceptable to TVB. Although *Five Easy Pieces* recorded a higher rating than *Fatherland*, TVB decided to cut it short and replace it with the last five episodes of *The Bund II* 《上海灘續集》, followed by Liza Wang's *King of Gambler* 《千王之王》. Before long, TVB regained lost ground, but RTV had already made an exceptional breakthrough. Moreover, although *Tears in a Sandstorm* was not successful, *Love Story* also made a mark for RTV as a creative story of puppy love. More importantly, the theme songs of *Fatherland* and *Love Story* were both very well received by audiences. The melodies and lyrics of the two songs were written by Michael Lai and Jimmy Lo, respectively (the former sung by Michael Kwan and the latter by Ruth Tsang 曾路得).

Michael Lai and Jimmy Lo had already established their music careers in the 1970s, but it was during their RTV collaboration that they developed into genuine competitors of the Joseph Koo and James Wong duo in the area of TV theme songs in the early 1980s. Michael Lai, a child actor in the 1950s, turned to the music sector to become a band leader when he grew up. He joined RTV in 1975 to team up with Nancy Sit 薛家燕 in the variety show *Nancy and Michael* 《家燕與小田》. He started writing television theme songs for RTV in 1976 (Nancy Sit's "Upper/Lower Class" 〈上下流〉), but due to the marginal status of the television company, his songs were not well received. In the shadow of Joseph Koo, who was the mainstay of TVB, he worked mainly with RTV in the late 1970s and early 1980s. The arrival of Jimmy Lo at RTV after the closure of CTV in 1978 later proved to be career-changing for Michael Lai. Thanks to the improved quality of the RTV dramas, and arguably the chemistry between the duo, RTV theme songs (such as "Chameleon" 〈變色龍〉; melody by Michael Lai and lyrics by Jimmy Lo, 1978) began to catch public attention. In the next few years, they produced numerous RTV theme songs, which could be compared with the "Fai and Wong" (Joseph Koo and James Wong) songs. After Joseph Koo left Hong Kong to further his studies in 1981, Michael Lai joined Capital Artists, a TVB subsidiary, in 1982 and truly shone in the music industry, collaborating with superstars like Leslie Cheung and Anita Mui. After a short spell with CTV, Jimmy Lo moved to RTV and teamed up with Michael Lai, "raising a thousand sails" in the Cantopop industry. The 1980 Gold Songs "Tear Drops on the Journey," "Decrepit Dream," and "Drama of Life" were their products. Michael Lai won the first-ever Best Lyrics Award in the RTHK Top Ten Gold Songs Awards in 1981 with the theme song "Unable to Find an Excuse" 〈找不着藉口〉 from the RTV drama *Hong Kong Gentlemen* 《浴血太平山》, whereas the Best Melody Award went to James Wong's "Forget Him" 〈忘記他〉 sung by Teresa Teng. As evident from the chart RTHK Top Ten Gold Songs, Michael Lai and Jimmy Lo were successful in challenging the dominant role of TVB theme songs, and they further developed their own styles and philosophies in soap opera songs such as "Drama of Life" and *wuxia* songs such as "Reincarnated" 〈天蠶變〉. However, unlike James Wong, Jimmy Lo was famous for his desolate tone, which could be seen as a perfect match for RTV's marginalized status in the television industry.

While TVB and RTV continued to produce many popular theme songs in the early to mid-1980s, the music scene also witnessed a drastic transformation. Television theme songs were no longer the overriding force in the Cantopop industry. This change can be seen in the RTHK Top Ten Gold Songs of 1981. Only three of the ten songs were related to television dramas: Adam Cheng's "A Free Life" 〈做人愛自由〉, Jenny Tseng's "Pearl of the Orient" 〈東方之珠〉, and Michael Kwan's "Drunken Red Dust" 〈醉紅塵〉. The revealing chart also spoke volumes for the popularity of movie theme songs. Sam Hui's "Impression" 〈印象〉 and George Lam's "Scent of a Woman" 〈活色生香〉 were theme songs of the movies *Security Unlimited* 《摩登保鑣》 and *All the Wrong Clues for the Right Solution* 《鬼馬智多星》, respectively. Sam Hui had indeed already made his mark in the movie sector in the 1970s, but more Cantopop singers began to cross over to the movie sector in the 1980s. As mentioned in the previous chapter, the use of Cantopop as movie theme songs continued in 1980, but later Hong Kong New Wave films no longer relied on theme songs. Notwithstanding this development, movie theme songs had become a common practice in the film industry in the early 1980s, and some of them even facilitated the career of Cantopop idols, including Danny Chan and Leslie Cheung, who were mentioned briefly in the previous chapter, and George Lam, among others. George Lam made his debut with *Money Trip* in 1978, but by then he was still not an established Cantopop singer. However, his *Jade Theatre* theme song "The Passenger" made him a rising Cantopop star. Shortly after the mediocre Shaw Brothers production *Disco Bumpkins* 《摩登土佬》, George Lam joined the newly established Cinema City & Films to develop his film career in *All the Wrong Clues for the Right Solution*. Cinema City later became the most influential film production company in Hong Kong in the 1980s, and George Lam was one of the successful examples of singer-turned-actor, which also signaled an era of cross-media Cantopop megastars.

Properly written, theme songs and movies created a win-win situation. Veteran lyricist Kwok-Kong Cheng said in an interview that he had seen *Homecoming* (a.k.a. *Years Flowing Like Water*) 《似水流年》 (1985) seven times before he finished writing the lyrics for the theme song, which was inspired by the last scene in the movie in which the female lead, Josephine Koo 顧美華, gazes at the vast sea. According to Kwok-Kong Cheng, the win-win situation could have been attributed to the synergy between the lyrics and the scenes in the movie, as well as the arrangement of the song by Michael Lai, who successfully gave the audience a feeling of flowing water.[6]

The synergy between images and songs was further enhanced by the appearance of music videos. While the influence of television drama theme songs was diminishing, the rise of music videos gave a new impetus to the expanding industry. Hong Kong television stations started airing music videos after MTV's launch in August 1981. Subsequently a revolutionary change occurred, resulting in a new creative synergy between television and popular music. Idol singers like Alan Tam, Leslie Cheung, and Anita Mui could use music videos to visualize their images in the songs. Cantopop became not only audio but also visual, and lyricists were thus prompted to use more concrete settings in their works. As noted by veteran lyricist Jolland Chan 向雪懷, the early 1980s was a period of experimentation. He enjoyed the luxury of testing innovative styles in his writing, one of which being the use of concrete images to enhance the mood of the songs.[7] A good example was Alan Tam's "Rain and Sorrow" 〈雨絲・情愁〉, in which Jolland Chan used images like rain showers and street lamps, which also inspired the set design of the music video, to evoke a melancholic mood. As music videos became increasingly popular, TVB launched two music video awards—Best Music Video Production Award and Best Music Video Performance Award—at its Jade Solid Gold Best Ten Music Awards Presentation in 1987 (won by Sandy Lam's 林憶蓮 "Passion" 〈激情〉 and Anita Mui's "Fiery Tango" 〈似火探戈〉, respectively). The growing importance of the visual dimension of Cantopop exerted a profound impact on the development of the idol industry in the 1980s.

New Cantopop Megastars

Thanks to the rapid growth of the television and record industries, a Cantopop star system took shape during the late 1970s. However, with the exception of Sam Hui, the fans of other Cantopop stars, such as Adam Cheng, Liza Wang, Roman Tam, and Paula Tsui, were somewhat restricted given free television's

---

6. Cited from Yiu-Wai Chu, *Songs of Your Life: On Hong Kong Cantopop* 《歲月如歌：詞話香港粵語流行曲》 (in Chinese) (Hong Kong: Joint Publishing, 2008), 89.
7. Chu, *Songs of Your Life*, 70–72.

emphasis on family audiences. Owing to their images and styles and, arguably, their ages, these Cantopop stars, albeit popular, could not genuinely captivate the young audience as idols. The swift development of the Hong Kong movie industry introduced a fresh impetus into the Cantopop star system at this particular juncture. The transformation of the movie industry in the 1980s reshaped the mediascape, which facilitated the production of cross-media megastars. At the turn of the decade, New Wave directors injected new life into Hong Kong cinema, which was dominated by Shaw Brothers and Golden Harvest during the 1970s. The otherwise aging industry was in dire need of new stars.

In response to this crisis, new film companies headhunted rising teenage singers to star in their productions, and youth was one of the most important genres. The teen film *Encore* 《喝采》 (1980), starring Danny Chan, Leslie Cheung, and Paul Chung 鍾保羅 (a disc-jockey idol), was a classic example. The theme song "Encore" 〈喝采〉 (a.k.a. "Heartening" 〈鼓舞〉) further developed Danny Chan's music career as a youth idol. In the semi-sequel *On Trial* 《失業生》 (1981), the theme songs "Sunflower" 〈太陽花〉 and "Having You" 〈有了你〉 also became all-time favorites of Danny Chan's fans. Meanwhile, the director of *Encore*, Clifford Choi 蔡繼光, also made the teen film *Teenage Dreamers* 《檸檬可樂》 for Shaw Brothers in 1982. Besides Rowena Cortes's 露雲娜 theme song "Lemon Coke" 〈檸檬可樂〉 (what the Chinese title of the film literally means), there was also the popular song "Gaze" 〈凝望〉 sung by Leslie Cheung. However, the time had not come for Leslie Cheung yet, who still had to wait a couple of years before he finally became a megastar.

Because of the contents of the teen films, young Cantopop singers were needed to perform the theme songs. During the early 1980s, many young singers got into the Cantopop industry, and with the help of movie theme songs they soon attracted many teenage fans. Ken Choi, a disc jockey-turned-singer, was one of these young singers.[8] When RTHK, in the face of competition from Commercial Radio Hong Kong, decided to market their disc jockeys as teen idols in the early 1980s, Ken Choi became one of the most successful cases. His first hit, "Her Shadow" 〈倩影〉, was one of the RTHK Top Ten Gold Songs in 1981. As the lead actor in the teen love story *Love* 《拖手仔》 (1982), he sang the theme song "Sparks of Love" 〈愛的火花〉 with Samantha Lam 林志美, who later sang the puppy-love classic "Coincidence" 〈偶遇〉, the theme song of the movie *A Certain Romance* 《少女日記》 (1984). The success

8. An anecdote in the history of Cantopop can be noted here. Ken Choi later became the host of the TVB music program *Jade Solid Gold*. In a 1985 quarterly award ceremony, he made a comment after Leslie Cheung received a Gold Song award: "A flash of glory may not last forever." It was widely reported by the media as a sour-grapes criticism, which was vehemently condemned by Leslie Cheung's fans. After this, Ken Choi's career hit rock bottom.

of these puppy-love songs can be attributed not just to the rising stars but also to the lyrics written by Kwok-Kong Cheng (the lyricist of the singers mentioned above), who was an expert at presenting teenagers' affections. Suffice it to say that these are just a few examples of the emerging trend of teen Cantopop, which significantly expanded its fan base.

The New Wave directors made a great impact on the filmscape of Hong Kong, allowing new companies to enter the market. These companies were of different sizes, and, among them, Cinema City & Films, established in 1980, was the new trendsetter. Cinema City knew very well what a new company had to do when entering the market. In response to George Lam's success in the movie *All the Wrong Clues for the Right Solution*, they spent big money to attract Sam Hui to star in the *Aces Go Places* 《最佳拍檔》 series, which proved to be hugely successful in terms of the box office. (Sam Hui was reportedly paid HK$2 million for the first episode of *Aces Go Places* in 1982, which was one-quarter of the entire budget.)[9] Sam Hui's Cantopop theme songs in the series further developed his status as a megastar in the music industry. George Lam's "Love Songs" 〈幾段情歌〉 in *All the Wrong Spies* 《我愛夜來香》 (1983) and "Big Step Forward" 〈邁步向前〉 in *Banana Cops* 《英倫琵琶》 (1984) were also big hits, boosting both his film and music careers.

It Takes Two 《難兄難弟》 (1982) was another example of Cinema City's keen insight into the synergy between film and popular music. Although the leading actors were Dean Shek 石天, Richard Ng 吳耀漢, and Cherie Chung 鍾楚紅, Cantopop singers George Lam, Alan Tam, and Frances Yip made special guest appearances in the film. At the time Alan Tam had not become a Cantopop megastar yet. One of his career-changing songs, "Illusion" 〈幻影〉, was the theme song of *Esprit d'amour* 《陰陽錯》, a 1983 Cinema City film in which he was the leading actor. Before the success of *Esprit d'amour*, Alan Tam also starred in several Cinema City films—*My Darling, My Goddess* 《愛人女神》 (1982), *Till Death Do We Scare* 《小生怕怕》 (1982), and *Play Catch* 《少爺威威》 (1983)—all featuring Cantopop theme songs. He was also the leading actor in later Cinema City films such as *Kung Hei Fat Choy* 《恭喜發財》 (1985) and *Mummy Dearest* 《四眼仔》 (1985). Another movie worth mentioning here is *Merry Christmas* 《聖誕快樂》 (1984), starring Karl Maka 麥嘉, Paula Tsui, Danny Chan, and Leslie Cheung. While Danny Chan's "Waiting" 〈等〉 from the movie became a great hit of the year, Leslie Cheung's performance stole the limelight. He later established a very good working relationship with Cinema City in the *A Better Tomorrow* 《英雄本色》 and *A Chinese Ghost Story* 《倩女幽魂》 series, from which many of his Cantopop classics came. There were many popular movie theme songs in the 1980s, and

---

9. Lisa Morton, *The Cinema of Tsui Hark* (Jefferson, NC: McFarland, 2001), 136.

they bore witness to the heyday of both Hong Kong cinema and popular music. During this period, it was Cinema City that exemplified this creative synergy between movies and popular songs.

Given the limited scope of this chapter, I will focus on only three Cantopop legends: Alan Tam, Leslie Cheung, and Anita Mui. As mentioned in the previous chapter, Alan Tam was the lead vocalist of the local band The Wynners in the 1970s. After they unofficially disbanded in 1978, Alan Tam had a short spell with TVB, cohosting the teen show *The Sound of Bang Bang* 《繽繽咁嘅聲》 with Carol Cheng (a.k.a. Dodo Cheng) 鄭裕玲, and starring in *The Youth Craze* 《青春熱潮》 and the *Jade Theatre* soap opera *Over the Rainbow* 《天虹》 (1979). Meanwhile, before The Wynners parted ways, Kenny Bee had already begun his film career in Taiwan in 1976. He was the male lead of Chelsia Chan's award-winning *Chelsia My Love* 《秋霞》 (directed by the renowned Taiwanese director Tsushou Sung 宋存壽). As Kenny Bee and Chelsia Chan fascinated the Taiwanese audience with their romantic love stories, Alan Tam was invited to develop his film career in the Taiwanese film *A Girl without Sorrow* 《忘憂草》 (1979). In the same year, he released his first solo Cantopop album, *Naughty Boy* 《反斗星》, which was quite a success in terms of sales (it won the IFPIHK Gold Disc Award in 1979).

At the same time Alan Tam shifted his base to Taiwan, and in the subsequent three years he made many Taiwanese movies, among which the most successful was *If I Were for Real* 《假如我是真的》 (1981), the masterpiece that earned him the Best Actor Award at the Eighteenth Golden Horse Awards. He did not give up the Cantopop market during his tenure in Taiwan, releasing his second and third Cantopop albums *Crazy in Love with You* 《愛到你發狂》 and *Can't Forget You* 《忘不了您》 in 1980 and 1981, respectively. The title song of the latter, "Can't Forget You" (a cover version of "Lover" 〈恋人よ〉 by the Japanese vocalist Mayumi Itsuwa 五輪真弓), was a great success, and "Imagining the Future" 〈想將來〉 won him an RTHK Top Ten Gold Songs Award. *Can't Forget You* won the Platinum Disc Award, with sales volumes of more than four times that of the minimum requirement. However, his fourth album, *My Darling, My Goddess*, when compared to his previous ones, was less popular, although the song "Rain and Sorrow," a cover version of the Japanese song "Revival" 〈リバイバル〉, composed by Mayumi Itsuwa, was very well-liked by audiences. With his fifth Cantopop album, *Spring . . . The Late Spring* 《春……遲來的春天》, the most popular hit was the title song "The Late Spring," which was, again, a Japanese cover version 〈遲來的春天〉. The theme song "Illusion" mentioned above was also included on this album, contributing a creative synergy between Alan Tam's film and music careers.

After this Alan Tam and his producers found the right track and began directing their focus on Japanese cover versions for his upcoming albums. The next album, *Fog of Love*《霧之戀》(1984), not only turned a new page in his career but also a new chapter in the history of Cantopop. While the rearranged version of "Illusion" was still in vogue, the title song "Fog of Love"〈霧之戀〉also became an all-time classic, along with other tracks like "Unyielding"〈傲骨〉, "Replacement Lover"〈愛的替身〉, and "Midnight Girls"〈午夜麗人〉, which were all very popular. Alan Tam had also established a successful formula with Andrew Lam 林敏驄, the up-and-coming lyricist of "Can't Forget You," "Illusion," and "Fog of Love." The Cantopop scene in the mid-1980s was overwhelmingly dominated by Alan Tam's famous love trilogy—*Fog of Love* and his two subsequent albums, *Source of Love*《愛的根源》(1984) and *Love Trap*《愛情陷阱》(1985)—which sold better than hotcakes. In 1984, Alan Tam set a record by winning three Gold Song Awards at the Second Jade Solid Gold Best Ten Music Awards Presentation with "Illusions," "Source of Love" (the theme song of the romantic comedy *The Other Side of a Gentleman*《君子好逑》, starring Alan Tam and Brigitte Lin 林青霞), and the song of the year, "Love in Late Autumn"〈愛在深秋〉. He was also awarded the Jade Solid Gold Most Popular Male Singer in four consecutive years before announcing at the Tenth RTHK Top Ten Gold Songs Awards Ceremony in 1988 that he had decided not to receive any awards that involved competition from then on. One of his reasons was that he had been fed up with endless idle talk in the music industry. He did not specify what he meant by that, but it was clear that he was referring to his competition with Leslie Cheung.

After winning the first runner-up at the Asian Music Contest held by RTV in 1976, Leslie Cheung started his entertainment career with the second-rate television company. At first he focused on English popular songs, and then he released the Cantopop album *Lover's Arrow*《情人箭》in 1979. Perhaps due to the disadvantages of being an RTV artist, his music career had a rocky beginning. In the early 1980s, he shifted his emphasis to television dramas and movies after a disappointing start to his singing career. Despite his impressive performances in teen films (*Encore, On Trial*, and *Teenage Dreamers* mentioned above), he lived in the shadow of Danny Chan. His talent was finally recognized by his nomination for Best Actor (*Nomad*《烈火青春》) at the Hong Kong Film Awards in 1983, but he still needed a big hit to turn around his Cantopop career. The opportunity to sign with Capital Artists, a new record label closely related to TVB, changed Leslie Cheung's career. With his first Cantopop album released by Capital Artists, Leslie Cheung had a big hit, "The Wind Continues to Blow",〈風繼續吹〉, a cover version of Japanese legend Momoe Yamaguchi's 山口百惠 "The Other Side of Goodbye"〈さよならの向う側〉. The same album also included the theme songs of his movie *The Drummer*《鼓手》(1983), which were also quite popular. Given the relation of Capital Artists to TVB, Leslie Cheung included TVB theme songs on his second album, *Craziness* 《一片痴》. He successfully built up a new image in that year, but, contrary to its immense popularity, "The Wind Continues to Blow" did not win any awards at the end of the year.

1984 was an important year in the career of Leslie Cheung. His performance in the TVB drama *Once upon an Ordinary Girl* 《儂本多情》 and the movie *Behind the Yellow Line* 《緣份》 (costarring Maggie Cheung 張曼玉 and Anita Mui, and produced by Jimmy Lo) stole the limelight. With respect to his music career, the star passed the acid test with his first top-ten hit "Monica" 〈Monica〉, and the cream rose to the top at long last. The strong dance beat in "Monica," a cover version of a Japanese pop song of the same title by Kōji Kikkawa 吉川晃司, was completely different from other mainstream love ballads. While the song gave Leslie Cheung the chance to showcase his charisma on stage, it was also trailblazing in bringing a new genre of love songs to mainstream Cantopop. (For example, Alan Tam's "Love Trap" released a year later, belongs to this genre.) The album *Monica* sold more than 200,000 copies, and Leslie Cheung became the only competitor of Alan Tam in the mid-1980s. Leslie Cheung's next few albums sold as well as Alan Tam's. His next album included the theme song of his film *For Your Heart Only* 《為你鍾情》 (1985), bringing his talent as a cross-media megastar into full play. The first hit, "Wild Wind" 〈不羈的風〉, "For Your Heart Only," and tracks like "I Do" 〈我願意〉 and "Devoted to You" 〈癡心的我〉 (the theme song of the movie of the same title) all helped to enhance his image as a romantic lover. "Wild Wind" won the Gold Song Award in both the TVB and RTHK award ceremonies, further advancing Leslie Cheung's career in the music industry.

Although the number of Gold Songs Awards won by Alan Tam at the TVB and RTHK award ceremonies was greater in 1986, Leslie Cheung already caught up with him by winning the TVB Gold Song Gold Award (given to the most popular song of the year) for "Who Feels the Same?" 〈有誰共鳴〉. After "Who Feels the Same?" Leslie Cheung joined Cinepoly Records Hong Kong, which brought his career to its peak. His album *Summer Romance*, released in 1987, turned out to be the best-selling album of the year. He won the TVB Gold Song Gold Award with "Don't Wanna Sleep" 〈無心睡眠〉, the top hit of the album, again in 1987. During these two years, he also made glittering performances in Cinema City's productions *A Better Tomorrow* and *A Chinese Ghost Story*, and their theme songs all became Leslie Cheung's golden hits (e.g., "The Love Then" 〈當年情〉 and "Tao of the World" 〈人間道〉). His subsequent albums, *Virgin Snow* and *Hot Summer*, continued to sell exceedingly well, and in the latter the song "Silence Is Golden" 〈沉默是金〉 was a classic collaboration between two Cantopop megastars: melody by Leslie Cheung and lyrics by Sam Hui. After Alan Tam's decision to decline music awards, Leslie Cheung swept all Cantopop award ceremonies, becoming the most popular male singer in Hong Kong and even across Chinese communities worldwide. Without a rival, however, Leslie Cheung's enthusiasm flagged. To the surprise of all his music fans, he announced his very early retirement from the music industry at the summit of his career and popularity in 1989. After his *Final Encounter* album and 33 farewell concerts—he was 33 years old at the time—at the Hong Kong Coliseum, he waved goodbye to the music industry. When Leslie Cheung returned to music after a five-year hiatus, he made spectacular breakthroughs, which will be discussed in the next chapter.

There were many succesful duos in the history of Cantopop, but the chemistry between Leslie Cheung and Anita Mui was unprecedented—they were both born for the perfoming arts, showing their mystic power of charisma once on stage. In the 1984 movie *Behind The Yellow Line* starring Leslie Cheung and Maggie Cheung, Anita Mui won Best Supporting Actress at the Hong Kong Film Awards. Later in 1988, she teamed up with Leslie Cheung again in Stanley Kwan's haunting romance *Rouge* 《胭脂扣》, and her amazing performance won her the Best Actress Award at the Hong Kong Film Awards, the Taiwan Golden Horse Awards, and the Asia-Pacific Film Festival Awards. Similar to Leslie Cheung, Anita Mui entered the music industry by winning the First New Talent Singing Awards organized by TVB in 1981. The Cantopop diva began her singing career at Lai Chi Kok Amusement Park when she was still a child, as her elder sister and she had to earn a living for her family after the early death of their father.[10] It was reported that Joseph Koo, one of the judges of the New Talent Singing Contest, "scored 99 points for Anita, the highest praise he has ever given anyone."[11] As the winner she won a contract with Capital Artists and started her music career with a TVB theme song.

Although Anita Mui showed enormous potential in her first hit "Debt of the Heart" 〈心債〉, the theme song of the 1982 TVB drama *Soldier of Fortune* 《香城浪子》, the record company did not show full confidence in the production of her first album, *Debt of the Heart*. Side B of the album included the songs of The Little Tigers, a Hong Kong boy band that also partcipated in the New Talent Singing Awards. It is interesting to note that in 1983 the Cantopop diva sang the theme song of a TVB-purchased program based on the Japanese manga *Dr Slump* 《IQ 博士》. Although the song did not match perfectly with the mature style of the songstress, it won her immense popularity, and this influenced the decision by Capital Artists to direct resources to developing her career. Anita Mui did not need long to showcase the talents

10. Tony Rayns, "Anita Mui: Actress and Singer Dubbed Hong Kong's Madonna," *The Independent* (January 2, 2004).
11. Cited from "Anita Mui: Number One and Only," http://archives.muimusic.com/foreverno1.htm; retrieved on March 15, 2016.

of a gifted singer. Her first genuine solo album, *Crimson Anita Mui* 《赤色梅艷芳》 (1983), reached five times the sales volume of a platinum disc as per Hong Kong standards. Dubbed by the media "Little Paula Tsui" (because she won the New Talent Singing Contest with Paula Tsui's classic "The Season of Wind" 〈風的季節〉), Anita Mui started to show her potential of becoming a *sui generis* "ever-changing" queen before long. While the album featured a hit entitled "Dedicate My Heart" 〈交出我的心〉, the theme song of the TVB drama *Woman on the Beat* 《警花出更》, and the cover versions of the theme songs of Momoe Yamaguchi's *The Crimson Doubt* 《赤的疑惑》 and *The Crimson Shock* 《赤的衝擊》 (TVB-purchased Japanese television dramas), she also showed her flair in handling different styles in the theme songs of the TVB Japanese manga series *Queen Millenia* 《千年女王》.

In her next album, she showcased the talents of a stage performer as vividly illustrated by the album's title: *Leaping in a Spotlight* 《飛躍舞台》 (1984). The title hit was the theme song of a classic TVB drama *The Rise & Fall of a Stand-In* 《五虎將》, starring five TVB up-and-rising "tigers" (the Chinese title literally means "Five Tigers"): Michael Miu 苗僑偉, Kent Tong 湯鎮業, Felix Wong 黃日華, Andy Lau 劉德華, and Tony (Chiu-Wai) Leung 梁朝偉. The song might not have been as popular as the tigers, but it gave Anita Mui the chance to shine on stage. Her versatility was further proved in the subsequent album entitled *Anita Mui (Homecoming)* 《似水流年》 (1985). The album included six theme songs from the TVB drama *Summer Kisses Winter Tears* 《香江花月夜》, in which Anita Mui was the female lead. The major hit of the album, "Homecoming," the theme song of renowned New Wave director Yim Ho's movie of the same title, was a cover version of Japanese master Kitarō's "Delight." Anita Mui handled the tenderness of "Homecoming," almost the opposite of the strong dance beat of "Leaping in a Spotlight," extremely well, which spoke volumes about her versatility. Another big hit on this album was "Dream Embrace" 〈夢幻的擁抱〉, the cover version of George Michael's masterpiece "Careless Whisper." She wore a man's suit in the music video of "Dream Embrace," and the well-received image was also used for the album cover, which paved the way for her "ever-changing" images in subsequent albums. "Bad Girl" 〈壞女孩〉 (the album sold 8 times more than the average platinum disc) won her not only the title of "Madonna of the East" but also the Most Popular Female Singer at music award ceremonies, and she had a stranglehold on the title in the latter half of the 1980s. With the help of her friend and image desginer, Eddie Lau 劉培基, she turned into an ever-changing diva—from a monster girl to a lady ("Monster Girl" 〈妖女〉 and "Lady" 〈淑女〉) and from tango to samba ("Fiery Tango" and "Lost Carnival" 〈失落嘉年華〉), among others. Anita Mui succesfully created a revolutionary image for Cantopop songstresses, which appealed not only to teens but also to mature women. Her signature images could be seen as expressions of the female sen-siblities of different characters and ages. Following the retirement of her best partner, Leslie Cheung, Anita announced hers in 1991, signaling the end of the golden age of Cantopop.

Pop Stardom and the Concert Industry

One of the reasons behind the rise of Cantopop singers to stardom was cross-media synergy. In the 1970s, television was the main source of multimedia stardom: "The interlocking relationships between these media in the 1970s and 1980s capitalized on the mass audiences' familiarity with television as the main source of multi-media stardom and the means to build[ing] the stars' subsequent popularity in films and popular music."[12] But as discussed above, television stars like Adam Cheng and Liza Wang did not really fare well in the movie industry. The transformation of the movie industry in the early 1980s provided a good opportunity for young rising stars to move between the television, movie, and music industries. Leslie Cheung and Anita Mui were prime examples of cross-media success. Modeled on the Japanese idol industry, the Cantopop industry began to invest more on the images of idol singers through a series of packaging strategies. In 1982, Paula Tsui released the first "double-cover" Cantopop album, which turned a new page in the design of album covers.[13] Thereafter, the Cantopop industry focused more and more on the visual effects of the albums; for example, Leslie Cheung's *For Your Heart Only* had a special white vinyl disc edition. The emerging stardom successfully expanded the fan base of Cantopop, hence the income of record companies increased significantly. They in turn invested more on the images of the super-stars, and, at least up to that point, there were all-win situations thanks to the vigorous growth of the Cantopop market.

Meanwhile, the newly built Hong Kong Coliseum, albeit unexpected at the outset, helped develop a highly profitable concert industry in Hong Kong and it later became *the* pop venue for Hong Kong people. The inauguration on April 27, 1983 of the Hong Kong Coliseum, a multipurpose indoor arena originally designed for sports activities, provided an unforeseen opportunity for the entertainment business to further develop. Before the Hong Kong Coliseum was inaugurated, the largest venue for concerts in Hong Kong was the Queen Elizabeth Stadium, which opened in 1980 with a seating capacity of 3,500. With 12,500 seats, the Hong Kong Coliseum immediately attracted the

---

12. Wing-Fai Leung, "*Multi-Media Stardom, Performance and Theme Songs in Hong Kong Cinema*," *Canadian Journal of Film Studies* 20, no. 1 (Spring 2011): 41.
13. Chi-Wah Wong, *Forty Years of Cantopop* 《粵語流行曲四十年》 (in Chinese) (Hong Kong: Joint Publishing, 1990), 14.

attention of superstars. The first Cantopop solo concerts in the Coliseum were held by Sam Hui on May 5, 6, and 7, 1983, followed by George Lam's concerts in July and Danny Chan's in September. The legendary Teresa Teng was the first female star to hold solo concerts in the Coliseum. In December 1983, she held six concerts there to celebrate the fifteenth year of her singing career. After that, more and more Cantopop stars held their concerts there. In the mid- to the late 1980s, superstars like Alan Tam, Leslie Cheung, Anita Mui, and Paula Tsui held hundreds of concerts in the Coliseum, and the record for the number of consecutive concerts held there was broken almost every year. In August 1984, Alan Tam held six consecutive concerts, which was soon leapfrogged by Paula Tsui's eight in February and then George Lam's thirteen in April 1985. Alan Tam reclaimed the record by holding twenty concerts in July in the same year. From December 1987 to January 1988, Anita Mui held a then record-breaking twenty-eight consecutive concerts. 1989 was an important year, in which Leslie Cheung held thirty-three shows of his farewell concert, *Final Encounter Concert*, in December 1989, and Paula Tsui also set a record of thirty-three from 1989 to 1990. In the same year, the highest number of total performances at thirty-eight was set by Alan Tam. In the 1980s, Alan Tam held in total more than a hundred concerts in the Hong Kong Coliseum. "Assuming that each ticket [cost] HK$125 on average, the ticket sales for the aggregate attendance of 1,350,271 for the year 1989 amount[ed] to HK$168 million, about half of the total record sales for local songs" (not including the HK$2 million from the 3,600-seat Queen Elizabeth Stadium).[14]

The concert business had a creative synergy with the music industry indeed. The record companies leveraged on the concerts of idol singers by linking them to their albums. For example, Leslie Cheung's *For Your Heart Only* album was released in lieu with his concerts bearing the same title. Songs like "I Do," "For Your Heart Only," and "Wild Wind" helped build his romantic lover image that proved to captivate fans across Chinese communities, which in the end contributed much to the sales of the album. When Hong Kong's "Father of Concerts," Yiu-Wing Cheung 張耀榮, passed away in March 2014, many Hong Kong singers expressed their condolences for him. He was remembered as a pioneer in turning Cantopop singers into legends through their Hong Kong Coliseum concerts. Back in the early 1980s, as Katie Chan 陳嘉瑛, the manager of Faye Wong 王菲 and Eason Chan 陳奕迅, recalled, "[T]he business wasn't too prosperous. There were few production firms for concerts . . . After Uncle Yiu-Wing got into the field, he brought a new level of vigor to the industry."[15] Yiu-Wing Cheung was willing to take a risk and invest

---

14. Choi, "Popular Culture," 543.
15. Cited from Stuart Lau and Vivienne Chow, "Hong Kong's 'Father of Concerts' Cheung Yiu-wing Dies," *South China Morning Post* (March 25, 2014).

big money in these concerts, bringing a new operational mode modeled after the Japanese pop concerts to the entertainment business in Hong Kong. His Yiu Wing Entertainment organized concerts for all the big names in Cantopop, including the Four Heavenly Kings 四大天王 in the 1990s—Andy Lau 劉德華, Jacky Cheung 張學友, Leon Lai 黎明, and Aaron Kwok 郭富城. The new styles introduced in these concerts (including, among others, image, fashion, and stage design) exerted a very profound impact—besides great profits—on the music industry, which was a further extension of Cantopop from the audio to the visual.

As noted by Wai-Chung Ho, "The emphasis of this type of 'show business' is on 'buying' the visual enjoyment of the entertainers' stage performance. This, and the way that fans uphold the notion of local sounds and scenes, indicates the growth of popular music as a presentation of image."[16] Not only did the concerts enhance stardom by enthralling the fans with sounds and images, they also became a venue for building a collective memory for Hong Kong people. Hong Kong had long been (in)famous for its disappearing culture. "In a city where everything is disappearing," as argued by Yiu-Fai Chow and Jeroen de Kloet, "[t]he permanence of certain public spaces, like the Hong Kong Coliseum, serves to comfort city dwellers with the feeling that something is staying, will stay essentially the same. . . . Pop venues are not only the embodiment of culture; they also help to construct and sustain a city and its culture."[17] Before the definitive Hong Kong Coliseum was built, Cantopop concerts were held in small venues like the Academic Community Hall (built in 1978) and the Queen Elizabeth Stadium (built in 1980) with a seating capacity of only 1,300 and 3,500, respectively. While the Coliseum became the venue for Cantopop stars to prove their popularity, it was also "a factory, literally, a production site, of collective memory, and a temple of experience and identity."[18]

That many Taiwanese singers continued to cross the Strait for greener pastures was a good example of Cantopop's being the center of Chinese popular music. Jenny Tseng and the legendary Teresa Teng, who had a brief spell with Cantopop in the early 1980s, were successful examples in the 1980s, as were Sally Yeh 葉蒨文 and Dave Wong 王傑. Born in Taiwan and educated in Canada, Sally Yeh entered the entertainment business in Taiwan with her debut movie *A Match* 《一根火柴》 and Mandapop album *Embossing Spring* 《春天的浮雕》 in 1980. She first came to Hong Kong for the swiftly growing film market in 1982, starring in *Crimson Street* 《殺人愛情街》 and *Marianna* 《賓妹》. Having increased her popularity in Hong Kong, she released her

---

16. Wai-Chung Ho, "Between Globalisation and Localisation: A Study of Hong Kong Popular Music," *Popular Music* 22, no. 2 (May 2003): 148.
17. Yiu-Fai Chow and Jeroen de Kloet, *Sonic Multiplicities* (Bristol and Chicago: Intellect, 2013), 108.
18. Ibid., 114.

debut Cantopop album *Sally Yeh* 《葉蒨文》 in 1984. The main plug in that album, "00:10" 〈零時十分〉, was a chart-topping hit, and thereafter Sally Yeh became one of the leading songstresses in the Cantopop industry. Her song "Blessing" 〈祝福〉, a cover version of a Taiwanese song, became the most popular song of the year in 1988, which was an extraordinary achievement as the industry was dominated by Alan Tam, Leslie Cheung, and Anita Mui. Her singing career reached summit after the retirement of Anita Mui, and she was awarded the Most Popular Female Singer by TVB's Jade Solid Gold for four consecutive years, from 1990 to 1993. Dave Wong was also an interesting case. Son of a Shaw Brothers' martial arts movie actor, he grew up in Hong Kong but started his singing career as a Mandapop singer in Taiwan. At the age of 17, he went to Taiwan and later became a stunt actor. He released his debut Mandapop album *A Game A Dream* 《一場遊戲一場夢》 with UFO Limited by Share Ltd. (Taiwan) in 1987, which won him instant fame. Back in his hometown as an up-and-coming superstar, he enthralled Hong Kong audiences with his debut Cantopop album *The Role of the Story* 《故事的角色》 in 1989, becoming arguably the last Cantopop superstar of the 1980s.

Diversification of Cantopop

In spite of the growing popularity of Cantopop, not all singers could hold a series of concerts in the Hong Kong Coliseum. Diversity was a key element in the vigorous development of the Cantopop industry in the 1980s. Thanks to the expanding market, there were also singers with target audiences different from those of megastars like Alan Tam, Leslie Cheung, and Anita Mui. Veteran singers from the 1970s, like Roman Tam, Jenny Tseng, George Lam, and Michael Kwan, continued to attract a large audience in the 1980s. With an eye toward the big potential of the developing market, record companies were willing to experiment with singers of different styles. As mentioned above, there were young rising stars like Danny Chan who fascinated teen fans, and there were also performers such as Johnny Yip who attracted mature audiences. There were dance kings/queens, such as Leslie Cheung and Anita Mui, and there were also performers who focused solely on singing, such as Michael Kwan and Paula Tsui. While songstresses like Elisa Chan, Teresa Carpio 杜麗莎, and Deanie Ip 葉德嫻 graced Cantopop with the sensibilities of mature women, teens like Priscilla Chan 陳慧嫻 and Sandy Lam also had the opportunity to realize their potential. Priscilla Chan stood out with her first major hit "Forgotten Promise" 〈逝去的諾言〉 among three teenage girls in an album packaged as *Girl Magazine* 《少女雜誌》 (1984). She went solo in her next album (except for one song coperformed with her two teammates), *Feelings of a Story* 《故事的感覺》 (1984). After the success of "Flower Shop"

〈花店〉 (1985), she signed with PolyGram in 1986, which helped her reach new heights in her singing career, with chart-topping hits such as "Dancing Street" 〈跳舞街〉, "Love and/as Accident" 〈痴情意外〉, and, above all, "Silly Girl" 〈傻女〉 (1998). Surprisingly, she chose to further her studies in the United States in 1989, which was reportedly a promise she had made to her family. Her popularity could be proved by the theme song of her farewell concert "Thousands of Songs" 〈千千闕歌〉, which was at least equally popular as Anita Mui's "Song of the Sunset" 〈夕陽之歌〉, both cover versions of Masahiko Kondō's 近藤真彦 "Song of the Sunset" 〈夕焼けの歌〉. Priscilla Chan did continue to release albums and resume her full-time singing career after she graduated in the 1990s, remaining as one of the mainstays in the golden age of Cantopop. (Priscilla Chan's career will be further discussed in the next chapter.)

In 1982, when she was still a secondary student, Sandy Lam started her career as a part-time disc jockey at CR2 with the name "611." She was later spotted by CBS Sony and released her debut Cantopop album *Lam Yik Lin* (her Chinese name) 《林憶蓮》 in 1985. The main plug was "Love, I Don't Know" 〈愛情 I Don't Know〉, a cover version of a Japanese popular song, and it marked her as a Japanese-styled teen idol. It was not a big success, but she managed to propel her career forward with *Self-Indulgence* 《放縱》 (1986), and with her next album, *Yik Lin* 《憶蓮》 (1987), her image became more mature, paving the way for a transformation to a dancing queen in *Grey* 《灰色》 (1987) and *City Rhythm* (1988). Sandy Lam was among the few Cantopop singers who were able to transform with different styles at different stages of their career. (Sandy Lam's career will be further discussed in the next chapter.) Meanwhile, Prudence Liew 劉美君 is a good example to show that the mainstream Cantopop industry, at least during the 1980s, was not as conservative and standardized as it was often criticized to be. Known for touching on sexual topics in her songs, she was one of the rare artists who tested the bottom line of the mainstream, as "occasional references to wild female sexuality . . . were frequently subjected to trivialization by the industry and censorship by the radio."[19] Her first major hit, "Midnight Love" 〈午夜情〉 (a cover version of a Korean pop song, lyrics self-written; 1986), the theme song of the movie *Midnight Beauties* 《午夜麗人》, touched on the topic of prostitutes. Despite the controversial topic, Prudence Liew managed to win the Most Promising Newcomer Award at the RTHK Top 10 Gold Songs Awards in 1987. Later, she became even more provocative in songs such as "Afterwards" 〈事後〉, which spoke frankly about sexual pleasure.

---

19. John Erni, "Moving with It, Moved by It," *Perspectives: Working Papers in English & Communication* 16, no. 2 (2004): 9.

Numerous singing contests were held to spot rising stars. The New Talent Singing Awards held by TVB, among others, was once the cradle of Cantopop stars in addition to Anita Mui, such as David Lui 呂方, Alex To 杜德偉 (a.k.a. Alejandro Delfino), Andy Hui 許志安, and, most notably, Leon Lai and Sammi Cheng 鄭秀文, who later became one of the heavenly kings/queens of Cantopop in the 1990s. These singers contributed different styles to the Cantopop industry, and hence further expanded its fan base. The trend of singer-songwriters in the late 1980s further diversified the styles of mainstream Cantopop. Sam Hui was indeed the first successful Cantopop singer-songwriter, but he represented more of an exceptional case than a trend. In the 1980s, in order to present a versatile image for singers, record companies put more emphasis on their creative talents. Alan Tam and Leslie Cheung, albeit occasionally, wrote their own melodies and lyrics. In addition to these sporadic attempts, some singer-songwriters did emerge and exerted a deep impact on the Cantopop scene. Anthony Lun 倫永亮 and Lowell Lo 盧冠廷, among others, were two remarkable examples of singer-songwriters who not only became Cantopop singers but also composers and producers who were mainstays in the industry. Regarding lyrics, Andy Lau and Hacken Lee 李克勤 were two notable examples of having consistently produced lyrics from the late 1980s to the present.

These singer-songwriters had their own styles and sensibilities, which were significantly different from mainstream composers and lyricists. For instance, Anthony Lun and Lowell Lo were famous for their unique styles. In his debut album *Bird in the Sky* 《天鳥》 (1983), Lowell Lo stunned the Cantopop scene with his musical talents and unique singing style. Anthony Lun also brought a brand new concept of music to Cantopop audiences with his debut *Anthony Lun's Collections* 《倫永亮創作歌集》 (1986), in which he was the singer, composer, lyricist, arranger, producer, and recording engineer. When he later won the Asia Popular Song Contest with the song "Lyrics" 〈歌詞〉 in 1986, his unique singing style drew a wider audience. Not only was he a successful singer-songwriter, he later became an influential producer who provided excellent collaborations with Cantopop singers like Anita Mui and Sandy Lam. In terms of the diversification of styles, these singer-songwriters exerted a positive impact on the Cantopop industry in the 1980s.

Violet Lam 林敏怡 is another composer worth noting here. The sister of the famous lyricist Andrew Lam, she was trained as a pianist and composer. Having given many piano recitals of contemporary works, she was also well-known for her popular songs, especially the theme songs and musical scores of Hong Kong movies. Some of the her best-known songs included "This Is Love" 〈這是愛〉 (sung by Teddy Robin, lyrics by Andrew Lam; 1981), "Illusion" (sung by Alan Tam, lyrics by Andrew Lam; 1983), "Love in a Fallen

City" 〈傾城之戀〉 (sung by Liza Wang, lyrics by Andrew Lam; 1985), "Heart of the Dragon" 〈誰可相依〉 (sung by Julie Sue 蘇芮, lyrics by Calvin Poon; 1986), and "Story of Oshin" 〈阿信的故事〉 (sung by Judy Ong 翁倩玉, lyrics by Kwok-Kong Cheng; 1986). Her "Empty Chair" 〈空〉 (sung by Danny Summer, lyrics by Richard Lam; 1985) won the Asia-Pacific Broadcasting Union Songwriting Contest in 1985. The rise of Violet Lam was just one of the examples that proved that the expanding music industry in the 1980s had a great demand for new talents, who helped diversify the styles of Cantopop. Such a diversification in turn expanded the fan base, giving the record companies more initiative to experiment with new types of songs, singers, composers, and lyricists. Meanwhile, Jimmy Lo's "non-love songs" movement is also worth noting as an activity that enhanced the diversification of the subject matter of Cantopop. In the midst of sentimental love ballads that had dominated the mainstream for years, he initiated a "non-love songs campaign" in 1983 to promote topics other than romantic love. Although he was the only one to openly advance the idea, he made a significant impact as he forced producers to take one "non-love song" for every four songs they asked him to write. Jimmy Lo successfully made use of his status in the music industry to write a series of "non-love" topics, including anti-war themes ("The Mantis and I" 〈螳螂與我〉) and idealism ("Don Quixote" 〈唐吉訶德〉). The irony was that despite the popularity of some of these songs, fewer and fewer producers invited Jimmy Lo to write lyrics for their songs. As one of the most prolific lyricists in the late 1970s and early 1980s, Jimmy Lo produced much fewer lyrics in 1985. Notwithstanding the fact that this one-man movement was doomed at the outset, it did inspire many lyricists to pay more attention to "non-love" topics. Calvin Poon was one of the influential lyricists who echoed Jimmy Lo's idea. His "Numbers and Life" 〈數字人生〉, for example, underscored the over-importance of numbers in real life by using lots of numbers in the lyrics to convey the theme, which was a ground-breaking attempt in the history of Cantopop. According to Calvin Poon, lyricists had the freedom to explore different topics in the mid-1980s, and so he could experiment with themes like his own worldview (e.g., Sally Yeh's "My Opinion" 〈一點意見〉) and national allegory (e.g., George Lam's "National Flag" 〈國旗〉).[20] The increased diversification of Cantopop genres could also be seen from, among other things, the wave of city folk songs in the early 1980s and band songs in the late 1980s.

Back in the late 1970s, when the Cantopop industry was developing rapidly in Hong Kong, there was a folk song movement across the Strait in Taiwan. Yang Hsien 楊弦, the "father" of the movement, released his *Collection of Modern Chinese Folk Songs* 《中國現代民歌集》 in 1975 (the lyrics in

---

20. Chu, *Songs of Your Life*, 110.

this album were adapted from the poems of internationally renowned poet Kwang-Chung Yu 余光中). In its aftermath, a number of concerts featuring folk songs were held on college campuses, triggering a new wave of folk songs in Taiwan. After the swift growth of the Cantopop industry in the late 1970s, some fans were already fed up with its commercialization. They were thus attracted to the sweet innocence of these campus folk songs from Taiwan, and subsequently a campus folk song movement in Hong Kong was mobilized, mainly by college students, in the early 1980s. There were many folk song concerts and contests held (e.g., the City Folk Songs Writing Contest organized by RTHK in 1981), and the Academic Community Hall was a famous venue for Hong Kong folk songs, which later became the collective memory of fans of folk songs in Hong Kong.[21] These folk song contests placed heavy emphasis on creativity, and thus there were many young talents participating with their own works—both melodies and lyrics. This in turn created an aura of original songs in the midst of cover versions. Outstanding works from these contests were sometimes collected in folk albums, such as *Collection of Hong Kong Campus Folk Songs* 《香港校園民歌創作專輯》 and *Hong Kong City Folk Songs* 《香港城市民歌》.

As the city and homeland were common topics of campus folk songs, a new genre of Cantopop appeared under their influence. The songs "Footprint" 〈足印〉 and "A Morning at Repulse Bay" 〈淺水灣的早晨〉 in *Collection of Hong Kong Campus Folk Songs* entered the pop chart of RTHK, one of the enthusiastic promoters of folk songs in Hong Kong. "On the Ferry Last Evening" 〈昨夜的渡輪上〉 was another signature example that had become a classic almost always heard at folk song concerts in Hong Kong, and it was so popular that Andy Lau performed a rearranged version in the 1990s. A notable example of folk albums was *Hong Kong City Suite* 《香港城市組曲》, in which Armando Lai 韋然 used different districts of Hong Kong as the subject matter, contributing unprecedented imaginaries of the city from different perspectives (e.g., "A Morning at Repulse Bay," "The Story of Lamma Island" 〈南丫島的故事〉, and "The Dust on Nathan Road" 〈彌敦道的塵埃〉). The folk song wave also brought new talents into the mainstream music industry. Among those who actively participated in these contests were singers like Samantha Lam and lyricist Lin Xi. Lin Xi's award-winning work, "A Lane in the Rain" 〈雨巷〉, inspired by modern Chinese poet Dai Wangshu's poem, was a good example in showing that it was possible to cross literary works with popular lyrics. According to Armando Lai, *Hong Kong City Suite* was unexpectedly profitable, proving to the music industry that folk content could also have great potential in this money-making business.[22] Not unlike other trends in

---

21. Chow and de Kloet, *Sonic Multiplicities*, 109–11.
22. Chu, *Songs of Your Life*, 122–24.

Hong Kong, the folk song wave came and went very quickly. The impact of folk songs on the music industry, however, had been rather positive in the sense of injecting new elements—subject matter and styles—into mainstream Cantopop (this will be further discussed in the next section).

If the short-lived folk songs movement changed the music scene in Hong Kong in the early 1980s, the band songs movement made an even deeper impact on the music industry in the latter half of the decade. The early 1980s witnessed different forms of Hong Kong consciousness, from the construction of a Hong Kong cultural identity and an emphasis on Hong Kong locality to a cross-cultural imaginary incorporating both China and Hong Kong. Different voices coexisted, but they were still very much in their initial stages, and more comprehensive developments did not appear until the mid-1980s. Hong Kong consciousness, after all the years of self-conscious construction, was able to withstand the test of time but not that of political changes. After the Sino-British Joint Declaration on the future of Hong Kong, the die was cast. Hong Kong people had to face the music, no matter how they saw their reunion with China. A considerable amount of cross-cultural imagination linking China and Hong Kong thus came to the fore in the mid- to the late 1980s. Popular bands were arguably the most outstanding spokespersons on this subject. The bands that came onto the scene in the mid-1980s in the Hong Kong popular music industry undeniably represented one of the most significant waves in the history of Hong Kong popular music.

As mentioned in the first chapter, there was a band wave in Hong Kong in the 1960s. Local popular bands such as Lotus, Teddy Robin and the Playboys, Joe Junior and the Side Effects, and Anders Nelsson and the Inspiration focused on English songs. Band sound remained all the rage until the late 1960s, but there was a brief revival of band music in the 1970s, such as The Wynners and the New Topnotes. Many former band members turned to Cantopop in the late 1970s (such as Alan Tam of The Wynners, George Lam of Jade, and Elisa Chan of the New Topnotes). The second band wave did not gather momentum until the 1980s. Different from their counterparts in the 1960s, the bands of the 1980s focused on Cantonese instead of English popular songs. One of the main characteristics was their strong emphasis on original compositions (at the time most Cantopop songs were cover versions of Western songs). These bands also experimented with different themes from mainstream love songs, and thus songwriters who previously had little in the way of free choice in subject matter experienced the luxury of being able to write about a range of different topics. The period between 1982 and 1985 was the creation stage of the second band wave. There were more than 40 local bands, but most of them were short-term, exerting no genuine influence on the music industry. Among the more influential bands at that time, the now legendary protest band Blackbird

黑鳥 was a notable example. All of their songs were in one way or another related to Hong Kong society and politics. There was populist resistance similar to Sam Hui's works in the 1970s (such as "Furious" 〈發火〉), attempts at reconstructing Hong Kong history (such as "Talking about the History of Hong Kong" 〈香港史話〉), and reflection on the relationship between China and Hong Kong (such as "Why Don't You Come Back?" 〈胡不歸〉). As Blackbird insisted on staying underground, their impact on Hong Kong popular music was intense but restricted. Fortunately, there were other bands that successfully caught the attention of the music industry, if not the public.

In 1985, Tom Lee Music, a local musical instrument company, collaborated with Carlsberg to launch the Carlsberg Pop Music Festival, which created "an overwhelming response from local musicians and widespread support from the music industry."[23] Besides market considerations, one of the reasons the music industry showed determined support was that members of some 1960s bands had already become part of the senior management of music companies (such as Ricky Fung of the Mystics and William Kwan 關維麟 of Teddy Robin and the Playboys). They believed that it was time for another wave of band music in Hong Kong. Moreover, after its rapid expansion in the early 1980s, the Cantopop industry had lost much of its youthful vigor, and the new wave of band music focusing on Cantonese songs brought an entirely new impetus to the music industry: "rising bands were like a shot in the arm, using their unique music packaged in local style to rock the music industry."[24] The champion of the first Carlsberg Pop Music Festival was Taichi 太極, a seven-man rock band that later became one of the mainstays in the second wave of band music in the mid- to the late 1980s. In the same year a three-man folk rock band, Small Island 小島, released their debut album *Legend of a Small Island*, lifting the curtain on a new era of band music in Hong Kong. Although Small Island, whose album was not particularly popular, disbanded soon after and reorganized later, other bands subsequently came onto the scene and successfully generated the second wave of band music in Hong Kong. Unlike the first one, the second band wave focused mainly on Cantopop. Among these were Beyond and Tat Ming Pair, the legendary bands with an uncompromising sense of social intervention that later influenced the development of popular music in Hong Kong for many years. The legendary rock band Beyond rocked the establishment by their call to arms in songs like "Goodbye My Dream" 〈再見理想〉, "Forever Waiting" 〈永遠等待〉, and "Metal Maniacs" 〈金屬狂人〉. In the meantime, the earlier works of Tat Ming Pair, such as "Roller

23. Cited from "Carlsberg Pop Music Festival & Carlsberg Music Expression (1985–1998)," http://www.tomleemusic.com.hk/events_1_1.php?id=200; retrieved on March 15, 2016.
24. Ping-Long Ngai, "It's All Because of College Students" 〈都是大專生做的好事〉 (in Chinese), *Hong Kong New Generation Biweekly* (November 7, 1986): 2.

Skating Gang" 〈溜冰滾族〉, "Angels on the Road" 〈馬路天使〉, and "Car Lost in the Night" 〈今夜星光燦爛〉, voiced the feelings of the lost generation in the face of a future marred by 1997, using the cityscape of Hong Kong as the backdrop for their chorus of bewilderment.

The second wave, similar to the first one, did not last long. With an eye only on profitability, music companies pushed numerous bands into the market in the late 1980s. Given the poor quality of some of these products packaged as "bands," fans were chased away and the market started to shrink before long. A burgeoning musical revolution would turn commercial, and in the end the music industry killed the goose that laid the golden eggs, leading to the premature decline of the second band wave. The disbanding of Tat Ming Pair in 1990 was generally considered the end of the second band wave in Hong Kong. This may be controversial as some bands such as Beyond continued to be productive, but there must be no denying that the accidental death of Ka-Kui Wong 黃家駒, the soul of Beyond, in Japan in 1993 was seen as the finale of the band era.

Hybridized in Hong Kong[25]

That Cantopop reached its apex in the 1980s could be accounted for by its increased diversity. While it was unabashedly commercial, the coexistence of mainstream and nonmainstream popular songs and their vibrant creative interaction effectively inspired the hybridity as well as the creativity of Cantopop. City folk songs and band songs in the 1980s, for example, proved that discursive space was available for nonmainstream attempts. Up to that point, Cantopop had to differentiate itself from the marketing economy that sold it, showing that the music industry and its commercialization cannot be seen as the main factor behind its later decline. As convincingly noted by Arjun Appadurai, when music, television, and other media make an impact on traditional forms, such as epic and folklore, new hybridized styles will come to the fore.[26] In this sense, popular media means much more than commercialization, and the hybridized products had the potential to inspire an emergent culture. Actually, Hong Kong culture had long been famous for its hybridity. Cantopop had been one of the biggest representatives of Hong Kong's hybrid media forms. The rise of Cantopop in the 1970s could be attributed to musical genres and cross-media hybridizations (e.g., Sam Hui and TVB theme songs, respectively).

25. Parts of this section are drawn from Yiu-Wai Chu and Eve Leung, "Remapping Hong Kong Popular Music: Covers, Localisation and the Waning Hybridity of Cantopop," *Popular Music* 32, no. 1 (January 2013): 65–78.
26. Arjun Appadurai, "Afterword," in *Gender, Genre, and Power in South Asian Expressive Traditions*, ed. Arjun Appadurai et al. (Philadelphia: University of Pennsylvania Press), 474.

In the 1980s, the rapidly growing Cantopop market (the CD format became popular in Hong Kong in 1985, which helped boost the sales of Cantopop albums) provided more discursive space for more hybridizations. As Lawrence Witzleben rightly claimed, Cantopop is "a unique and often bewildering mixture of Chinese, other Asian and Western elements."[27] If one were to change "mixture" to "hybridization," it would be even more accurate in describing the characteristics of Cantopop in its heyday. In the 1980s, Cantopop was able to promote linguistic/cultural hybridity on the one hand, and foster connections between various kinds of music (such as the mainstream and the underground/indie scene) on the other. A vigorous pop scene needs both types of cross-fertilization. As noted above, city folk songs and band songs had proved that discursive space was available for nonmainstream attempts, and the vibrant creative interaction between mainstream and nonmainstream popular songs effectively inspired the hybridity as well as the creativity of Cantopop.

In regard to language, Cantonese served as an everyday "low" language when compared to English as the auxiliary "high" language.[28] The "lowness" of the language constitutes an important marker of difference. Cantopop lyricists had been successful in introducing a restricted use of Cantonese in their lyrics, generating a unique hybridized style mixing Cantonese and standard Chinese.[29] This typical hybridized language style not only made Cantopop hybridized in its distinctive way, but it also provided the people of Hong Kong with an interesting sense of belonging over the past thirty years or so, articulating, together with other media such as film and television, a typical kind of Hong Kong cultural identity.[30] "Cover music" also played an important role in the hybridity of Hong Kong popular music. As noted in the previous chapter, the use of cover music had long been a common practice in Hong Kong since the 1970s. Owing to the growth of the market, the industry needed much more musical materials than before, and "[a]lthough technological innovations and consumer demand allowed the industry to produce and sell many more records and CDs than in previous periods, the creative capability within the industry

---

27. Lawrence Witzleben, "Cantopop and Mandapop in Pre-postcolonial Hong Kong: Identity Negotiation in the Performances of Anita Mui Yim-Fong," *Popular Music* 18, no. 2 (May 1999): 241. It has to be stressed that while Cantopop was diverse and hybridized, it was not necessarily more hybrid than Mandapop. As convincingly noted by an anonymous reviewer, Witzleben's claim can also be used for Mandapop and Chinese rock.

28. Martha Pennington, *Forces Shaping a Dual Code Society: An Interpretive Review of the Literature on Language Use and Language Attitudes in Hong Kong* (Hong Kong: City Polytechnic of Hong Kong, 1994).

29. James Wong, "The Rise and Decline of Cantopop: A Study of Hong Kong Popular Music (1949–1997)" 《粵語流行曲的發展與興衰：香港流行音樂研究 1949–1997》 (in Chinese) (Hong Kong: PhD thesis, the University of Hong Kong, 2003), 132–34.

30. David Parker, *Through Different Eyes: The Cultural Identity of Young Chinese People in Britain* (Aldershot: Avebury, 1995), 152.

was out of step with the trend."[31] Record companies used cover music as a quick and easy way to produce profit-making popular music. Cover music was chosen according to its popularity in its local market. If a record company chose a song that topped the music chart in its own market, it would be very likely that the song would enjoy similar success in Hong Kong when it was covered locally. There were thus many one-tune-two-version examples (such as "Careless Whisper"). Another important factor was that production costs could be kept to a minimum; Hong Kong music companies only had to pay the copyright fee to the original composer/music company and the costs of rewriting the lyrics. The Hong Kong lyricists received only a fixed amount but not the future royalties generated by the song for cover versions. When compared to the music production fees of a song locally composed, using cover music was cheaper, and it was also quicker to produce and publicize the song. Therefore, cover music slowly overtook local productions in Hong Kong. Later in the 1980s, the success of superstars such as Leslie Cheung, Alan Tam, and Anita Mui was a result, at least in part, of Japanese cover music. Cover versions of Japanese pop songs were very popular in the 1980s, as "the typical Japanese pop song melody line is well suited to Asian listeners, in particular Chinese audiences, in that it is different but not too strange."[32] One of the most remarkable examples was Masahiko Kondō's "Song of the Sunset", which had three Cantonese cover versions: Anita Mui's "Song of the Sunset", Priscilla Chan's "Thousands of Songs", and Blue Jeans's "Time Hangs Heavy on Our Hands" 〈無聊時候〉. At that time the popular music market in Taiwan, let alone the Mainland, was rather closed, and thus Cantopop had plenty of space to develop.

In Hong Kong, mainstream audiences' major concern was whether the songs were easy to listen to; they did not pay much attention to who the composers or the arrangers were or whether they were foreign or local. Moreover, lyricists played an important role in Chinese popular songs, as audiences appreciated the lyrics to a greater extent in the Chinese context, thanks to the close relationship between the lyrics and the literary tradition. This kind of listening habit changed the priorities of the Hong Kong audience. They considered Japanese cover music to be their local "Hong Kong" music as long as it was being sung in Cantonese.[33] In short, the music industry used cover versions

---

31. Masashi Ogawa, "Japanese Popular Music in Hong Kong: Analysis of Global/Local Cultural Relations," in *Globalizing Japan: Ethnography of the Japanese Presence in Asia, Europe, and America*, ed. Harumi Befu and Sylvie Guichard-Anguis (London and New York: Routledge, 2001), 24.

32. Ogawa, "Japanese Popular Music in Hong Kong," 124.

33. James Wong argued that the localization of foreign popular songs was one of the distinctive characteristics of Cantopop, and the waning of this was one of the reasons behind its decline. Wong, "The Rise and Decline of Cantopop," 175–76.

primarily for effective productions and bigger profits in the expanding market in the 1970s and the early 1980s. Hybridity might only be an unexpected side product of the operation of the music industry, but in the end it was the key element of Cantopop's success in its heyday.

J-Pop (Japanese pop) was just one of the examples of different music styles adopted by Cantopop. It also assimilated different music styles in the 1980s, and the two genres, city folk songs and band songs, discussed in the previous section, were noteworthy examples. When Taiwanese city folk songs generated a wave of popularity in Hong Kong, music companies expended a great deal of effort on city folk songs in order to ride the crest of the latest wave of popularity. This new genre also happened to arouse considerable local interest in the development of Cantopop, which could be traced back to Sam Hui's "Eiffel Tower above the Clouds." Unlike mainstream popular songs, the city folk songs introduced a fresh sensibility with simple melodies, graceful lyrics, and simple instruments such as guitar and piano. The folk song movement introduced an important theme to Cantopop: local consciousness. Social parodies also had to transform themselves in order to deal with the rapid social changes of the 1980s, as they no longer focused solely on the hardships of life. Consumerism, among other factors, became one of the most important topics.[34] Cantopop of the 1980s concerned itself less with populist resistance and more with consumer sensitivity in a late-capitalist society. However, songs about consumerism in a general sense appeared to lose the sense of Hong Kong locality inherent in the parodies of the 1970s. The empty space was filled by a series of songs about the future of Hong Kong and its reunion with China in 1997. A number of Hong Kong–oriented concept albums appeared between 1980 and 1982, including *Hong Kong City Folk Songs* and *Hong Kong City Suite*, which were typical examples that foregrounded the locality of Hong Kong. In the songs on these concept albums, Hong Kong was neither a skin-deep signifier nor a brief stop on the diasporic journey of Chinese people. Although songs like "Morning at Repulse Bay," "The Story of Lamma Island," "Dreaming of Shatin," and "The Dust on Nathan Road" did not exhibit much in the way of an extensively in-depth cultural imaginary of Hong Kong, there was nonetheless a comprehensive representation of Hong Kong locality, as apparent in the title of the albums, for the first time in the Hong Kong music industry. The albums marked a point from which singers and songwriters began to use Hong Kong as a means of presenting local sensibilities.

Meanwhile, the Hang Seng Index suffered far more than Margaret Thatcher did when she slipped on the stairs of the Great Hall of the People in Beijing

---

34. Chi-Wah Wong, "A Cultural Prejudice" 〈一種文化偏好〉 (in Chinese), in Elizabeth Sinn ed., *Hong Kong Culture and Society* (Hong Kong: Centre of Asian Studies, the University of Hong Kong, 1995), 184.

after her meeting with Deng Xiaoping about the 1997 issue. There was a wave of emigration and a general loss of confidence—the early 1980s were a repetition of 1967 in this sense. In this particular context, the local awareness instilled by city folk songs into mainstream Cantopop offered different contributions to the issue of the future of Hong Kong, from a positive advocacy of a spirit of unity (such as Jenny Tseng's 1982 "The Pearl of the Orient") to a more negative escape from reality (such as Danny Summer's 夏韶聲 1983 "Drunk" 〈醉〉). Later, Hong Kong people began to regain confidence, and those who chose to stay or leave the country had already made their decisions. Popular songs were then able to embark on a program of remapping Hong Kong from different perspectives. Among such attempts, the "homeland" series, which in part evolved from earlier city folk songs, represented a rather typical imaginary which incorporated both China and Hong Kong. Songs like Teddy Robin's 泰迪羅賓 "Homesick" 〈鄉愁〉(1984) and Lowell Lo's 1985 "Root" 〈根〉 (1985) were attempts at searching for the cultural roots of Hong Kong. The political changes of the early 1980s had forced the people of Hong Kong to mature. Identity had become the major concern, and "Hong Kong" was being fashioned in different ways from different positions. The Hong Kong imaginary had been transformed from the representation of lifestyles to the articulation of ideologies.

The early 1980s witnessed different forms of Hong Kong consciousness, from the construction of a Hong Kong cultural identity to an emphasis on Hong Kong locality and a cross-cultural imaginary incorporating both China and Hong Kong. Different voices coexisted, but they were still very much in their initial stages, and more comprehensive developments did not appear until the mid-1980s. The articulation of ideologies witnessed further developments in band songs popular in the late 1980s. Ping-Long Ngai, a local disc jockey, offered a convincing account of the rise of band music in the mid-1980s: "College students and intellectuals were lost in a highly materialized, soulless society. They felt being lost and dejected, and band music was an effective means to express their anti-establishment sentiments."[35] On the one hand, band songs introduced different music styles into Cantopop, such as Beyond's hard rock and Tat Ming Pair's cutting-edge electronic music. On the other hand, their music hybridized effectively with the sensibilities of their lyricists. The subject matter of band songs was significantly different from the romantic stories of mainstream Cantopop ballads. These bands touched on different cultural, social, and political issues of the local society.

As noted by Tat Ming's lyricist, Keith Chan 陳少琪, at a time of rapid economic development and looming anxiety over the 1997 handover, he had

---

35. Ngai, "It's All Because of College Students," 2.

the freedom to choose his own style to present the social reality of Hong Kong, and he decided to use many urban settings, such as roller-skate malls, highways, and the Queen's Statue Park, to draw a picture of the city with his lyrics in "Roller Skating Gang," "Angels on the Road," and "Car Lost in the Night."[36] Yiu-Fai Chow 周耀輝, another lyricist working closely with Tat Ming Pair, highlighted the importance of freedom provided by the duo, offering him the chance to explore nonmainstream topics such as queer politics in "Forgot He or She"〈忘記他是她〉. In his debut "Love in the Time of Cholera"〈愛在瘟疫蔓延時〉, he was able to bring in Gabriel García Márquez's literary classic, contributing a dimension rarely touched by mainstream Cantopop. In addition, legendary rock band Beyond brought not only social critiques but also national allegories to the mainstream in "Vast Land"〈大地〉 and "Great Wall"〈長城〉. Gene Lau 劉卓輝, the lyricist of many Beyond classics, noted in an interview that he enjoyed the discursive space provided to him, without which he was not able to delve into politically sensitive topics.[37]

The cross-cultural Mainland Chinese and Hong Kong imaginary at this stage exhibited mixed feelings of worry, puzzlement, and paradox. While Beyond voiced the feeling of many Hong Kong people—"On the roads opening out to the world, how many ideals have been disillusioned?" ("Vast Land")— Tat Ming Pair also raised a question buried in the hearts of Hong Kong people by asking "Do You Still Love Me?"〈你還愛我嗎？〉. Apparently, Hong Kong people were feeling very insecure about their reunion with China at that time. The locality in city folk songs had also evolved into another stage in band songs. Those who could not or would not emigrate had to reconsider their relationship with China on the one hand, and try to develop a kind of local sense of identity on the other. "Angels on the Road" and "The Lovely New World"〈美好新世界〉 are typical examples which used the city to foreground a sense of Hong Kong local imaginary. ("New World" was the shopping center where teenagers liked to hang out in the 1980s.)

The June Fourth Incident in Tiananmen Square brought about a radical change in the music industry in Hong Kong, but one that proved to be temporary. In the year following the Incident, mainstream singers, one after another, began to sing about the future of China in their songs. Given the music industry's continuing focus on profit and commercial priorities, this overwhelming emphasis on political issues had certainly been unimaginable in the past. Cantopop artists who had previously sung almost exclusively mainstream love songs participated in the "June Fourth" wave. Against this political backdrop songwriters discovered that the topic was suddenly commercially viable. June Fourth songs became so popular that for a certain period there were almost

---

36. Chu, *Songs of Your Life*, 128–30.
37. Ibid., 133–36.

more June Fourth songs than there were love songs. When Tat Ming Pair broke up after *Crazy*, a beautiful collage of the courage, anger, selfishness, cowardice, and even self-deception of the Hong Kong people in 1989, Hong Kong people also waved goodbye to the innocence of the 1970s and 1980s. Despite its rapid decline, the second band wave contributed some very important talents to the mainstream music industry, who later became masters during the heyday of Cantopop in the early and mid-1990s: composers such as Kwong-Wing Chan 陳光榮 ("Fundamental"), Kenneth Fong 方樹樑 ("The Wind Group" 風之 Group), and Kubert Leung 梁翹栢 ("Life Exhibition and Ukiyo-e" 浮世繪); and lyricists such as Lin Xi (Raidas), Keith Chan (Tat Ming Pair), Gene Lau (Beyond), and Yiu-Fai Chow (Tat Ming Pair). Not unlike the first band wave, this one also offered creative space for rising stars and nurtured them into becoming successful musicians. Their impact lasted long as the composers and lyricists entered the mainstream in the 1990s, instilling fresh impetus to the music industry which had been aging after a decade of swift development.

All-Round Development of the Music Industry

The rise of megastars and the diversification of singers and genres were closely related to the all-round development of the Cantopop industry in the 1980s. Eyeing the great potential of the expanding market, more and more record companies directed resources to Cantopop. Back in the 1970s, there were mainly the transnational labels Polydor and EMI in the Hong Kong music industry, and at first they focused mainly on English popular songs. In the late 1970s, they began investing in Cantopop stars and became the market leaders in the 1980s. As noted by veteran disc jockey Joe Chan 陳任, the main players increased from two to five in the 1980s.[38] Besides Polydor and EMI, CBS Sony and Warner Music also entered the Cantopop market, and together with the local company Capital Artists, they became the market leaders in Hong Kong in the 1980s. Besides the big labels, local companies like Crown Records and Wing Hang Music continued to operate. Moreover, there were new companies like the local Contec Sound Media that set up in 1981 and collaborations like Cinepoly Records Company, jointly founded by Polygram and Cinema City in 1985. The former had just a few singers but all were big stars (e.g., Sam Hui, Paula Tsui, and Michael Kwan), whereas the latter signed, among others, Leslie Cheung and Beyond. There were also new small companies coming onto the scene. One of the most eye-catching examples of this in the early 1980s was Jenny Tseng's Gold Music Limited 金音符, founded in 1980. The label,

---

38. Stephanie Po-Yin Chung, "On the Birth of DJ Culture in Hong Kong" (in Chinese), *Media Digest*, RTHK (December 15, 2008), http://app3.rthk.hk/mediadigest/content.php?aid=852; retrieved on March 15, 2016.

albeit short-lived, focused not only on Jenny Tseng's own albums, but also new endeavors such as Danny Summer's *Hair of Trouble: Night Prowl*《煩惱絲‧夜徘徊》(1983). There were two examples from the pop charts that showed that the demand for Cantopop was on the rise in the late 1980s. In 1987, RTHK increased the number of songs on its pop charts from ten to fifteen. In the following year, TVB also increased the number of new plugs from four to seven per week. It was apparent that the number of songs produced was growing at that time.

The expanding market was able to support other small to mid-sized record companies, and this was an essential factor of the diversification of Cantopop genres (e.g., IC Records published Small Island's album that generated the band wave in the late 1980s). Apparently, the growing number of record companies would be followed by an increasing demand for talents. Besides headhunting from different sources, there were also various singing contests, among which the New Talent Singing Contest organized by TVB was the biggest and most influential one in the 1980s. In addition to award winners like Anita Mui, David Lui, Alex To, Leon Lai, and Andy Hui mentioned above, many participants later also became mainstays in the Cantopop industry in the 1990s; to cite a few examples, Hacken Lee, Vivian Chow 周慧敏, The Grasshoppers 草蜢, Shirley Kwan 關淑怡, Ekin Cheng 鄭伊健, and Edwin Leung 梁漢文. ATV later followed suit and organized the First Future Idol Contest in 1985. Owing to the much smaller impact of the television company, the contest did not exert long-term influence on the music industry, but winners like Norman Cheung 張立基 and Yolinda Yan 甄楚倩 were also once popular, albeit briefly, in the late 1980s. The influence of the New Talent Singing Contest was profound because, in addition to the fact that it was organized by TVB, it had a close relationship with Capital Artists. The winners of the contest were guaranteed a contract with the record label, and participants of great potential were also invited to sign with the company.

Mass media could be a very important promoter of the music industry. Besides the New Talent Singing Contest, TVB also played an important role in the music industry by launching the music show *Jade Solid Gold* in 1981 and subsequently the *Jade Solid Gold Best Ten Music Awards Presentation* in 1983. When it was launched, *Jade Solid Gold* aired during prime time on Saturdays, featuring mainly Cantopop music videos and interviews. In 1986, it set up a JSG chart, which became one of the indexes of the popularity of Cantopop singers (the other being the RTHK pop chart). Besides TVB and RTHK, Commercial Radio Hong Kong also became a key player when its Channel 2 (CR2) shifted emphasis from English to Cantonese popular songs. CR2 was the most popular channel among the younger generation. In the face of big competition from RTHK, its image as an English pop channel changed in the early 1980s. Its disc jockeys set up a "6 Pair and a Half" 六啤半 group and released a Cantopop album. Between 1983 and 1984, "[i]nstead of catering to the exclusive and rapidly diminishing foreign popular song audience, CR2 broadened its audience base somewhat by putting in more talk shows and giving Cantonese songs more airtime."[39] Cantopop further gathered momentum after Winnie Yu 俞琤, one of the members of this group, took up the post of general manager of Commercial Radio in 1988. Shortly before she assumed her new post, she expressed her views toward her plans in an interview. She confessed in the interview that her first and foremost task was to make Commercial Radio Hong Kong a "profitable" radio station. When she took office, a policy of promoting local Cantopop was implemented. One of her strategies was to use her brainchild, "All Chinese Pop Music Station," to pave the way for a Cantopop chart and subsequently an award ceremony. (By the end of the 1980s, there were pop charts and award ceremonies organized by TVB, RTHK, and CR2. In addition to these, there were also awards presented by the Composers and Authors Society of Hong Kong Ltd.).[40]

In a press conference on February 1, 1988, Winnie Yu declared that CR2 would become an "All Chinese Pop Music Station" beginning March 21, 1988. The new program ordained that only Chinese songs, including Mandarin and Cantonese songs, were allowed to air on its Channel 2 (hereafter abbreviated as CR2), which was the most popular radio channel among the younger generation in Hong Kong. The group of veteran disk jockeys and administrators who initiated the format was paradoxically those who had contributed most to familiarizing the Hong Kong audience with Anglo-American popular music in the past. While it is not unusual for many countries to put forward "protectionist" plans to enhance the development of local popular songs, in Hong Kong such an "All Chinese Pop Music Station" format was unprecedented. Later that year, CR2 further expanded the plan to include a "Round the Clock with Original Pop" format once a week on Mondays, in which no cover versions would be aired. The "All Chinese Pop Music Station" format started in March 1988 but began to fade out by the end of the same year. Although short-lived, it was influential to the development of local Hong Kong pop music. Despite the backdrop of commercial considerations, this format clearly encouraged local music economically by giving it greater radio airplay. If properly developed, such a format might also have foregrounded and developed local identity through promoting local music culture. But as CR2 focused

---

39. Choi, "Popular Culture," 542.
40. Since the 1980s, the Composers and Authors Society of Hong Kong Ltd. (CASH) has awarded "Winners of the CASH Song Writers Quest," "Best Chinese (Pop) Melody and Lyrics Awards," and "Most Performed Cantonese Pop Work on Radio and TV." See Ho, "Between Globalisation and Localisation," 147.

its attention only on an "All Chinese Pop Music Station" format to pave the way for "The Supreme Pop Chart," it failed to connect broadcast policy and local music industry development. Owing to the lack of support provided to the music industry, the quality of local Cantopop remained more or less the same as the quantity significantly increased. Interestingly enough, in the case of New Zealand, the radio industry argued that "there is not enough local music to fit their airplay formats, and that too much of what is available is qualitatively inferior to overseas product."[41] In contrast, in the case of Hong Kong, it was the music industry that made the complaint. In any case, a lack of communication between the two industries hindered the use of a cultural policy to develop local music culture. It should be apparent that as long as there was no industry policy to lift the standards of local productions, there would not be enough high-quality local products. Without the continuous supply of good quality local pop songs, the "All Chinese Pop Music Station" format could not last long.

The "All Chinese Pop Music Station" format appeared in 1988 during the heyday of Hong Kong Cantopop. Starting in the mid-1970s, Hong Kong Cantopop was considered almost identical to Hong Kong pop songs. In other words, Cantopop was hailed as the dominant genre of pop songs in Hong Kong for the last thirty years or so. When Cantopop reached the apex of its development in the late 1980s, it was very popular in Mandarin-speaking regions. From the mid-1990s onwards, the situation gradually changed. The rise of a global Chinese media network set up an aura more suitable for Mandapop to develop. Keith Negus stated that in the global era, the music industry shifted to pay more attention to the "global" market in terms of aesthetics (such as melody and rhythm), semiotics (such as the images of the singers), politics (such as political or religious taboos), economics (such as the notion of a globalized market), marketing (such as distribution strategies), and practical needs (such as copyrights).[42] The resulting shift of emphasis in the global market changed not only the criteria for choosing a singer but also the language of pop songs to a more "global" one. With respect to Chinese pop songs, as Mandarin was more widely used in Greater China, the market for Mandapop became more globalized than that of Cantopop. Thereafter, the Cantopop market shrank. One need only look at the great number of Hong Kong singers who moved their career base to Taiwan to be convinced of this phenomenon.[43]

41. Roy Shuker, *Understanding Popular Music* (London and New York: Routledge, 1994), 52.
42. Keith Negus, *Music Genres and Corporate Cultures* (London and New York: Routledge, 1999), 155–56.
43. Yiu-Wai Chu, "Developing Local Popular Songs in Hong Kong: A Study of the 'All Cantonese Pop Music Station' Format," *Media International Australia Incorporating Culture and Policy* 105 (November 2002): 147–62.

The "All Chinese Pop Music Station" format, by no means an isolated contingent attempt, must be interpreted alongside the Supreme Pop Chart, which was touted as "a totally unbiased pop chart," by CR2. Not long after CR2 became an "All Chinese Pop Music Station," the Supreme Pop Chart was launched on March 27, 1988. Since the Supreme Pop Chart used the airplay frequency of a particular song as the basic criterion of ranking, CR2 claimed that it was the "fairest" music awards program in Hong Kong. On January 16, 1989, the first Supreme Music Awards was held, and the whole series of CR2's plans climaxed. It was the trend of localization, as well as the marketing strategy of the radio station, that would steal the limelight. As Hong Kong had long been famous for its laissez-faire policy, it was not surprising to find that Hong Kong did not have any specific cultural policy to foster local popular songs production. The "All Chinese Pop Music Station" format was the first of its kind, which exerted a profound influence on the local music industry. The extremely controversial plan exerted an enormous impact on the music scene in Hong Kong. Some argued that local composers and lyricists would have a better opportunity to develop their talents, whereas critics argued that choices would became limited and would result in the development of Cantopop in terms of quantity, but not quality. Others opined that such a format made room for the genre of Cantopop to take shape. Some did commend CR2's reforms but others found it far from "fair." Differences in responses notwithstanding, the series of reforms did become the talk of the town at that time. Some Cantopop legends were created as a result of these reforms. The debut album of the new group Dream Theatre, for instance, topped the Supreme Pop Chart for three weeks, and it was unimaginable in the past for a new group to attain such an outstanding achievement. Besides, since the disc jockeys had to find more Chinese songs to air, some previously marginalized songs had the chance to be introduced to audiences. These reforms evidently exerted a positive impact in terms of the diversity of pop songs.

Statistically speaking, the quantity of local Cantopop benefited greatly from CR2's reforms. According to the figures compiled by Chi-Wah Wong, "among the 223 songs in the 30 albums premiered in the first quarter of 1989, 142 (63.67%) are works of local composers."[44] In 1988, the percentage was less than 50 percent. Thus, there seemed to be little doubt that CR2's reforms did exert a positive impact on local Cantopop in terms of quantity. On the other hand, as noted by another famous Hong Kong music critic, Chi-Chung Wong, the increased number of Cantopop did not necessarily mean the successful

---

44. Chi-Wah Wong, "Statistics on the 'Population' of Local Composers in the First Quarter of 1989" 〈1989 年本地作曲家「人口」統計〉 (in Chinese), *Music Bus* 143 (April 14, 1989), page number missing.

localization of Hong Kong popular songs.[45] In other words, quantity could not be put on a par with quality. Chi-Chung Wong believed that the standards of the audience were a more important factor. However, as the series of reforms were very much oriented to Winnie Yu's goal of making Commercial Radio Hong Kong a "profitable" radio station, there were no other follow-up activities (such as music education) to promote local music culture. In addition, there were no adequate channels of communication among the broadcasting institutions, music companies, and other media. As the "All Chinese Pop Music Station" format was oriented far more toward short-term returns (such as the increase in the size of the audience) than the long-term development of local Cantopop, it ended with its promises far from realized.[46] The "All Chinese Pop Music Station" format was short-lived but influential. Although it only lasted about nine months, local popular songs still accounted for about 90 percent of airplay.[47] Whether or not the format was a success, that Cantopop was used by a popular radio station as a marketing strategy was patent proof of its popularity and status in the late 1980s.

Afterword

By the end of the 1980s, Hong Kong became the largest center of Chinese popular music worldwide. "In 1989, the Coliseum held 129 nights of concerts by local artists, selling 1.35 million tickets. Toward the end of the decade the industry was producing more than 300 Cantopop albums a year and locally produced albums outsold imported albums by around 2 to 1."[48] The actual figures are cited in Table 4.2:

Table 4.2
Distribution of sales in record market, 1989*

Type	Amount (Million HK Dollars)	Percentage
Local popular music	336	56
Foreign popular music	144	24
Non-popular music (including classical music and Cantonese operatic songs)	120	20

*Choi, "Popular Culture," 539.

45. Chi-Chung Wong, "Original Music Should be Encouraged"〈創作風氣應推崇〉(in Chinese), *Breakthrough Teenagers* 132 (November 1, 1989): 4.
46. For a detailed account of the format, see Yiu-Wai Chu, "Developing Local Popular Songs in Hong Kong," 147–62.
47. Ho, "Between Globalisation and Localisation," 147.
48. Cited from "Hong Kong Pop: English Style," Department of English, Hong Kong Institute of Education, https://home.ied.edu.hk/~hkpop/music/hkpophistory.html; retrieved on March 15, 2016.

While Cantopop was orchestrating a spectacle of consumerism, it was not hopelessly standardized; although it was unabashedly commercial it was also vigorously hybridized. Cantopop was dominated by mainstream love ballads, but other genres like city folk songs and band songs proved that discursive space was available for nonmainstream attempts. New singers, composers, and lyricists came onto the scene and injected new life into the music industry. Not unlike Hong Kong, which assimilates different cultures, Cantopop's renditions of Euro-American, Japanese, Mandarin, and even Korean songs made it a vibrant hybrid of different music cultures. Having its vitality spilled over to other sectors such as movies, concerts, and advertisements, Cantopop further expanded into a multimedia industry, becoming so popular that it attracted those who did not speak Cantonese. "In its heyday in the 1970s and 1980s, Cantopop defined the look, feel and—with its lush, ultra-refined production values—even the sound of Chinese cool."[49]

While the music industry celebrated swift growth, inherent problems were swept under the carpet. After Alan Tam, Leslie Cheung, and Anita Mui retired, in a different sense of the word, the Cantopop industry had to find new stars to keep its momentum. More importantly, a new trend of globalization was silently reshaping cultural industries across the world after the fall of the Berlin Wall in 1989. The Mainland market unexpectedly began to open up after 1989, when China entered a "post-new" era of cultural industry according to Chinese critics.[50] The government relaxed its control over the development of cultural industries in the aftermath of the June Fourth Incident. As the Cantopop industry was still enjoying success after unprecedentedly swift growth over the decade, the gradual reconfiguration of the Asian mediascape was left unnoticed.[51] The rise of the Four Heavenly Kings in the early 1990s gave the music industry the opportunity to kick the can down the road. Whether it was a blessing to the development of Cantopop or not it is not easy to tell, but it is safe to say that the industry was ignoring the danger of thin ice when it stuck with its success formula, even as the ecology of Asian cultural industries was changing radically. Many deep-seated problems surfaced when the Cantopop industry faced a shrinking market in the mid- to the late 1990s.

---

49. Geoff Burpee, "As Sun Sets on British Empire in Hong Kong, Industry Gears for Return to China." *Billboard* 108, no. 43 (October 26, 1996): APQ-1.

50. "Post-new" era was used by Mainland critics to analyze Chinese culture in the 1990s; see Zhang Yiwu, "Postmodernism and Chinese Novels of the Nineties" (trans. Michael Berry), *Boundary 2* 24, no. 3 (Autumn, 1997): 247.

51. Asian popular culture was undergoing significant transformation in the early 1990s; for details, see, among others, Lorna Fitzsimmons and John A. Lent, eds., *Asian Popular Culture in Transition* (New York: Routledge, 2013).

5 | The Best of Times, the Worst of Times
The 1990s

Introduction

The eye-catching title of an essay published in *Billboard* in 1999, "The Cantopop Drop," advertised the sad but all-too-true fact that the golden days of Cantopop had passed.[1] It was no coincidence that James Wong, the godfather of Cantopop, used 1997 as the end boundary for the timeline of Cantopop in his doctoral thesis, "The Rise and Decline of Cantopop 1949–1997." It is widely believed that the fall of Cantopop was caused by a combination of a bad economy, piracy, and file sharing. Nevertheless, considering the rapid recovery of Mandapop after the Asian financial crisis, this explanation is less helpful. Mandapop, facing problems similar to those faced by Cantopop, rapidly bounced back and reclaimed its lost turf, gaining even more ground in the Hong Kong market. The common belief in the Hong Kong music industry that file sharing was the key reason for the drastic drop in record sales was problematic. According to Felix Oberholzer-Gee and Koleman Strumpf's empirical study, file sharing seemed to translate into an effect on album sales that was "statistically indistinguishable from zero."[2] While Oberholzer-Gee and Strumpf's study is problematic, it is reasonable to say that one needs to look at the issue from different perspectives.

In addition to explanations such as piracy and file sharing, there were other reasons behind the steady loss of Cantopop's popularity. Some of the important reasons were outlined by James Wong in his doctoral thesis, which posited that there were seven major reasons behind the fall of Cantopop since 1997.[3]

---

1. Ann Tsang and Debe Campbell, "The Cantopop Drop," *Billboard* 111, issue 9 (February 27, 1999): APQ-1. Part of the introduction has appeared in Yiu-Wai Chu, *Lost in Transition: Hong Kong Culture in the Age of China* (Albany: SUNY Press, 2013), 121–22.
2. Felix Oberholzer-Gee and Koleman Strumpf, "The Effect of File Sharing on Record Sales: An Empirical Analysis," *Journal of Political Economy* 115, no. 1 (2007): 3.
3. James Wong, "The Rise and Decline of Cantopop: A Study of Hong Kong Popular Music (1949–1997)"〈粵語流行曲的發展與興衰：香港流行音樂研究 1949–1997〉(in Chinese) (Hong Kong: PhD thesis, the University of Hong Kong, 2003), 169–78.

One of those reasons was related to piracy, but it also involved the short-sightedness of the music industry. At that time, Hong Kong's music culture was overwhelmed by a music industry that was complacent with its success in the good old days, not only sticking to the old formula but also further concentrating resources on those who were selected by the formula. When record sales dropped because of piracy, record companies, rather than trying to develop the market, counted on the successful formulae of the Cantopop kings/queens to make a profit. Furthermore, record companies, with an eye toward profits brought not by record sales but from commercials and karaoke copyrights, targeted mainly teenage fans who were the main consumers of those commodities. These factors led to the standardization of products and an over-emphasis on packaging. Advertising was hardly new in a commercial society like Hong Kong, but when Cantopop developed into a multimedia transnational business, the scale of its production had to be much larger. To be profitable, mass production must be accompanied by mass consumption, which can be facilitated by the strategy of commodity fetishism and consumption. Thus, the music industry had to rely upon idol worshipping much more than it did in the 1980s. Moreover, when production costs rose, sales of albums could no longer guarantee good returns for the record companies' investments. In short, record sales were no longer the main source of income and the music industry became increasingly dependent commercially on media it did not itself control. These developments contributed to the stereotypical impression that Cantopop gave its audiences in the 1990s: "the sentimental lyrics, the melancholic melody, and the banality of romance."[4]

The situation would not have been so bad had these developments not happened at the dawning of the age of global media. Previously, Hong Kong, as a cosmopolitan city, was notorious for its small number of media channels, having only two free television stations and three radio stations for a very long period of time. In the past, these limited channels had a stranglehold on what audiences saw and heard. In the early 1990s, however, the scene changed. The broadcasting of cable and satellite television multiplied the number of media channels by several times. As far as music was concerned, the channels provided by these new media were mostly Mandarin-speaking, as the Mandarin market was obviously considerably larger. The new choices did provide Hong Kong audiences with the chance to listen to Mandapop from Taiwan, Singapore, Malaysia, and Mainland China, but it seemed to be having adverse effects on Cantopop. In this particular context, the development of the Chinese music industry became transnational and media consumption was deterritorialized in the early 1990s, which led the Hong Kong music industry to face an irreversible

---

4. John Nguyet Erni, "Like a Culture: Notes on Pop Music and Popular Sensibility in Decolonized Hong Kong," *Hong Kong Cultural Studies Bulletin* 8/9 (Spring/Summer 1998): 60–61.

structural change it did not realize at the outset. This at first facilitated the success of Cantopop stars in Asia but later exposed standardized Cantopop to harsh competition with Mandapop from different music cultures. Moreover, the music industry had to work closely with the media to maintain the star system, and record companies had to spend tons of money on marketing and buying time on television and radio channels. As other media and the income generated dominated the operation of the music industry, music companies directed most of their resources to the big stars. As a result, cross-genre hybridity of Cantopop started diminishing in the time of the Four Heavenly Kings, which exerted harmful impacts on its later development. As the Cantopop market started shrinking and the record companies diverted more attention to the Mandapop market in the late 1990s, the Cantopop industry was about to fall into an abyss it refused to recognize at that time.

The Four Heavenly Kings

After Alan Tam quit pop music award ceremonies and Leslie Cheung retired from the music industry, Hong Kong needed new megastars to further develop its Cantopop business. Still the trendsetter of Chinese popular culture, it did not take long for Hong Kong to push its cultural industries to new heights. The rise of the Four Heavenly Kings, namely, Andy Lau, Jacky Cheung, Leon Lai, and Aaron Kwok, dominated not only the local market but also almost all Chinese communities around the world. The term "Four Heavenly Kings" was reportedly coined in 1992 to name the four male artists who dominated the industry. Before his retirement in June 2013, Man-Sun Cheung 張文新, broadcasting veteran and former assistant director of broadcasting, mentioned that he came up with the name during the RTHK "Solar Project" event that he masterminded. At that time Aaron Kwok, a Hong Kong–born entertainer popular in Taiwan, had just moved back to Hong Kong for career advancement. Man-Sun Cheung saw great potential in him, and thus used the term the Four Heavenly Kings when he introduced him along with Andy Lau, Jacky Cheung, and Leon Lai—who were already Cantopop superstars—for the sake of marketing.[5] The Four Heavenly Kings, who subsequently generated a Cantopop craze across Chinese communities, helped the industry to develop into a transnational business venture. Jacky Cheung's Cantopop album *Overthrow of True Love* 《真情流露》 (1992), for example, sold more than 450,000 copies in Hong Kong, which was totally unimaginable before. The success of the Four Heavenly Kings was not only in the realm of popular music.

---

5. "The Good Old Days: Man-Sun Cheung" 〈流金歲月張文新〉, *Ming Pao Weekly* 2327 (June 2013). Available at: http://www.mingpaoweekly.com/easyview/content.php?type=1&section=2327&id=1389266952189; retrieved on March 15, 2016.

Like Leslie Cheung and Anita Mui, they also crossed over to wider audiences through concerts, movies, and, more importantly, commercials for artistic recognition as well as financial gain. While they helped usher Cantopop into a new era of the cross-media cultural industry, ironically, their multiple talents also contributed, at least partly, to the later fall of Cantopop.

Among the Four Heavenly Kings, Andy Lau was the first to win TVB's Jade Solid Gold Most Popular Male Singer Award in 1990. He was also the first to start his entertainment career at TVB back in the early 1980s. As noted in the previous chapter, he was one of the "Five Tigers," who were up-and-coming television actors in the early 1980s. He captured the limelight in the TVB drama *Eagle Hunter* 《獵鷹》 in 1982. The *wuxia* masterpiece *The Legend of the Condor Heroes* 《神雕俠侶》, which premiered the following year, brought new fame to the young actor. It was very common at that time for television and movie actors to pursue a singing career to boost their popularity. With an eye toward developing his career in the swiftly growing Cantopop industry in the mid-1980s, Andy Lau released his debut album, *Just Know I Still Love You Now* 《只知道此刻愛你》, with TVB's sister company Capital Artists in 1985. Owing to a contract controversy with TVB, he later signed with EMI and focused more on developing his film career in the late 1980s, as Cantopop showbiz was dominated by Leslie Cheung and Alan Tam. Despite this situation, he released some chart-topping hits, such as "Forbidden Zone of Love" 〈情感的禁區〉 and "Back to You" 〈回到你身邊〉. The album *Forbidden Zone of Love* (1987) sold more than 50,000 copies, winning him his first platinum disc award. Before he became the most popular male singer, he was already a big movie star. His popular movies, including *As Tears Go By* (1987), won him popularity that paved the way for his later success in the Cantopop industry. In the late 1980s, Andy Lau directed more emphasis toward his singing career, owing perhaps to the fact that the Cantopop industry needed new superstars to fill the gaps left behind by Alan Tam and Leslie Cheung. It was perfect timing for him to win the Most Popular Male Singer Award in 1990, which signaled that he had formally picked up the baton from Leslie Cheung and Alan Tam, becoming "probably the most successful example of an actor-turned-singer."[6]

In 1990, Andy Lau signed with the new record company In-Co Music Publishing 寶藝星, a joint venture of PolyGram and Entertainment Impact 藝能娛樂, and released two Cantopop albums in the same year, *Would It Be Possible?* 《可不可以》 and *Goodbye* 《再會了》. Both albums went triple platinum (more than 150,000 copies each), and the title songs "Would It Be Possible?" and "Goodbye" topped Cantopop charts, helping him to become the Most Popular Male Singer in Hong Kong at TVB's Jade Solid Gold Top 10

---

6. Cited from Wing-Fai Leung, *Multimedia Stardom in Hong Kong: Image, Performance and Identity* (Abingdon, Oxon and New York: Routledge, 2015), 98.

Awards, and he had a stranglehold on the award for three consecutive years (after that, he became the Asia Pacific Most Popular Hong Kong Singer). It did not take long for him to break his own record. In 1991, he released three more Cantopop albums, *Never-ending Love*《愛不完》, *The Days We Went through Together*《一起走過的日子》, and *Believe in Destiny*《不可不信……緣》. All of the albums topped sales charts, with *The Days We Went through Together* selling more than 300,000 copies. The synergy between the Hong Kong film and music industries reached new heights, as shown in the immense popularity of "The Days We Went through Together" and "Believe in Destiny," which were featured in the Andy Lau movies *Casino Raiders 2*《至尊無上 II 之永霸天下》 and *Savior of the Soul*《九一神鵰俠侶》, respectively. Andy Lau staged twenty shows of his debut concert at the Hong Kong Coliseum in January 1993, and twenty more in both 1994 and 1996, further extending the glory days of the Cantopop concert industry.

The music awards won by Andy Lau are indeed too many to be detailed here. I would rather focus on one of his achievements that arguably surpassed those of his predecessors. As mentioned in the introduction, the landscape of Chinese popular culture was changing in the early 1990s due to the rapid growth of the Mandarin popular song market. Andy Lau's fan base was enormously expanded by his knack for performing Mandapop. His predecessors did turn to Mandarin-speaking markets, but it was Andy Lau who genuinely enthralled Mandapop fans. Thanks to the Mandarin renditions of his movies popular across Chinese communities, he was much loved by Mandarin-speaking fans. He released his Mandarin album *Inevitable to Make Mistakes*《難免有錯》 in 1990, and the 1994 album *Forget Love Potion*《忘情水》 reportedly sold more than 3 million copies, which was his best-selling album. *True Forever*《真永遠》 (in Mandarin) was the first album Andy Lau released with his new company, Music Impact Entertainment 藝能動音 in 1995, which was also a big success in terms of sales.[7] Thereafter, Andy Lau divided his energy between the Cantopop and Mandapop markets. His songs topped music charts in Hong Kong, Taiwan, and Mainland China, and he kept on sweeping both Cantopop and Mandapop awards. By April 2000, with 292 awards for his singing career, Andy Lau entered the Guinness World Records for "Most Awards Won by a Cantopop Male Artist."[8]

---

7. "Since 1992, Andy's albums were produced by his own production house—New Melody Production (renamed NMG in 2000), which gave him a new channel to experiment with different styles and approaches, bringing new music elements to his music. Whereas the distribution of his albums were handled by the record companies." Cited from AndyLauSounds. Available at: http://www.andylausounds.com/?page_id=110; retrieved on March 15, 2016.

8. Cited from "Andy Lau and Jackie Chan Entering Guinness World Records," *Wen Wei Po* (October 17, 2000). Available at: http://paper.wenweipo.com/2000/10/17/EN0010170001.htm; retrieved on March 15, 2016.

Unlike the "actor-turned-singer" Andy Lau, Jacky Cheung was a "singer-turned-actor." He started his music career after winning the Hong Kong 18-District Amateur Singing Contest in 1984. He signed with PolyGram and released his debut Cantopop album, *Smile*, in 1985. As mentioned in the previous chapter, the mid-1980s witnessed an amazing growth of the Cantopop market. Jacky Cheung's *Smile* reportedly sold a mind-blowing six-times platinum (more than 300,000 copies), an amazing amount for a rookie, and his second album, *She is Afar, Amour* 《遙遠的她 Amour》, reportedly sold more than eight-times platinum. He won the Best New Artist Award at the Eighth RTHK Top 10 Chinese Gold Songs Awards, and his golden hits included, among others, "Love Is Gone" 〈情已逝〉, "Half Moon" 〈月半彎〉, and "She Is Afar" 〈遙遠的她〉. Jacky Cheung's first four Cantopop albums sold more than two million copies in total, and he held six consecutive concerts in the Hong Kong Coliseum in 1987, just the third year of his music career. In the 1980s, it was rather common for Hong Kong popular singers to cross over to movies, and Jacky Cheung also directed his attention to the movie industry. Perhaps with the exception of Wong Kar Fai's famous debut in *As Tears Go By* 《旺角卡門》, which won him Best Supporting Actor at the Hong Kong Film Awards in 1988, Jacky Cheung's film career did not create a dynamic synergy between the two industries. It was even more unexpected that he went from hero to zero after the sales of his fifth album, *In My Dream Last Night* 《昨夜夢魂中》, dropped to a miserable 20,000 copies.[9] Jacky Cheung blamed early fame exposure for his unruly attitude, which brought him to the lowest point in his career. The problem of negative media reporting (such as becoming dependent on alcohol) delved deeper into the continued struggles of the rising star in 1988, and it was not until 1989 that he escaped his career doldrums with *One Love One Life* 《只願一生愛一人》. It was perfect timing for Jacky Cheung to bounce back at this particular juncture, when the semi- or full retirement of Alan Tam and Leslie Cheung brought new opportunities for new male Cantopop singers.

The early 1990s was a turning point in Jacky Cheung's music career. He managed to rally from his brief downturn in the late 1980s, greeting the new decade with *Summer Dream* 《夢中的你》. In hindsight, this may not be among the most important albums by Jacky Cheung, but the song "Li Xianglan" 〈李香蘭〉, which later stood out as being very different from other mainstream love ballads, gave him the chance to showcase his vocal talents, which the other Heavenly Kings did not quite possess. *Uncontrolled Passion* 《情不禁》,

9. Cited from the interview with Jacky Cheung: "Jacky Cheung Popular for 30 Years" 〈張學友長紅三十年〉 (in Chinese), published in *Business Weekly* 《商業周刊》 1413 (December 11, 2014). Available at: http://www.businessweekly.com.tw/KWebArticle.aspx?ID=56754&path=e; retrieved on March 15, 2016.

released in 1991, was undoubtedly a career-changing album for Jacky Cheung. The all-time classic "Love You More Each Day" 〈每天愛你多一些〉, a cover version of the Japanese group Southern All Stars' "Midsummer Fruit" 〈真夏の果実〉, included in this album won him almost all of the prestigious awards, including, *inter alia*, TVB's Gold Song Gold Award and Commercial Radio's The Most Beloved Song Award. In 1992, the album *Overthrow of True Love* mentioned above brought his career up another notch. It was unprecedented that nine of the eleven songs entered popular charts, five of which were top hits: "Breaking up on Rainy Days" 〈分手總要在雨天〉 (TVB's Gold Song Gold Award), "My Love Is Deeper Than Yours" 〈愛得比你深〉, "Secret Admirer" 〈暗戀妳〉, "When the World Ends Tomorrow" 〈明日世界終結時〉, and "Missing You amidst Wind and Rain" 〈相思風雨中〉. The unparalleled success of this album made Jacky Cheung the rival of Andy Lau at music award ceremonies. In a sense, Jacky Cheung won the battle when Winnie Yu, former Deputy Chairman and veteran disc jockey of Commercial Radio Hong Kong, publicly crowned Jacky Cheung the new "God of Cantopop" at TVB's Jade Solid Gold Top 10 Awards presentation in early 1993. Thanks to Winnie Yu's special status in the music industry,[10] Jacky Cheung succeeded Sam Hui to become the new God of Cantopop. Jacky Cheung's continued success proved that he was not unworthy of the title. As early as 1994, he was named the most popular singer in Asia at the US Billboard Music Awards. In 1997, he played a leading role in Hong Kong's first modern musical, *Snow Wolf Lake* 《雪狼湖》, which he masterminded, with 103 performances around the world—still a record for Chinese musicals. He won countless music awards after that, and his immense popularity straddled the new millennium. One of the remarkable examples of his success is the Guinness world record he set in 2012: the largest combined audience for a live act in 12 months, with 2,048,553 audience members.[11]

Similar to Andy Lau, Jacky Cheung's achievements also extended to Chinese communities across the globe. The fame he accumulated first through Cantopop helped him establish a large fan base, which was further expanded by his involvement in Mandapop. He released his first Mandapop album, *Homeless Love* 《情無四歸》, in 1986, but it was not until the release of the 1993 album *Goodbye Kiss* 《吻別》, which sold almost five million copies around the world,

---

10. Winnie Yu was hailed by *Time Out Hong Kong* in 2008 as "the most powerful person working in broadcasting in Hong Kong." Cited from "Winnie Yu Tsang," *Time Out Hong Kong* (September 20, 2008). Available at: http://www.timeout.com.hk/around-town/features/14233/winnie-yu-tsang.html; retrieved on March 15, 2016.

11. "The record-setting Jacky Cheung 1/2 Century Tour ran from 30 December 2010 to 29 December 2011, with 105 live concerts in 61 cities across China, USA, Malaysia, Singapore and Australia." Available at: http://www.guinnessworldrecords.com/news/2012/6/jacky-cheung-performs-for-largest-combined-audience-42990/; retrieved on March 15, 2016.

that he conquered the swiftly growing Mandapop market. The title track, "Goodbye Kiss," was so popular that it was later covered in an English version by the Danish pop band Michael Learns to Rock. Thereafter, Jacky Cheung adopted a two-pronged approach—both Cantopop and Mandapop—to further his music career. The astounding sales volumes of *True Forever* and *Goodbye Kiss* prompted more and more Hong Kong record companies and singers to switch more resources to Mandapop, with an eye toward the larger market. As noted above, the Hong Kong music industry was facing an irreversible structural change it did not realize at the outset, which at first facilitated the success of the Heavenly Kings in Asia, but later exposed Cantopop to harsh competition with Mandapop, which was increasingly popular in the new mediascape (this will be further discussed later in this chapter).

Leon Lai, born in Beijing, moved to Hong Kong at the age of four and began his entertainment career after winning the Bronze Award at the New Talent Singing Contest organized by TVB in 1986. However, he did not have a chance to release his first Cantopop album, *Leon*, until 1990. He spent several years as a TVB actor after signing a singing contract with Capital Artists, the sister company of TVB. Although his performance in the television sector was reasonably good, he did not have an opportunity to start his singing career until his popular Taiwanese television drama, *A Turbulent Era* 《風雲時代》, aired. Reportedly owing to contract problems, Leon Lai was shut out by TVB, and he thus had to shoot a Chinese Television Company drama in Taiwan. His insert song "Cloud of Dust" 〈風雲塵煙〉 (in Mandarin) in the drama became so popular that the Cantopop industry saw his great potential and brought him back from Taiwan in 1990. He then released his debut Cantopop album, *Meeting in the Rain* 《相逢在雨中》, with PolyGram. His career gathered momentum in 1991 with several big hits, including "What If This Is Love" 〈如果這是情〉, "It's Love, It's Destiny" 〈是愛是緣〉, "Sorry, I Love You" 〈對不起我愛你〉, "My Feeling" 〈我的感覺〉, and "Will You Come Tonight?" 〈今夜你會不會來〉. A quick glance at the titles easily reveals that Leon Lai excelled at, except for "My Feeling," romantic ballads targeted at young female audiences. Owing to his origin in Beijing and his popularity in Taiwan, his singing career was two-pronged from the outset. He released Cantopop and Mandapop albums, with some songs having two versions (such as "Will You Come Tonight?"), and he managed to establish a big fan base in the early 1990s. In 1992, he continued to develop his image as a prince of romantic ballads with chart-topping hits such as "Wish I Could Be More Than Just a Friend" 〈但願不只是朋友〉, "I Will Be As Foolish As You" 〈我會像你一樣傻〉, "Dear My Love" 〈我的親愛〉, and "I Love You OK?". He was fully baptized into stardom after holding his first ten concerts at the Hong Kong Coliseum in October 1992. Meanwhile, it is interesting to note that in 1992 Leon Lai sang a song entitled "I Came from

Beijing"〈我來自北京〉, which also topped pop charts. According to the lyricist Gene Lau, "I Came from Beijing" marked the transformation of mainstream Hong Kong audiences' attitude toward Mainland culture.[12] Back in the 1980s, it would have been unimaginable for a singer to highlight his or her Mainland background (see the account of Faye Wong later in this chapter). In hindsight, it is safe to say that the song was an early signal of a later paradigm shift from Cantopop to Mandapop.

The 1993 album *Summer Love*《夏日傾情》propelled Leon Lai's career to new heights. Not only was the title song "Summer Love" another chart-topping love song, it was also the theme song of a new telecom television commercial. The commercial was enormously popular, hitting the fancy of many females. While using Cantopop in television commercials was by no means new, the song, thanks to the booming industry of mobile phones, generated a new creative synergy between the music and advertising industries. The unexpected success of this venture also earned Leon Lai TVB's Jade Solid Gold Most Popular Male Singer Award for the first time in 1993. After "Summer Love," Hutchison Telecom rolled out a new large-scale advertising campaign in 1994, with Leon Lai as the leading character. "Love between Sky and Earth," the theme of the campaign, was also the title of Leon Lai's album released that year. The music video (MV) for the title song, "Thinking of You Every Day" 〈那有一天不想你〉, financed by a handsome budget provided by the telecom giant, told a movie-like story in the commercial. The out-of-the-box production of the MV-cum-commercial generated a new wave of Cantopop crossover with commercials, especially those of the telecom industry, which was experiencing soaring demand at that time. The sequels to "Thinking of You Every Day" included, among others, "You're the Love of My Life"〈一生最愛就是你〉, "Words of Love Not Yet Spoken"〈情深說話未曾講〉, "Just Love Me for One Day"〈只要為我愛一天〉, "Love You, Not Love You"〈愛你不愛你〉, and "I Love You So Much"〈我這樣愛你〉. Most of the storyboards for these commercials adopted the success formula from "Love between Sky and Earth," which told a story between two lovers while showing their affection through mobile devices. It is safe to say that Leon Lai attained genuine superstardom in the music industry through this series of Cantopop songs. Before "Thinking of You Every Day," despite often being juxtaposed with Andy Lau and Jacky Cheung, Leon Lai was often seen as third in rank. From 1991 to 1994, he received the Bronze Award for Best Male Singer at the Commercial Radio Annual Awards Ceremony. Thanks to the success of his love songs in commercials, he won the Gold Award for Best Male Singer for the first time

---

12. Cited from Yiu-Wai Chu, *Songs of Your Life: Talks on Hong Kong Cantopop*《歲月如歌：詞話香港粵語流行曲》(in Chinese) (Hong Kong: Joint Publishing, 2009), 161.

in 1996. Furthermore, similar to Andy Lau and Jacky Cheung, Leon Lai also had countless fans across Asia. In this regard, his influence in South Korea was especially remarkable. In 1998, his Korean song "After Loving You" reached top 10 on Korean pop charts, the first time a Hong Kong singer managed to achieve this.[13] Like some of his predecessors, Leon Lai announced to the public in 1999 that he would no longer accept music awards in Hong Kong.

As mentioned above, when Aaron Kwok moved his base from Taiwan back to Hong Kong, the trio of Andy Lau, Jacky Cheung, and Leon Lai had already accumulated huge popularity in the early 1990s. Actually, Aaron Kwok's entertainment career, like Andy Lau and Leon Lai's, could be traced back to TVB when he joined the leading broadcaster in 1984 as a dancer trainee. His talent for dancing and, more importantly, his captivating looks were quickly spotted by audiences. TVB later transformed him into an actor, but he mainly played supporting roles in TVB dramas. Aaron Kwok turned his career around for the better with a Taiwanese motorcycle TV commercial in 1990. He enthralled Taiwanese—and actually Hong Kong as well—audiences with his handsome, innocent face in the commercial, which won him instant fame. The Taiwanese music industry seized the opportunity to turn him into a superstar with his debut Mandapop album, *Loving You Endlessly* 《對你愛不完》, in 1990, which sold more than 1 million copies across Asia. He also had a chance to showcase his dancing talent with the fast-paced love song bearing the same title. Aaron Kwok once said, "My musical style is energetic and passionate and I go to great lengths to show myself off to the best of my ability. I belong to the stage, so I think this is my own unique style which has developed during my music career."[14] He released two more albums in the following year, *In the End Who Can Tell Me?* 《到底有誰能夠告訴我》 and *Should I Leave Quietly?* 《我是不是該安靜的走開》. Despite being Mandapop, the songs from these albums won him the Best New Artist Gold Award at the RTHK Top 10 Gold Songs Awards in 1991. This award came out of the blue given the dominant role of Cantopop not only in Hong Kong but also across Asia.

Riding on his quickly accumulated popularity after the motorcycle commercial, Aaron Kwok decided to move his base back to his hometown in 1992, as Hong Kong was clearly the trendsetter of Chinese popular music then. Aaron Kwok's debut Cantopop album, entitled *Dance Endlessly, Love Endlessly, Sing Endlessly* 《跳不完・愛不完・唱不完》, was released in 1992. Notwithstanding the similarity of the titles, it was not a Cantonese rendition of *Loving You Endlessly*. While "Why Did I Let You Go?" 〈我為何讓你走〉 was

---

13. Cited from "Leon Lai, as Mei Lanfang," CCTV.com (November 11, 2008). Available at: http://www. cctv.com/english/special/meilanfang/20081111/106557.shtml; retrieved on March 15, 2016.

14. Cited from "Chinese Pop Music History 20 Years Special—Aaron Kwok," CRIEnglish.com (April 23, 2007). Available at: http://english.cri.cn/4406/2007/04/23/47@219380.htm; retrieved on March 15, 2016.

a fluid, romantic ballad with a typical touch of sensuality, "The Fourth Night Feelings" 〈第四晚心情〉 could be seen as an example of his signature dance songs. Aaron Kwok continued to advance his career in the Cantopop industry in the mid-1990s. With the tremendous success of the energetic dance song "Wild City" 〈狂野之城〉 in 1994 (winner of CR2's Ultimate Song of the Year Award), he went from innocent to wild, signaling a significant metamorphosis of his music career. Dubbed the "Hong Kong Michael Jackson" by the media, Aaron Kwok stood out as the dancing king among the four Cantopop megastars. He officially entered the temple of Cantopop after holding his first sixteen concerts at the Hong Kong Coliseum in the same year (not including the birthday concert organized by CR2 in 1993). In subsequent years, on the one hand, Aaron Kwok continued to focus on his dance songs, such as "Temptation of the Iron Mask" 〈鐵幕誘惑〉, "The Legend of Innocence" 〈純真傳說〉, and "The GIG Kingdom" 〈最激帝國〉, while on the other hand, he experimented with new topics with his agent May May Leung 小美, a renowned female lyricist in Hong Kong. They introduced new themes into their Cantopop dance songs, contributing a new discursive angle different from the mainstream love ballads. "Memorandum of Amnesia and Understanding" 〈失憶諒解備忘錄〉 and "The Emperor's New Song" 〈國王的新歌〉, for example, were social allegories with strong dance beats—the former a satire of people's purposeful amnesia and the latter an adaptation of the famous tale about pluralistic ignorance.[15]

Not unlike the other Heavenly Kings, Aaron Kwok also crossed over to other media. His golden hit "The Call of Love" 〈愛的呼喚〉 was the theme song of a commercial for the telecommunication service provider One2Free, a rival of Leon Lai's client Hutchison. It is worth noting here that Aaron Kwok was the first Chinese pop singer to sign with a global promotion project—Pepsi Cola—in late 1997. Their collaboration started with "Sing This Song" 〈唱這歌〉, the theme song of a Pepsi commercial in 1998 (which had both Cantonese and Mandarin versions). Later, in 1999, he had the opportunity to work with Janet Jackson, singing the Chinese version of the song Janet Jackson wrote for Pepsi—"Ask for More" 〈渴望無限〉. The commercial was undoubtedly a big success, prompting Pepsi to enter him into their Music Hall of Fame in 2002. As Aaron Kwok started his singing career in Taiwan, it was not surprising that in the 1990s he had been walking with two legs—Cantopop and Mandapop. "Ask for More," however, did mark a paradigm shift, showing that Cantopop had gradually been taken over by Mandapop by the end of the 1990s. When compared to the other three Heavenly Kings, Aaron Kwok started his Cantopop career a bit later, and thus it was not surprising that it took him

---

15. For a detailed analysis of the lyrics, see Yiu-Wai Chu, *A Study of Hong Kong Popular Lyrics* (in Chinese) (Hong Kong: Joint Publishing, 1998), 351–53.

the longest to come to the throne at popular music award ceremonies. He won his first Jade Solid Gold Best Singer Award in 1997 (and twice more in 1998 and 2000) and the Gold Award for Best Male Singer at the Commercial Radio Annual Awards Ceremony in 1998. Soon after he reached the apex of his music career, he directed more energy to the movie sector in the new millennium, a time that witnessed the waning of not just the Four Heavenly Kings but also Cantopop per se.

When Cantopop Turned Visual

Both the rise and decline of Cantopop in the 1990s boiled down to the transformation of the mediascape. In the early 1990s, when global capitalism swiftly crossed borders and transformed the landscape of the popular culture industries in Asia, Cantopop stars took advantage of becoming singing icons across Chinese and other Asian communities. New cross-media synergy was spawned and expanded to the realms of other media such as advertising and karaoke. The Four Heavenly Kings spontaneously became the favorite stars of major advertising campaigns. For instance, telecommunication service was expanding fast in Hong Kong in the 1990s, and the Four Heavenly Kings starred in big-budget advertising campaigns for telecommunication providers and/or products. Leon Lai's telecommunication commercial series noted above won unprecedented success, and many of his greatest hits were related to those commercials. Meanwhile, Andy Lau, Jacky Cheung, and Aaron Kwok also played the lead in commercials for Ericsson mobile phones, Smartone Telecommunications Limited, and One2Free Mobile Service, respectively. Some of the advertising campaigns were not just local but also global. For instance, Andy Lau, Aaron Kwok, and Faye Wong became Asian superstars when they endorsed Pepsi-Cola, joining international celebrities such as Michael Jackson, Tina Turner, and Janet Jackson. Songs that were tailor-made to promote other commodities had a close relationship with the visual images of the commercials, turning Cantopop from audio to visual. Commercial Radio organized an election of "Sanctuary-Level" Cantopop lyrics of the decade, and out of the three finalists, two were theme songs for commercials ("Thinking of You Every Day" and "The Call of Love"), proving that they had taken over the TV and movie songs of the 1970s and 1980s. In the meantime, the budget for promoting these commercials was three times that of the production of a Cantopop song. As argued by James Wong, the music industry was not attending to its proper duty, its goal now being set at attracting advertising clients rather than music fans.[16]

---

16. Wong, "The Rise and Decline of Cantopop," 176.

Advertising was nothing new to the popular music industry, but the point of concern was that image had at times become more important than the songs. Unlike the commercial songs in the 1980s (e.g., Willie & The City Band's 威鎮 樂隊 "Sunlight and Air," the theme song of a Hong Kong Towngas commercial, was so popular that it was expanded and turned into a popular song), the Heavenly Kings' songs were carefully designed to be songs that substantiated the themes of the commercials. Jolland Chan, a veteran lyricist and producer who had participated in many joint ventures of record and advertising companies, made clear in an interview that advertising agencies were willing to spend tons of money on the production of the songs and their music videos, and songs were in a supporting role in commercials and the stars' overall images, so to speak. As these stars had to create eye-catching and consistent images, their songs had to be standardized. Moreover, record sales were no longer the main source of income and the music industry became increasingly dependent commercially on media it did not itself control.[17] According to Jolland Chan, despite the fact that "Thinking of You Every Day" (he was the lyricist and producer of this song) was immensely popular, the revenue from record sales was not comparable to the huge budget and profits from the commercials and other related channels.[18] In theory this should have been a win-win situation. Even though the theme songs had to highlight the products and/or services in the commercials, sometimes there was a kind of chemistry between the theme and the song. For instance, the songs in Leon Lai's telecom commercial series were penned by different lyricists (e.g., "Thinking of You Every Day" by Jolland Chan, "Words of Love Not Yet Spoken" by Calvin Poon, and "Just Love Me for One Day" and "I Love You So Much" by Lin Xi), but the different styles of the lyricists were not incorporated into the songs. The problem was that later on record companies were dominated by advertising clients when they had to rely on commercials for the major part of their incomes, and as noted by Jolland Chan, this exerted an adverse impact on the operation of the music industry and hence the quality and variety of Cantopop.[19]

What was more important to the development of Cantopop was that its huge budget brought about a radical structural change in the music industry, one in which small record companies did not have the budget to compete for airplay. While B-list singers also relied more on the income from shooting commercials than from selling records, they were not able to lure major advertising clients due to their lack of big fame outside Hong Kong. The Cantopop industry was thus increasingly dominated by big stars and labels. When

---

17. Simon Frith, "The Popular Music Industry," in *The Cambridge Companion to Pop and Rock*, ed. Simon Frith, Will Straw, and John Street (Cambridge: Cambridge University Press, 2001), 44.
18. Chu, *Songs of Your Life*, 144.
19. Ibid., 146.

Jolland Chan was interviewed in 2007, he bemoaned the lack of Cantopop superstars to succeed the role played by the Four Heavenly Kings in the 1990s, since Cantopop singers could no longer have a long-term relationship with the major advertising campaigns that had turned to Mandapop stars to promote their commodities.

The rise of karaoke also dealt a significant blow to the Cantopop industry. The impact of karaoke, which constituted a distinctive and important cultural practice, on Cantopop was not just negative. In the late 1980s, small-scale karaoke venues became popular in Hong Kong. They helped disseminate popular songs and contributed to the expansion of the fan base for Cantopop. When the first karaoke box chain, "Big Echo," was introduced in Hong Kong in the early 1990s, it created an unexpected impact on local audiences and the music industry. Later, a number of karaoke box chains entered the market, completely altering the ecology of the local music industry. As claimed by Asia's regional managing director of EMI Music, one of the world's biggest record companies, "If you can't sing it in karaoke, it won't be a hit."[20] In brief, karaoke's impact was at least twofold, affecting both the style of Cantopop and the business venture of record companies. The collaboration between record companies and karaoke corporations was profit-making, as the Cantopop industry had a new platform on which to publicize their products. Karaoke later transformed to form a new medium of music entertainment, which was used as a tool for strategic marketing. The big-budget MVs sponsored by advertising agencies were an additional medium used to reach audiences. As the popularity of the songs in karaoke boxes guaranteed sales volume, record companies tended to produce tailor-made "k-songs" that were not only easy to listen to but also easy to sing, as songs are sung aloud in karaoke. Moreover, as karaoke box chains were highly profitable, record companies had to work closely with them to make more money. The income from selling the copyright of a certain hit song to karaoke box chains could be considerably higher than that from record sales. This caused a kind of structural change in the music industry, in which it began to produce k-songs for amateur singers rather than songs for professional listeners.

Closely related to karaoke was the production of MVs. As part of its formula, karaoke must include MVs, and the MVs in the 1980s were a hybrid of records; however, in the 1990s, they were a hybrid of commodities.[21] Karaoke MVs began as low-budget productions, some of which were a hodgepodge of scenes from movies or television programs. Owing to fierce competition in the emerging market of karaoke, more money was chipped in to

---

20. Timothy Dean Taylor, *Global Pop: World Music, World Markets* (New York and London: Routledge, 1997), 200.
21. Frith, "The Popular Music Industry," 44.

produce high-quality MVs to lure fans. At first, the record companies had more resources and inspiration to create the videos, but the problem was that very soon they found that they had to spend much more money on MVs than on the songs themselves. This in turn shifted Cantopop from audio to visual. The idol-worshipping logic highlighted by the industry additionally directed the attention of music fans from the songs to the images of the entertainers. This change fascinated some audience members, but other listeners who preferred songs of quality to flamboyant images were chased away. This also made it more difficult for small record companies to stay in the market. Furthermore, easy-listening/singing k-songs also had a negative impact on the quality of the singers. Some Cantopop singers could not perform live if the songs were not karaoke-style.[22] James Wong slammed the rise of karaoke when he argued that the music industry was putting the cart before the horse, as the music industry was focused on producing k-songs tailor-made for the purgation of fans' feelings.[23]

A related point to note is that idol worshipping even extended to the production team. Not only did managers change their roles,[24] star producers, composers, and lyricists were being marketed with the same operational logic as the singers. Beginning in the mid-1990s, star producers like Michael Au 歐丁玉, composers like Mark Lui 雷頌德 and Keith Chan 陳輝陽, and lyricists like Lin Xi, Wyman Wong 黃偉文, and Canny Leung 梁芷珊 attracted more limelight than commonplace singers did. All of these developments contributed to the stereotypical impression that Cantopop presented to its audiences in the 1990s. However, as mentioned above, if one pays closer attention to the Cantopop of the 1980s, one will observe that Cantopop singers and songs with different styles once coexisted in the mainstream. The problem of standardization did not surface when business was running smoothly. Unfortunately, with the bursting of its bubble economy after the Asian financial crisis, Hong Kong's economic situation was thrown into unprecedented dire straits. One of the consequences of this situation was that the sales of Cantopop dropped drastically and were later taken over by Mandapop.

The Homogenization of Mainstream Cantopop

The 1990s was the decade of the Four Heavenly Kings, and that of Cantopop as well. These male artists bagged all of TVB's Jade Solid Gold Best Male Singer Awards during the 1990s, and from 1991 to 1998, they also shared the Gold Award (and most of the Silver and Bronze Awards) for Best Male Singer

---

22. Chu, *Songs of Your Life*, 146.
23. Wong, "The Rise and Decline of Cantopop," 178.
24. Frith, "The Popular Music Industry," 48.

at the Commercial Radio Annual Awards Ceremony, the two most representative music awards ceremonies in Hong Kong (the RTHK ceremony did not present solo singer awards). As mentioned in the introduction, it was the best of times in the sense that the Four Heavenly Kings dominated showbiz across Chinese communities around the world; it was, however, also the worst of times in the sense that music was no longer the central concern of these multimedia stars. The images of these Heavenly Kings, among others, had utmost importance in the eyes of the investors. Aaron Kwok made a confession in an interview in 2013: "There were many layers of packaging [on me]. The record company gave you an image to do your job. They're extremely protective. They made you think that your image is very important; it's so firmly linked to your work that the two simply couldn't be separated."[25] The multitalented Heavenly Kings further developed the Cantopop industry with record-breaking album sales, full-house concert series, top box-office movies, and unprecedentedly successful commercials. Each of them had their own fans, and the large fan base they created turned Cantopop into a highly profitable business. Although the Heavenly Kings did have their own endeavors in experimenting with new styles, as noted above, they were significantly framed by the music industry to perform mainly easy listening love songs. The sweet melodies and lyrics were tailor-made for audiences, especially female teenagers, to conjure up romantic fancies. One need only to look at the names of the songs, such as "Never-ending Love," "Love You More and More Each Day," "I'm Sorry, I Love You," and "The Call of Love," to identify the key theme of the Heavenly Kings' songs. However, it would be wrong to assume that the mainstream Cantopop industry was not dominated by love songs. Hong Kong Cantopop has almost always been criticized for being overly flooded with love songs. As noted by the renowned lyricist Calvin Poon, "The problem is not that there are too many love songs; it is that there are not enough good love songs."[26] Of course, one might have different definitions of a good love song, but the overemphasis on the standardized success formula of the Four Heavenly Kings would definitely jeopardize the appearance of different styles of love songs targeted at different kinds of audiences, which had a bigger development space in the mainstream Cantopop industry in the 1970s and 1980s.

If Theodor Adorno's criticism of popular music—that it is a standardized commodity[27]—was not applicable to the Hong Kong music industry in the

---

25. Cited from "Aaron Kwok: A Man of Many Parts," *Time Out Hong Kong* (April 10, 2013). Available at: http://www.timeout.com.hk/film/features/57683/aaron-kwok-a-man-of-many-parts.html; retrieved on March 15, 2016.

26. Cited from Chi-Wah Wong, *Taking Music Seriously* 《正視音樂》 (in Chinese) (Hong Kong: No Frills, 1996), 72.

27. Theodor Adorno, "On Popular Music," in *On Record: Rock, Pop and the Written Word*, ed. Simon Frith and Andrew Goodwin (New York: Pantheon Books, 1990), 301–14.

1980s, it was by the 1990s. Despite the fact that Adorno's claim has been debunked in popular music studies, I revert to it again here to underscore the over emphasis on the success formula of mainstream idols. Commercialization is an important aspect of the record industry, and the binary between commercial and creative is unproductive. However, the commercialization of the record industry, as argued by the late James Wong, had become overly short-sighted in the 1990s.[28] During the heyday of the Four Heavenly Kings, nearly all songs were being produced in a similar way, rendering them vulnerable to Adorno's critique of standardization and pseudo-individualization. The trend of teenage groups after the unexpected success of Twins, including Cookies (and later Mini Cookies), 2R, Shine, and Boy'z, is another typical example of how pseudo-individualization operates. This is not to say that there were no songs with other styles, but as the products of the Heavenly Kings were so profitable, record companies were more than happy to stick to the winning formula. The star system existed in the past, but starting in the early 1990s, it developed into a far more mature network. If in Leslie Cheung's and Alan Tam's albums seven to eight out of ten songs were either wistful love ballads or dance-floor jingles, sometimes ten out of ten were so in the albums of the Four Heavenly Kings. In this sense, the Cantopop drop in the late 1990s and the new millennium can be interpreted as a side effect of the Four Heavenly Kings' domination of the market. In the 1980s, when Alan Tam and Leslie Cheung competed to be the King of Cantopop, singers with different styles and target audiences, such as George Lam and Michael Kwan, could also survive. Tina Liu, channel director at 104 FM Select, the Metro Station in Hong Kong, rightly pointed out that in the early 1980s, there was a better balance between pop idols and "non-idols." But in the 1990s, when the Four Heavenly Kings overwhelmed the market, their market share was so large that singers with different styles had to look for opportunities elsewhere. When the mainstream became excessively powerful, popular music culture was marginalized to the extent that it could not make an impact on the music industry. While the sounds of Faye Wong and Anthony Yiu-Ming Wong, among others, can be considered as countering Adorno's claim, some Hong Kong singers that could not survive in the Cantopop industry had to move to Taiwan and later made an impact there. This had already sounded the alarm for Cantopop, which, sadly enough, could not be heard by those who were enjoying big gains guaranteed by the successful formula.

Alex To and Karen Mok (a.k.a. Karen Joy Morris) 莫文蔚 were two of the successful cases of Hong Kong singers moving to Taiwan to further their singing careers in the mid-1990s. Alex To was the winner of TVB's Fourth New Talent Singing Awards in 1985. Like other New Talent winners and participants,

---

28. Wong, "The Rise and Decline of Cantopop," 171–72.

he started his singing career with Capital Artists. He was among the luckier ones, having had the chance to release his debut album, *Just Wanna Stay* 《只想留下》, in 1987. The title song from this album topped the pop charts of TVB and RTHK (at that time CR2 had not yet launched its pop chart), turning Alex To into a rising star in the industry. Actually, the song was a Cantonese rendition of David Was and Don Was's "Where Did Your Heart Go?" (covered by Wham! In 1986), showing that Alex To, probably owing to the musical background of his Filipino-singer father, was not simply a middle-of-the-road Cantopop singer. Some of his songs were heavily influenced by Western soul music, which was not common in mainstream Cantopop. His next album, *Waiting for Dawn* 《等待黎明》, was also a success, with two chart-topping songs—"Waiting for Dawn" and "Hold Me Tight" 〈抱緊我〉. In the next few years he continued to introduce soul and R&B into his Cantopop, which was not totally welcomed by Cantopop fans but he still managed to fare reasonably well in the local market. In 1990, he released his first Mandapop album, *Talk about Love* 《談情說愛》, in Taiwan. With the rise of the Four Heavenly Kings in the early 1990s, Alex To found that his music style was not a good fit for the mainstream Cantopop industry, and he decided to leave Hong Kong and focus on the Taiwanese market in the mid-1990s. Although he did not win any major music awards in Taiwan, he was widely recognized as an outstanding singer. He was hailed as "Outstanding Male Singer" (Taiwan) by The Pop Charts of Chinese Original Music in 2001, and *Follow Me Your Whole Life* 《跟着我一輩子》 (2000) was one of the Ten Best Albums awarded by HitRadio in Taiwan.

Karen Mok was a similar and very successful case of a Hong Kong songstress developing her career in Taiwan. Although Karen Mok entered show business as a Cantopop singer in 1993 with her debut album *Karen*, she was arguably better known by Hong Kong audiences as an actress, thanks to her performance in the remarkable Stephen Chow two-part classic *A Chinese Odyssey* 《大話西遊》 in 1995. She confessed in an interview almost twenty years after the release of her debut album that "[a]t the very beginning, when I first started in show-business, everything was more conservative. I was literally forced to wear some really 'princessy' outfits. That was kind of the way everyone did it."[29] Apparently Karen Mok was not happy with the "princess" style, and thus her singing career did not start well. With increased popularity after *A Chinese Odyssey*, she signed with Rock Records to release another Cantopop album, *Karen Mok in Totality* 《全身莫文蔚》, in 1996. In Cantonese "in totality" (literally "whole body") and "completely new" are homonyms. The album

---

29. Cited from "Karen Mok," *Time Out Hong Kong* (September 12, 2012). Available at: http://www.timeout.com.hk/feature-stories/features/53116/karen-mok.html; retrieved on March 15, 2016.

was made with experimental styles to show Cantopop audiences a brand new Karen Mok—"a completely new team of musicians, an exemplary work in totality (with whole body)," as reflected by the promotion slogan. To echo the theme of the album, she even showed her whole body from the back, lying on a sofa, in the cover photo. In the end, however, the album won decent reviews but failed in terms of sales, showing that Karen Mok's attempt to crossover from mainstream to avant-garde music (e.g., the main plug being "Wet" 〈潮濕〉) did not pay off. Her debut Mandarin album, *To Be* 《做自己》, released in Taiwan in 1997, was a sharp contrast in terms of popularity. She was so well liked by Mandapop audiences that the next year she won the Most Popular Female Singer Award at the Super Live Awards Taiwan. It was thus understandable that in subsequent years she concentrated on the Mandapop market. She did not need long to sweep many Mandapop awards, including the Most Popular Female Singer of the Year at the China Music Chart Awards in 2000.

The diva did not forget her native Cantonese, though (she was born in Hong Kong to a half-Chinese, half-Welsh father and a half-Chinese, one-quarter Iranian, and one-quarter German mother). In 2001, she tested the Cantopop waters again with another Cantopop album, *Golden Flower* 《一朵金花》, with new experiments of hybridizing electronic music, such as techno and breakbeat, with Chinese instruments. The outcome in terms of reception by audiences proved to be far from promising once more. After that she focused on the Mandapop market and went on to make history in Hong Kong popular music by being the first female artist from Hong Kong ever to win the Best Female Mandarin Artist at Taiwan's prestigious Golden Melody Awards in 2003. In a 2012 interview she was asked if she felt she had to turn to the Mainland or Taiwan to be more experimental. Her answer was in a sense cryptic: "I've been really lucky branching out to different markets and territories very early on in my career. Taiwan and Mainland China are bigger markets so they embrace more versatility."[30] Hailed by *Billboard* as an "Asian Superstar,"[31] Karen Mok turned global in 2013 with her first English album, *Somewhere I Belong*. Her international fame, ironically enough, did not have much to do with Cantopop, the genre of her mother tongue. In short, Karen Mok and Alex To are two prominent examples who, although known for different music and performing styles, were not well received in Hong Kong in the 1990s. They had to move to Taiwan for greener pastures, where they further developed their music careers.

---

30. Cited from "Karen Mok."
31. "Asian Superstar Karen Mok Explores New Territories with 'Belong'," *Billboard* (February 28, 2013). Available at: http://www.billboard.com/articles/news/1550124/asian-superstar-karen-mok-explores-new-territories-with-belong; retrieved on March 15, 2016.

Transformation of the Mediascape

In terms of sales, the decline of Cantopop started in the mid-1990s. In the early 1990s, the swift development of global media had a very significant impact on the Cantopop industry, which later proved to be a heavy blow to its operation. As mentioned above, the development of the Chinese music industry became transnational and media consumption was deterritorialized in the early 1990s, which led the Hong Kong music industry to face an irreversible structural change it did not realize at the outset. The globalization of the mediascape in the early 1990s created a market environment favorable to the swift development of Mandapop, which later led to the downfall of Cantopop in the late 1990s. In the new globalized Chinese music industry, the prospect of Mandapop was much brighter than that of Cantopop. Record companies, with an eye toward the growing Mandapop market, redirected their resources to the production of Mandapop before long. Steve Jones's account of American popular music can well be applied to the situation in Hong Kong: to achieve commercial success, the commerce of commerce is more important than the commerce of music.[32] In an era of "Two Sides of the China Strait," to borrow James Wong's words,[33] this at first facilitated the success of the Cantopop Kings in Asia, but later exposed standardized Cantopop to harsh competition with Mandapop from different music cultures. The mediascape in Hong Kong also transformed very rapidly in the early 1990s, with the rise of transnational karaoke companies and broadcasters, and "the relocating of cores of production . . . affect[ing] how widely consumed cultural forms [were] made."[34]

Meanwhile, the transformation of the mediascape in the early 1990s was also reflected in the deterritorialization of media consumption. Previously, Hong Kong, as a cosmopolitan city, was notorious for its small number of media channels: only two free television stations and three radio stations. In the past these limited channels had a stranglehold on what audiences saw and heard. In the early 1990s, the scene changed. The broadcasting of cable television and satellite television in the early 1990s multiplied the media channels by several times. While the localization of free television and the movie industry in the 1970s led to a glorious era of Hong Kong popular culture, the globalization of the mediascape in the early 1990s ironically led to its downfall. As far as music is concerned, the channels provided by these new media were mostly Mandarin-speaking, as the Mandarin market was obviously considerably

---

32. Steve Jones, "Who Fought the Law? The American Music Industry and the Global Popular Music Market," in *Rock and Popular Music: Politics, Policies, Institutions*, ed. Tony Bennett et al. (London: Routledge, 1993), 94.
33. Wong, "The Rise and Decline of Cantopop," 151.
34. Taylor, *Global Pop*, 200.

larger. The new choices did provide Hong Kong audiences with the chance to listen to Mandapop from Taiwan, Singapore, Malaysia, and Mainland China, but it seemed to be having adverse effects on Cantopop. Record companies, with an eye toward the growing Mandapop market, redirected resources to the production of Mandapop before long. At first, the influence could be said to be mutually beneficial. Record companies such as Music Factory, which later became Rock Records, came to Hong Kong and released some excellent albums such as *Queen's Road East*, which mapped the best post-1989 imaginaries of Hong Kong's relationship with Mainland China. However, it was very disappointing from the view of Cantopop lovers when Rock Records later shifted its attention to the market in Mainland China and ceased to produce Cantopop. In the fans' view, Hong Kong was just used as a springboard to the huge market in Mainland China, which was reinforced by the outlook of Greg Rogers, senior VP at MCA Music Entertainment International, Asia-Pacific: "Mandarin is an increasingly important language for music in the region. That will probably accelerate somewhat, and then, for Chinese repertoire at least, Hong Kong becomes increasingly irrelevant to the equation."[35]

The change of the mediascape lured Cantopop singers, including the Four Heavenly Kings, to woo the Mandapop market. The rise of an international repertoire profoundly influenced how record companies marketed their products: "It is those artists who have previously achieved international success and who are releasing a new album who will have little difficulty attracting radio play and media coverage and gaining sales."[36] To court huge markets by thinking more "internationally," record companies and Cantopop singers actively turned to Mandapop. Starting from the early 1990s, many leading Hong Kong Cantopop singers released more Mandapop than Cantopop albums. Worse yet, while Cantopop singers turned to Mandapop for more opportunities, Mandapop singers encroached into the Hong Kong market. Before the advent of Mandapop stars in the mid-1990s, Hong Kong audiences enjoyed the privilege of listening to Cantopop sung by Mandapop singers. In the beginning, Mandapop singers such as Nicky Wu 吳奇隆 and Jeff Chang 張信哲 still had to follow the successful Taiwanese singers in the 1980s, that is, to sing Cantopop to please the local audience. But it did not take long for Mandapop singers to gain the upper hand and enthrall Cantopop audiences with their own Mandapop.

---

35. Geoff Burpee, "As Sun Sets on British Empire in Hong Kong, Industry Gears for Return to China," *Billboard* 108, Issue 43 (October 26, 1996): APQ-1. As perceptively noted by an anonymous reviewer, the story that Cantopop was once strong and later taken over by Mandapop with the rise of China reads a bit oversimplistic. In terms of music industry, Mandapop has also been facing a crisis, and in recent years its revenues came primarily from performances, not from record sales. Furthermore, in terms of scholarly attention, as noted above, both Cantopop and Mandapop have received very little scholarly attention.

36. Keith Negus, *Music Genres and Corporate Cultures* (London and New York: Routledge, 1999), 157.

In the new millennium, when Cantopop was struggling hard to keep afloat, Jay Chou, Stefanie Sun 孫燕姿, and F4 overtook the Four Heavenly Kings and Sammi Cheng in terms of commercial viability. Instant stardom was no longer the monopoly of the Hong Kong pop industry. "While Cantopop marches on in Hong Kong, Chinese pop has moved elsewhere, on to Mandarin singer/songwriters, Taiwanese folk artists, Beijing rockers, Singapore balladeers."[37]

Faye Wong (a.k.a. Shirley Wong 王靖雯) is a prime example of the paradigm shift from Cantopop to Mandapop. When she started her singing career back in the late 1980s, she used the name Shirley Wong (in Cantonese "Ching-Man Wong"). Born in Beijing, Faye Wong moved to Hong Kong in 1987 to join her father who was working there. Actually, her singing career began before she left Beijing. In 1985, she was selected by a record company in Beijing to release her first album, *Where Does the Wind Come From?* 《風從哪裡來？》, featuring the songs of Teresa Teng, who was arguably the most popular singer in the Mainland then. From 1985 to 1987, she released a total of six cassettes before she left for the then British colony. In Hong Kong she gradually picked up Cantonese, and after two years of lessons with a renowned Hong Kong music teacher who had previously tutored Leon Lai, she was introduced to Cinepoly Records, a subsidiary of PolyGram. Faye Wong grabbed the limelight by winning the Bronze Award at the Asia-Pacific Popular Song Contest in 1989 with "Still the Old Sentence" 〈仍是舊句子〉, a typical love ballad, which was later included on her first Cantopop album, *Shirley Wong* 《王靖雯》, the new Hong Kong–style name given to her by the record company to replace her "Mainland-sounding" name. It is worthwhile noting that she might have been destined to meet Lin Xi, who penned the lyrics of the main plug of the album, "The Other Day, Helpless" 〈無奈那天〉, and later became her dream collaborator. In 1990, she went on to release two big sellers, *Everything* and *You're the Only One*, which were so popular that they won her the Bronze Award for Best Female Singer at the Commercial Radio Annual Awards Ceremony. Her music, while mainstream, was not without style. The R&B cover versions of EPO, Diana Ross, and Karyn White songs in *You're the Only One* did let her stand out from other new Cantopop singers at the time. But image packaging was perhaps another thing. "During the late 1980s and early 1990s mainland Chinese singers were stigmatized by Cantopop industry executives and music consumers as lacking the fashionable and cosmopolitan qualities of their Hong Kong counterparts."[38] As the record company was determined to groom her for stardom, they provided her with not just a new name but also a Hong Kong–style look. As she lamented in an interview: "What I wore

---

37. Burpee, "As Sun Sets on British Empire in Hong Kong, Industry Gears for Return to China."
38. Michael Curtin and Anthony Fung, "The Anomalies of Being Faye (Wong): Gender Politics in Chinese Popular Music," *International Journal of Cultural Studies* 5, no. 3 (2002): 263–90.

was picked by other people, and my name was changed, too. Everything was decided by other people, that's not who I was at all."[39] At that point, triggered by unsettled issues in her contract, she decided that she did not fit into showbiz. Having no sense of direction and suffering from a personality crisis, she went to the United States for some time off.

The New York trip did give her new inspiration, and, more importantly, she met her new agent, Katie Chan 陳家瑛, after she returned to Hong Kong, who offered her a plinth to become a new Faye Wong in her next album, *Coming Home*, released in 1992. The English name "Faye"—a homophone of her own Chinese name—appeared on the cover of the album, although in Chinese she was still called "Ching-Man Wong." It was nonetheless symbolic, showing that the diva-to-be was determined to claim herself back. The 1992 album incorporated an R&B style and included the English song "Kisses in the Wind," but strictly speaking it was not totally different from her previous works. The song "An Easily Hurt Woman" 〈容易受傷的女人〉, a cover version of Miyuki Nakashima's "Rouge," topped pop charts and hit karaoke boxes, winning her not just awards but also capital to make further changes in her subsequent albums. In an interview with CNN in 1998, she made it clear that "An Easily Hurt Woman" did not represent her. Described by the CNN anchor as a performer who can "break away from the typical mode of performance in Asia,"[40] Faye Wong's genuine change arguably began in *No Regrets* 《執迷不悔》 released in 1993. She was still using the Hong Kong–style Chinese name on the album cover, but she was definitely no longer the "Ching-Man Wong" packaged by the Cantopop industry. The album included two versions of the song "No Regrets," in Cantonese and Mandarin (the lyrics of the Mandarin version were written by Faye Wong), bringing her mother tongue back into her singing career. "Ching-Man Wong" continued her metamorphosis in the album released later that year, *One Hundred Thousand Whys?* 《十萬個為什麼？》. She played a greater role in its production, as shown in her own work "Crush" 〈動心〉—both melody and lyrics. The most popular hit on that album was "Cold War" 〈冷戰〉, a cover version of Tori Amos's "Silent All These Years." The chemistry between the melody, Lin Xi's lyrics, and Faye Wong's performance helped the songstress find a different kind of style in the midst of mainstream Cantopop ballads. Not only did she make a breakthrough in her music style, her avant-garde images, such as the "pineapple-styled" hairdo and see-through dress with mohair underwear-like shorts, shocked audiences, who gradually disremembered the old "Ching-Man Wong."

39. "An Interview with Faye Wong by Yang Lan" (January 31, 2011). Available at: https://www.youtube.com/watch?v=IZiyMI8z440; retrieved on March 15, 2016.
40. Cited from the interview "Faye on CNN." Available at: https://www.youtube.com/watch?v=fR6RG9_2XmE; retrieved on March 15, 2016.

In Faye Wong's career, 1994 was a year of significance. That year she released *Random Thoughts* 《胡思亂想》, the last time she relied mainly on cover versions. For the first time her own Chinese name, "Fei Wang," appeared on the cover, probably a signal that she had left her "Ching-Man Wong" years behind. The two cover versions of the Scottish post-punk group Cocteau Twins' "Bluebeard" and "Know Who You Are at Every Age"—"Random Thoughts" 〈胡思亂想〉 and "Know Yourself and Your Enemy" 〈知己知彼〉—marked her effort to distinguish herself from other mainstream Cantopop songstresses. She also started working with Wei Dao 竇唯 and Yadong Zhang 張亞東, alternative Beijing musicians. The title of the next Cantopop album she released in the same year, *To Please Myself* 《討好自己》, spoke a thousand words. She wrote the lyrics of the title song, showing her determination to use her music to please herself. Her indifferent, if not hostile, attitude toward the media— perhaps a marketing strategy—was a good example of her reticent character. As was noted, "[i]n the political economy of music, Faye challenges, distorts and transforms the prevailing market logic, and by that twisting, she further commodifies her image and her music while at the same time enhancing her cultural capital."[41] Interestingly enough, the song that stood out on that album was "The Edge between Love and Pain" 〈愛與痛的邊緣〉, a relatively mainstream Cantopop love ballad similar to "An Easily Hurt Woman" (the lyrics of both songs were penned by Calvin Poon). Faye Wong might not have been totally pleased, but that song won her more capital, including TVB's Jade Solid Gold Most Popular Female Singer Award and the Asia Pacific Most Popular Hong Kong Female Singer Award, so that she could complete her metamorphosis. The irony was that deep down in the heart of the new Cantopop diva was Mandapop. In fact, she also released two Mandapop albums in 1994— *Mystery* 《迷》 and *Sky* 《天空》—which were so popular, not only in Taiwan but also in the emerging Mainland market, that they paved the way for her "return" to Mandapop. The song "I Do" 〈我願意〉 in *Mystery* became one of the all-time classics in the history of Mandapop.

In 1995, Faye Wong released her last full Cantopop album, *Di-Dar* (excluding later EPs such as *Toys* 《玩具》), and after that she recorded mostly in her native Mandarin. Faye Wong graced the cover of *Di-Dar* like a charming and delightful butterfly, signaling the completion of her metamorphosis. The lyrics of all the songs (except for the only Mandarin one, "Shooting Star" 〈流星〉) were written by Lin Xi, and this was the beginning of a beautiful friendship and collaboration. Lin Xi, the lyricist par excellence, composed some of the most beautiful Chinese lyrics for Faye Wong in subsequent albums, the most remarkable ones being the first five songs that explored the theme of searching for love in the 2000 album *Fable* 《寓言》. "Di-Dar" and "Ambiguous" 〈曖昧〉 were

41. Curtin and Fung, "The Anomalies of Being Faye (Wong)," 286.

among the more well-known songs on that album. As noted above, Faye Wong did have some new Cantopop EPs released after she left Cinepoly to join EMI to focus mostly on Mandapop. Thanks to Cinepoly's market calculations, Faye Wong's Cantopop fans continued to have the chance to listen to her new Cantopop (recorded before she left Cinepoly) in different albums, including the EPs *Toys* and *Help Yourself* 《自便》in 1997. "Undercurrent" 〈暗湧〉and "Rendezvous" 〈約定〉on *Toys*, lyrics written by Lin Xi, have become two of the most romantic songs in the history of Cantopop—the former evincing one's disbelief in love and the latter one's belief in love. "Rendezvous" was in a sense ironic for die-hard Cantopop fans—Faye Wong was turning her eyes to the Asian market by producing Mandapop, English, and Japanese songs. After shifting her focus, her reputation soared in Asia. The Cantopop songstress successfully transformed into a world diva when *Time* magazine dubbed her a songbird joining "the chorus of women heard around the world."[42] Her decision was in this sense correct, but her often-reported distaste for the commercial Hong Kong entertainment industry was not justified. Some of her greatest Mandapop hits that topped pop charts (e.g., "I Do," "Red Bean" 〈紅豆〉, and "The Moon Back Then" 〈當時的月亮〉) were actually rather traditional romantic ballads. Be that as it may, the profit-oriented Cantopop industry was able to make megastars in the 1990s. From Shirley to Faye, a new diva of pop was born. But the sound of her voice later took on a sad tone when Cantopop witnessed a paradigm shift that led to its decline and the rise of Mandapop.

The Heavenly Queens

Faye Wong was not the only Cantopop diva in the 1990s. Shortly before the semi-retirement of Anita Mui, female singers Sally Yeh, Sandy Lam, and Priscilla Chan had already come on the scene in the late 1980s. Until she ceased to accept music awards, Anita Mui bagged almost all of the Most Popular Female Singer awards. In the early 1990s, Cantopop fans had a chance to witness the rise of a new Cantopop songstress to stardom. Sally Yeh was the first one to be crowned as the new Cantopop Queen. She won TVB's Jade Solid Gold Most Popular Female Singer Award for four consecutive years beginning in 1990. Before achieving this title, Sally Yeh won a Jade Solid Gold Song Award with "00:10" in 1984. She was a popular Cantopop songstress, as well as film actress, but her singing career was overshadowed by the legendary Anita Mui in the late 1980s. While her "Blessing" 〈祝福〉received the Gold Song Gold Award at the Jade Solid Gold Awards in 1988, she had to wait until the turn of the decade to succeed Anita Mui to become the Most Popular Female Singer.

---

42. "The Divas of Pop," *TIME* cover (October 14, 1996).

Unlike Anita Mui's famous ever-changing image, which sometimes crossed gender stereotypes, Sally Yeh's style was typically feminine. Most of her songs were about a woman's longing for love and pain of separation. Her master-pieces, such as "Burning My Heart with Fire" 〈焚心以火〉 and "A Woman's Weakness" 〈女人的弱點〉, were prime examples of women's willingness to sacrifice for love and women's weakness in a relationship, which was also the typical female emotions of Faye Wong's early songs.

While Sally Yeh dominated TVB's Jade Solid Gold Awards in the early 1990s, Sandy Lam was the favorite of CR2's award ceremonies. She won the Gold Award and the Bronze Award for Best Female Singer at the Commercial Radio Annual Awards Ceremony for three consecutive years, beginning in 1990, until the rising Faye Wong took her place in 1994. In other words, between the reigns of Anita Mui and Faye Wong, Sally Yeh and Sandy Lam shared the queen's throne of Cantopop. Sandy Lam also started her singing career in the 1980s. Her debut album, *Lam Yik Lin* (her Chinese name), was released in 1985, and her image was just an "I Don't Know Love" kind of teenage girl. Then she turned into a dancing queen in, among others, *Grey* 《灰色》 (1987) and *City Rhythm* (1988). She was very popular but, not unlike Sally Yeh, she was dancing under the shadow of Anita Mui. In the 1990s, she transformed her image to a less mainstream singer, voicing alternative female sensibilities. In *Dream, Crazy, Tired* (a.k.a. *Drifting*) 《夢了倦了瘋了》 she experimented with a new R&B style with Singaporean composer Dick Lee 李炳文, paving the way for her transformation in *Wild Flowers* 《野花》 toward a more-than-mainstream image. The most successful song in the album was arguably "Without You, I Still Love You" 〈沒有你還是愛你〉, a cover version of Beverley Craven's signature song "Promise Me." In the meantime, Sandy Lam was also developing her Taiwanese market. Her first two Mandapop albums, *Home Again without You* 《愛上一個不回家的人》 (1990) and *City Heart* 《都市心》 (1991) were testing the waters with her style branded in Hong Kong in the late 1980s. She started working with renowned Taiwanese musician Jonathan Lee 李宗盛 on her third Mandapop album, *Don't Care Who I Am* 《不必在乎我是誰》 (1993), which was not only career-changing but also life-changing for her. Not long after they sang "When Love Fades Away" 〈當愛已成往事〉 (included in that album), the theme song of Chen Kaige's *Farewell My Concubine* 《霸王別姬》, they fell in love and later got married in 1998. Sandy Lam did release some Cantopop albums in the mid-1990s, but once she established her relationship, her main interest was no longer in the mainstream Cantopop market.

Cass Phang's 彭羚 first song was a duet sung with Louis Yuen 阮兆祥 in 1989, which was not a big hit but it was able to enter the CR2 pop chart. Dubbed "Commercial Radio's daughter-in-law" by the media, Cass Phang was the favored female singer of CR2, alongside Sandy Lam. She not only received awards from CR2, but later she also won TVB's Jade Solid Gold Most Popular Female Singer Award in 1995, succeeding the legendary Faye Wong. Cass Phang released her debut album, *With Love*, with the small record company Rock-In in 1990. Although she was awarded the Bronze Award for New Female Singer by Commercial Radio, she had to wait until the next year for her first chart-topping song, "I'll Wait Even If I Was Hurt" 〈愛過痛過亦願等〉, included in her second album, *Somewhere in Time*. Despite the fact that her next two albums released by Rock-In had decent sales, her career did not soar until she moved to EMI and released *So Beautiful . . . To Be With You* 《有著你⋯⋯多麼美》 in 1994. The main plug, "If I Can't Have Love" 〈如果得不到愛情〉, topped the charts of all major media, showing that Cass Phang was not just the favorite of CR2. Thereafter, she began to bag song awards from all mainstream media, and 1995 was a year of significance in her career. Her "Still Love You Most" 〈仍然是最愛你〉 (theme song of the TVB drama *Fate of the Clairvoyant* 《再見亦是老婆》), "All Because of You" 〈完全因你〉, theme song of Chow Yun Fat's movie *Peace Hotel* 《和平飯店》), "Awake from Dreams" 〈如夢初醒〉, and "Small Token of Love" 〈小玩意〉 were all big hits, helping her win the Most Popular Female Singer awards at both Jade Solid Gold and CR2. As apparent in the tiles of those songs (and in fact many others as well), Cass Phang's songs were about romantic love from the eyes of a girl and later a young woman. According to Sandy Cheung 張美賢, lyricist of "I'll Wait Even If I Was Hurt," the female stereotype could have been attributed to market demand. Only the leading lyricists had bargaining power to present alternative imaginaries.[43] Sandy Cheung later did articulate the importance of female subjectivity in the songs of Cass Phang and other female singers, such as "I Have My Own World" 〈我有我天地〉. Furthermore, since Cass Phang wanted to be a singer more than an idol, she maintained a relatively low profile compared with other Cantopop divas. In the next couple of years she continued to release several decent-selling albums, but as reported by the media she was dating the CR2 idol disc jockey Jan Lamb 林海峰 then, so she was not focusing solely on her music. After their marriage in 1998, Mrs. Lamb continued to have some golden hits, but they were phased out after the 1999 album *A Flower* 《一枝花》, in which "To All the Boys I Loved Before" 〈給我愛過的男孩們〉 was one of her greatest hits.

As Cass Phang reached the peak of her career in 1995, another Cantopop Queen was ready to make a transformation. Sammi Cheng, after a long vacation owing to a contract row with Capital Artists, signed with Warner Music to turn a new page in her career. The first chapter of her singing career

---

43. Sandy Cheung said this in an interview; cited from Chu, *Songs of Your Life*, 169–70.

was written with Capital Artists after she won the Bronze Award in the New Talents Singing Competition at the age of 15 in 1988. Because of her age, in the next couple of years she had just two duets with David Lui, a New Talents winner who was already an established singer then, which were songs from the TVB martial arts drama *Secret of the Linked Cities* 《連城訣》. In 1990, Sammi Cheng was mature enough to release her Cantopop debut, *Sammi* 《鄭秀文》. She was a promising new star but did not truly shine until she tested a brand new image, after the successful dance song "Red Hot Motion La La La" 〈火熱動感 La La La〉 (with Aaron Kwok, Andy Hui, and Edmond Leung 梁漢文) in her fourth album, *Sammi Cheng's Labyrinth of Happiness* 《鄭秀文的快樂迷宮》 (1993). The main plug, "Chotto, Wait, Wait" 〈Chotto 等等〉, was a fast-beat dance song that significantly distinguished her from other leading songstresses. While she continued to produce romantic ballads (such as "Do You Really Have Me in Your Heart?" 〈其實你心裡有沒有我〉, a love duet classic with Andy Hui) and dance songs (such as "Ding Dong" 〈叮噹〉), a contract issue kept her out for nine months until she came back with *Can't Afford Losing You* 《捨不得你》 in November 1995. It sold more than triple platinum (150,000 copies) in Hong Kong, and not only the main plugs but also some side cuts (e.g., "The Love Story in Autumn and Winter" 〈秋冬愛的故事〉, "The Swansong of Love" 〈愛的輓歌〉, and "A Shot of Tequila" 〈Tequila 一杯〉) entered the pop charts. Starting with that album, perhaps inspired by Anita Mui, Sammi Cheng's "Can't Afford Losing You" and "Gentlemen, You're So Fine Today" 〈男仕今天你很好〉 articulated two different, if not opposite, kinds of female emotions—the former an archetypal woman's love song and the latter a strong dance-beat mockery of men's dominant position in society. Sammi Cheng's (de)construction of female stereotypes further developed in her next album with two similar endeavors, namely "Can't Let Go" 〈放不低〉 and "Beware of Women" 〈小心女人〉. In the same year, she held her first Hong Kong Coliseum concert, which was immensely popular, and her Nike-esque eyebrows became one of the most iconic looks in Cantopop history. Her transgression of gender stereotypes offered a unique image among the Cantopop divas, and she collected Most Popular Female Singer awards in 1996. In the latter half of the 1990s, similar to some other leading Cantopop singers, she diverted more time to the Mandapop market in Taiwan. Doing well in the Taiwanese market, she also managed to produce Cantopop hits. Her song "Episode" 〈插曲〉 won the Gold Song Gold Award (1999) at the Jade Solid Gold Awards, and she became the second female singer to achieve this prize in the decade of the Four Heavenly Kings (the first was Sally Yeh in 1990).

When Sammi Cheng had a brand new start in 1995, another Cantopop Queen released her debut Cantopop album. That year Kelly Chen 陳慧琳

starred in the film *Whatever Will Be, Will Be* 《仙樂飄飄》, together with Heavenly King Aaron Kwok, and the theme song "Everything's Wonderful Just Because of You" 〈一切很美只因有你〉 was, not surprisingly, a big hit. In the same year, after her collaboration with three other new stars in the album *Open the Sky* 《打開天空》 she released her debut solo album, *Charming Lover* 《醉迷情人》, masterminded by Mark Lui, a rising star musician and composer of "Everything's Wonderful Just Because of You." Mark Lui began his experiments with different combinations of musical instruments, such as synthesizer, drum, and guitar, back in his school days in England. His experimental arrangements brought a new character to mainstream Cantopop in *Charming Lover*, helping Kelly Chen get her career off to a good start. That year she bagged almost all of the new talent awards at various music award ceremonies, becoming the most eye-catching female rising star. She quickly ascended in her professional career with her next album, *Wind, Flower, Snow* 《風花雪》 (1996), the title song of which was the theme song of the film *Lost and Found* 《天涯海角》. As the female lead of the film, she benefited from the synergy between the two industries (which was very common in the 1980s and gradually disappeared in the new millennium), and the song "Wind, Flower, Snow" swept many music awards at the end of the year. It also helped her score her first concert at the Hong Kong Coliseum in January of the following year, and in less than two years after her debut she had already become a Cantopop Queen. Her next album, *Starry Dream of Love* 《星夢情真》, could be considered a side-product of her "Starry Dream" concerts held in Hong Kong Coliseum later that year, attesting to the popularity of the new Queen. As arguably the Cantopop celebrity who had the least amount of gossip reported by the media, she steadily developed her career and was crowned the Most Popular Female Singer for the first time by TVB's Jade Solid Gold Awards in 1999. She was among the few Cantopop stars who continued to fare well in both the music and movie industries in the new millennium.

As outlined above, most of the gold hits of the Cantopop divas were in one way or another love ballads embodying female sensibilities. That was not the whole picture though. Amanda Lee 李蕙敏, ex-member of the female duo Echo, which disbanding in 1992, started her solo career after a short spell with Commercial Radio as a disc jockey. While her debut album *Debut* (1994) was unexceptional, the second one, *Goodbye My Love in Yokohama* 《橫濱別戀》 (1995), did make noise for her. Though the main plug, a typical love story as seen from the title, was popular, another song really stood out from the rest—"Live a Life Better Than Yours" 〈活得比你好〉. The lyrics were penned by Wyman Wong, Amanda Lee's partner in her CR2 radio program who later became a leading lyricist-cum-fashion trendsetter, which abandoned the stereotypical image of a woman having lost her love. The sequel to this song,

"You Won't Have (a Good Ending)" 〈你沒有（好結果）〉, deconstructed Cantopop's female image by openly wishing bad things to happen to her departed lover. But the energy of the new woman did not last long. The next few albums did have similar songs, such as "I Live for Myself" 〈我為我生存〉 and "Revenge of the Princess" 〈公主復仇記〉, but they failed to make the same impact as the previous ones. The styles of the Cantopop Queens were in fact more diversified than the Heavenly Kings' (given the limited space, we cannot touch upon some other songstresses like Shirley Kwan, Vivian Chow 周慧敏, and Vivian Lai 黎瑞恩). But in a sense, no matter the Kings or the Queens, they were mainly singing the theme of love. One needs only to look at the titles of the songs to be convinced. Love is of course the main theme of most, if not all, popular songs, but in the 1990s, the mainstream was so popular that other topics and genres found it difficult to survive.

Alternative Imaginaries and Undercurrents

Despite the fact that the 1990s were dominated by the Heavenly Kings and Queens, there were also undercurrents which kept the music industry heterogeneous to a certain extent. As noted in the previous section, some female singers did embody the image of traditional women longing for love, but there were also others who crossed the gender boundaries to problematize that image. Interestingly enough, these alternative imaginaries were often penned by male lyricists (such as Lin Xi, Wyman Wong, and Thomas Chow 周禮茂). Hong Kong Cantopop had long been dominated by male lyricists, but some of them were in a sense androgynous. In the Chinese literary tradition, lyrics, as opposed to poetry, were commonly seen as a genre of personal feelings, and thus highly suitable for expressing intimate emotions. When compared with the love ballads of the Heavenly Kings, the Queens were able to explore different possibilities. From "A Woman's Weakness" and "An Easily Hurt Woman" to "Beware of Women" and "You Won't Have (a Good Ending)," the male lyricists were able to empathize with women from different angles. The latter's famous deconstruction of the traditional female image by Wyman Wong, for instance, successfully injected into the mainstream an alternative imaginary. A related alternative attempt was queer discourse. Cantopop, like most other popular songs, was dominated by heterosexual love. Homosexual relationships were seen by many as taboo in mainstream popular songs. In the midst of the standardized romantic ballads of the 1990s, there were some courageous attempts to diversify love relationships in Cantopop. Although Tat Ming Pair did have similar attempts back in the late 1980s ("Forbidden Color" 〈禁色〉 and "Forget He or She" 〈忘記他是她〉), and Grasshopper's "Paradise Lost" 〈失樂園〉 was also a similar daring challenge of traditional values, fans had to wait until Leslie Cheung came back from retirement to see a beautiful crossing of gender boundaries.

During the heyday of the Four Heavenly Kings, Leslie Cheung made a comeback in 1995 after a six-year retirement from the music industry. His first "comeback" album, *Beloved* 《寵愛》, was a tremendous success (the best-selling Cantopop album of the year), mostly due to the popularity of the theme songs of his movies, such as "Song at Midnight" 〈夜半歌聲〉 and "Chase" 〈追〉. Undoubtedly, he enthralled Cantopop fans with his increased charisma, but in terms of making a genuine breakthrough, it was with the 1996 album *Red* 《紅》. In one of his signature movies, the Cannes Film Festival award-winning *Farewell My Concubine*, Leslie Cheung played a gender-bending role that stole the limelight. His androgynous style began to shine in *Red*. "Grieving Man" 〈怨男〉, among others, showcased the unique beauty of a man, which was unprecedented in the Cantopop industry. In the following year he starred in Wong Kar-Wai's *Happy Together* 《春光乍洩》, an exotic romance between two handsome men. During his World Tour 97, a bustlingly spectacular series of concerts, he blew his fans away with his red high heels. "The rhetoric of cross-dressing in his concerts, as Cheung explained, [was] meant to express a femininity that he had within."[44] In the 1999 album *Count Down with You* 《陪你倒數》, the main plug "Left Hand Right Hand" 〈左右手〉, swept song awards presented by RTHK, Commercial Radio, and Metro Radio, becoming one of the most popular songs of the year. The interesting point was that, as a mainstream love ballad, the lyrics written by Lin Xi were in a way cryptic: "Since then I have fallen in love with my left hand; since then I have despised my right hand." Bearing the Chinese saying of "male left female right" in mind, it was not unreasonable for audiences to presume that the song was about homosexuality. In the same album there was another song, "Comrade" 〈同道中人〉, that reinforced this speculation. But Leslie Cheung never openly declared his sexual orientation; however, it was noted that "Cheung [was] a queer icon because—not in spite—of his ambivalence."[45] Even in his later Mandapop song "I Am What I Am" 〈我〉, a self-confession inspired by *La Cage Aux Folles*, he still remained ambiguous: "I have no need to hide; I live my life the way I like." No matter what these songs were implying, that a pop legend was willing to use songs like "Left Hand Right Hand" as main plugs did mean something. As convincingly noted by Natalia Sui-Hung Chan, a big fan of and an expert on Leslie Cheung, "[t]he endless varieties of cross-gender performances Cheung

---

44. Natalia Sui-Hung Chan, "Queering Body and Sexuality: Leslie Cheung's Gender Representation in Hong Kong Popular Music," 137. Yau Ching, ed., *As Normal As Possible: Negotiating Sexuality and Gender in Mainland China and Hong Kong* (Hong Kong: Hong Kong University Press, 2010), 137.
45. Helen Hok-Sze Leung, *Undercurrents: Queer Culture and Postcolonial Hong Kong* (Vancouver and Toronto: UBC Press, 2008), 88.

pioneered on stage are unprecedented in Hong Kong's performing arts and popular music. While these performances are legendary, they have also broken a major social taboo."[46] Leslie Cheung's comeback set off spectacular fireworks of different colors in the relatively dull Cantopop industry in the mid- to late 1990s. His pioneering effort was duly recognized at music award presentations. One example was the RTHK Golden Needle Award (1999), the highest honor of the RTHK Top 10 Chinese Gold Songs Awards. Another anecdote worth mentioning here is that Leslie Cheung sang a duet with Alan Tam after he signed with Universal Music Group, Alan Tam's music company, previously known as PolyGram, in 1999. It was a sweet reminder of the good old days of the 1980s, which was especially memorable at a time when Cantopop was about to face a drop in the new millennium.

While the 1990s relished the comeback of Leslie Cheung, it suffered a big loss when the mainstay of Beyond, Ka-Kui Wong, passed away in an accident in Japan in 1993. The legacy of the band wave did inject alternative energies into the Cantopop industry in the 1990s. Stepping into the new decade, Beyond continued to speak truth to power for the Hong Kong people, and, more importantly, their social consciousness went from local to global. While they slammed the operational logic of Hong Kong's music industry in "Face-Giving Party" 〈俾面派對〉, they also shouted for peace in "Amani"; and while they despised the authoritarian regime in "Great Wall" 〈長城〉, they also paid tribute to Nelson Mandela in "Days of Glory" 〈光輝歲月〉. After the 1993 "Under a Vast Sky" 〈海闊天空〉, Beyond went to Japan in search of more space for their creative intervention in society, as voiced in the lyrics, "All these years confronted with disdain and jeers, I have always refused to abandon the dream in my heart." It was incongruous that the tragic death of Ka-Kui Wong resulted from a stage accident in Tokyo. Beyond continued to rock throughout the 1990s in the absence of their soul. Songs such as "The Paradise Afar" 〈遙遠的 Paradise〉 and "Life Is Wonderful" 〈活著便精彩〉 still captivated rock fans, but Hong Kong music had suffered a great loss that proved to be too hard to bear. More than twenty years later, "Under a Vast Sky" became the unofficial theme song of the Umbrella Movement in Hong Kong, speaking volumes for the role of Beyond in the history of Hong Kong music as well as social involvement.

Tat Ming Pair took a very different road. In 1990, the duo parted company after the classic album *Nerves* 《神經》, an amazing collection of different imaginative critiques of the June Fourth Incident. Anthony Yiu-Ming Wong (the Ming of Tat Ming Pair) was supported by Music Factory in the production of two later albums, *Trust, Hope and Love* 《信望愛》 (1992) and *Borrowing*

---

46. Chan, "Queering Body and Sexuality," 139.

Your Love 《借借你的愛》 (1993). (In the album that best represents a typical Hong Kong and Chinese imaginary of the early 1990s, *Capital* 《首都》, Music Factory focused on the political context of Hong Kong in the late-transitional period. "Capital" 〈首都〉 and the two parts of "Mother" 〈母親〉 extended the national allegories of Tat Ming Pair.) In those two albums, almost every song was in one way or another related to the fate of Hong Kong, but most of them were little more than sequels to the songs that Tat Ming Pair produced back in the 1980s. Some songs reimagined the June Fourth Incident, such as "Dance, Dance, Dance" 〈舞吧舞吧舞吧〉, which used Shanghai to symbolize Hong Kong; "Never-Fading Love" 〈不夜情〉, which reexamined Hong Kong's current situation; "Out There May Be Heaven" 〈哪裏會是個天堂〉 and "You Are So Great" 〈你真偉大〉, which reconstructed the relationship between China and Hong Kong. A number of different kinds of Hong Kong–Chinese imaginaries were on offer in one album. Likewise, the music company BMG backed Tats Lau (Tat)'s album *Tats Lau and Dream* 《劉以達與夢》 in 1992, in which the songs were very much like those in *Trust, Hope and Love*. The songs primarily addressed the June Fourth Incident, and the album was in a sense an extension of the political allegories of Tat Ming Pair. Ironically enough, before long Music Factory was restructured and incorporated into the transnational recording label Rock Records and Tapes. Two years later, Rock Records decided to focus solely on the Mainland market and stopped producing Cantonese albums. The ideology behind such a transformation should be self-evident: Hong Kong was simply a springboard for developments in the Mainland market. Not long before the 1997 handover, Anthony Yiu-Ming Wong released a beautiful swansong. In *The More Beautiful the Later at Night* 《愈夜愈美麗》 (1995), he no longer directed his critique toward a northbound imaginary. His signifiers pointed away from the Mainland and back toward the here and now of Hong Kong. The title of the album referred to the situation in Hong Kong in the last couple of years before the handover: would the scene become more beautiful the later it was at night? Tat Ming Pair also briefly reunited to produce an album called *A Thousand Years, A Thousand Years, Thousands and Thousands of Years* 《萬歲萬歲萬萬歲》 in 1996, seemingly another brilliant allegory of the late-transitional period. In the album, the title of the song "The Cruel Story of Youth" 〈青春殘酷物語〉 poignantly highlighted the fact that Cantopop, and perhaps even Hong Kong, was no longer young when it got later into the night.

The Hong Kong music industry faced another significant change in the mid-1990s, when another wave of nonmainstream music took place in which more interesting images of Hong Kong were being represented. Anthony Chau-San Wong 黃秋生 was one of the more remarkable examples, producing songs that were in a way similar to those of the group Blackbird, with a strong emphasis on national identity (Tat-Nin Kwok 郭達年, the soul of Blackbird, wrote songs for Wong). Unfortunately, the independent label that produced Anthony Chau-San Wong's first album, DIY, was later sold to Rock Records and Tapes, and Wong's position in the market was in a sense commodified before its maturity, shifting from independent creative productions to the mainstream. The odd duo Softhard 軟硬天師 also deserve a note here, as their songs could be regarded as providing a cultural record of a local Hong Kong popular lifestyle, particularly that of the younger generation, extending Sam Hui–styled parodies into the realm of teenagers. The songs touched on various social issues, including consumerism ("Commes des Garçons vs. Yohji Yamamoto" 〈川久保玲大戰山本耀司〉), fetishism ("The Fan Incident on Broadcast Drive" 〈廣播道fans殺人事件〉), the drug problem ("No. 14 Sky City" 〈十四號天空城〉), AIDS ("Why Do We Need a Condom?" 〈點解要大家笠〉), and the like. Their albums offered a multi-perspective picture of the postmodern consumer society in Hong Kong. Above all, their songs exposed the problems that the "abandoned Hong Kong child" would have to face. These problems had become much more complicated than those represented in the works of Sam Hui in the 1970s, and a simple economic grand narrative could no longer sum them up. In this sense, Softhard can be said to have supplemented a kind of innocent intervention in the Hong Kong cultural imaginary no longer available in other national allegories.

While band music became marginalized in the 1990s owing to the immense popularity of the Kings and Queens, the alternative music scene was still robust. Companies such as G.I.G. (Global Independent Generation), Sound Factory, and Music Communication continued to produce nonmainstream music, and there were a number of bands, such as A.M.K., Anodize, Black & Blue, Black Box, . . . Huh!?, Virus, and Zen, that were active at the margins. Unlike the bands of the 1980s, they mainly stayed at the margins, creating different voices with different music styles, from noise pop to heavy metal. In 1995, Channel 2 of Commercial Radio of Hong Kong, the most popular channel among teenagers, held a band concert at Hong Kong Coliseum that aimed to provide a crossover between the mainstream and the nonmainstream. Unfortunately, as argued by local music critic Chi-Chung Yuen 袁智聰, "[c]an one concert change it all? Several hours of cross-over cannot but be just a flash in the pan." In the late 1990s, there were no dominant bands or styles, except for a series of overworked formulas written on the basis of the success of the Four Heavenly Kings. The radio program "Band Time," which aired on Channel 2, might have been able to offer a discursive space for local bands to rock in, but the real impact exerted on the mainstream music industry did not surface until the formation of LMF (a.k.a. Lazy Mutha Fucka), a merging of the underground bands Anodize, Screw, and N.T. and local hip-hop star DJ

Tommy in 1998. In early 1999, LMF produced a self-financed EP, generating a hip-hop wave across the territory. Later, LMF signed a contract with D.N.A., a label of Warner Music Group. The album *LMF*, launched in 2000, was a big success in terms of not only sales volume but also song quality. Soon after their success, the members of LMF began to feel strangled by the operational logic of the music industry. As slammed by MC Yan, the mainstay of LMF, music companies simply sold hip-hop as a trend rather than as a culture, thus missing the anti-authoritarian spirit of hip-hop culture. It was thus not surprising that LMF disbanded in 2003 to pursue other interests.

The Decline of Cantopop and the Localization Campaign[47]

In response to Cantopop's sudden drop in sales in the mid-1990s, most record companies directed their resources toward winning formulae to guarantee their profits. But as a whole, the music industry had to do something more to boost the declining sales and market share of Cantopop. CR2, under the leadership of Winnie Yu, which had the experience of launching an "All Chinese songs" format in the late 1980s, initiated in 1995 a controversial campaign that only original songs could be aired on CR2. This could be seen as a strategic plan to hit two birds with one stone: to promote/protect local popular musicians and advocate local consciousness at the same time. As the number of radio channels in Hong Kong was surprisingly low, radio stations had been exerting great influence on record companies, as the latter had to struggle for limited space in which to air their products. Thus, the "Original Songs Campaign" launched by Commercial Radio of Hong Kong in 1995 exerted a great impact on the local music industry. As one of the most popular radio stations actively encouraged the use of local products over cover music, cover music lost its eligibility to enter the music charts on the radio stations. Music companies had to rethink their position of using cover music extensively. Gradually, the use of cover music in the Hong Kong music market diminished, and the music that was "plugged," that is, music that was promoted extensively, was produced locally. The swift change was shown in the RTHK Gold Songs Awards in 1995: all of the Top 10 Gold Songs were composed by local composers. This reflected the sharp and sudden decrease in cover music. Whether the "success" was a result of localization, one could not easily tell, but it was certain that the campaign had profound influence on the local soundscape, which turned out to be much more negative than positive.

---

47. Part of this section has appeared in Yiu-Wai Chu and Eve Leung, "Remapping Hong Kong Popular Music: Covers, Localisation and the Waning Hybridity of Cantopop," *Popular Music* 32, no. 1 (January 2013): 65–78.

Although piracy and illegal downloading/file sharing did contribute to the downfall of actual sales figures, they were not the only factors that caused the decline of Cantopop. In fact, there were adverse effects on the sales figures that came from CD/cassette tapes and, even later, with the advanced use of the USB stick MP3 format.[48] When profits dropped, music companies became more conservative. Instead of trying to use different tactics, they tended to play it safe by distributing resources to selected target audiences according to those would-be winners. Lachlan Rutherford, senior VP of Warner Music South East Asia, confessed that Warner had no choice but to channel its investments into its top-ranking artists.[49] When the target audiences of Cantopop became limited to teenagers only, Cantopop inevitably became more and more homogeneous. In short, the shrinking of the Cantopop market on the one hand and the rapid rise of the Mandapop market on the other had forced Cantopop to become less hybridized in terms of music styles, lyrics, and target audience groups. The inherent problems of the Cantopop industry can be unearthed by measuring it against the benchmarks set by Richard Caves's theory of creative industries. According to Caves, truly "differentiated" products are the key factor of a successful creative industry.[50] In the face of the shrinking market and crisis of identity shortly before 1997, the Cantopop industry redirected resources toward success formulae and promoted local consciousness without long-term policies. However, it failed to observe that the future of Cantopop must depend on a reform of the operational logic of the industry that had been placing most, if not all, emphasis on idol worshipping alone.[51] This was one of the main reasons Cantopop was not adequately responsive to the technological developments and related global changes in the popular music industry, which was one of the main reasons behind its decline.

Another major problem was the lack of local popular music talents. The Hong Kong government was infamous for having no long-term planning for nurturing local creative talents. As a result, the number of local talents could not meet the sudden demand for locally produced music, which later proved to have hit the market hard. For years, cover music dominated the Hong Kong music market and suppressed local productions. Local musicians had difficulty

---

48. "However, record companies were already aware of these problems and had begun to shift their revenue-generating focus from selling music to operating as an all-round media business. They achieved this by signing so-called '360 Contracts' with artists, such as those offered by Gold Label, in order to generate as much revenue and profit as possible." For details, see Chu and Leung, "Remapping Hong Kong Popular Music," 71–72.
49. Cited from Tsang and Campbell, "The Cantopop Drop."
50. Richard Caves, *Creative Industries: Contracts between Art and Commerce* (Cambridge: Harvard University Press, 2000), 2–9.
51. Yiu-Wai Chu, "Can Cantopop Industry Be Creative? The Transmission and Transformation of Hong Kong Popular Songs," in *Chinese Culture: Transmission and Transformation*, ed. Lawrence Wong et al. (Hong Kong: Chinese University Press, 2009), 461.

finding creative jobs in the industry, and many had to take on side jobs, such as performers and other music-related positions. The change in the number of people who worked full time in the music industry spoke volumes for this problem. As a result, this directly affected the quality of local productions in the Hong Kong music industry, as the gap left by cover music, in terms of both quantity and quality, was unable to be filled by local talents.[52] The extra space created by the localization campaign was mostly occupied by mainstream stars, and thus the mass productions of the Heavenly Kings and Queens continued to dominate the market. While a select few of the local musicians, such as Anthony Yiu-Ming Wong, were hailed as creative in the Hong Kong music industry, the media began to comment on the relatively subordinate music quality of purely local productions. Actually, this "poor" quality was caused by the overwhelmingly commercial demands of the music industry. Karaoke-style songs were preferred and hence local musicians wrote exclusively for that genre, and the music styles were almost indistinguishable from one another. That karaoke-style music was the dominant genre in the music industry was not the problem. The problem lay in the reduction of space for nonmainstream attempts in the mainstream. This in turn had adverse effects on the hybridity of Cantopop.

The local media launched such a localization campaign less for local identity construction than as a marketing gimmick to raise the market profile of radio stations.[53] Although this strategy could have been a way of making money while being culturally significant at the same time, and other music industries (such as Taiwan and Korea) proved to do better, the problem was that in the cases of Taiwan and Korea, their governments had taken an active part in using cultural/broadcasting policies to enhance the development of local popular music. In other words, they were already treating popular music as an important sector of the creative industries. In Hong Kong, however, the government was only paying lip service to fostering local popular music. In hindsight, it would be safe to conclude that it was a painful misrecognition if the localization campaign was planned as a way to resist the swift rise of Mandapop. It proved to be a failure. In the end, the campaign admittedly failed to provide more discursive space for diversified local productions, as increased air time was still mostly occupied by the big stars. And thus it did not contribute to the hybridity of Cantopop; on the contrary, the lack of high-quality local productions forced many listeners to turn away from Cantopop. The localization campaign might have exerted positive effects if there were other related policies such as

52. "Many people who were passionate about music and wanted to contribute to the industry had difficulties getting started: there were not enough open auditions through which new and enthusiastic talent could begin the process of becoming fully fledged musicians, and outsiders viewed the Cantopop industry as a closed one." Chu and Leung, "Remapping Hong Kong Popular Music," 73.
53. Chu, "Can Cantopop Industry Be Creative?" 453–59.

education of local music talents. This could have been an admirable attempt to avert the shrinking of the Cantopop market, which in the end proved to be inevitable. But without long-term planning and related policies, it could not provide discursive space for local talents to develop their creativity. Contrary to what the campaign promised at the outset, it neither nurtured local music talents nor enhanced the diversity of popular music genres. To make things worse, it came at a point when Cantopop was facing a big crisis brought forth by the transformation of the Chinese popular music industry. In the new millennium, the swift rise of China and its cultural industries created an environment not favorable to the hybridity of Cantopop.

After the Fall

In the early 1990s, the swift development of global media had a very significant impact on the Cantopop industry, which later proved to be a heavy blow to its operation. "It was the best of times; it was the worst of times." Charles Dickens's famous words from *A Tale of Two Cities* perfectly describe the Hong Kong music industry at that time. It was the best of times in the sense that Cantopop further expanded its business in Asia and around the world. Cantopop stars continued to be the trendsetters of popular culture across Chinese communities. The rise of the Four Heavenly Kings—Andy Lau, Jacky Cheung, Leon Lai, and Aaron Kwok—who dominated not only the local market but also almost all of the Chinese communities around the world, helped Cantopop develop into a transnational business venture. The success of the Four Heavenly Kings was not limited to the realm of popular music. Like Leslie Cheung and Anita Mui, they also crossed over to wider audiences through concerts, movies, and, more importantly, commercials in pursuit of artistic recognition as well as financial gain. It was the worst of times in the sense that music was no longer the central concern of these multimedia stars. As the Mandapop market expanded, the fan base of Cantopop kept shrinking, to such an extent that it fell into a vicious cycle: the lack of support made it difficult for different styles of Cantopop to survive, which in turn chased fans away as they looked for other genres.

During the late transitional period after the Sino-British Joint Declaration was signed in 1984, 1997 had long been seen as the *fin die siècle* of Hong Kong, but in the end "one country, two systems" proved to be working effectively, at least in the first few years after the handover. What was not working was the operational logic of Hong Kong Cantopop, if not Hong Kong popular culture per se. As rightly noted by Wyman Wong, "I thought we were facing an era of drastic change, but nothing really big or significant happened [in 1997]—we had already experienced that in 1989."[54] Nothing dramatic happened in

---

54. Cited from Helena, "Feeling Wyman Wong," *Heineken Music Magazine* 2 (1997), no page numbers.

the few years after 1997, apart from the collapse of the Hong Kong economy. Expectations were high that 1997 would provide the climax to the ongoing Hong Kong drama. But, just like Hong Kong's economy at the time, it proved to be rather anti-climactic for Hong Kong popular culture. The handover of sovereignty in 1997 showed later that it represented a fitting endgame to Cantopop. The most remarkable composition to come out of the 1997 handover was perhaps Andy Lau's Mandarin song "Chinese" 〈中國人〉. As one of the most prominent and commercially successful idol singers in Hong Kong, Andy Lau could be seen as emblematic of the Hong Kong music industry and its operational logic. "Chinese" could of course be viewed as an expression of national sentiment, but it could also be interpreted as a kind of northbound imaginary that masked commercial considerations with the grand narrative of nationhood. In that song, "Hong Kong" unabashedly became "Chinese." As Chinese national sentiment reached its apotheosis, Hong Kong Cantopop had come to a point of no return. In this regard, the song "Queen's Road East" 〈皇后大道東〉 was precursory:

> There is a noble friend on the back of my coin.
> Forever young, her name is "Queen."
> I have to carry her through every business transaction.
> Though she has no expression on her face,
> It is the converging point of all accomplishments.
> My dear friends leave the city with a "bye bye,"
> New developments are left to the great comrades.
> The real-estate market is running as usual,
> But perhaps Mongkok [a busy shopping area] needs a new name.[55]

If Sam Hui was the representative of the *vox populi* in the social parodies of the 1970s, and bands and groups such as Tat Ming Pair provided the soundtrack of the 1980s, then Music Factory could be regarded as the voice of the 1990s. In 1991, Music Factory, led by Luo Dayou 羅大佑, arrived in Hong Kong from Taiwan, and their plan for Hong Kong domination was officially launched. Their pioneering work, "Queen's Road East," was very popular and was even regarded as a liminal soundtrack to the in-betweenness of Hong Kong.[56] The witty lyrics of Lin Xi's "Queen's Road East" sketched the complex political and cultural conditions of Hong Kong, but the contextual situation of its production told an even more interesting story. The critic Chi-Wah Wong described it as "[t]he most encouraging song to be released this year [1991]." But the later discovery that it represented merely the first step of the Rock Records

---

55. English translation cited from Rey Chow, *Ethics after Idealism: Theory-Culture-Ethnicity-Reading* (Indianapolis and Bloomington: Indiana University Press, 1998), 165–66.
56. Chow, *Ethics after Idealism*, 165–66.

and Tapes company's "plan to develop [the] Hong Kong market" was cause for great disappointment.[57] The later rise of the Mainland market exerted adverse effects on the "in-betweenness" of Hong Kong—Hong Kong lost its once singular and prolific position between China and the world, as China became the world.[58] The fall of Cantopop as well as Hong Kong cinema also diminished the synergy between the two once-leading cultural industries in Chinese communities around the world. "The Wheel of Time turns, and ages come and pass, leaving memories that become legend," as Robert Jordan's famous saying goes.

---

57. Wong, *Taking Music Seriously*, 10.
58. Chu, *Lost in Transition*, 3.

6 | After the Fall
The New Millennium

Introduction

As noted in the previous chapter, there was a rapid and widespread change in the mediascape in the 1990s, leading to the rise of Mandapop. While the repercussions of the Heavenly Kings and Queens could still be strongly felt, the aging Cantopop industry was struggling to keep its leading role. The swift rise of China and its soft power in the new millennium did not need long to kill off Cantopop's lingering effects. In the new millennium, diminishing record sales stimulated record companies and Cantopop singers to switch to the Mandapop market in Taiwan and Mainland China, producing more Mandapop albums than Cantopop albums. During this time, record sales dropped from HK$17 billion in 1997 to HK$0.56 billion in 2006.[1] It was not surprising that people thought Cantopop had died. In 2003, a year of significance in the history of not only Cantopop but also Hong Kong society per se, the passing away of Cantopop legends Leslie Cheung and Anita Mui seemed to symbolize the end of the era of Cantopop. Hong Kong was struck by the outbreak of SARS (Severe Acute Respiratory Syndrome) in early 2003, hitting hard its already weak economy. When the media reported that Leslie Cheung had leapt to his death from the twenty-fourth floor of the Mandarin Oriental Hotel on April 1, 2003, Hong Kong people would rather have believed that it was just an April Fool's Day joke. Unfortunately, it was not, and the horrible news rubbed salt into the wounds of the Hong Kong people. While Hong Kong's economy bounced back from the bottom of its recession after SARS, Cantopop was dealt a further deadly blow by the untimely deaths of Cantopop stars. The cancer-stricken Anita Mui passed away on December 30, 2003, adding another dark day to this bleak year in the history of Hong Kong. Shortly before the death of the legendary songstress, cancer also robbed the life of the lyric master

---

1. Hong Kong Heritage Museum, *Riding a Melodic Tide: The Development of Cantopop in Hong Kong* (Hong Kong: Hong Kong Heritage Museum, 2007), 13.

Richard Lam on November 16, 2003. This was followed almost a year later by the decease of the godfather of Cantopop, James Wong, on November 24, 2004, which was arguably the last straw that broke the camel's back. The late Dr. Wong hinted at the death of Cantopop in his doctoral thesis, and his own departure summed up controversies about the death of Cantopop:

> When did Hong Kong popular music die? Theories abound as to the death of Hong Kong pop songs delivered in the local language of Cantonese, or Cantopop. Some say it died when Hong Kong was handed over by the British to the Beijing authorities in 1997. Others say that it died along with its two international superstars, Leslie Cheung and Anita Mui, in 2003.[2]

In terms of record sales, it was no exaggeration to say that Cantopop had died. But the shrinking market might not have been directly attributed to the quality and diversity of the genre. Simon Frith astutely identified a very important point to note in popular music studies: "popular music culture isn't the effect of a popular music industry; rather, the music industry is an aspect of popular music culture."[3] In this sense, the excessively powerful mainstream marginalized popular music culture to the extent that it could not make its due impact on the music industry, which meant that Cantopop had nowhere else to go but hopelessly downhill. Consequently, the fall of Cantopop was a side effect of the excessively dominant role of Cantopop stars. If every cloud has a silver lining, perhaps it was the drastic fall of record sales, which forced the record companies to be less reluctant to experiment with new styles and genres. In addition, despite its fall from fashion, Cantopop nonetheless retained its important function of voicing Hong Kong people's discontent whenever there was a crisis, as it played a big role in times of social unrest.

Whether Cantopop was dead or diminishing was not the key question; the crucial point was whether it could regain the vibrant hybridity it once had. As veteran lyricist Yiu-Fai Chow argued in the book *Sonic Multiplicities*, coauthored by Jeroen de Kloet, "Hong Kong pop is not dead, but it has transformed, mutated, and altered, and the authors want to encourage people to see, listen, and think in new and altered ways."[4] There must be no denying the fact that Cantopop was no longer the trendsetter of Chinese popular culture in the new millennium, and it had a mountain to climb in the age of China and its soft power. However, fans did witness the transformation of Cantopop, albeit incomplete, in the twenty-first century. Before I move on to how it has

---

2. Subashini Navaratnam, "Hong Kong Pop and Its Discontents: Sonic Multiplicities," *Pop Matters* (March 4, 2013). Available at: http://www.popmatters.com/review/168667-sonic-multiplicities-by-yiu-fai-chow-and-jeroen-de-kloet/; retrieved on March 15, 2016.
3. Simon Frith, "The Popular Music Industry," in *The Cambridge Companion to Pop and Rock*, ed. Simon Frith, Will Straw, and John Street (Cambridge: Cambridge University Press, 2001), 27.
4. Navaratnam, "Hong Kong Pop and Its Discontents."

mutated and altered, it is necessary to examine its inherited role as a star production industry. After Cantopop established its star system in the late 1970s, it remained as the center of superstar productions for more than two decades. Singers from Taiwan and the Mainland—such as Jenny Tseng and Faye Wong—had to come to Hong Kong to be baptized into superstardom. However, with diminishing record sales and market share, Hong Kong was eventually taken over by Mandapop centers like Taipei and Shanghai. But those who emerged as rising stars in the late 1990s still found that, to reverse the two signature lines of a famous Chinese poem, "although it was close to the evening, the sunset was still in full glory."

New Four Heavenly Kings

Capital Artists was one of the main players that contributed to the building of the Cantopop star system in the 1980s. Thanks to its close relationship with TVB, it became the cradle of TVB's new singers who made noise at the New Talent Singing Awards. Capital Artists gradually lost its leading role in the 1990s owing to the departure of superstars like Leon Lai, Sammi Cheng, and Andy Hui. Because of poor sales, the music production section of Capital Artists was discontinued in 2001, signaling the end of an era. Before its end, Capital Artists managed to nurture some new talents in the late 1990s, who, in the shadow of the Heavenly Kings and Queens, had to wait until the new millennium to fully realize their potential. Andy Hui was one notable example. Andy Hui signed with Capital Artists after he won the silver prize at the Fifth New Talent Singing Awards in 1986. Not long after this he established his place in the Cantopop industry with his collaboration with Anita Mui in "Breaking the Iceberg" 〈將冰山劈開〉. But in subsequent years, due to the overwhelming domination of Alan Tam, Leslie Cheung, and then the Four Heavenly Kings, he remained a second-tier Cantopop singer, despite occasional chart-topping hits such as "Somersault" 〈翻騰〉 (1991), "Love You the Way You Are" 〈喜歡你是你〉 (1992), and "Sunshine after the Rain" 〈雨後陽光〉 (1993). In 1996, he had a career-turning hit, "The Most Unbearable Pain of a Man" 〈男人最痛〉, and with improved performance over the next couple of years after signing with his new manager Paco Wong and Go East Entertainment in 1997, he managed to win Commercial Radio's Ultimate Best Male Singer Gold Award in 1999 and 2000. But he still had to wait until the phasing out of the Four Heavenly Kings in the new millennium to win the Jade Solid Gold Most Popular Male Singer Award in 2001.

Meanwhile, Edmond Leung, entering the entertainment business via the New Talent Singing Awards, had a comparable development trajectory to Andy Hui's. Although he did not win a trophy at the singing contest, he was spotted by Capital Artists and became a professional singer in 1990. He was one of Capital Artists' rising stars, as apparent in his participation in the Capital Artists' song "Red Hot Motion La La La" with Aaron Kwok, Sammi Cheng, and Andy Hui. Similar to Andy Hui, he did have occasional chart-topping hits, such as "Breath" 〈呼吸〉 (1996) and "Good Friend" 〈好朋友〉 (1997), but he was eclipsed by the tsunami of popularity of the Four Heavenly Kings in the late 1990s. His singing career came to a temporary halt after his Capital Artists contract expired in 2001. After signing with his new manager Paco Wong, he released his most successful album—*No. 10* 《10 號》—in terms of popularity among fans. In 2004, he released another successful album in terms of popularity among music critics, *03/Four Seasons* 《03/四季》, which was a concept album that was considered an epic history of Hong Kong in the year 2003. Thanks to the golden touch of Paco Wong, Edmond Leung was named one of the "New Four Heavenly Kings," along with Andy Hui, Hacken Lee, and Leo Ku 古巨基 by Alan Tam, nicknamed the "Principal" of the Cantopop industry. The interesting point to note is that all of the New Kings, having long curricula vitae, were by no means "new" stars.

Hacken Lee, the most experienced among the New Four Heavenly Kings, started his singing career during the heyday of Alan Tam and Leslie Cheung after winning the Hong Kong 19-District Amateur Singing Contest in 1985 (the first winner being Jacky Cheung). He then signed with PolyGram and released his debut EP the following year. One of his distinguishing characteristics, besides his voice, which was later commended as "immaculate," was that he wrote the lyrics of "A Hand Watch" 〈手錶〉, one of the songs in the album *Signs of Life* 《命運符號》 released in 1987, and the lyrics for two other songs. After that, he wrote lyrics not only for himself but also for other singers, becoming one of the most productive singer-lyricists. The song "Half Moon Serenade" 〈月半小夜曲〉, a cover version of a Japanese song by Naoko Kawai, was quite popular, but it was not until the 1988 album *Summer Legends* 《夏日之神話》 that he truly made a mark in the industry. The title song, "Sumer Legends," and "City Hall Auditorium" 〈大會堂演奏廳〉, the lyrics of both penned by Hacken Lee (however, the former was coauthored), climbed pop charts quickly, and the rising airplay contributed to the popularity of the rising star. The young star continued to impress with new chart-topping hits such as "Deep, Deep, Deep" 〈深深深〉 (1989), "Never Change in This Lifetime" 〈一生不變〉 (1989), and "One Thousand and One Nights" 〈一千零一夜〉 (1990). At that point Hacken Lee's performance was so promising that Alan Tam, in an interview shortly after he announced that he would no longer accept music awards, noted that Hacken Lee would be his successor.[5]

---

5. Alan Tam, *The 40th Anniversary of Alan Tam's Entertainment Career* 《譚詠麟走過的銀河歲月》 (Hong Kong: Joint Publishing, 2015), 215.

With this blessing the media called him one of the "Three Musketeers" of Cantopop, the other two being Jacky Cheung and Andy Lau.[6] However, he did not live up to Alan Tam's expectations, owing to the swift rise of Leon Lai and Aaron Kwok, whose handsome looks were more attractive to fans.

Hacken Lee went through several ups and downs in his career in the 1990s. His inspirational song "Red Sun" 〈紅日〉 (1992), a cover version of Daijiman Brothers Band's "The Most Important Thing" 〈それが大事〉, with lyrics penned by Hacken Lee, became an all-time classic. It did not bring him any major awards though. His career further developed after he moved to a new company, Star Records 星光唱片, in 1993, with "Look Back" 〈回首〉, but it was short-lived. Owing to, among other things, contract problems, his singing career experienced two years of lows after he held his first concerts at the Hong Kong Coliseum to full houses in 1993. His popularity bounced back briefly after he moved to Music Impact in 1996, but it was not until he signed with Universal Music (formerly PolyGram) that he eventually saw the chance to realize his potential. It was good timing for him to turn a new page in his music career. After his career hit a new low in the late 1990s, Hacken Lee shifted his emphasis to the television sector. Having established a good relationship with TVB, he sang the theme song "Thinking about You Once Again" 〈再一次想你〉 for a TVB drama in which he was the male lead in 2000. The success of this song paved the way for his return to Cantopop, which was in dire need of new stars to succeed the Four Heavenly Kings. Although he was not "new," his career reached new heights with two popular albums, *Flying Flowers* 《飛花》 (2001) and *Let's Celebrate* 《李克勤大派對》 (2002). His five "comeback" concerts at Hong Kong Coliseum in January 2002 signaled the (re)birth of a Cantopop king. He won the Jade Solid Gold Most Popular Male Singer Award in 2002 and collaborated with his mentor Alan Tam in a series of "Alan and Hacken" concerts, which were among the most popular Cantopop concerts in the new millennium. He went on to attain the Jade Solid Gold Most Popular Male Singer Award in 2003 and 2005, with the remarkable achievement of Commercial Radio's Ultimate Best Male Singer Gold Award in 2003, given the fact that his work relationship with the commercial radio station was known to have been poor for many years. Hacken Lee won numerous awards thereafter, and at long last he took the baton from the former Cantopop superstar who named him his successor more than ten years earlier. He was the only Cantopop singer who managed to win music awards in four different decades—from the 1980s to the 2010s.

Among the four New Kings, Leo Ku had the shortest resume. His entertainment career began as a TVB actor in 1991. He signed with Music Impact in 1994 and ventured into the Cantopop industry. While Hacken Lee was

---

6. Cited from "Hacken Lee Leaving Universal for TVB in July," *3 Weekly* 762 (May 2014): 44.

handpicked by Alan Tam to be his successor, Leo Ku was the choice of Leslie Cheung. In a Commercial Radio talk show in 1994, Leslie Cheung made a precursory remark that the green singer had the potential to make an impact in the Cantopop industry.[7] During the mid- to late 1990s, he made steady progress and released many popular albums, with chart-topping hits every year, including "The Second Most Beloved" 〈第二最愛〉, "Enjoy Yourself Tonight" 〈歡樂今宵〉, and "Roman Holiday" 〈羅馬假期〉. Singing in the shadow of the Four Heavenly Kings, just like the other three male singers already mentioned, he did not manage to reach the summit of his career. In the new millennium, he decided to sail into new waters, developing his career in the Mainland market, which was not very mature at the time. As the male lead in two Chiung Yao 瓊瑤—a renowned veteran Taiwanese writer—television dramas highly popular in the Mainland, *Romance in the Rain* 《情深深雨濛濛》 (2001) and *My Fair Princess 3* 《還珠格格3》 (2002), he accumulated considerable economic as well as symbolic capital. Instead of further developing his television career in the swiftly growing Mainland market, he decided to shift his emphasis back to Hong Kong Cantopop and signed with the prime manager Paco Wong, who proved him right by guiding him to instant success in his new company, Gold Label 金牌娛樂. Leo Ku made clear the reason behind this decision when he received Commercial Radio's Ultimate Most Popular Song Award in 2003 with the song "Fatal Blow" 〈必殺技〉. He memorably burst into tears when he confessed, "I truly love singing." Leo Ku was able to retain the title the following year with another great hit, "Love and Honesty" 〈愛與誠〉. On top of this success he also won the Ultimate Best Male Singer Gold Award in 2004. The two songs were both main plugs in two concept albums, *Games* 《遊戲—基》 and *Nobita* 《大雄》, the former using electronic games and the latter manga (Nobita Nobi is the protagonist of the Japanese manga series *Doraemon*) as the main themes. His 2005 album *Star Track* 《星戰》 was another concept album hybridizing *Star Wars* and Cantopop oldies. His experience in the industry and successful marketing strategy focusing on kidult culture helped him establish a rather broad fan base. He staged two rounds of "Leo Ku in Concert 2005" in March and April 2005, the tickets of which were sold out fast.

Leo Ku received the Ultimate Best Male Singer Silver Award for four consecutive years, from 2005 to 2008, second to Eason Chan in the first three years and Khalil Fong 方大同 in the last one, and he gained the recognition of TVB by winning the Jade Solid Gold Most Popular Male Singer Award from 2008 to 2011. He continued to use concept albums to brand his music, but the kidult grew up and life became the main theme of *Human* 《我生》 (2006). "Too

---

7. Cited from Sandra Ng and Wyman Wong's talk show, Commercial Radio Hong Kong (1994). Available at: https://www.youtube.com/watch?v=vvoGWIR_jmE; retrieved on March 15, 2016.

Late for Love" 〈愛得太遲〉, with lyrics penned by Lin Xi, in *Human* was exceptional in the sense that it won the Ultimate Most Popular Song Award as a nontraditional love ballad—it was about the importance of expressing one's love to all those you care about, before it is too late. While the next album, *Moments* (2007), also focused on different aspects of life (such as home and fortune), Leo Ku continued to sing mainstream love songs, as indicated by the title of the 2008 album *I'm Still Your King of Love Songs* 《我還是你的情歌王》. In 2009, he left Gold Label for Emperor Entertainment Group (EEG) for a career change. He was still very much into the concept album idea, and *The Age* 《時代》 (2010) was a beautiful attempt at narrating the stories of Hong Kong people from different perspectives.

To borrow the words from the American playwright George Martin, "[w]hen the sun has set, no candle can replace it." To be fair, the New Four Heavenly Kings did make contributions to the Cantopop industry. However, unlike their predecessors, they were facing a shrinking market in an age of Mandapop. They also graced the Cantopop industry with their creative endeavors. As mentioned, the New Kings wanted to transform from romantic ballads tailor-made for the teen market to other genres, but the changing mediascape and shrinking fan base significantly limited their new directions. More importantly, the New Four Heavenly Kings were not newcomers, as they ventured into the industry in the 1980s and 1990s. Their rise, perhaps overdue, implied that a succession crisis had already surfaced in the new millennium if not earlier. The problem was not that there was a lack of talented young singers ready to take the baton from the superstars, but rather that the Cantopop industry had probably lost its ability to make stars in the age of Mandapop. Ironically enough, the New Four Heavenly Kings—Mandapop instead of Cantopop—were crowned by the media in 2012: Jay Chou, Leehom Wang 王力宏, JJ Lin 林俊杰, and Show Luo 羅志祥. Two decades after the coinage of the term, sadly enough, Cantopop had to pass it on to Mandapop. And this has extended beyond the scope of this book.[8]

The New Cantopop Divas

While the Cantopop industry moved into a post–Four Heavenly Kings era, it was in dire need of new queens as well. Sammi Cheng and Kelly Chen continued to lead the market, but as Faye Wong and Cass Phang were no longer active (the former turning to Mandapop and the latter retiring after marrying Jan Lamb), new Cantopop divas were needed to boost the market. As noted earlier, the impact of Capital Artists could still be felt in the new millennium.

---

8. As noted by an anonymous reviewer, the issue can be complicated by pointing at the regional entanglement: Hong Kong is still playing a role in the shift from Cantopop to Mandapop.

Miriam Yeung 楊千嬅, who was working as a nurse at Princess Margaret Hospital, signed with Capital Artists after winning the Bronze Award at the Fourteenth New Talent Singing Awards in 1995. Like her predecessors, she had the chance to release her debut album, *The Boy Who Cried Wolf* 《狼來了》, the following year. It was still the heyday of Cantopop at the time, and thanks to the influence of Capital Artists, she managed to win new talent awards at RTHK (Excellence Award) and Commercial Radio (Bronze Award). In the next few years, she continued to make steady progress with popular hits, among which the most remarkable was "Goodbye Nichome" 〈再見二丁目〉 (1997) collected in the album *Instinct* 《直覺》. The song was not particularly popular when it was released, although it topped the Jade Solid Gold pop chart. The lyrics, penned by Lin Xi, were later recognized as one of the signature works of the lyric master, catching the attention of many fans of Cantopop lyrics. Interestingly enough, Lin Xi later noted in an interview that Miriam Yeung impressed him by performing the song in an unexpectedly touching way, making him pay more attention to this new songstress. Miriam Yeung was among the rising stars touted by Capital Artists, as shown in her participation in the 1998 song "Great Violent Thoughts" 〈大激想〉, co-sung with Eason Chan and Edmond Leung. As the Cantopop scene was dominated by Faye Wong, Sammi Cheng, and Kelly Chen, the rising star had to gradually and quietly build up her fan base in the late 1990s. Shortly before the turn of the millennium, she released a career-changing hit entitled "Lift up My Head" 〈抬起我的頭來〉. The song helped Miriam Yeung hold her head high in the competition for the crown of the Heavenly Queen.

Miriam Yeung did not need long to be crowned. Shortly before she signed with Cinepoly Records, she released her last Capital Artists album, *Play it Loud, Kiss me Soft* (a double EP), in 2000. It was a huge success, perhaps to the surprise of the company that let her go. "A Maiden's Prayer" 〈少女的祈禱〉 (with no direct connection to Tekla Bądarzewska-Baranowska's piano masterpiece), the lyrics of which were penned by Lin Xi, won Miriam Yeung two major song awards: TVB's Gold Song Gold Award and The Best Song Award, jointly presented by the four broadcasting stations in Hong Kong. In September 2000, she held two debut concerts entitled "My Concert" at Hong Kong Coliseum, another confirmation of her rising status in the Cantopop industry. Her career soared to new heights after she joined Cinepoly Records. A series of chart-topping hits, including "Sisters" 〈姊妹〉 and "Wild Child" 〈野孩子〉 in *Miriam* (2001), "Miriam Yeung" 〈楊千嬅〉 and "Shining" 〈閃靈〉 in *M vs M First Half* 《M vs M 上半場》 (2002), and "Tears in My Smile" 〈笑中有淚〉 and "It's a Pity I Am an Aquarius" 〈可惜我是水瓶座〉 in *Miriam's Music Box* (2002), led to her Jade Solid Gold Most Popular Female Singer Award and Ultimate Most Popular Female Singer Award in 2002. In the same year she also crossed over to the film sector, starring in *Love Undercover* 《新紮師妹》 and *Dry Wood Fierce Fire* 《乾柴烈火》. Her film career became so successful that later she devoted quite a portion of her time to Hong Kong movies.[9] Despite this, she still fared well in the music industry, which can be attributed at least in part to the transformation of her image over the years.

Unlike other Cantopop Queens, it was noted that Miriam Yeung "emphasizes her ordinariness, and that she is not beautiful but friendly and approachable. Ordinary women can see their experiences reflected in Yeung."[10] Miriam Yeung continued to reflect ordinary women's experiences during her tenure at Gold Label and A Music. When she grew up, she changed from a maiden to "Fierce Lady" 〈烈女〉 (2005) and "Woman with a Past" 〈有過去的女人〉 (2005) who talked about "My Way of Survival" 〈我的生存之道〉 (2006) and "Collective Memory" 〈集體回憶〉 (2007). With the assistance of Lin Xi's exceptional lyrics, she was among the few Cantopop stars who could age gracefully with their audience. She looked back at her own development after getting married in 2009 (from an interview in 2011): "In previous albums my songs were a kind of self-therapy. . . . I used to sing about sadness, breakups, heartache. Now my songs are much happier; they show solutions to relationship problems."[11] Miriam Yeung regained, among other awards, the Jade Solid Gold Most Popular Female Singer Award in 2008 and 2009, which was sound proof of her successful transformation.

One year after Miriam Yeung won an award at the New Talent Singing Competition, Denise Ho 何韻詩 became the champion in 1996. In 1997, when Hong Kong reverted back to China, the contest was rebranded as the International Chinese New Talent Singing Championship. Ironically enough, despite its high-sounding expansion, it gradually lost its function as the cradle of new Cantopop stars thereafter. Denise Ho's singing career, similar to other New Talent winners, began with Capital Artists. But unlike her predecessors, Denise Ho did not have the chance to release her own album after signing with the company. Instead, she spent the first several years as a presenter for TVB music and travel programs. Denise Ho, who won the New Talent Singing Competition with Anita Mui's song "Woman's Heart" 〈女人心〉, repeatedly stressed that she was a crazy fan of Anita Mui, and perhaps it was destiny that it was the late Cantopop legend who later mentored her in the music industry. Having been Anita Mui's background singer, she had the chance to collaborate with her mentor in 1999 on the song "Women's Worries" 〈女人煩〉.

9. Wing-Fai Leung, *Multimedia Stardom in Hong Kong: Image, Performance and Identity* (Abingdon and New York: Routledge, 2015), 75–79.

10. Leung, *Multimedia Stardom in Hong Kong*, 78.

11. Jill Triptree, "Acting Her Age," *Luxury Insider* (December 2011). Available at: http://www.luxury-insider.com/features/2011/interview-miriam-yeung?page=3; retrieved on March 15, 2016.

Denise Ho's first recording was eventually cut five years after she won the singing contract. In 2001, she released her debut EP, *first*, the style of which was significantly different from other mainstream new singers. The main plug, "Home of Glory" 〈光榮之家〉, a rock ballad about abandoned utilities in our everyday lives (Wyman Wong's ingenious lyrics touched on a topic rarely discussed in Cantopop), brought Denise Ho her first chart-topping hit. She had to find a new home, however, as Capital Artists discontinued its music production later that year. With hindsight, it was perhaps a blessing in disguise. The protégé of Anita Mui moved to EMI, where the major label provided the platform for her to enjoy mainstream success. She further developed her own style in the album *Hocc2* released in 2002, in which another chart-topping hit, "Angel Blues" 〈天使藍〉, accumulated more fans for her. In the same album there was another remarkable song, "Rosemary" 〈露絲瑪莉〉, the lyrics of which were also penned by Wyman Wong who later became her regular team player. A touching lesbian romance, the song did not receive its due attention until its sequel, "Goodbye . . . Rosemary" 〈再見露絲瑪莉〉, was released in her next album, *Free[Love]* (2002). The song became one of the most popular songs of the year, showing that queer romance could also be a mainstream topic.[12] She went on to release the concept album *Dress Me Up!*, which was about the different stages of life—birth, aging, illness, and death—in 2003, before she left EMI.

After her brief tenure at EMI, Denise Ho moved to East Asia Records in 2004, looking for more discursive space for her critical inquiries. As she stated in an interview: "Anyone who knows me knows I'm a person with my own very strong opinions. . . . I can't be convinced to do anything I don't want to."[13] Her first East Asia album, *Glamorous* 《艷光四射》 (2005), unlike her previous androgynous presentations, featured an alluring image that paid tribute to her mentor Anita Mui, who passed away in December 2003. Denise Ho, with the assistance of Wyman Wong, then went through a metamorphosis in her next concept album, *Butterfly Lovers* 《梁祝下世傳奇》, which was based on a musical in which she was the female lead and music director. The Ho and Wong team developed queer imaginaries by deconstructing gender and love with a Chinese legendary love story. "Rolls and Royce" 〈勞斯萊斯〉, inspired by a love story, described a gay romance that shook the mainstream. The theme was so successful that Denise Ho kept going in her *Our Time Has Come* (2006) and *We Stand as One* (2007), with hits like "Wish I Knew How to Quit

---

12. Wyman Wong noted in an interview that the success of "Goodbye . . . Rosemary" was remarkable in the sense that it was arguably the first openly queer song that topped pop charts in Hong Kong; Yiu-Wai Chu, *Songs of Your Life: On Hong Kong Cantopop* 《歲月如歌：詞話香港粵語流行曲》 (in Chinese) (Hong Kong: Joint Publishing, 2008), 176.

13. Cited from "Mini Mui," *South China Morning Post* (January 20, 2005). Available at: http://www.scmp.com/article/486234/mini-mui; retrieved on March 15, 2016.

You" 〈願我可以學會放低你〉 (inspired by Ang Lee's *Brokeback Mountain*) and "Illuminati" 〈光明會〉. Denise Ho successfully cultivated and turned her queer and indie edge into mainstream success.[14] Her first Hong Kong Coliseum concert held in October 2006 and Commercial Radio's Ultimate Female Singer Gold Award in the same year were solid evidence of this. However, it would not be fair to say that the attention was slanted heavily toward her queer inquiry.

After being crowned a new Cantopop Queen, she carried on with her nonmainstream experiments in the mainstream with concept albums like *Ten Days in the Madhouse* (2008) and *Heroes* (2009), the former exploring mental health and problems faced by the underprivileged and the latter using supernatural heroes to radiate positive energy in a gloomy society. In the face of a shrinking market still overwhelmed by mainstream love ballads, Denise Ho decided to venture to Taiwan for greener pastures, and her Mandapop album *Anonymous Poetry* 《無名・詩》 (2010) brought her into the top five female singers in Taiwan's prestigious Golden Melody Awards in 2010. She confessed in an interview: "After the 2009 concerts, I felt exhausted. I decided to tour first in Taiwan and then in the Mainland to rekindle my passion. No more restrictions and concerns, I could sing my beloved music."[15] In a sense, Denise Ho was similar to Karen Mok, and that they had to develop their music careers in Taiwan told a sad story about the Cantopop industry: the local market was not able to accommodate different styles. Despite this, Denise Ho did not change her strong attitude. She was the first Hong Kong Cantopop songstress to openly come out of the closet in 2012. During the Umbrella Movement in late 2014, she was one of the leaders who supported the protest for genuine universal suffrage and the first cultural celebrity to be arrested at the protest site.[16] The Occupy Central Movement's anthem "Raise the Umbrella" 〈撐起雨傘〉, sung by Denise Ho, Anthony Yiu-Ming Wong, and other pop singers, might be used as a footnote to not only the fight for democracy in Hong Kong but also diversity in the music industry.

Whether it was a sheer coincidence that the new Cantopop songstresses were able to sing in the city of Hong Kong is not easy to tell, but Kay Tse 謝安琪 was arguably the only Heavenly Queen to sing "Raise the Umbrella" alongside Denise Ho. It should not be surprising because Kay Tse was nicknamed

14. Cheuk-Yin Li, "The Absence of Fan Activism in the Queer Fandom of Ho Denise Wan See (HOCC) in Hong Kong," in *Transformative Works and Cultures* 10 (2012). Available at: http://journal. transformativeworks.org/index.php/twc/article/view/325/286; retrieved on March 15, 2016.

15. Cited from "Paco's Meetings with Celebrities" 〈PACO 名人會〉 (in Chinese), *Headline Daily* (August 5, 2013). Available at: http://news.stheadline.com/dailynews/headline_news_detail_columnist.asp?id=249014&section_name=wtt&kw=109; retrieved on March 15, 2016.

16. Vivienne Chow and Danny Lee, "Denise Ho First Celebrity to Be Arrested at Protest Site," *South China Morning Post* (December 12, 2014). Available at: http://www.scmp.com/news/hong-kong/article/1661308/denise-ho-first-celebrity-be-arrested-protest-site?page=all; retrieved on March 15, 2016.

the "Grassroots Heavenly Queen"—an oxymoron after she began enjoying mainstream success. The well-deserved title came as an acknowledgment of her concern about social issues in Hong Kong, from local tea restaurants to minivan trips and poverty problems. The winner of a singing contest at her alma mater—the University of Hong Kong—in 2002, she was spotted by producer and University of Hong Kong alumnus Adrian Chow 周博賢, who invited her to sign with his independent label Ban Ban Music. After that, they established a close partnership in the music industry, be that at the margin or the center. Kay Tse's debut album *Kay One*, released in 2005, did not bring her instant fame in the Cantopop industry, but her campus-style social satires, such as "Beauties" 〈姿色份子〉 (in Cantonese it is a homonym of "intellectuals") and "Happy Reading" 〈開卷快樂〉, won her many nonmainstream fans. The former was a pointed critique of the body slimming and cosmetic surgery phenomenon, whereas the latter was a piercing mockery of tabloid culture.

Kay Tse's alternative style was not widely recognized by mainstream media, but she still managed to win the Bronze Award of Commercial Radio's Ultimate New Singers in 2005. Her second album, *K sus2*, continued to focus on local cultural and social issues. Having established a fan base in indie music circles, she was able to attract more attention with "Gloomy Festival" 〈愁人節〉 and "Filipino Love Song" 〈菲情歌〉, articulating the problems faced by the underprivileged and domestic helpers, respectively. She also won loyal followings who were concerned about local culture with songs like "A Deadly Trip" 〈亡命之徒〉 and "I Love Tea Restaurants" 〈我愛茶餐廳〉, both of which were about local daily life—from transportation to food. She released her third album, *The First Day*, after signing with Cinepoly in 2007, an album of three new songs plus remixes of her greatest hits, bringing her fame from indie circles to the mainstream. Interestingly enough, one of the new songs was entitled "New Branch from a Knot" 〈節外生枝〉—in Chinese it also means a new problem that complicates the issue—which sounded like a confession from a songstress who got pregnant while she was developing her singing career. It might have been a problem for the new company but definitely not for Kay Tse, who got married and gave birth to a baby boy in 2007. To the surprise of many, her career soared to new heights despite "the new branch from a knot."

The album *3/8* (implying that there were eight stages in one's life, and Kay Tse had completed three of them) was released in December 2007, shortly after her maternity leave. It was so successful that it won the lavish praise of *South China Morning Post*: "Thanks to Kay Tse, there's still hope for Cantopop."[17] The album comprised three new songs plus greatest hits, an attempt similar to that of *The First Day*. All of the three new songs, "3/8," "Wuyen" 〈鍾無艷〉,

---

17. "Cantopop at Its Best," *South China Morning Post* (March 10, 2010). Available at: www.scmp.com/article/621855/canto-pop-its-best; retrieved on March 15, 2016.

and "Retired Life of Wonder Woman" 〈神奇女俠的退休生活〉, entered pop charts, with the latter two being chart-topping hits. This essentially paved the way for her career breakthrough in the following year. The 2008 album *Binary* turned Kay Tse into a household name. Among other hits, the melodic "Wedding Card Street" 〈囍帖街〉 (melody by Eric Kwok and lyrics by Wyman Wong) truly stood out, winning her at the end of the year almost all of the major awards, including Commercial Radio's Ultimate Supreme Song Award, Commercial Radio's Ultimate Most Popular Song Award, and TVB's Gold Song Gold Award. The song was about the preservation of Lee Tung Street—also known as Wedding Card Street—in the old district of Wan Chai on Hong Kong Island, and it stirred up reflections on urban renewal and collective memory under the shell of a romantic ballad. The lyricist Wyman Wong ingeniously crossed a mainstream love theme with a hotly debated social issue, an often highlighted item on Kay Tse's resume. The creative synergy enabled the song to become song of the year, and also brought a grand slam of personal awards to Kay Tse—Commercial Radio's Ultimate Most Popular Female Singer, Commercial Radio's Ultimate Female Singer Silver Award, and Media Awards for the Best Song, for the Best Singer, and for the Best Album presented by the four broadcasting stations in Hong Kong.

In 2008, the year of "Wedding Card Street" as well as Kay Tse, she was formally baptized into superstardom at the Hong Kong Coliseum with her seven concerts in May 2009. The new Cantopop Queen merged seamlessly into the mainstream, but her "grassroots" style remained her trademark. Her subsequent albums, *Yelling* (2009), *Slowness* (2010), and *Your Happiness* 《你們的幸福》 (2011), tried to strike a balance between mainstream constraints (such as romantic ballads) and her own local and social sensitivity. In terms of popularity they were quite successful, as shown by the fact that Kay Tse was able to retain the Ultimate Female Singer Silver Award for four consecutive years starting in 2008. In order to develop a greater market she turned to Mandapop in 2010. Yet she still had her own plan in mind. In an interview with the online music platform KKBOX, she made it clear that what she enjoyed most was using her music to record social events.[18] This was the reason behind her

---

18. According to Kay Tse, "this also had impacts on my career, such as increasing demands from the people surrounding me, as well as criticism that follows. For a period of time, even though I acted upon good intentions, my actions were read as bad through the influence of external reporting outlets. When I sang love songs, I was criticized for deviating from who I am as a person, thus undeserving of the continuing support from my audience. And when I produced Mandarin songs, I have been criticized for inclining towards the Mainland Chinese music market. Suddenly, it seemed that a lot of things were not permitted. The endless amount of pressure has made my work difficult for me in the past." Cited from "Kontinue: Kay Tse" 〈幸福待續─謝安琪〉 (in Chinese), KKBOX (October 27, 2014). Available at: http://www.kkbox.com/hk/tc/column/interviews-44-565-1.html; English translation cited from http://hkxasampuff.tumblr.com/post/101157215321/kay-tse-interviewed-by-kkbox-for-her-newest-album; retrieved on March 15, 2016.

decision to return to her original mode in 2014, signing with a new company, Maya Entertainment, which allowed her team to have "more independence in terms of music production, investment and copyrights."[19] Going back to her indie roots, she released *Kontinue* in 2014, focusing overtly on her favorite themes, such as social justice ("The Best Moment" 〈最好的時刻〉, paying homage to Martin Luther King, Jr.), personal values ("The Lone Village" 〈獨家村〉), national allegory ("Ka Ming" 〈家明〉, implying the "future of the country"), and Mainland–Hong Kong conflict ("Grandmaster of Suitcase" 〈篋神〉, teasing free-tour Mainland tourists). If Kay Tse is able to continue in her signature style, the *South China Morning Post*'s claim that "there's still hope for Cantopop" may be true.

The Last Megastars? Eason Chan and Joey Yung

There is no denying that the New Heavenly Kings and Queens emerged in the new millennium, but beautiful sunsets should not be mistaken for a dawn. The shrinking Cantopop market significantly limited the possibilities of new stars, and most, if not all of them, had to direct their attention to the growing Mandapop market. These new kings and queens, with the exception of Kay Tse, were all experienced singers coming onto the music scene in the 1990s or even the 1980s. More importantly, the power of these New Kings and Queens in influencing the events of Chinese pop culture, compared with their predecessors, was greatly reduced. Strictly speaking, in terms of market share and industry status, they were not as prominent as the Cantopop megastars in the 1980s and 1990s. Among the new generation, it was Eason Chan and Joey Yung 容祖兒 who could categorically be put on a par with the Heavenly Kings and Queens before the turn of the millennium.

Eason Chan won two awards—the Gold Award and a newly established "Personal Style" prize in 1995 in the New Talent Singing Competition, a cradle for new stars in the 1980s. In the 1990s, the event might have been less influential given the increasing number of media channels, but in the fourteenth competition it witnessed the birth of another Cantopop superstar. Like his predecessors, Eason Chan also won a contract with Capital Artists after winning the contest. Among the luckier ones, he was able to release his debut Cantopop album the following year. The 1996 album *Eason Chan* 《陳奕迅》 was not especially well liked by listeners at the time, given the overwhelming supremacy of the Four Heavenly Kings. Songs like "Song of the Era" 〈時代曲〉 and "A Heartbreaking Letter" 〈傷信〉 later proved to be longtime favorites of

---

19. Grace Choi, "Kay Tse," *HK Magazine* (October 25, 2012). Available at: http://hk-magazine.com/city-living/article/kay-tse; retrieved on March 15, 2016.

Cantopop fans. Notwithstanding this, he was able to win the Silver Award for New Male Singers at the Commercial Radio Award Presentation Ceremony in 1996. In the next few years, he continued to produce solid work, including some now-monumental albums such as *Always with Me* 《與我常在》 (1997), *My Happy Era* 《我的快樂時代》 (1998), and *God Bless My Lover* 《天佑愛人》. Had it not been the era of the Heavenly Kings, these albums would have helped Eason Chan grab many more awards with ease. The latter two albums were awarded Supreme Album of the Year by Commercial Radio in 1998 and 1999, respectively, a truly exceptional achievement for a relatively new singer besieged by the Heavenly Kings.

The turn of the millennium witnessed the dawning of the era of Eason Chan. He signed with Music Plus under EEG, a swiftly expanding record company that later became the market leader. With a larger budget and more freedom, he had the opportunity to further develop his personal style. His first Music Plus album, *Some Like It Hot* 《打得火熱》 (2000), was a tremendous success. Besides the title song, another major plug, penned by Lin Xi, "King of K-Songs" 〈K 歌之王〉, a mimicry of karaoke love songs, ironically captured all karaoke fans and turned out to be the most popular Cantopop song of the year, winning countless awards for him. He came to the throne of Cantopop in 2000 by winning the Media Award for the Best Singer presented by the four broadcasting stations in Hong Kong. A happy era began for the fans of Eason Chan. His career soared higher the following year with two new albums, *Shall We Dance (Shall We Talk)* and *The Easy Ride*. The song "Shall We Talk," like "King of K-Songs," swept all music award presentations and firmly established the new reign of Eason Chan. At this point, Eason Chan had proved to the judges granting him the "Personal Style" prize that they made the right choice. Unlike the Heavenly Kings, Eason Chan relied on neither handsome looks nor groovy dance steps. "Shall We Talk," "Space Odyssey 2001" 〈2001 太空漫遊〉, "Bicycle" 〈單車〉, "Gift from an Angel" 〈天使的禮物〉, and "Monster" 〈怪物〉 explored different subject matter as well as music styles. Wyman Wong's lyrics in the "psycho" love song "Eyes Wide Shut" 〈大開眼戒〉 were not only highly creative but also a perfectly apt portrayal of Eason Chan's style: "If you like an eccentric, I am actually very beautiful." It would be no exaggeration to say that the styles of Eason Chan's songs up until that point had been more diversified than those of the Four Heavenly Kings in aggregate. It was still a happy era for Cantopop back then.

The Line Up (2002) was another fascinating experiment. As reflected by the title, Eason Chan lined up two teams of foremost composers and lyricists for this album: Keith Chan 陳輝陽 and Lin Xi, and Carl Wong 王雙駿 and Wyman Wong (each team was responsible for five songs). In the end "Next Year Today" 〈明年今日〉, written by Chan and Lin, became the song of the year, but the other songs were all well received by fans as well as critics. Although Eason Chan won TVB's Gold Song Gold Award twice with "Shall We Talk" and "Today Next Year" in 2001 and 2002, respectively, he was not the favored male singer of TVB. He was awarded Commercial Radio's Ultimate Best Male Singer Gold Award in 2001 and 2002, but the Jade Solid Gold Most Popular Singer Award was handed to Andy Hui, Hacken Lee, and even back to Andy Lau between 2001 and 2005. His next album, *Live for Today* (2003), also came off with flying colors, but the eccentric Cantopop King was not satisfied with his achievements. He signed with a new manager, Katie Chan, Faye Wong's manager, in 2004, and left Music Plus for Cinepoly. His collaboration with the new company enabled chemical reactions in his album *U-87* (2005), which pushed him to new heights. Lin Xi's lyrics for "Infinite Beauty of the Setting Sun" 〈夕陽無限好〉 (inspired by a classical Tang poem), which became the song of the year, added a philosophical dimension to Eason Chan's music. Meanwhile, Wyman Wong's "Flamboyant" 〈浮誇〉 made an ingenious use of Eason Chan's public image to let the singer voice his deep feelings, and "When the Grapes are Ripe" 〈葡萄成熟時〉 reflected life wisdom under the shell of a romantic ballad. All of these songs contributed to a more mature yet still energetically diversified Eason Chan. The subsequent years were his era. With dazzling projects like *Life Continues* (2006), *What's Going On . . .?* (2007), and other Mandapop best-sellers, he ascended to genuine superstardom in Asia. At long last he conquered Jade Solid Gold by winning the Most Popular Singer Award in 2006 and 2007. He went on to release many classic Cantopop albums, including *H³M* (2009), *Time Flies* (2010), *Taste the Atmosphere* (2010), *3mm* (2012), and *The Key* (2013), and had a stronghold on Commercial Radio's Ultimate Best Male Singer Gold Award—from 2001 to 2013, he won this title a remarkable ten times. In short, Eason Chan was probably the only genuinely international superstar produced by Hong Kong Cantopop after the Four Heavenly Kings.

While Eason Chan was the Cantopop King of the 2000s, Joey Yung was indisputably the Queen in terms of awards. She was reared into superstardom by EEG. A major label established in 1999, EEG replaced Capital Artists and emerged to become "one of the market leaders of the music industry in the Asia-Pacific region."[20] From 2003 to 2014, she won Commercial Radio's Ultimate Best Female Singer Gold Award nine times, and the Jade Solid Gold Most Popular Female Singer Award ten times. Joey Yung had been a frequent participant in singing contests since she was 15 years old. After winning a karaoke singing contest, she signed with Go East Entertainment and released

---

20. Cited from EEG's website. Available at: http://www.emperorgroup.com/en/ourbusinesses.php?id=4; retrieved on March 15, 2016.

the song "The First Time I Want to be Drunk" 〈第一次我想醉〉, the theme song of the movie *Those Were the Days* 《4個32A和一個香蕉少年》 (1996). But perhaps due to her age, she had to wait until she had the chance to join EEG before she released her debut, *EP*, in 1999. The main plug, "Not Yet Known" 〈未知〉 (a cover version of Jennifer Paige's "Crush") surprised everyone, probably including herself, by helping *EP* remain at the top of the pop charts for ten weeks, bringing the "not-yet-known" teenage songstress to center stage. With the support of the expanding EEG, her next EP, *Don't Miss* 《不容錯失》, and her first full album, *Who Cares to Love Me* 《誰來愛我》, were both great successes. Just in the second year of her career, excluding her brief Go East Entertainment tenure, she managed to snatch Commercial Radio's Ultimate Best Female Singer Bronze Award in 2000. In the same year, she also held her first concert at Hong Kong Coliseum in November. After a dream start for a new talent, it was smooth sailing from there on. The year 2001 was a significant year for Joey Yung, in which she successfully turned into a Heavenly Queen with the tremendous success of albums like *Love Joey* 《喜歡祖兒》, *All Summer Holiday* 《全身暑假》, and *Solemn on Stage* 《隆重登場》. The main plug in the combined new songs and greatest hits album *Love Joey* (which won the best-selling album award of the year from IFPI Hong Kong), "Painful Love" 〈痛愛〉, rode a wave of "self-harm" love songs and topped the pop charts of different media. Thanks to the proactive promotional strategy of EEG, she became the brand ambassador of many famous labels, including, among others, Nikon, Compass Visa, and Kao.

Joey Yung needed just two more years to reach the summit of the Cantopop industry. In 2003, her "My Pride" 〈我的驕傲〉 swept countless awards, including TVB's Gold Song Gold Award, and helped her win The Most Popular Female Singer awards from both TVB and CR2. In 2004, after Eason Chan left Music Plus, a subsidiary of EEG, Joey Yung became the sole mainstay of the entertainment giant. In the next few years, she won almost everything in the Cantopop industry. The immense popularity of "Painful Love," "My Pride," and other hits in karaoke boxes earned her the title of "Karaoke Queen," which at first enhanced but later restricted the development of her Cantopop career. The 2006 album *Ten Most Wanted* was a remarkable endeavor for the Karaoke Queen. Not complacent with her domination of the Cantopop scene, Joey Yung apparently made an attempt to broaden her music style in this album. The songs presented not only Joey Yung's "ten most wanted" things, but also a diversification of the character of her music as well as lyrics. For example, the two songs written by Taiwanese singer-songwriter Mavis Fan 范曉萱 (melody) and veteran lyricist Yiu-Fai Chow (lyrics), "Doing Aerobics with Jane Fonda" 〈跟珍芳達做健身操〉 and "Split Tongue" 〈舌尖開叉〉, were funky experiments that went beyond Joey Yung's well-received mainstream karaoke style. The most popular song in that album, however, turned out to be "Snow on Barren Land" 〈赤地雪〉, a J-Pop (Japanese pop music)–style theme song of a commercial series for the Broadway Electronics Group. Compared with her previous albums, this one was less successful in terms of sales and number of hits on the pop charts. It was not without irony that this song implied "rebirth," one of the things Joey Yung most wanted in her planned year of transformation.

When asked in a 2010 interview whether she would like to try something different, Joey Yung confessed that she had thought about it—and she actually did—but given her role as an artist with endorsement deals, there had to be "one or two songs that could be used for commercials." She was optimistic enough to see this as an opportunity though:

> There are times when I can't do what I want and I would get annoyed but I'm an optimistic person. When you think about it, in a time when the music industry is struggling, life would be harder without these sponsors supporting us. So we would sit down with them and negotiate a compromise on certain decisions.[21]

She did have the ability to negotiate a compromise and she continued to succeed in the Cantopop industry despite an incomplete rebirth. On top of her numerous concerts held around the world, she became the first Chinese female singer to perform at the prestigious Royal Albert Hall in London, following her mentor Roman Tam who was the first Chinese singer ever to hold a concert there. She managed to win numerous Cantopop awards, including the TVB special award "Most Popular Singer for Ten Years" in 2015 for setting the record of winning the Jade Solid Gold Best Female Singer Award ten times. During the twelve years since Joey Yung first won the Jade Solid Gold Best Female Singer Award in 2003, she managed to retain the title ten times, with only Miriam Yeung winning the award twice in 2008 and 2009. This was indeed a remarkable achievement for the Cantopop diva, but it also sounded the alarm about the lack of effective succession planning in the Cantopop industry.

The Twins Effect

While the Cantopop industry relied upon the successful formulae of the Cantopop Kings and Queens, it tried figuring out new succession plans, but owing to the rise of Mandapop in the millennium as noted in the introduction and the previous chapter, most, if not all, of these plans turned out to be much

---

21. Leon Lee, "Hot Seat: Joey Yung," *Timeout Hong Kong* (August 18, 2010). Available at: http://www.timeout.com.hk/big-smog/features/36283/hot-seat-joey-yung.html; retrieved on March 15, 2016.

less effective than those in the 1980s and 1990s. The unexpected success of the female duo Twins (Charlene Choi 蔡卓妍 and Gillian Chung 鍾欣桐), formed in the summer of 2001 and signed by EEG, was arguably an exception that at once shed new light on the industry. Hailed as the "most successful pop music duo in China's history" that once dominated the East Asian music market,[22] Twins gave a new impetus to the Hong Kong music industry. Unfortunately, though, the impact was short-lived, owing not only to the infamous Edison Chen 陳冠希 sex photos scandal in 2008, but also structural problems inherent in the Cantopop industry (as will be described). Twins released their debut EP *Twins (AVEP)* in the summer of 2001, the prime time for the teen market. The EP contained six songs and three music videos, in which Twins appeared as secondary school students. Songs like "Love Tutorial"〈明愛暗戀補習社〉and "Boy Student in a Girl School"〈女校男生〉stood out and became great hits among teenage fans. As apparent from the titles, their target audience was secondary school students. This album also adopted a different strategy to market its products, which gave the industry a much-needed shot in the arm on the one hand but exerted an adverse effect on it on the other hand. The record company collaborated with MSN to design web games to promote the album. To lure the teenage audience, in addition, EEG bundled coupons and gifts with the album, such as skin care products, sushi gift vouchers, and dance course coupons, all geared to the tastes of teenagers. When fans bought the album, they got far more for the price of the album if all the coupons were used. This strategy crucially changed the age group of Cantopop's target audience, which has since become younger and younger. The lyrics of one of the greatest hits by Twins can best illustrate their target audience: "I haven't grown up yet, and so let me be shallow. I only know love means more than the world to me." Obviously, the sole target audience was teen fans.[23] Their second and third EPs, *Twins' Love* and *Twins*, stuck with the strategy of featuring both songs and music videos, using the image of Twins to spur the fancy of teen fans by both audio and visual means. Having said that, it is also necessary to note the reason behind Twins' popularity. As convincingly argued by Anthony Fung, examining Twins' image from the perspective of the fans can contribute to understanding the role of Twins in popular culture. Thanks to Twins' school uniform image, their teen fans found it easy to project the images of Twins onto themselves, helping create a sense of group identity among themselves.[24]

---

22. Lisa Funnell, *Warrior Women: Gender, Race, and the Transnational Chinese Action Star* (Albany: SUNY Press, 2014), 153.
23. Yiu-Wai Chu, *Lost in Transition: Hong Kong Culture in the Age of China* (Albany: SUNY Press, 2013), 123.
24. Anthony Fung, *Hong Kong Popular Music Culture*《香港流行音樂文化》(in Chinese) (Hong Kong: Wheatear Publishing, 2004), 2–19.

Having passed their examinations with flying colors, Twins released their debut album *Our Souvenir Book* in 2002, which featured ten new songs and two music videos. Their next album, *Amazing Album*, adopted the same strategy, which proved to be efficacious as Twins were able to hold their first Hong Kong Coliseum concerts in September 2002; at 19 years old, Charlene Choi became the youngest singer to hold a concert in the temple of Cantopop. Twins' effect lasted long, and the young duo needed just another year to secure Commercial Radio's Ultimate Best Group Gold Award. In the next couple of years, they continued to diversify their endeavors by releasing children's albums (e.g., *Singing in the Wonderland*) and starring in Hong Kong movies. Teens grow up fast, and so did Twins. In 2004, they tried to make a transformation with the album *Girl Power*, in which they showcased their "Scent of a Woman" 〈女人味〉 along with depressing love songs such as "Shame" 〈丟架〉. This album also came with lots of gifts and coupons, including scratch-and-win lucky draw cards and mini posters, and the record company was willing to spend a handsome budget on packaging the album—a large cardboard book-like set wrapped with colored fabric bands. While they were no longer the teenage school girls gossiping about the boy student in their girls' school, their fans wished they could stay forever young. "As for the young teen groups," argued John Erni, "their rise to stardom [was] part of the industry's response to a large teenage audience seeking ultrapositive personae of their own age as a point of social encouragement in difficult and uncertain times."[25] This was proved by their shifting back to school uniform girls on their cover of their debut Mandapop album, *Trainee Cupid* 《見習愛神》. In the Cantopop album *The Missing Piece* 《一時無兩》, released in the same year, the most popular hit was "Kindergarten" 〈幼稚園〉, a song expressing the wish to go back to childhood—"Please don't force me to grow up"—as shown in the lyrics by Wyman Wong. Despite this return to their school girl image, they did work hard to diversify their music with such dance songs as "Samba Queen" 〈森巴皇后〉 and "Summer Vacation" 〈熱浪假期〉. In 2007, they won the Jade Solid Gold Most Popular Female Singer in Asia-Pacific Award, and in January 2008, they won the Jade Solid Gold Most Popular Group Award, showing that their transformation was well received among their fans. No sooner had they won these honors than the untimely sex photos scandal struck Gillian Chung, which later forced the duo to announce its "temporary dissolution." Although they reunited two years later for EEG's tenth anniversary concert and released another Cantopop album, *2 Be Free*, in 2012, things had changed so much that the youthful innocence of not only the duo but also their fans was gone. Lost time is never found again.

---

25. John Erni, "Moving with It, Moved by It," *Perspectives: Working Papers in English & Communication* 16, no. 2 (Fall 2004): 24–25.

Twins' cross-media achievements—pop songs, movies, and commercials—prompted many record companies to emulate their success. Similar girl groups such as Cookies (which later became Mini Cookies), 2R, and Hotcha, and boy groups such as Shine and Boy'z (the male version of Twins) came onto the scene and stole the limelight for a very short period, but none managed to make similar sustained achievements. The duplication of the Twins formula aggravated the problem inherent in the Cantopop industry. In the face of a shrinking market, record companies distributed more resources to the teen market, which exerted a negative impact on the fan base of Cantopop. Teen fans have always been a very important part of Cantopop's audience members, but it was less homogeneous back in the 1970s and 1980s. While Danny Chan and Leslie Cheung enthralled teen fans back in the 1980s, others subscribed to mature singers such as Michael Kwan and Paula Tsui. There was no denying the fact that the youthful, innocent image of Twins was a successful packaging strategy, and that songs such as "Love Tutorial" and "Boy Student in a Girl School" were very effective in constructing that image for the two female singers. The problem, however, was that the focus on teenage audiences trapped Cantopop in a vicious cycle: mature audiences shunned Cantopop and, in turn, the market shrank further, and the further the market shrank, the more resources were directed toward the teenage audience. The contracting fan base limited the development of the singers. When the young idols grew up, they could not transform into mature singers targeting different audiences. A bigger age range in audiences was important to the long-term development of the music industry. As James Wong argued in his doctoral thesis, while the stars were aging, the target audience remained focused on the teens.[26] This was one of the reasons behind the shrinking Cantopop market in the new millennium.

Yesterday, Once More

The lack of new superstars and the focus on the teen market had a side effect on the Cantopop industry—many adult fans were being forced to turn to the good old days. The Cantopop industry ushered in the comeback phenomenon with the return of Sam Hui after the 2003 SARS Incident. When the city of Hong Kong remained persistently gloomy after the SARS period, Sam Hui decided to cheer Hong Kong people up with his music. Sam Hui once wrote in the preface of a book about him, "I have written many melodies and lyrics. I am not sure whether these songs can have resonance in society and impact in the cultural arena. I have never thought my works would become the topic of

---

26. James Wong, "The Rise and Decline of Cantopop: A Study of Hong Kong Popular Music (1949–1997)"《粵語流行曲的發展與興衰：香港流行音樂研究 1949–1997》(in Chinese) (Hong Kong: PhD thesis, the University of Hong Kong, 2003), 174–75.

Hong Kong cultural studies."[27] Hong Kong fans assured him of his contributions to and impacts on Hong Kong by embracing his comeback with open arms in 2004. Not unlike "Eiffel Tour above the Clouds" and "Staying on the Same Boat," his "Keep on Smiling" 〈繼續微笑〉 and "2004 Blessings" 〈零四祝福你〉 were written to remind Hong Kong people to stay home and strive for a better future. In 2004, he staged three rounds of "Keep on Smiling" comeback concerts (a total of thirty-eight) at the Hong Kong Coliseum, the tickets of which were reportedly sold out in a short while. His concerts "generated great excitement among adults ordinarily considered above the age of pop star fandom."[28] Hong Kong people saw hope in Sam Hui, who dressed in a tailor-made suit with the signature Hong Kong red-white-and-blue fabric for his concerts. From "La Tour Eiffel above the Clouds" to "Staying on the Same Boat," Sam Hui underscored the importance of the local in the Hong Kong imaginary, as they were articulated at the outset and during the heyday of the golden era of Cantopop. "If the first Sam Hui phenomenon in the 1970s marked the rise of local culture, the excitement around his return to the stage indicated a return to the local in Hong Kong culture after more than a decade of rushing toward becoming a 'world city'."[29]

Sam Hui's comeback this time invoked not just the local but also the golden age of Cantopop. A great number of comeback concerts were held in 2005. Paula Tsui, Sally Yeh, Sandy Lam, and George Lam, among others, staged sold-out comeback concerts at the Hong Kong Coliseum, drawing a big crowd of mature Cantopop fans back to the temple of Cantopop. These superstars were regular hosts at the Hong Kong Coliseum in the 1980s and 1990s, and their comebacks were not surprising to the audience. However, that the dance group Grasshoppers, who came onto the scene back in the 1980s, held three rounds of concerts at the Hong Kong Coliseum between 2005 and 2007 carried an important message. Grasshoppers held their debut concerts (three in total) at Hong Kong Coliseum in 1995, and perhaps they could not imagine ten years later that they would become even more popular than when they were young. In the next couple of years, veteran Cantopop stars like Shirley Kwan, Vivian Chow, and David Lui rode on the comeback wave and continued to bring Cantopop fans back to the good old days: "the older audience group would consider these stars as representatives of 'a golden age'."[30] The comeback was not restricted to mainstream singers. Band groups also came back for audiences. Tat Ming Pair reunited to celebrate their twentieth anniversary, with

27. Sam Hui, "Preface," Chun-Hung Ng, *Here and Now: Sam Hui* (Hong Kong: Enrich Culture, 2007), 9.
28. Leung, *Multimedia Stardom in Hong Kong*, 52.
29. Janet Ng, *Paradigm City: Space, Culture, and Capitalism in Hong Kong* (Albany: SUNY Press, 2009), 148.
30. Leung, *Multimedia Stardom in Hong Kong*, 53.

four shows at the Hong Kong Coliseum in December 2004, and again in their "Round & Round" concerts in April 2012 (Part 2 at Hong Kong AsiaWorld-Expo in August 2012). In July and August 2006, Softhard held their "Long Time No See" comeback concerts at the Hong Kong Coliseum, generating another wave of nostalgia for the trendy good old days. The most significant aspect of the works of the witty duo was that they fully captured the trendy youth culture and lifestyle back in the early 1990s, which also stretched to include Sam Hui's parodies in the realm of teenagers. They were thus considered icons of trendy Hong Kong culture in the 1990s. In 2012, Softhard crossed over with Grasshoppers and staged 12 full-house shows entitled "Grasshoppers' Samba vs. Softhard's Fans" at Hong Kong Coliseum, showing that the comeback phenomenon extended well into the 2010s. The key question was whether it was the success of the groups remaining trendy for more than a decade or the failure of the Cantopop industry to make new icons.

Meanwhile, Donald Cheung 張偉文 was another remarkable phenomenon in the midst of this wave. An old-timer who started his singing career back in the late 1970s, he was not very popular and became a back-up singer in 1985. He was among the best local back-up singers, but perhaps his fans could not expect a rebirth of his solo career in the new millennium. In 2003, he released an album entitled *Encore* 《唱好女人》 in which he covered golden hits by Cantopop divas such as Anita Mui and Sally Yeh. It went platinum almost immediately, and with this surprising success he held four concerts at the Queen Elizabeth Stadium, an arena with 3,500 seats, in the same year. They were so popular that he had encore concerts in 2004 and 2005, and his fan club was also founded in 2005. In May 2007, he staged two debut concerts at the Hong Kong Coliseum, three decades after the start of his singing career. Donald Cheung was not an isolated case. Prudence Liew, who enjoyed short-term popularity with her sexually explicit songs in the late 1980s, also held her debut concerts at the Hong Kong Coliseum in April 2008, after releasing her comeback album *Crossing the Boundary of Sex* 《大開色界》. Whereas Cantopop records had not sold well in the decade prior, the sales of these collections of golden hits were remarkable. The effect was not long-lasting, however: "The commercial success of the comeback albums and concerts of the previous generation of pop stars illustrate[d] the strength of the mass market for indigenous media as well as its subsequent fragmentation."[31]

After the Four Heavenly Kings, the industry relied on new Kings who had already been around for quite a while. As a major segment of fans turned away from Cantopop, the record companies realized that their power to make new stars was gone. The industry chose to ride on the nostalgic wave generated by the rising local consciousness related to the conservation of Star Ferry's Pier

31. Ibid.

and Queen's Pier. Although some of the old stars released new songs, such as Shirley Kwan's "Something about Me" 〈關於我〉 (2005) and Sandy Lam's "True Color" 〈本色〉 (2005), they were less well received by fans than their 1980s golden hits. The comeback phenomenon was largely triggered by the longing for the good old days of Hong Kong. As the 1980s was seen as the heyday of not just Cantopop but also Hong Kong culture per se, it was an era that could not be surpassed. The surplus value of the 1970s and 1980s' stars was exhausted before long. Although the comeback phenomenon extended into the 2010s, the impact of individual stars did not last long. When Sam Hui released his new album *Life's So Good* 《人生多麼好》 in 2007, for example, it was less galvanizing than the 2004 one. It would not be fair to read the comeback concerts simply in terms of nostalgia, as some comebacks—such as the metamorphosis of Leslie Cheung and the pointed critique of current social affairs of Tat Ming Pair—did breathe new life into Cantopop. (Meanwhile, nostalgia can also be critical at once; see below.) However, it is safe to say that the Cantopop industry could not rely on the comeback of superstars in the long run, especially as it had fallen behind considerably in the new mediascape of Chinese popular culture. As argued by James Wong in his doctoral thesis, one of the reasons that led to the decline of Cantopop in the late 1990s was that it lived on its own fat when the market was changing.[32]

Alternative Voices in the Mainstream

It would be wrong to assume that the record companies did not try to win the market over. Owing to shrinking sales, the Cantopop industry was more willing, compared with the 1990s, to experiment with new styles and genres. The Cantorap wave generated by Lazy Mutha Fucka (LMF), a hip-hop band formed by a merging of the underground bands Anodize, Screw, and N.T. and local hip-hop star DJ Tommy in 1998, was a prime example of this willingness at the turn of the millennium. According to Chi-Chung Yuen, because of the new technology available, the new millennium witnessed a vigorous recovery of indie music in Hong Kong.[33] As music production software became popular and recording costs were significantly lowered, more indie bands found that they could afford to produce their own albums. DIY music production, and in some cases home recording, provided indie bands with the opportunity to produce their own works. At first, LMF benefitted from the change of production mode and seized the chance to make noise, swiftly developing

---

32. Wong, "The Rise and Decline of Cantopop," 171.
33. Chi-Chung Yuen, "Autonomous Voice of the Epoch: Exploring the Ecology of the Development of Hong Kong Indie Music" 〈劃時代自主呼聲：探討香港獨立音樂發展生態〉 (in Chinese) (August 26, 2012). Available at: http://blog.sina.com.cn/s/blog_aeb7c18e01015xqx.html; retrieved on March 15, 2016.

into one of the most popular bands in Hong Kong. After the success of their EP *Lazy Mutha Fucka* (1999), LMF moved aboveground and signed (in the name of their recording studio "A Room") with DNA, Warner Music HK's independent label, in 1999. The next album, *LMF 《大懶堂》* (2000), created a stir in the mainstream music industry, and the main plug, "Lazy Mutha Fucka," was a Cantorap song that paid tribute to Sam Hui's songs about the working class. In the new millennium, LMF successfully generated a hip-hop wave in Hong Kong with their subsequent albums *LMFamiglia* (2001) and *Crazy Children 《嘻武門》* (2002). However, commercial success did not bring satisfaction to members of the band. Feeling strangled by the operational logic of the popular music industry, they decided to disband after the album *Finalazy* in 2003 to strive for further developments in different fields. They briefly reunited in 2009 to commemorate their tenth anniversary, and the song "Holding onto Your Middle Finger" (in Cantonese "middle finger" is a homonym of "principle") 〈揸緊中指〉 was a typical example of their fight for freedom—it was a blistering critique of the privileged in an increasingly unjust world. According to MC Yan, the mainstay of LMF, Cantorap aspired to free speech, which provided an effective platform for social critiques.[34] In 2014, they reunited again to release a new song, "An Age of Evil" 〈惡世紀〉, showing that Hong Kong did not get any better after fifteen years, but it was in a sense fortunate that LMF was still determined to speak truth to power.

Although the short-term success of LMF did not bring structural change to the music industry, it did boost the morale of indie bands. More indie labels came onto the market, and in the midst of this indie wave, The Pancakes, Primary Shades, King Ly Chee, 3P, and Site Access brought different kinds of music to Hong Kong. The Pancakes' debut album *Les Bonbons Sont Bons*, for instance, sold more than 11,000 copies (a sale of 200 copies covered the production cost),[35] which was even more promising than the achievements of many mainstream Cantopop stars. The expanding market was also able to support more labels. Among these new labels, People Mountain People Sea and 2nd Floor Rear Block stood out, owing to their relationship with established bands such as Anthony Yiu-Ming Wong (Tat Ming Pair) and Beyond, respectively. Two of the labels that contributed a genuinely indie dimension to band music were 89268 Music and Harbor Records. Kelvin Kwan, a member of AMK and founder of Harbor Records, made it very clear: "While they are running a business, we are not . . . we are trying to embody the spirit of independence."[36] During this period, Hong Kong indie music was heterogeneous, but no sooner

---

34. For further details, see Yiu-Wai Chu, "The Importance of Being Free: Fu©Kin Music as Alternative Pop Music Production," *Inter-Asia Cultural Studies* 12, no. 1 (2011): 62–76.
35. Yuen, "Autonomous Voice of the Epoch."
36. Cited from Yuen, "Autonomous Voice of the Epoch."

had the bands found their voice than the new Web 2.0 age arrived. As argued convincingly by Chi-Chung Yuen, the consumption model of music fans drastically changed in the age of Web 2.0, and CDs were no longer popular among them. That Web 2.0 technologies exerted adverse effects on record sales may not be necessarily bad, but in this context the new indie groups had fewer chances to produce their own albums, and due to limited fan base it has become more difficult for their songs to reach the audience. To make things worse, the Hong Kong government launched a project to revitalize industrial buildings, in which many studios were located. Many bands could no longer afford the rent, which went up swiftly after government intervention. As a result, the production of indie labels slowed down after 2005.[37]

MC Yan said in an interview that one of most serious problems of the Cantopop industry was the overemphasis on cultural trends.[38] Hip-hop should have been a sustained culture, not simply a trend, but the record companies packaged it like other trendy products, and thus it was not long-lasting enough to make a genuine impact on the operational logic of the music industry. After the wave of hip-hop and indie bands, the Cantopop industry promoted another alternative in the mainstream in 2005: singer-songwriters. A number of singer-songwriters, including Vicky Fung 馮穎琪, Ivana Wong 王菀之, Chet Lam 林一峰, and Pong Nan 藍奕邦, emerged on the music scene, making fans think that the mainstream industry was eventually willing to try something new. Singer-songwriters were, of course, not new to Cantopop. Sam Hui was a prime example back in the 1970s. Behind the comeback of singer-songwriters was the record companies' marketing strategy to lure fans back to Cantopop. Given that these singer-songwriters were allowed to have their own personal styles, the strategy did inject some new blood into the industry. Chet Lam's cultural *Travelogue* trilogy—*Travelogue 1* 《遊樂》 (2003), *Travelogue, too* 《一個人在途上》 (2004), and *travelogue, three* 《城市旅人》 (2008)—among others, introduced a newfangled idea to Cantopop. Pong Nan's first two albums, *The Unadorable Pong Nan* 《不要人見人愛》 and *Almost Happy* 《無非想快樂》, were a young man's reflections on himself and society, with original acoustic music and topics ranging from local culture (e.g., "Ice House at 3pm" 〈三點冰室〉) to national allegory (e.g., "June" 〈六月〉). Having written songs and lyrics for mainstream Cantopop singers like Sammi Cheng and Kelly Chen for many years, Vicky Fung released her solo concept album *Never Home . . .* 《想回家》 in 2005. Shortly after her second album, *The Journey of Present* 《擁抱現在》, she shifted back to the role of composer.

---

37. Yuen, "Autonomous Voice of the Epoch."
38. Cited from an interview with MC Yan by the author at Festival Walk, Hong Kong, September 18, 2009.

Among these singer-songwriters, Ivana Wong was perhaps the one who was most able to merge into the mainstream. After winning the Twelfth CASH Song Writers Quest (2000), she started writing songs for mainstream Cantopop singers. She had the chance to sing the song "I Am Really Hurt" 〈我真的受傷了〉 (2001, in Mandarin) with the Heavenly King Jacky Cheung (for whom the song was originally written) at his 2004 concert, which stole the limelight and won her the chance to release her own album with Universal Records in 2005. Trained as a classical pianist, she showcased her musical talents with her unique sound and delicate lyrics in two albums, *Ivana* (EP) and *I Love My Name*, which established a sound basis for her singer-songwriter career. Not surprisingly, she won several awards at the end of the year, including the Ultimate Song Chart Singer-Songwriter Bronze Award (2005), the Jade Solid Gold Most Popular Singer-Songwriter Silver Award (2005), and the Jade Solid Gold Most Popular New Female Singer Silver Award (2005). More resources were directed to her up-and-coming start in her next album, *Poetic Feeling, Picturesque Sense* 《詩情・畫意》 (2006). The melodies of the two main plugs, "Poetic Feeling" and "Picturesque Sense," were composed by Ivana Wong. The lyrics, penned by Lin Xi, added poetic and picturesque charm to the beautiful tunes, building a solid career for her in the mainstream music industry.

To recognize her achievements, RTHK Top Ten Gold Songs Awards conferred on Ivana Wong the CASH Best Singer-Songwriter Award in 2006. Her 2007 album *Read My Senses . . .* continued to impress, and with her popularity accumulated through her previous album and chart-topping hit "Mask" 〈面具〉, she went on to grab both the Ultimate and the Jade Solid Gold Singer-Songwriter Gold awards in 2007. More importantly, unlike the sporadic endeavors of other singer-songwriters, her works continued to enter pop charts. After she moved to East Asia Records, she managed to have pop-chart hits every year, including, "I Came from Mars" 〈我來自火星〉 (2008), "The Moon Says" 〈月亮說〉 (2009), "Open Cage Bird" 〈開籠雀〉 (2010), "Water Lily" 〈水百合〉 (2011), and "Leave Blank" 〈留白〉 (2012), and the latter even won her TVB's Gold Song Gold Award, a remarkable achievement for a singer-songwriter in the Cantopop industry. Moreover, she held her debut "Water Lily" concerts at Hong Kong Coliseum in October 2012, making her one of the very few singer-songwriters who entered the Cantopop shrine. As Ivana Wong once remarked in an interview, "I seldom compromise my creativity for popularity because as a singer-songwriter I have a responsibility to bring more music to the audience rather than being bound by the media."[39] Unfortunately, she was among the few singer-songwriters who could survive in a shrinking market with their creativity.

---

39. Arthur Tam, "Ivana Wong," *Timeout Hong Kong* (November 7, 2012). Available at: http://www.timeout.com.hk/feature-stories/features/54388/ivana-wong.html; retrieved on March 15, 2016.

That the Cantopop industry was more willing to experiment with new styles and genres may be true, but it should also be noted that these genres, as stressed by MC Yan, were simply packaged as trendy styles in a short-sighted manner. Neither hip-hop nor singer-songwriters lasted long. The singer-songwriter Candy Lo 盧巧音 would be a very good example in exposing the morbid side of the Cantopop industry. As the lead vocalist of the rock band Black & Blue, Candy Lo made an impact in the band wave back in the 1990s. She went solo in 1998 after signing with Sony Music. Her debut EP *Not Necessary . . . To Be Terribly Perfect* 《不需要……完美得可怕》 (1998) and subsequent albums *Miao . . .* (1998) and *Get Close to Candy Lo* 《貼近盧巧音》 (1999) were reasonably popular given her pioneering effort of mixing rock and pop. Her performance was steady in the new millennium, with popular hits like "Deep Blue" 〈深藍〉 (2000) and "Wind Chime" 〈風鈴〉 (2001). Her 2002 album *Appreciate the Taste of Life* 《賞味人間》 went triple platinum (more than 90,000 copies sold), owing to the immense popularity of the song "Please Let Me Go" 〈好心分手〉, both the solo version and the version featuring Leehom Wang. The style of the song (melody by Mark Lui and lyrics by Wyman Wong) was not quite similar to Candy Lo's previous pop rock, but it turned out to be one of the most popular songs of the year. Candy Lo bagged many song awards with that song, among which was "The Most Popular Karaoke Song" awarded by RTHK. Candy Lo, with her rapidly increasing fame, was baptized into stardom in her two debut Hong Kong Coliseum concerts "True Music 1st Flight Live 2003."

Apparently, the female rocker was not satisfied with her success in the mainstream. After *Flower Talks* 《花言・巧語》 (2003), which claimed to be a concept album about flowers, she released a truly avant-garde concept album entitled *Evolution Theory* 《天演論》 in 2005. She wrote the tunes of eight of the ten songs (plus two Mandarin versions) in the album (the other two were written by her producer Kubert Leung), and the lyrics examined life from philosophical and scientific perspectives—as indicated by the title of the album. The songs touched on controversial topics like the ancestor of human beings ("Lucy" 〈露茜〉), religion ("The Opposite Shore Goddess of Mercy" 〈隔岸觀音〉, and death ("Sutra for Seeing Souls Off" 〈送魂經〉), to name a few. The return of her band soul was welcomed by some of her fans, but it sounded too highbrow for ordinary audiences to join in the chorus. Despite excellent reviews, the album did not sell well, which became a turning point in Candy Lo's mainstream career. She left Sony, joined WOW Music, and released another album, *Process*, in 2007. While she refused to compromise her individuality for popularity, the sad fact was that the narrow fan base of the mainstream Cantopop industry made it difficult for singers with an attitude to survive.

It is important to recognize that the Cantopop industry had inherent problems, but thanks to the untiring efforts of some mainstream industry players, creative vigor could still be introduced into the aging industry. Wyman Wong and Lin Xi are two major examples of this phenomenon. An acclaimed lyricist famous for his creativity, Wyman Wong contributed innovative ideas to Cantopop by, among other means, crossing different themes (e.g., "Wedding Card Street" mentioned in a previous section). As already noted in Chapter Three, Cantopop was not true to its name, with most songs written in standard Chinese rather than Cantonese, and to use 100 percent Cantonese in writing lyrics would be considered unofficial, if not vulgar. Against all odds, Wyman Wong decided to launch, in collaboration with composer Ronald Ng 伍樂城, a "New Cantonese Songs Campaign" to promote songs written in 100 percent Cantonese. One of the more important examples of this string of songs was Rain Li's 李彩樺 "You Don't Love Me Anymore"〈你唔愛我啦〉, which was known as the "Cantonese Experiment No. 1." Love songs are rarely written in Cantonese, but Wyman Wong was determined to revolutionize the language style of Cantopop with this project. Thanks to the innovative use of Cantonese, and especially the word "la" 啦 (which can be said in different tones to imply subtly different meanings), this was a successful attempt to use the different tones of Cantonese to present a Hong Kong girl's views on love. According to Wyman Wong, he had hoped to produce an album with all songs written in Cantonese, but in the end, due to the lack of support, only some of the songs were collected in different albums by different singers.[40] There were six other "experiments," but, except for the relatively popular "Silly Boy"〈傻仔〉(No. 2) by Miriam Yeung, the others were not well received by fans.[41] It was a shame that even Wyman Wong, as one of the two most influential lyricists from the mid-1990s to the early 2010s, could not succeed in persuading the record companies to publish an album written in 100 percent Cantonese. This may be attributed to the lack of appreciation for those kinds of songs among fans. It also revealed the fact that, more importantly, the Cantopop industry did not have the courage to promote genuinely experimental styles in the mainstream. Despite the incomplete experiment, Wyman Wong introduced new language styles with his perceptive handling of Cantonese. He was among the few lyricists who made tactful use of a hybrid of Cantonese and standard Chinese, a style more common among the lyricists in the 1970s, in his lyrics

---

40. Chu, *Songs of Your Life*, 226–27.
41. The other five were: Patrick Tang's 鄧健泓 "Don't Think I'm Crazy"〈你咪當我傻〉(No. 3); Patrick Tang and William So's 蘇永康 "Afraid of You"〈怕咗你〉(No. 4); Miriam Yeung, Rain Li, and Charmaine Fong's 方皓玟 "What We Want" (No. 5); Miriam Yeung, Rain Li, Charmaine Fong, William So, Patrick Tang, and Alex Fong's 方力申 "Make Me Mad" (No. 6); and Charmaine Fong's "You Have a Car?"〈你有車嗎〉(No. 7).

(for example, in the line "Those being built, one has to accept, will topple one day" "築得起，人應該接受，都有日倒下" from "Wedding Card Street," the word "*dou*" 都 is a Cantonese expression, and the use of it makes the line sound better than using a standard written Chinese expression).

It would be one-sided, however, to assume that the Cantopop industry focused mainly on romantic ballads, which has been an unfair stereotype for many years. Lin Xi, the lyricist who dominated the industry since the late 1980s, launched an unofficial "non-love songs movement," similar to the one by Jimmy Lo in the 1980s, in the new millennium. Lin Xi had long been famous for his signature love songs, which touched the hearts of countless fans. In the new millennium, he started writing more non-love songs to expand the vision of Cantopop. Some of the golden hits mentioned above, such as "Infinite Beauty of the Setting Sun" and "Too Late for Love," were songs of the year that touched on less mainstream topics such as life philosophies. Interestingly enough, Lin Xi entered the industry by winning a "Non-Love Song Writing Competition" with the song "Once" 〈曾經〉 back in 1985. At the outset of his career, he caused a stir with his "non-love" lyrics penned for the group Raidas. After many years of focusing mainly on love, he realized, especially after his recovery from an anxiety disorder in 2006,[42] that the themes of Cantopop had been too narrow. He decided to introduce new themes, including the uneven distribution of resources (e.g., Hacken Lee's "Tin Sui Wai: The Besieged City" 〈天水圍城〉), political allegory (e.g., Eason Chan's "June Snow" 〈六月飛霜〉), and Daoist philosophy (e.g., Juno Mak's 麥浚龍 "Three Thousand Fathoms of Weak Water" 〈弱水三千〉). The three songs in Juno Mak's album *Innate Dreams* 《天生地夢》 (2009), "Three Thousand Fathoms of Weak Water," "Life and Death Are Wearing Me Out" 〈生死疲勞〉, and "Inverting the Dream" 〈顛倒夢想〉, were all "hard-core" life philosophies inspired by Taoism and Buddhism. Thanks to Juno Mak's independent production budget, composers and lyricists had relatively more space to articulate their own ideas. Lin Xi was also able to introduce his life philosophies into love ballads through mainstream Cantopop stars, including Eason Chan and Joey Yung (such as "Not Wearing One Thread" 〈一絲不掛〉 and "In Search of the Supernatural" 〈搜神記〉, respectively, the former a Buddhist-inspired examination of love and the latter a self-reflexive contemplation of the importance of self-love). One of the contributions of Lin Xi was that he was able to pioneer philosophical themes into mainstream Cantopop, demanding the audience to have in-depth understanding of the songs. Meanwhile, Yiu-Fai Chow, the

42. "The God of Lyrics Feels Unwell" 〈林夕病詞神〉 (in Chinese), *Headline Daily*. Available at: http://hd.stheadline.com/living/living_content.asp?contid=11780&srctype=g; retrieved on March 15, 2016.

lyricist of the other three songs of Juno Mak's album *Innate Dreams*, has also been introducing alternative elements into the mainstream. As noted above, his funky experiments in Joey Yung's *Ten Most Wanted* is a good example to show his refusal to submit to mainstream styles. His collaborations with Juno Mak, such as "Androgynous"〈雌雄同體〉, "Queer"〈酷兒〉, "Step with Left Foot, Step with the Right Foot"〈彳亍〉 and "Door"〈門〉, are avant-garde imaginaries of gender and/or life philosophy rarely seen in the main-stream. He has also been working closely with new singers such as Eman Lam 林二汶 and Ellen Loo 盧凱彤 on bold endeavors to explore the possibilities of Cantopop lyrics. For example, "Rampant"〈囂張〉, winner of "2013 CASH Golden Sail Best Lyrics Award," highlights the importance of self-esteem through a Kafkaesque presentation of talent shows. His lyrics can be summed up in this: "mainstream but unconventional, alternative yet tenderly sensitive." In short, the cross-fertilization between the mainstream and the alternative, as shown in Chapter Four, was one of the most important sources of the creativity of Cantopop in the 1980s. This could also be seen in the third wave of band music in Hong Kong.

The Third Band Wave

As LMF was arguably the only band that made an impact on the mainstream music industry in the first few years after the turn of the millennium (similar to the situation in the 1990s, when Beyond was the only popular band), the sound of "one hand clapping" was not widely heard. Moreover, although pre-band wave energy emanated in a stable market, unlike that of the 1980s, the market for local popular music was shrinking swiftly. Both bands and mainstream singers faced an uphill battle in this market, and thus it took much more time for another wave of band music to gather momentum. While indie music made its impact, as mentioned in the previous section, it was arguably not until 2008 that the mainstream music industry felt the new wave of band music. In 2008, major labels in Hong Kong, such as Universal Music, Gold Typhoon, and BMA Records, formally absorbed band music into their marketing plan. Mr., a quintet recommended to Universal Music by famous Cantopop star Alan Tam, released their first album (Universal Music released an EP for them to test the waters in 2008) entitled *If I Am . . .* in 2009. Based on the title of their first hit, "If I Were Eason Chan"〈如果我是陳奕迅〉, Mr., formerly an indie band known as White Noise, was determined to enter the mainstream. (The voice of the lead vocalist for Mr., Alan Po, was considered similar to Eason Chan's.) When their commercial venture started in 2008 with a major label, they were considered a "sell out" by many in Hong Kong's indie rock scene, and Alan Po responded by stressing that "the band would rather focus on making good music than to get all hung up on whether they are making 'rock' music."[43]

RubberBand, founded in 2004, was signed by Gold Typhoon and they released their first album entitled *Apollo 18* in 2008, making noise in the music industry with their fusion/funky rock. Meanwhile, Soler, a rock duo signed to BMA Records in 2008, released their first all-Cantonese album *Canto* in the same year. C AllStar is another band worth mentioning here. Founded in 2009, C AllStar was different from other rock bands. The four members were first interested in a cappella; later, they successfully stormed pop charts with their hybridized, college-style jazz, rock, and R&B in their debut album *Make it Happen*, which was released in 2010. The absorption of band music into the mainstream was seen as a sign of band music's comeback. In short, band music songs stormed pop charts in Hong Kong and were later recognized at year-end music award ceremonies in 2009, signaling the generation of the third wave of band music. Whether the mainstream ventures of band music was a "sell out" or not, as criticized by some die-hard rock fans, is a complicated question that calls for a more nuanced account; it is safe to say, however, that the third wave of band music made room for other alternative attempts in the mainstream music industry. For instance, Dear Jane, a rock band founded in 2003, was signed to See Music Ltd. and Music Nation Group before moving to Warner Music Group in 2011. Most of these bands remained peripheral in the music industry, but some made a significant impact on the mainstream.

The songs by these bands, like those of their counterparts in the 1980s, voiced their discontent with the Hong Kong society. The music lyrics had specific meanings, and "the 'content' of rock music [was] not merely grounded in the musical form of the songs."[44] The themes of these songs fell into three general categories: to speak truth to power, to stay young, and to imagine alternatives. In the aftermath of the financial tsunami, Hong Kong's economy suffered a serious setback, aggravated by the problem of the uneven distribution of wealth. The lack of upward mobility, a notorious problem for Hong Kong over the past decade, generated widespread anger among the younger generation. Rock band music, at this particular juncture, empowered their social participation. The song "Black Fanatic" by Mr., for instance, used the color

---

43. Cheong Poh Kwan, "Hong Kong Rock Band Mr. Grateful for Success," *The Straits Times* (November 10, 2012). Available at: http://stcommunities.straitstimes.com/music/2012/11/10/hong-kong-rock-band-mr-grateful-success-0; retrieved on March 15, 2016.
44. For the meanings of the rock lyrics, see Peter Christenson and Donald Roberts, *It's Not Only Rock & Roll: Popular Music in the Lives of Adolescents* (Cresskill: Hampton Press, 1998), 63–64, 153, 179. Moreover, "[o]n the one hand this 'content' is determined by the contexts which its fans give it, and on the other hand it is also preconditioned by the social relations of its production and distribution together with the institutional contexts in which these stand." Peter Wicke, *Rock Music: Culture, Aesthetics and Sociology* (Cambridge: Cambridge University Press, 1990), ix.

black as a symbol of opposition against institutional power. In a similar vein, RubberBand's "Open Your Eyes" asked Hong Kong people not to turn a blind eye to the demolition of old communities and other forms of social inequalities. While Mr. and RubberBand were signed by major music labels and their songs were in a way commercial (for instance, "Black Fanatic" was the theme song of the promotional campaign for Coca-Cola), rock band music exerted the special function of locating its fans as oppositional, as noted by Lawrence Grossberg: "Rock and roll locates its fans as different even while they exist within the hegemony," serving as an "insider's art that functions to position its fans as outsider[s]," and "[t]his 'encapsulation' may sometimes be produced through ideological representations which either explicitly attack the hegemony or define an alternative identity for those living within its affective alliances."[45]

To stay young is another central theme of rock band music, which has the function of taking its listeners back in time. Mr., among others, forth-rightly expressed their wish to go back to the good old days in their version of "Yesterday." C AllStar's "Our Woodstock" paid homage to global as well as local deceased music legends, from John Lennon to Leslie Cheung, while highlighting the importance of using music to disseminate "the world will live as one" message. "Pop Songs of the Post-1980s," a collage of Cantopop hits from the 1980s, also aimed at taking the audience back to the good old days of Cantopop in particular and Hong Kong culture in general. The seeming nostalgia in these works must be understood as another way of imagining the future. It is in this sense that these works exhibited a longing for the past: "music stands for the alternative: freedom from the restraints of authority and the right to seek pleasure in one's own way and in the moment."[46] While rock music offers an opportunity for the audience to provisionally escape from the oppression of social reality and stay young, it empowers the agency of its audience, as noted succinctly by Simon Frith in his monumental study on the sociology of rock: "The rock audience is not a passive mass, consuming records like corn-flakes, but an active community, making music into a symbol of solidarity and an inspiration for action."[47] This inspiration can be seen, for example, in the alternative imaginaries in band songs. In its portrayal of a world threatened by environmental destruction and pandemics, "The New Prophecy" by C AllStar asserted that as long as one firmly believes that there is a better future, it will become true one day. RubberBand's "World Cup on the Street" used soccer as a means to unite different walks of life, advocating racial harmony through soccer and music. Moreover, "Keenly Felt Pain" by C AllStar

45. Lawrence Grossberg, "Another Boring Day in Paradise: Rock n' Roll and the Empowerment of Everyday Life," *Popular Music* 4 (1984): 234.
46. Christenson and Roberts, *It's Not Only Rock & Roll*, 59.
47. Simon Frith, *The Sociology of Rock* (London: Constable, 1978), 198.

was an open statement of their pacifist sentiments, adding a much-neglected anti-war dimension to Cantonese popular songs.

"Rock music had become 'progressive,' or at least this was how musicians, as well as journalists and fans, referred to the music which distinguished itself by virtue of its artistic and political ambitions from the purely commercial products of the music market."[48] At times, the "progressive" nature of rock music made it a target for political incorporation. The Hong Kong Dome Festival saga is an interesting example of the complex dynamics between rock band music and the power network. The Hong Kong Dome Festival took place on July 1, 2013, featuring Korean pop stars and groups, including BoA, Shinee, f(x), EXO, and Henry from Super Junior M. Mr. and RubberBand were the two bands representing Hong Kong in the show. As tickets were being sold at an incredibly low price of HK$99, the organizers were widely criticized for using the show to tempt young people away from the annual pro-democracy march customarily held on the same day. Fans of the two local bands voiced their discontent, asking them to boycott the show organized arguably for the sake of "social stability." The two bands decided to play, but they also issued an apology to their fans and pledged that they would donate all their earnings to charities and join the march after the event. Notwithstanding the fact that these bands were signed to major commercial labels, they were able to position themselves as being "progressive," contributing an important dimension absent from the mainstream Cantopop industry. Simon Frith once predicted that world popular music will take the form of one of three parallel music entities in the near future: (1) the mainstream pop/rock business; (2) the essentially chaotic illegal music business involving both straightforward crooks ripping off rights holders by bootlegging and experimental and political artists who refuse to accept the constraints of copyright laws; and (3) genre music scenes in which semi-commercial local players are connected through websites and digital radio with aims of neither fame nor profit.[49] There have been "semi-commercial" local bands in between the mainstream and the underground, and more discursive spaces have been available since the major labels absorbed band music into their marketing agenda.

Kolor is an interesting example of in-between rock. A four-man rock band founded in 2005, Kolor was brought onto the music scene by Ka-Keung Wong 黃家強, the brother of the legendary Ka-Kui Wong of Beyond. They later produced their album under their own label, Lead Harmony Limited. According to their introduction on their website, Kolor "represents their diversities both musically and personally. Coming from different backgrounds, it is as though there are four artists working on a single composition, each infusing his unique

48. Wicke, *Rock Music*, 92–93.
49. Frith, "The Popular Music Industry," 50.

perspective, ultimately creating music as a group that is both powerful and meaningful." One of their most innovative endeavors is the project "Law of 14"—uploading a song to the Internet for free listening every month on the 14th—which began in January 2010. They worked closely with lyricist Pak-Kin Leung 梁柏堅, and because of their flexible mode of production, they acted promptly and offered timely commentaries on social issues. Two remarkable examples of this are "The Gang of Heaven and Earth" and "The Apocalypse of Gambling." The former echoed the TVB program *When Heaven Burns* by slamming a dying city lost in finance-dominated capitalism. By the end, the song voiced the role of rock music in a dying city: "The city will not die, as long as there is rock music breaking the walls." The latter song was uploaded in March 2012, shortly before the election of Hong Kong's chief executive. The election campaign was blemished by scandals, which were vividly depicted in the song as the indecent tactics of the candidates. For instance, the illegal structures found in the luxury house of one of the candidates, Henry Tang, were alluded to in the song, along with vehement condemnations of the candidates' conduct.

Another notable example of speaking truth to power from beyond the mainstream is My Little Airport (MLA). MLA was first heard on the Internet and quickly gained recognition due to their creative style and poignant social critiques. Hitting the fancy of young netizens, their songs have had hundreds of thousands of hits. One need only look at the name of their earlier representative song—"Donald Tsang, Please Go Die"—to understand why it appealed to the public, who had long been fed up with the poor governance of the former chief executive of Hong Kong, Donald Tsang. Needless to say, it would be unimaginable to speak for the *vox populi* in such a direct and piercing manner in the music industry.[50] MLA's records were produced by Harbor Records, an indie label established in 2004. Financially independent from the mainstream music industry, MLA was able to sing what they thought—from political satires to sex dreams, all taboos in the mainstream industry. The success of MLA can be attributed to, besides pointed social and political commentaries, their creative imagination in blending local issues with a global vision, as seen in the title of one of their representative songs, "Being Poetic in between Paris and Mong Kok." (Mong Kok is one of the busiest and most densely populated districts on Earth.) While Kolor slammed political figures hard, MLA made

---

50. In August 2010, John Tsang 曾俊華, the financial secretary of Hong Kong, visited Taipei in the capacity of honorary chairperson of the Hong Kong–Taiwan Economic and Cultural Co-operation and Promotion Council. During his visit to Eslite Bookstore, he was escorted by Wen-Jie Wu 吳旻潔, daughter of the chairman of the Eslite Groups. Wu picked a CD for John Tsang, which, interestingly enough, turned out to be an MLA album. One can imagine how embarrassed John Tsang was when he listened to the song "Donald Tsang, Please Go Die," a curse against his then boss. This is an interesting anecdote that attests to the popularity of MLA in Taiwan.

use of satires in a lighter manner. As shown in their album title *Hong Kong Is One Big Shopping Mall* (2011), MLA also has harsh criticism for finance-dominated capitalism.

Despite the shrinking market of Cantopop, greener pastures were available to indie labels with the comeback of band music in 2008. While Harbor Records ran its business with an alternative mode of music production, which was basically independent from the mainstream, there were other indie labels operating in a different manner. Redline Music is a representative example. Its indie productions were distributed by East Asia Music Publishing Limited, a major label in the market. Like other major labels, Redline Music relied on resources from commercial sponsorships. Its mission was to absorb resources from the mainstream and use them to support the indie music scene. Notwithstanding reservations about a lack of independence, Redline Music was able to support local indie bands in releasing their albums, such as Peri M and Supper Moment.[51] Peri M (short for Perimeter), named for the outermost limits of a confined area and range of vision, aimed at expressing the viewpoint that band music was about every aspect of the people and the world. Musically, the style of Peri M could be categorized as Melodic Rock. With a focus on creating a sonic landscape for its audience, Peri M persisted in using rich and tight musical arrangements as the backbone to support its melodic vocal lines. Meanwhile, Supper Moment, influenced by Mr. Children and John Mayer, is a four-man band focused on pop rock. Without the vehement social criticisms of Kolor, their songs presented similar messages: the importance of staying young and to dare to dream for a better tomorrow. In their representative album *Heartbeat Once Again* (2011), they used "Soap Bubble" to symbolize, despite being extremely transient, the wish to fly high for dreams. After saying "Goodnight City," they still reminded the audience to strive for a better tomorrow. Their "Explaining Love to Children" may be interpreted as an attempt to explain the importance of believing in fairy tales, echoing Jean-François Lyotard's postmodernist take on childhood: "What would happen if thought no longer had a childhood?"[52] Lyotard approached this question by underlining the importance of childhood as the season of possibilities. It may be true that "the illusions which once assigned to rock music the power to undermine social relations, to explode them and to build a more human, a 'better' world in their place have long since faded away."[53] However, at least in the case of Hong Kong, the third wave

51. I owe this to my graduate student Eva Leung, whose thesis offers a comprehensive account of the mode of operation of indie labels in Hong Kong.
52. Jean-François Lyotard, *The Postmodern Explained* (Minneapolis: University of Minnesota Press, 1993), ix.
53. Wicke, *Rock Music*, 174.

of band music has shown otherwise: the people still resort to "illusion"—be that as it may—to rock the city and strive for a better world.[54]

Afterword: The New Mediascape

Unlike their counterparts in the 1980s, these bands have been facing a swiftly shrinking market. Small independent companies could have diversified music genres with experimental projects, but their impacts could not be capitalized on without a robust industry. Meanwhile, the music awards, no matter those of TVB, CR2, or RTHK, gradually lost their influence. As noted in Chapter Four, mass media was a very important promoter of the music industry, and the music awards presentations, such as Jade Solid Gold, the Ultimate Awards, and the Ten Gold Songs Awards, played an important role in amplifying the influence of Cantopop. In the new millennium, however, the popularity of these awards gradually diminished. Worse yet, the controversy between TVB and Hong Kong Recording Industry Alliance Limited (HKRIA) dealt a further blow to the credibility of Jade Solid Gold, if not other music awards as well. TVB fought with HKRIA over copyright fees in 2009,[55] and as they failed to resolve the dispute, TVB decided to ban singers from the four big companies—the founding members of HKRIA, including Universal, Warner, Sony, and EMI—from their programs, including the Jade Solid Gold Music Awards in early 2010. It was perhaps the first time since its launch back in the 1980s that many best-known names were edited out of the awards lists. Without Eason Chan, Hacken Lee, Kay Tse, and other big names, it was not surprising that the awards ceremonies failed to impress fans. When TVB gave the Most Popular Male Singer in the Asia-Pacific Region Award to their own actor-turned singer Raymond Lam 林峯 (actually three years in a row), many music fans simply turned their backs and refused to believe that the decision was

---

54. There are many bands with different styles, but given the limited scope of this chapter, I cannot go into more detail here. Other representative bands include, among others, Chochukmo, a five-piece indie rock and experimental band. Unlike the bands on which I have focused here, Chochukmo plays English songs, so it was not covered. I am indebted to an anonymous reviewer for noting that it is unsophisticated to use language as the sole defining characteristic of a music genre. For example, the songs of MLA are in both Cantonese and English (actually the songs of many Cantopop stars, especially those in the 1970s, are in both English and Cantonese). This is an important topic related to Hong Kong popular music per se, which is worthy of its own full-length study. As the focus of this book is Cantonese songs, my analysis is cursory and I would leave this as critical reflection here.

55. "The alliance had planned to charge 0.45 per cent of TVB's advertising revenue in 2008—HK$10.8 million of HK$2.4 billion—saying the rate fell within the world standard of 0.13 per cent to 1.2 per cent. The amount was more than double the figure—less than HK$5 million a year—TVB used to pay the four labels." Vivienne Chow, "TVB to Edit Top Singers out of Awards Shows as Row with Major Labels Takes Centre Stage," *South China Morning Post* (January 8, 2010). Available at: http://www.scmp.com/article/703093/tvb-edit-top-singers-out-awards-shows-row-major-labels-takes-centre-stage; retrieved on March 15, 2016.

impartial. In the Jade Solid Gold 2012 awards presentation, the Most Popular Male Singer in the Asia-Pacific Region Award, apparently owing to the lack of home-grown stars (Raymond Lam had already received the Most Popular Male Singer Award), went to the Taiwanese group Lollipop, which was the first time in twenty years that the title was awarded to a non-Cantopop unit. The TVB-HKRIA controversy dragged on for several years, and, regarding the diminishing influence and popularity of TVB's prime popular music programs, it was arguably the last straw that broke the camel's back. When the dispute was settled in January 2013, serious damage had been done and it was by no means easy to win back the hearts of the fans.

The situation would not have been that bad had Hong Kong been able to have more media channels. Compared with the major music outlets around the world, the number of broadcasting channels in Hong Kong was infamously low. There were only two free-to-air television companies after the closing of Hong Kong Commercial Television in 1978, and, arguably, RTV had not been fully functioning for many years due to poor management. In addition, there were only three major radio stations—RTHK, Commercial Radio, and Metro Radio—until Digital Broadcasting Corporation was founded in 2008 (it closed in October 2012 and relaunched in December 2013). TVB has been the market leader for decades, and its music programs' fall from grace exerted a very negative impact on the star-production mechanism of the media industries in Hong Kong. As repeatedly mentioned in previous chapters, the creative synergy among the popular music, film, and television sectors contributed enormously to the success of Hong Kong's cultural industries, and during their heyday these industries saw a win-win situation. In the face of the stellar rise of cultural industries in the Mainland and in Asian countries such as South Korea, the once trendsetter Cantopop significantly lagged behind. While the government was not aware of this, its promotion of Hong Kong creative industries was hopelessly framed by its "Brand Hong Kong" mentality. Simon Frith has perceptively identified a very important point to note in popular music studies: "Popular music culture isn't the effect of a popular music industry; rather, the music industry is an aspect of popular music culture."[56] Unfortunately, Brand Hong Kong, the promotional program that packaged Hong Kong as "Asia's World City" and distinguished it from other Mainland cities, uses "industry" to define "culture."[57] The Brand Hong Kong program, which has been trying to highlight "Hong Kong's existing strengths in areas such as financial services, trade, tourism, transport, communications,

---

56. Frith, "The Popular Music Industry," 27.
57. Chu, *Lost in Transition*, 139.

and as a regional hub for international business and a major city in China,"[58] came to dominate the Hong Kong government's attitude toward the local music industry, which has been handcuffed by its enduring enthrallment with branding: how to brand local culture and sell it to the global market. The government launched Entertainment Expo Hong Kong in 2005, bringing together key events from Hong Kong's entertainment calendar for film, TV, digital entertainment, music, and other cutting-edge media. The Hong Kong Music Fair and the Asian Pop Music Festival (since 2011) were key events for popular music, but as the government placed an emphasis on financing and networking, not on producing Hong Kong popular music, the event did not have much to do with inspiring creativity and hybridity.

James Wong stressed in his doctoral thesis that the achievement of Cantopop is similar to Hong Kong's legendary economic success, in that it is the result of a closed political environment on the Mainland and in Taiwan.[59] Taiwan and, subsequently, the Mainland turned from being fans of Cantopop to being its chief competitors. Instant stardom was no longer the monopoly of Hong Kong's pop industry. As Hong Kong ceased to be the center of Chinese popular music, only those established Cantopop singers such as Eason Chan could make a significant impact on the Mandapop market. Although the Hong Kong singers who turned to Mandapop in a sense made Hong Kong popular music more hybridized, in terms of Cantopop per se this further worsened the lack of creative space. In short, if one considers the late 1980s the golden age of Cantopop, the new millennium must belong to Mandapop.

---

58. Hong Kong Special Administrative Region Government, *The Report on the First Five Years of the Hong Kong Special Administrative Region of the People's Republic of China* (Hong Kong: Hong Kong SAR, 2002), 41.
59. Wong, "The Rise and Decline of Cantopop," 183.

7 | Epilogue
Cantopop in the Age of China

In the new millennium, Cantopop has been overtaken by Mandapop as the trendsetter of pan-Chinese popular culture. During its heyday from the 1980s until the early 1990s, Cantopop was hybridized, although it was highly commercial and had begun to cross borders. "As a small, wealthy, then-British colonial protectorate cum Chinese semi-autonomous region, Hong Kong has the mixture of economic wealth and cultural eclecticism that fosters hybrid media forms."[1] Cantopop was once among the most representative hybrid media forms in Hong Kong. Cantopop was able to blend the global and the local into a significantly hybridized, "glocal" culture, similar to what Homi Bhabha implied with his "vernacular cosmopolitanism."[2] Before the mid-1990s, Hong Kong Cantopop achieved remarkable success; however, in the 1990s, the globalization of Chinese media changed the ecology of Chinese popular music industries, and the Cantopop industry failed to make effective responses to these changes. Further aggravating the situation was the fundamental change Hong Kong experienced after the 1997 reversion to China. Before 1997, Hong Kong had been trying hard to identify ways in which it could retain autonomy after its return to Chinese sovereignty. However, Hong Kong witnessed a dramatic change in its attitude toward Mainland China after the handover, followed by the economic downturn in 1998 and 1999, which shattered Hong Kong's myth of economic success and put Hong Kong people in dire straits in the aftermath of the Asian financial crisis.

Many Hong Kong people willingly turned to the Mainland, not because of the Hong Kong government's edification of national consciousness, but because of China's surprisingly swift economic growth in the new millennium. The rise

---

1. Marwan M. Kraidy, *Hybridity, or the Cultural Logic of Globalization* (Philadelphia: Temple University Press, 2005), 8.
2. Homi K. Bhabha, "Unsatisfied Notes on Vernacular Cosmopolitanism," in *Text and Narration: Cross-Disciplinary Essays on Cultural and National Identities*, ed. Laura García-Morena and Peter C. Pfeifer (Columbia, SC: Camden House, 1996), 191–207.

of China and its soft power in the first decade of the new millennium contributed to Hong Kong's increasing dependence on the Mainland market. After China's soft power gathered momentum in the new millennium, Mandarin became the *lingua franca* of many Chinese communities. In this context, Mandapop became more and more popular. The shrinking of the Cantopop market on the one hand and the rapid expansion of the Mandapop market on the other forced Cantopop to become less diversified in terms of music styles, lyrics, and target audiences, as record companies directed their resources only to would-be winners. At that point the loss of hybridity was the major reason for the decline of the Hong Kong music industry, which was caused by the rise of the economic, political, and cultural influence of Mandarin-speaking Mainland China and the lack of competence in the industry in dealing with the resulting shifts in the media landscape.

In the face of the shrinking market, music companies did not invest in rising stars, and, subsequently, fewer and fewer young musicians joined the industry. Only a handful of new stars were able to survive; many left the industry altogether and took up related jobs such as acting or modeling to sustain their entertainment careers. Meanwhile, newcomers to the industry were not full-fledged musicians. Often poorly trained, they simply used their music career as a stepping stone into the wider entertainment industry. Releasing records was seen as merely a means to increase media exposure, which would then bring about further opportunities such as performing at private functions and establishing themselves as multitalented artists. The lack of dedicated creative talents in the mainstream market led many listeners to turn to Mandapop, which had become much more diverse than Cantopop. As Hong Kong increasingly began to rely on the Mainland market, it became more Mainland-oriented, exerting an adverse effect on its cultural variety. According to a survey by Siu-Kai Lau 劉兆佳, the former head of the Central Policy Unit of Hong Kong Special Administrative Region, a new identity of "Hong Kong Chinese" surfaced not long after 1997, evincing the growing importance of "Chineseness" in the formation of local Hong Kong identity.[3] After national identity and Chineseness became an important dimension in Hong Kong's education system, the social status of Putonghua rose to unprecedented heights. The rise of China and its soft power in the new millennium also contributed to the social significance of Putonghua in Hong Kong. In the age of globalization, Cantopop also had to face an important problem besides the rising status of Putonghua. In the new globalized Chinese music industry the prospect of Mandapop was apparently

---

3. Siu-Kai Lau, *Hongkongese or Chinese: The Problem of Identity on the Eve of Resumption of Chinese Sovereignty over Hong Kong* (Hong Kong: Hong Kong Institute of Asia-Pacific Studies, the Chinese University of Hong Kong, 1997), 41; see also Yiu-Wai Chu, *Lost in Transition: Hong Kong Culture in the Age of China* (Albany: SUNY Press, 2013), 132.

much brighter than Cantopop, as Mandarin was more widely used in Chinese communities.[4] If the late 1980s and early 1990s was considered the golden age of Cantopop, then the 2000s must be that of Mandapop. With the emergence of a national popular music culture in China, Mandapop will become more and more important in shaping Chinese identity.

As mentioned in the previous chapter, the success of Hong Kong Cantopop, similar to Hong Kong's legendary economic achievements, was the result of a closed political environment in the Mainland and Taiwan. Taiwan and, subsequently, the Mainland later turned from the markets of Cantopop and became its chief competitors. Instant stardom was no longer the monopoly of Hong Kong's pop industry. Mandapop singers encroached into the Hong Kong market, including Taiwanese singers such as Jay Chou, who overtook the Four Heavenly Kings in terms of commercial viability. "While Cantopop marches on in Hong Kong, Chinese pop has moved elsewhere, on to Mandarin singer-songwriters, Taiwanese folk artists, Beijing rockers, Singapore balladeers."[5] To court huge markets, record companies and Cantopop singers proactively turned to Mandapop. Since the early 1990s, for instance, Hong Kong musicians have sought to break into the Taiwan market by producing Mandapop, which was later also seen as a way to enter the enormous market in the Mainland. Although Hong Kong singers who turned to Mandapop in a sense made Hong Kong popular music more hybridized, for Cantopop per se this further worsened the lack of creative space. Other than those very established Cantopop singers such as Eason Chan, very few Hong Kong singers could make a significant impact on the Mandapop market. And thus Hong Kong singers who turned to Mandapop could not revitalize the local Hong Kong entertainment industry.

Recent discussions on the globalization of culture have dwelled upon whether the global would erase the local. From the recapitulation of the development of Cantopop in the last few decades, it seems that Cantopop rose with the localization of Hong Kong popular culture in the 1970s and began to fade away in the dawn of globalization. To place the fall of Cantopop in the context of globalization, it is easy to draw the conclusion that it lost its local characteristics when it became global. In popular music studies, however, scholars

---

4. As noted by Greg Rogers, senior VP at MCA Music Entertainment International, Asia-Pacific, "Mandarin is an increasingly important language for music in the region. . . . That will probably accelerate somewhat, and then, for Chinese repertoire at least, Hong Kong becomes increasingly irrelevant to the equation." Cited from Geoff Burpee, "As Sun Sets on British Empire in Hong Kong, Industry Gears for Return to China," See *Billboard* 108, no. 43 (October 26, 1996): APQ-1.

5. Burpee, "As Sun Sets on British Empire in Hong Kong, Industry Gears for Return to China." It also has to be stressed that this is to highlight that Cantopop was no longer the trendsetter of Chinese popular music. The simplistic narrative cited here has overshadowed the complex transformation and diversification of Chinese pop. For example, Beijing rock also had its heydays in the late 1980s and early 1990s, after which it declined. I am indebted to an anonymous reviewer for pointing this out.

have also noted that the global-local dichotomy cannot fully capture the new cultural dynamics in the age of globalization.[6] The arguments presented in this book have pointed toward a different interpretation: Cantopop failed to retain its popularity for reasons other than becoming global. The Chinese population gently turned its back on Hong Kong music and one reason for doing so was the economic recession in 1997, which never recovered from its boom in the 1980s and 1990s. Another reason was Hong Kong's localization campaign, which failed to create new space to increase the diversity of Cantopop. As the market became smaller, there was a serious lack of diversity, as well as hybridity, in Cantopop, which in turn caused more listeners to go elsewhere to find other genres of popular songs. A vicious circle appeared as a result of these failures. Therefore, the decline of Cantopop cannot be blamed solely on its commercialism or piracy or a bad economy. I propose that the transformation of mediascape, the rise of a Chinese music industry in the region, and the subsequent loss of Cantopop's hybridity are the major reasons behind its recent decline. Meanwhile, some see the fall of Cantopop as a chance for a more diversified Hong Kong pop to emerge.[7] "Hong Kong's music scene was dead and flat for so long because of Cantopop," said Riz Farooqi of the Hong Kong hardcore group King Ly Chee.[8] With this I can only partly agree. This is true of the standardized Cantopop with its limited teenage fan base, but I beg to differ if he is referring to Cantopop in general, as it was once an important part of Hong Kong's music scene.

It is important to point out that Cantopop was vigorously hybridized from the outset. As Lawrence Witzleben rightly claimed, Cantopop is "a unique and often bewildering mixture of Chinese, other Asian and Western elements."[9] If one were to change "mixture" to "hybridization," it would be an even more accurate description of the characteristics of Cantopop in its heyday. Hybridity, a term used by Homi Bhabha in postcolonial discourse to hint at the possibility of resisting the colonizer, is often believed to be a strategy used to achieve a new cosmopolitanism.[10] For instance, Ray Allen and Lois Wilcken used the example of Caribbean–New Yorkers' music to illustrate how the hybridization of different music cultures can exert a dual function of "creating a dialogue across ethnic boundaries and helping to negotiate relations between different

6. See, for instance, Jan Fairley, "The 'Local' and 'Global' in Popular Music," in *The Cambridge Companion to Pop and Rock*, ed. Simon Frith, Will Straw, and John Street (Cambridge: Cambridge University Press, 2001), 272–89.

7. I have analyzed the impact of "internationalization" on Cantopop; see Chu, *Lost in Transition*, 135–36.

8. Cited from Davena Mok, "Getting in the Groove," *Asiaweek* (August 10, 2001).

9. Lawrence Witzleben, "Cantopop and Mandapop in Pre-postcolonial Hong Kong: Identity Negotiation in the Performances of Anita Mui Yim-Fong," *Popular Music* 18, no. 2 (1999): 241.

10. Homi Bhabha, "Unsatisfied: Notes on Vernacular Cosmopolitanism," in *Text and Nation*, ed. Laura Garcia-Morena and Peter C. Pfeifer (Columbia, SC: Camden House, 1996), 191–207.

cultural groups or between a minority and the dominant culture."[11] There will surely be winners as well as losers in the transforming field of popular music production, just as there were in earlier stages. But from the wider perspective of the global Chinese music industry, the development of Cantopop might also benefit Mandapop in the sense that cultural interaction and hybridity can stimulate the creative vigor of Chinese popular music per se. The survival of a more diversified Cantopop can contribute to the development of the music industries of both Hong Kong and the Mainland. It is not necessarily a zero-sum game.

In concluding this book, I will briefly discuss the possibility of a "new" Cantopop in this context. The above account suggests that the emergence of Cantopop is linked to the rise of a Hong Kong–born generation who identifies themselves as Hongkongers. Despite increasing influence of Chineseness on the Hong Kong identity, the people of Hong Kong have refused to forfeit their sui generis identity. Hong Kong people accumulate their sense of identity through mass media and practices in their daily lives, and Cantopop is one of the significant sources from which Hong Kong people find their sense of belonging. I will start with the possible sites of resistance for Cantopop in the new mediascape. Theodor Adorno's famous critique of the standardization and pseudo-individualization of popular music[12] is often used to appraise the quality of Cantopop, which has been cited as the major reason behind its fall. Adorno's point might be used to account for the operational logic of the popular music industry in Hong Kong, but it is necessary to dissociate the quality of Cantopop from the industry that produces it. The preceding chapters have demonstrated that despite being commercial products, Cantopop songs are not necessarily standardized commodities without cultural/social values. Furthermore, the audience might also have their own modes of listening to the products of the popular music industry,[13] and some songs also exhibit their own styles and oppositional potentials.[14] Given the special conditions of the Hong Kong market, not all popular music theories are applicable to Cantopop;[15] however, it is safe to say that it is still possible for the minority to make choices and articulate their

11. Ray Allen and Lois Wilcken, "Introduction," *Island Sounds in the Global City: Caribbean Popular Music and Identity in New York* (New York: New York Folklore Society, 1998), 2.

12. Theodor Adorno, "On Popular Music," in *On Record: Rock, Pop and the Written Word*, ed. Simon Frith and Andrew Goodwin (New York: Pantheon Books, 1990), 301–14.

13. Keith Negus, *Popular Music in Theory* (Hanover and London: Wesleyan University Press, 1996), 12–35.

14. Dick Hebdige, *Subculture: The Meaning of Style* (London: Methuen, 1979), in *Resistance through Rituals: Youth Subculture in Postwar Britain*, ed. Stuart Hall and Tony Jefferson (London: Hutchinson, 1976).

15. For example, David Riesman argued that there are two different kinds of audiences—majority and minority—and the latter have their own choices of popular music; David Riesman, "Listening to Popular Music," in Frith and Goodwin, *On Record*, 5–6. It must be noted that owing to the size of the Hong Kong market, the majority is notoriously dominant; for instance, unlike many other markets, rock is widely considered to be an alternative choice of the "minority."

feelings in the mainstream music industry with the limited space available,[16] which has the potential to become a kind of "meaning of style," to borrow the term from Dick Hebdige's theory of subculture.[17] However gloomy the Cantopop industry may appear to be, the "minority" is still there to resist the operational logic of not only the industry but also society at large. In the aftermath of the Severe Acute Respiratory Syndrome (SARS) in 2003, Sam Hui's "Keep on Smiling" and "2004 Blessings" rekindled Hong Kong people's hope and sense of belonging.

As discussed in the previous chapter, Cantopop also played an important role in the Umbrella Movement in 2014. Unlike what "Eiffel Tower above the Clouds" and "Below the Lion Rock" successfully highlighted three decades ago, "Lion Rock Spirit" evolved into "2.0" version: striving for human right and democracy. During the movement, a group of rock climbers who called themselves "The Hong Kong Spidie," hung a spectacular huge yellow banner—reading "I want real universal suffrage"—from the highest point of the Lion Rock on October 22, 2014. Known as the "regional anthem" of Hong Kong, "Below the Lion Rock" has been seen as being able to evoke the spirit of the "Hong Kong story." The group later released a video online to show how and why they hung the banner, using the legendary band Beyond's Cantorock "Under a Vast Sky," the unofficial theme song of the Occupy Central with Love and Peace movement, as the background music. Besides "Raise the Umbrella" mentioned in the previous chapter, there were also "umbrella songs" sung by young singer/group-songwriters, such as Michael Lai's 黎曉陽 "I promise you an Umbrella" 〈撐著〉 (lyrics by Yiu-Fai Chow) and New Youth Barbershop's 新青年理髮廳 "Blue Ribbon" 〈藍絲帶〉. This has spoken good volumes for the importance of Cantonese songs in articulating "Lion Rock Spirit 2.0" for the younger generation. Meanwhile, "Sail On" 〈同舟之情〉, the theme song of a "Hong Kong, Our Home" campaign launched by the government via the BrandHK platform in 2013 to boost a local sense of belonging, was the government's attempt to use "Below the Lion Rock" (part of which is incorporated into the new song) to inspire Hong Kong people. Unfortunately, "Sail On," which was seen as not being able to reflect the social reality, was not well received, as the overwhelming top-down national consciousness is something most Hong Kong people cannot fully accept. The song did catch the public's attention but for the wrong reasons. The lyricist, Abrahim Chan 陳詠謙, said in an interview that the original version, which focused more on conflicts, was "harmonized." Although he penned the "harmonized" version, he could not help blaming the government for being inept in trying to mask the conflicts

---

16. Negus, *Popular Music in Theory*, 13–14; Stuart Hall and Paddy Whannel, *The Popular Arts* (London: Hutchinson, 1964), 276.
17. Hebdige, *Subculture: The Meaning of Style*.

apparent in the Hong Kong society.[18] In short, Cantopop has been functioning as an important vehicle through which the people of Hong Kong articulate their identity in a bottom up manner.[19]

The emphasis should not be solely placed on the younger generation—usually considered the major component of the "minority" listeners—as they are traditionally seen as the main target audience by the Cantopop industry in Hong Kong. As argued by Gary Clarke, while subculture theories focus on the minority, the possible agency of the majority is glaringly neglected.[20] Regarding this, Iain Chambers's point is more pertinent to Cantopop: mainstream music industry products might be appropriated by the audience as a form of symbolic resistance.[21] In other words, the audience might appropriate popular music products, as suggested by Michel de Certeau, John Fiske, and Simon Frith, for their own everyday practice.[22] Stuart Hall's often cited theory of decoding can be borrowed here to generalize different kinds of audience reception: preferred, negotiated, and oppositional.[23] Having said this, it is also necessary to state that the agency of the audience should not be the sole concern. Lawrence Grossberg made it clear that while it is possible for the audience to create their own texts, the texts also create their own audiences.[24] The intervention into the operational logic of the music industry should not be de-emphasized. The globalization of the mediascape has brought the Cantopop industry into a very difficult situation, and this distinctive genre has to imagine a future at this particular juncture. To be brief, I have chosen to focus on three aspects: indies, new media, and research aura.

---

18. Hin-Leung Lo, "A Rising Star: An Interview with Abrahim Chan" 〈陳詠謙：填詞超新星〉(in Chinese), *Sing Tao Daily*, February 2, 2014, A10.

19. It has also to be noted that, as noted by singer-songwriter and left-wing activist Billy Bragg, protest music is no longer "an agent of change" as the relationship between music and activism has changed: "I think the idea from the 1960s that, if we all sang these songs together that the world will change, was really – it wasn't naïve, it was that it came from the fact that music was the only social medium available to people back then, so everything went through music." Bragg also blogged about the different situation in our time: "the notion you can change the world by singing songs can only serve to undermine activism." The role of the musician is to articulate what society thinks and feels: "We are a catalyst, but not an agent." Cited from Eleanor Peterson and Bonnie North, "Brit Singer Billy Bragg: Protest Music is 'Not an Agent' of Change," *NPR News in Milwaukee*, September 23, 2013: http://wuwm.com/post/brit-singer-billy-bragg-protest-music-not-agent-change#stream/0; retrieved on March 15, 2016.

20. Gary Clarke, "Defending Ski Jumpers: A Critique of Theories of Youth and Subcultures," in Frith and Goodwin, *On Record*, 68–80.

21. See Iain Chambers, *Urban Rhythms: Pop Music and Popular Culture* (London: Macmillan, 1985).

22. Michel de Certeau, *The Practice of Everyday Life* (Berkeley, Los Angeles, and London: University of California Press, 1984); John Fiske, *Understanding Popular Culture* (London and New York: Routledge, 1991); Simon Frith, *Sound Effects: Youth, Leisure and the Politics of Rock 'n' Roll* (New York: Pantheon, 1981).

23. Stuart Hall, "Encoding/Decoding," in *Culture, Media, Language: Working Papers in Cultural Studies 1972–1979* (London: Hutchinson, 1980), 128–38.

24. Lawrence Grossberg, *We Gotta Get out of This Place: Popular Conservatism and Postmodern Culture* (New York: Routledge, 1992), 41.

As noted in Chapter Six, despite the shrinking market of Cantopop, greener pastures have been available to indie labels since 2008. In a sense, these indie groups are "making do," to borrow Michel de Certeau's term, with a space that "without leaving the place where [they have] no choice but to live and where it lays down its law for [them], [they establish] within it a degree of plurality and creativity."[25] While mainstream popular music has an eye mainly on profits, underground and indie singers and groups continue to sing truth to power. Small independent companies, or indies, function as an effective resistance to the operational logic of the music industry. In the 1980s, for instance, the bands in Hong Kong, albeit not exclusively products of small independent companies, rocked the Cantopop industry with their indie spirit. Despite the fact that they were not able to radically change the operational logic of the music industry, they exerted a significant impact on the development of Cantopop in the 1990s. More importantly, small independent companies are more willing to experiment with new genres; for example, American small independent companies have triggered, among other styles, waves of rhythmic blues and salsa.[26] Back in the heyday of Cantopop, small independent companies sometimes functioned as talent scouts for the major labels. Some indie labels were even acquired by major labels to become their diffusion lines (such as the acquisition of Indie Era by Rock Records in 1996). It is wrong to assume that all indie music sings truth to power with high-quality songs. However, indies have contributed significant impacts on the development of the Cantopop industry over the past forty years. They will have a more important role to play in the years to come, thanks to the rise of new media and mainstream Cantopop's fall from popularity.

In recent years, alternative groups such as My Little Airport and Supper Moment have won acclaim not only in Hong Kong but also in the Mainland. While mainstream Cantopop has lost its role as a trendsetter in the idol business, in the indies arena Cantopop has the ability to take the lead thanks to the freedom of speech and information flow in Hong Kong, which is not available in many Chinese and/or Asian cities. The rise of new media has also made it easier for indie groups to disseminate their works to audiences. Kolor, among others, made good use of their online project "Law of 14" to reach their intended audience. The rise of new media has facilitated not only creative works but also music criticism. As noted in the Introduction, back in the 1980s, music criticism was scattered across newspaper and magazine columns. The number of these columns has fallen over the past two decades, and most of those remaining few can be said to be "bean curd" criticism—very short columns of only three to four hundred words. As argued by Chi-Wah Wong, who is

---

25. de Certeau, *The Practice of Everyday Life*, 30.
26. Negus, *Popular Music in Theory*, 42–43.

a veteran music columnist, "bean curd" music criticism has exerted negative impacts on Cantopop by (1) lowering the quality of the fans; (2) denying composers and lyricists feedback with which they can make improvements; and (3) souring the quality of music criticism.[27] This may sound dogmatic to many ears (whether the quality of the fans and music criticisms has declined or not needs to be further explored), but it is reasonable to think that decent criticism would provide the necessary impetus for singers, composers, lyricists, and even the record companies to improve, pushing them to produce more high-quality products. Hopefully, the rise of new media has provided more discursive space in which fans can voice their opinions, but it is also necessary to note that not all online music criticism is well researched. It is exactly in this regard that academic research can play a role. The study of Cantopop can be facilitated by enhancing the aura of criticism in the academia as well as in the public arena. Despite the rising popularity of interdisciplinary research in academia, Cantopop, which straddles various disciplines, including Chinese language and literature, cultural studies, music, communication, sociology, and the like, is still being glaringly neglected.

Regarding the development of the quality and diversity of Cantopop, cultural policy is also a relevant topic.[28] Debates on the thin line between cultural industries (seen by many as equivalent to the mass production of low-quality commodities) and creative industries have shown that the transformation of cultural industries into creative industries involves intricate processes.[29] As popular music, television, and film are often regarded as profit-making industries closer to mass communication than culture, they have rarely been discussed in relation to cultural policy in Hong Kong until recently. In fact, cultural industries should receive more critical attention precisely because they are popular. During the heyday of Hong Kong popular culture, however, there was no policy to facilitate the development of cultural industries. There was thus a lack of research on how cultural/media policies could be used to foster the development of the music industry. Hong Kong did not have a general plan for a cultural policy before 1997; in other words, it was a kind of "policy without a policy." It was arguably not until the Disney deal in 1999, when the government officially took an active part in creative industries, that Hong Kong's cultural policy formally waved goodbye to the libertarian championing of the

---

27. Chi-Wah Wong, "Random Thoughts on 'Bean-Curd' Music Criticism"〈「豆腐塊樂評」隨想〉(in Chinese), *CASH Flow* 26 (July 1998): 5–6.

28. For an account of how broadcasting policy has exerted an impact on Cantopop, see Yiu-Wai Chu, "Developing Local Popular Songs in Hong Kong: A Study of the 'All Cantonese Pop Music Station' Format," *Media International Australia Incorporating Culture and Policy* 105 (November 2002): 147–62.

29. See, for example, David Hesmondhalgh, *The Cultural Industries* (London: Sage, 2002) and Richard Caves, *Creative Industries: Contracts between Art and Commerce* (Cambridge: Harvard University Press, 2002).

market.[30] According to the document prepared by the Hong Kong Culture and Heritage Commission (already dissolved), the Hong Kong government was no longer beholden to a laissez-faire policy. Instead, it began trying to implement policies to develop local cultural industries. The Commission published a report on the future development of Hong Kong in 2002, in which music was one of the cultural industries being studied.[31] At almost the same time, the Hong Kong Central Policy Unit began a study on creative industries, trying to map the past and current developments of the creative industries in Hong Kong. All of these policies and studies show that the government planned to develop the popular music industry into a form of creative industry. But the problem was how to sketch these plans with a vision beyond proposals, such as asking the government "to take an active role in developing a suitable environment for local popular music, to elevate the standard of local music listeners and in the long run to establish a mechanism involving both the government and the industry to facilitate local music development."[32] In 2002, the Hong Kong Central Policy Unit launched a project on creative industries, with reference to a study in the United Kingdom, and popular music was one of the creative industries examined in the study. According to the report, in order to develop the music industry it was necessary to consolidate copyright laws, strengthen the structure of music production companies, enhance Hong Kong's "star-making effect," create and sustain local music talents, and develop the Mainland China market.[33] There were hardly any objections to these suggestions, but it seemed that the local cultural policy that promoted popular music activities and/or education programs was equal, if not more important, to the future of Cantopop.

Cantopop was once the trendiest music genre in Chinese communities across the globe. This book has offered a sweeping account of its rise and fall over the past sixty years or so. Back in the 1980s and 1990s, Cantopop could attract those who did not speak Cantonese. In less than twenty years, it was abandoned by its local fans. The 1990s was the best of times, and it was also the worst of times. After the Four Heavenly Kings and, arguably, Eason Chan, Hong Kong Cantopop lost its magic power to make stars, but both the record companies and the government insisted on sticking with the "heavenly-king" strategy to promote Cantopop. As the market shrunk, Cantopop lost its sense of diversity, which in turn caused more listeners to turn to other popular

---

30. See, for instance, Thomas Yun-Tong Luk, "Postcolonial Culture Policy in Hong Kong," *Media International Australia Incorporating Culture and Policy* 94 (February 2000): 154–55.

31. Hong Kong Culture and Heritage Commission, *Policy Recommendation Report* (Hong Kong: Culture and Heritage Commission Secretariat, 2003), 49.

32. Hong Kong Centre for Cultural Policy Research, *Baseline Study on Hong Kong's Creative Industries* (Hong Kong: Centre for Cultural Policy Research, the University of Hong Kong, 2003), 119.

33. Hong Kong Centre for Cultural Policy Research, *Baseline Study on Hong Kong's Creative Industries*, 116–18. Given the scope of this book, I will not go into detail here.

genres. As repeatedly argued in this chapter, one of the major problems facing the Hong Kong popular music industry is its lack of diversity.[34] In the heyday of Cantopop, as the market was considerably bigger, this problem seemed less serious. When the Cantopop market began to shrink in the mid-1990s, the problem surfaced and was subsequently aggravated. Hong Kong Cantopop was later dominated by young idols whose target audience was limited to teenagers, and audiences over the age of twenty had to look elsewhere for their favorite songs. As warned by music critics, because of its promotional packaging in recent years, Hong Kong's Cantopop audience base has shrunk further, and thus the problem of homogenization and standardization has become more and more serious. One example is the "formulaic, sappy karaoke love ballad" stereotype that has been firmly embedded in the minds of many fans, which has resulted in these fans turning to either other genres of popular songs or the golden hits of the good old days. In short, the loss of hybridity is the major reason behind the decline of the Hong Kong music industry. This was caused by both the rise of the economic, political, and cultural influence of Mandarin-speaking Mainland China and the Hong Kong music industry's incompetence in dealing with the shifts in the media landscape. Trapped in a vicious circle, the Cantopop industry failed to revitalize itself in a shrinking market, which made it unable to compete with other rising music industries such as K-Pop (Korean pop songs). As the Hong Kong popular music industry aged, the younger generation undoubtedly went elsewhere to find new trendy popular songs. By this time, it was too late for the record companies to realize that they could no longer rely wholly on the old success formulae. Although they were more willing to invest in alternative endeavors such as bands and singer-songwriters, the diminishing influence of Hong Kong popular culture at large made it difficult for Cantopop to lure the audience back. Moreover, without a broad fan base, it was also difficult for the Cantopop industry to make a sustained promotion of different music genres and styles.

The decline/demise of Cantopop has almost become a cliché since the late 1990s. In 2005, the popular *Southern Metropolis Daily* 《南方都市報》, published by the giant Southern Media Group based in Southern China, featured a special story on the decline of the Hong Kong popular music industry, rightly underscoring the fact that the main reason behind Cantopop's fall from grace was not illegal downloads but the lack of diversity—"It lost to itself."[35] As noted in the introduction, this book, aiming to show how the rise of Cantopop is

---

34. See, for instance, Yiu-Wai Chu, *A Study of the "Chinese Songs Campaign"* 《音樂敢言：香港「中文歌運動」研究》 (in Chinese) (Hong Kong: Infolink, 2001) and Yiu-Wai Chu, *A Study of the "Original Songs Campaign"* 《音樂敢言之二：香港「原創歌運動」研究》 (in Chinese) (Hong Kong: Bestever, 2004).

35. Yiu-Wai Chu, *Lyrics of Your Life* 《歲月如歌：詞話香港粵語流行曲》 (in Chinese) (Hong Kong: Joint Publishing, 2009), 8.

related to an upsurge of Hong Kong culture in general, is not only a concise history of Cantopop but also of Hong Kong. With the decline of Cantopop in the 1990s, Hong Kong culture in general has also been declining, as foregrounded in the title of my previous book *Lost in Transition*.[36] Hong Kong continued to be shaped as a commercial city after its reversion to China, and the four traditional key industries in Hong Kong, financial services, tourism, trading and logistics, and professional and producer services, remain to be the driving force of Hong Kong's economic growth.[37] Ironically enough, while cultural and creative industries are seen by the government as "emerging" industries, the Hong Kong Cantopop industry has been scarred by a waning growth in recent years. Owing to the changing mediascape in Asia, the regionalization of the music industry has turned Hong Kong into one important node, rather than a primary producer, and the same is happening in cinema and television as well. In a sense Cantonese pop music may be less popular, but the role of Hong Kong in cultural production in the Sinosphere may still be strong.[38] This is perfectly summed up by the Beijing-born diva Faye Wong, who moved back to her hometown after her phenomenal success in Hong Kong: "Beijing is my home. Hong Kong is the office."[39] Unless Hong Kong people are willing to take Hong Kong as their office, Hong Kong must diversify its economies and continue to be a site of cultural production. Borrowing the title of a Cantopop album by the local group C AllStar, *Cantopopsibility* is pertinent to the future of Cantopop. The lyrics of "A Fickle Love Song" 〈薄情歌〉, one of the main plugs in the album, penned by Wyman Wong, are a creative crossing of the themes of romantic love and the fate of Cantopop: "I had once expressed all the sad feelings on earth, turning tears into poetic ballads. But all of a sudden you don't care to appreciate me anymore." The crisis Cantopop has been facing over the past few years has more to do with the overall image of Cantopop and Hong Kong pop culture at large, and "the question is how to win back the lost love of the audience."[40] Whether the sunset can be turned into a new dawn, only history will be able to tell, but it is safe to conclude that Cantopop can only be revitalized by exploring different possibilities for the aging genre.

---

36. See the section "Lost in Transition: Hong Kong Is Not Hong Kong Any More?" in Chu, *Lost in Transition*, 15–17.
37. Census and Statistics Department, *The Four Key Industries and Other Selected Industries in the Hong Kong Economy* (Hong Kong: The Government of the Hong Kong Special Administrative Region, 2016).
38. I am indebted to an anonymous reviewer for this astute remark.
39. Cited from Anthony Fung and Michael Curtin, "The Anomalies of Being Faye (Wong): Gender Politics in Chinese Popular Music," *International Journal of Cultural Studies* 5, no. 3 (2002): 277.
40. Chi-Wah Wong, "Cantopop Disapproved by the Younger Generation," 〈粵語歌不獲新生代認同〉 (in Chinese), *Hong Kong Economic Journal* (November 5, 2013): LifeStyle Journal page.

Appendix
Chronology of Major Events[1]

1935

- "Lullaby" 〈兒安眠〉, a song from the movie *Lifeline* 《生命線》, is arguably the first Cantonese popular song.

1937

- "Triumph Song" 〈凱旋歌〉 and "Gut-Wrenching Lyrics" 〈斷腸詞〉, from the movie *Stories on Canton 3 Days Massacre in 1650* 《廣州三日屠城記》, are popular anti-Japanese invasion songs.

1941

- On Christmas Day, the British garrison in Hong Kong surrenders to the Japanese.

1942–1945

- During the three years and eight months of Japanese occupation, a special genre of "New Songs of Illusion" 幻景新歌, possibly the prototypes of Cantopop, is very popular in Hong Kong.
- Britain restores its control over Hong Kong on August 29, 1945, ending the Japanese occupation of Hong Kong, which lasted for three years and eight months.

---

1. The 1930s to the 1990s is based on Chi-Wah Wong's works in Chinese. Available at: http://blog. chinaunix.net/uid/20375883.html.

1947

- "Never Too Late to Come Home" 〈郎歸晚〉, theme song of the first Cantonese movie after the end of Japanese occupation, is released in January.

1948

- The government broadcaster GOW (renamed ZBW in 1929; Chinese channel ZEK established in 1934) is officially renamed Radio Hong Kong 香港廣播電台.

- Among the four theme songs in the first color production in the history of Hong Kong cinema, *Madame Butterfly* 《蝴蝶夫人》, "Sing and Dance" 〈載歌載舞〉 is especially very well received (later rewritten to become the Cantopop classic "Sigh of Bettors" 〈賭仔自嘆〉).

1949

- Radio Rediffusion 麗的呼聲 is established in Hong Kong and launches its programs on March 1, featuring the wired distribution of one English-language channel and one Chinese channel, with the addition of a further Chinese channel in 1956.

- The People's Republic of China is founded on October 1.

1951

- The highly popular Cantonese ditty "Blooming Beauty by the Silver Pond" 〈銀塘吐艷〉 (a.k.a. "Fragrant Water Lily" 〈荷花香〉 in the Cantonese opera movie *Hongling's Blood* (Alias: *Mysterious Murder*) 《紅菱血》 is released.

1952

- Harmony Records 和聲唱片 releases the first batch of albums (eights songs in four albums) that is packaged with the term "Cantopop" in Chinese on August 26.

- EMI opens its Hong Kong office.

1953

- Harmony Records continues to release "Cantopop" albums, and Chung Chow 周聰, Hung Lu 呂紅, and Kwan-Min Cheng 鄭君綿 are popular Cantopop singers.
- Rediffusion launches the first Cantopop radio program "Studio Dance Hall" 空中舞廳.

1954

- The movie *Belle of Penang* 《檳城艷》 premieres on March 11, featuring Yuet-Sang Wong's 王粵生 theme songs and musical scores with extensive use of Western musical arrangements.

1957

- The Cantonese opera *The Flower Princess* 《帝女花》 premieres in June. The ditty, extracted from the section "Fragrant Sacrifice" 〈香夭〉, becomes an all-time classic.

1958

- The movie *Two Fools in Hell* 《兩傻遊地獄》, featuring the early Cantopop classic "Teddy Boy in the Gutter" 〈飛哥跌落坑渠〉, a Cantonese version of "Three Coins in the Fountain," premieres on September 3.

1959

- Thanks to the rising popularity of song and dance, Cantonese movie songs such as Patricia Lam's 林鳳 "Young Rock" 〈青春樂〉 and "The Fragrance of Durians" 〈榴槤飄香〉 gradually broadens Cantopop's fan base.
- Commercial Radio begins its first broadcast on August 26.

1962

- Commercial Radio starts using theme songs to promote radio dramas in the early 1960s, and the theme song of the Commercial Radio drama *Love of Rose* 《薔薇之戀》 (in Cantonese) sung by Kitty Lam 林潔 (in Mandarin) is very popular.

1964

- The Beatles visit Hong Kong on June 8, generating an instant rock band wave in Hong Kong, and rock band music becomes the vogue of the time.

1965

- The local record company Diamond Music 鑽石 issues many band albums. Local bands (singing English songs) such as Lotus, Teddy Robin and the Playboys, Joe Junior and the Side Effects, Anders Nelson and The Inspiration, Mystics, D'Topnotes, and Kontinentals steal the limelight.

- Singaporean singer Low-Won Seong Koon's 上官流雲 "Walk Faster Please" 〈行快啲啦〉 and "Thinking of My Lovely Beauty" 〈一心想玉人〉, Cantonese cover versions of the Beatles' classics "Can't Buy Me Love" and "I Saw Her Standing There," respectively, trigger a rock wave in Hong Kong.

1966

- The movie *The Story between Hong Kong and Macao* 《一水隔天涯》 (literally "World of Water Apart" in Chinese) premieres on New Year's Day, and the title tune sung by Winnie Wei 韋秀嫺 is exceptionally well received.

- The title tune of the movie *Lady Bond* 《女殺手》 (premiered on August 1; starring Connie Chan 陳寶珠) becomes a Cantopop classic, and the teen musical *Colorful Youth* 《彩色青春》 (premiered on August 17; starring Connie Chan and Josephine Siao 蕭芳芳) sets the trend of the decade.

1967

- Large-scale riots erupt on May 6 and escalate in the second half of the year.

- Television Broadcasts Limited (TVB) 無線電視 is established on November 19.

1968

- Joseph Koo 顧嘉煇 and James Wong 黃霑 start writing songs for movies; examples include Koo's works in *A Time for Reunion* (Alias: *Auld Lang*

Syne)《春曉人歸時》(in Mandarin) and Wong's works in *The Blossoming Rose* (Alias: *The Forsaken Love*)《青春玫瑰》(in Cantonese).

1969

- Taiwanese singers generate a heated wave of Mandapop in Hong Kong; Yao Surong's 姚蘇蓉 "I'm Not Going Home Today"〈今天不回家〉, among others, becomes a huge hit.

1971

- *The Hui Brothers Show*《雙星報喜》, hosted by Michael Hui 許冠文 and Sam Hui 許冠傑, premieres on TVB on April 23.
- Sam Hui releases his first album, *Time of the Season* (in English).
- In the midst of the heated wave of Taiwanese Mandapop, there are also very popular Cantopop hits, such as "Sound of the Bell at the Zen Temple"〈禪院鍾聲〉and "Tears of Love"〈相思淚〉by Singaporean singers Kam-Cheong Cheng (Kim-Chong Tay) 鄭錦昌 and Lisa Wong 麗莎, respectively.

1972

- Joseph Koo writes the first TVB theme song for the drama *Star River*《星河》(sung by Judi Jim 詹小屏 in Mandarin).
- Sam Hui performs his first Cantopop hit, "Eiffel Tower above the Clouds"〈鐵塔凌雲〉(original title: "Here and Now"〈就此模樣〉), on *The Hui Brothers Show* on April 14.

1973

- TVB launches the Jade Theatre 翡翠劇場 series with *Romance in the Rain*《煙雨濛濛》on March 19, which is the first TV drama featuring a Cantopop theme song sung by Adam Cheng 鄭少秋.
- The TVB-inspired movie *The House of 72 Tenants*《七十二家房客》premieres on September 22 and breaks the box-office record set by the legendary Bruce Lee 李小龍, paving the way for the later comeback of Cantonese movies.
- Hong Kong economy experiences a major recession owing to the oil crisis and the stock market crash.

- Radio Rediffusion, granted a free-to-air broadcasting license on April 6, is renamed Rediffusion Television Limited (RTV) 麗的電視.

1974

- TVB releases the drama *A Love Tale between Tears and Smiles* 《啼笑因緣》 in the *Chinese Folklores* 《民間傳奇》 series on March 11, and the Cantopop theme song sung by Sandra Lang 仙杜拉 is so popular that it effectively changes the image of Cantopop among Hong Kong fans.

- Joseph Koo wins the "Hong Kong Popular Song Contest" organized by TVB on September 21, with the song "Shau Ha Ha" 〈笑哈哈〉 (sung by Sandra Lang in English and Mandarin), and the first runner-up is James Wong's "L-O-V-E Love" (sung by The Wynners 溫拿樂隊 in English).

- Michael Hui and Sam Hui's Cantonese movie *Games Gamblers Play* 《鬼馬雙星》 premieres on October 17, and the theme songs by Sam Hui trigger a tidal wave of Cantopop.

1975

- In August, Radio Television Hong Kong (RTHK) launches a new program entitled *New World* 新天地 (later renamed *Chinese Pop Chart* 中文歌曲龍虎榜, a weekly top chart for Chinese—de facto Cantonese—songs in 1976) to broadcast Cantonese songs on Channel 2, the popular music channel.

- Commercial Television (CTV) 佳藝電視 goes on air on September 7, becoming the third free-to-air broadcast television station in Hong Kong.

- Chelsia Chan 陳秋霞 wins the "Hong Kong Popular Song Contest" held on September 28 with her English song "Dark Side of Your Mind."

- The Wynners sing their first Cantopop songs in the movie *Let's Rock* 《大家樂》 directed by James Wong (premiered on December 24).

1976

- TVB spends a handsome budget on *The Book and the Sword* 《書劍恩仇錄》 (premiered on June 28). The two versions of the title tune by Adam Cheng and Roman Tam 羅文 set a new trend of *wuxia* (martial arts hero) theme songs.

- In the movie *Jumping Ash* 《跳灰》 (premiered on August 26), which is generally considered a pioneering work that sets the scene for the later New Wave Cinema, there are two very popular Cantopop songs, "A Real Man" 〈大丈夫〉 and "Ask Me" 〈問我〉.

- The theme song of TVB's Jade Theatre drama *The Hotel* (Alias: *Raging Tide*) 《狂潮》 (written by Joseph Koo and James Wong) premieres on November 1 and pioneers a new style of Cantopop.

- Michael Hui and Sam Hui's *The Private Eyes* 《半斤八兩》 premieres on December 16 and breaks the box office record for Hong Kong cinema. The movie and the theme songs bring Sam Hui's career to new heights.

1977

- The International Federation of Phonographic Industry Hong Kong (IFPIHK) hosts the first Gold Disc Award Presentation on March 26.

- Leslie Cheung 張國榮 attains first runner-up at the Asian Music Contest held by RTV on May 9.

- The title tune of TVB's *A House Is Not a Home* 《家變》 (premiered on August 1), sung by Roman Tam, surpasses "Raging Tide" in terms of popularity.

- The Composers and Authors Society of Hong Kong Limited (CASH) starts operating on October 1.

1978

- A series of TVB's Jade Theatre theme songs written by Joseph Koo and James Wong, including "Vanity Fair" 〈大亨〉 (sung by Paula Tsui 徐小鳳), "The Giant" 〈強人〉 (sung by Roman Tam), and "Conflict" 〈奮鬥〉 (sung by Jenny Tseng 甄妮), take the craze of Cantopop TV songs one step further.

- CTV shuts down on August 22.

- The founding Hong Kong New Wave film, Ho Yim's 嚴浩 *The Extra* 《茄喱啡》 features the Cantopop theme song "An Extra in Life" 〈人生小配角〉, sung by Michael Kwan 關正傑. A creative synergy is subsequently created between Cantopop and Hong Kong New Wave.

- The Wynners unofficially disbands after the movie *Making It* 《追趕跑跳碰》, and members pursue solo careers.

- George Lam 林子祥, who has been focusing on English popular songs, releases his first Cantopop album, *Money Trip* 《各師各法》.

1979

- "Below the Lion Rock" 〈獅子山下〉, the unofficial regional anthem of Hong Kong, is released in January.
- The First RTHK Top 10 Gold Songs Awards (1978) is held on February 20.
- Sam Hui becomes the first Hong Kong singer to participate in the Tokyo Music Festival on June 17. The song he sings, "You Let Me Shine" 〈你令我閃耀〉, is bilingual—Cantonese and English.
- Alan Tam 譚詠麟 releases his debut solo Cantopop album *Porky's* 《反斗星》 in February.
- Leslie Cheung turns to Cantopop with *Lover's Arrow* 《情人箭》 in September. Meanwhile, Danny Chan 陳百強 releases his debut Cantopop album *First Love/Tears for You* 《初戀／眼淚為你流》 in December, raising the curtain on the era of Cantopop idols in the 1980s.

1980

- The TVB theme song "The Bund" 〈上海灘〉, sung by Frances Yip 葉麗儀, generates a huge wave across Chinese communities, including the Mainland, which just adopted the Open Door Policy, after the drama premieres on March 10.
- The Queen Elizabeth Stadium, with a seating capacity of 3,500, becomes the largest venue for concerts in Hong Kong after it opens on August 27.
- The new campaign "Raising a Thousand Sails" 千帆並舉展繽紛 launched by RTV on September 1 is a successful, albeit short-lived, challenge to the leading role of TVB. It changes the landscape of TV theme songs.

1981

- Television theme songs no longer dominate the Cantopop industry: only three of the RTHK Top 10 Gold Songs in 1981 are from television dramas.
- Folk song concerts and contests are very popular, and the Academic Community Hall becomes the cradle of folk singers.

- Alan Tam, while based in Taiwan, continues to release Cantopop albums. His *Can't Forget You* 《忘不了您》 (released on August 13) establishes a sound basis for his Cantopop career.

- TVB launches the music show *Jade Solid Gold* 《勁歌金曲》 on October 10.

- The Amateur Lyric Writers' Association of Hong Kong 香港業餘填詞人協會 is founded in December.

1982

- Joseph Koo is presented the first Highest Honour Award at the Fourth RTHK Top 10 Gold Songs Awards (1981).

- James Wong and Jimmy Lo 盧國沾 win the first-ever Best Melody Award and Best Lyrics Award at the Fourth RTHK Top 10 Gold Songs Awards (1981) with "Forget Him" 〈忘記他〉 and "Unable to Find an Excuse" 〈找不着藉口〉, respectively.

- Anita Mui 梅艷芳 wins the First New Talent Singing Awards 新秀歌唱大賽 organized by TVB on July 18.

- On September 22, soon after then British Prime Minister Margaret Thatcher slips on the stairs in front of the People's Hall in Beijing, the Hong Kong economy also falls sharply.

- Capital Artists 華星唱片, a TVB subsidiary founded in 1971, establishes its records department.

1983

- The inauguration of the Hong Kong Coliseum, a multipurpose indoor arena originally designed for sport activities, on April 27, provides a perfect venue for Cantopop concerts.

- Sam Hui holds the first concerts at Hong Kong Coliseum in May.

- Anita Mui's first solo album, *Crimson Anita Mui* 《赤色梅艷芳》, records a five-times platinum disc sales volume as per Hong Kong standard.

- Jimmy Lo initiates a "Non-Love Songs" campaign to promote more subject matter besides romantic love.

1984

- TVB hosts the First Jade Solid Gold (JSG) Music Awards Presentation (1983) on January 28.

- The competition between Alan Tam and Leslie Cheung brings sales volumes and the influence of Cantopop to new heights.

- Jacky Cheung 張學友 wins the 18 Districts Amateur Singing Competition held on September 1.

- In response to Jimmy Lo's "Non-Love Songs" campaign, RTHK organizes a "Non-Love Lyrics Writing Contest." The winner, Lin Xi 林夕 (a.k.a. Albert Leung 梁偉文), later becomes one of the leading lyricists in Hong Kong for more than thirty years.

- The Sino-British Joint Declaration is signed on December 19, according to which Hong Kong will be reverted to China in 1997.

1985

- Tickets for Cantopop concerts held at Hong Kong Coliseum sell like hot cakes. New records are set throughout the year.

- Tom Lee Music, a local musical instrument company, collaborates with Carlsberg to launch the Carlsberg Pop Music Festival, which later generates a band wave that sweeps the territory in the late 1980s.

- Danny Summer 夏韶聲 wins the First "Asia-Pacific Popular Song Contest" organized by the Asia-Pacific Broadcasting Union on August 10 with the song "Empty Chair"〈空凳〉(melody by Violet Lam 林敏怡 and lyrics by Richard Lam 林振強).

- Asia Television (ATV; formerly RTV) organizes the First Future Idol Contest 未來偶像爭霸戰 to emulate TVB's New Talent Singing Awards.

- The CD format becomes popular in Hong Kong, which helps boost the sales of Cantopop albums.

1986

- TVB sets up a JSG pop chart on February 1, which becomes one of the indexes of the popularity of Cantopop singers and songs.

- The fierce competition between Alan Tam and Leslie Cheung continues. While the number of Gold Song Awards won by Alan Tam is greater,

Leslie Cheung wins the TVB Gold Song Gold Award (given to the most popular song of the year) with "Who Feels the Same?" 〈有誰共鳴〉.

- Band music becomes a new trend as Beyond, Tai-chi 太極, and Tat Ming Pair 達明一派 enter the mainstream.

- According to Chi-Wah Wong 黃志華, local Chinese record companies, such as Crown Records 娛樂唱片, are taken over by international labels owing to their outdated operation.

1987

- The legendary rock band Beyond signs with Cinepoly 新藝寶 and releases their first mainstream debut EP *Waiting Forever* 《永遠等待》 in January (their first cassette *Goodbye Ideals* 《再見理想》, released in 1986, was self-financed).

- RTHK increases the number of songs on its pop chart from ten to fifteen, a sign of the growing number of Cantopop songs.

- RTHK organizes the band show "Fly High with Bands" on May 17, after which the band wave gradually recedes.

- Cantopop concerts continue to be highly profitable. Paula Tsui and Anita Mui set new records of twenty-two and twenty-eight shows at Hong Kong Coliseum, respectively.

1988

- Alan Tam announces at the Tenth RTHK Top 10 Gold Songs Awards Ceremony (1987) held on February 13 that he has decided not to receive any awards involving competition from then on.

- Sally Yeh's 葉蒨文 "Blessing" 〈祝福〉, a cover version of a Taiwanese song, becomes the most popular song of the year, an extraordinary achievement as the industry is dominated by Alan Tam, Leslie Cheung, and Anita Mui.

- TVB increases the number of new plugs from four to seven per week, showing that the number of Cantopop songs continues to grow.

- Winnie Yu 俞錚, invited to return to Commercial Radio as general manager, declares on February 1 that CR2 will become an "All Chinese Pop Music Station" beginning March 21.

- ATV turns its Future Idol Contest into a trans-region competition to include participants from Guangzhou and Macau.

1989

- Commercial Radio holds the First Ultimate Song Chart Awards Presentation (1988) on January 16.

- "Concert for Democracy in China" 「民主歌聲獻中華」 is held at Happy Valley on May 27 to support the student democratic movement in Beijing, which is later cracked down on June 4.

- Alan Tam sets a new record of thirty-eight shows at Hong Kong Coliseum, which began on July 31.

- On September 17, Leslie Cheung announces his very early retirement from the music industry at the summit of his career and popularity after his *Final Encounter* album and thirty-three farewell concerts at the Hong Kong Coliseum.

- The CASH organizes the First CASH Popular Song Writing Contest in December, and the winner is "The Flow of Time" 〈光陰流轉〉 (sung by Kit-Man Mak 麥潔文, melody by Ching-Yue Wong 王正宇, and lyrics by Keith Chan 陳少琪).

1990

- RTHK presents the "Top Ten Hong Kong Entertainers in the 1980s" on March 10, and five of the awardees are Cantopop singers: Alan Tam, Leslie Cheung, Anita Mui, Paula Tsui, and Liza Wang 汪明荃. In addition, Jackie Chan 成龍 and Yun-Fat Chow also release Cantopop albums.

- Anita Mui announces on October 7 that she will no longer receive any music awards.

- Tat Ming Pair disbands after the album *Nerve* 《神經》, signaling the end of the band wave.

- More and more Taiwanese singers, such as Jeremy Chang 張洪量, Harlem Yu 庾澄慶, and Sky Wu 伍思凱, test the waters of the Hong Kong market.

- Andy Lau 劉德華 signs with the new record company In-Co Music Publishing Ltd. 寶藝星, a joint venture of PolyGram 寶麗金 and Entertainment Impact 藝能娛樂, and releases two chartbusting Cantopop albums, *Would It Be Possible?* 《可不可以》 and *Goodbye* 《再會了》.

1991

- Jacky Cheung releases his career-defining album *Uncontrolled Passion* 《情不禁》 in January, which includes his all-time classic "Love You More and More Each Day" 〈每天愛你多一些〉.

- Music Factory 音樂工廠, led by Luo Dayou 羅大佑, arrives in Hong Kong from Taiwan, and their pioneering work "Queen's Road East" 〈皇后大道東〉 is very well received by Hong Kong people.

- Metro Broadcast Corporation Limited 新城電台, founded on July 1, begins broadcasting on August 12.

- The career of Leon Lai 黎明 gathers momentum with big hits such as "Sorry, I Love You" 〈對不起我愛你〉 and "Will You Come Tonight?" 〈今夜你會不會來〉.

- Sandy Lam 林憶蓮 shines in *Wild Flowers* 《野花》 (released in December), with a transformation toward a more-than-mainstream image.

- The age of compact discs begins as local record companies stop producing vinyl discs.

1992

- Anita Mui completes her farewell concerts "Anita Mui Final Concert" in January.

- Aaron Kwok 郭富城 moves his base back to Hong Kong from Taiwan and releases his debut Cantopop album *Dance Endlessly, Love Endlessly, Sing Endlessly* 《跳不完・愛不完・唱不完》 in February.

- Sam Hui holds his farewell concerts, beginning on March 18 in Hong Kong and ending in a US-Canada tour in September.

- Danny Chan goes into a coma on May 19 and passes away on October 25, 1993.

- "Four Heavenly Kings" 四大天王 is coined at the RTHK summer event "Solar Project" to name the four male artists—Andy Lau, Jacky Cheung, Leon Lai, and Aaron Kwok—who are dominating the Cantopop scene.

- California Red 加州紅 opens the first karaoke venue, with a computerized song selection system, in Wan Chai, marking a new era of the karaoke industry.

1993

- Winnie Yu publicly crowns Jacky Cheung the new "God of Cantopop" at TVB's JSG Music Awards Presentation in January.

- Jacky Cheung's album *Goodbye Kiss* 《吻別》, selling almost five million copies around the world, conquers the swiftly growing Mandapop market.

- Ka-Kui Wong 黃家駒, the soul of Beyond, passes away on June 30 after a stage accident during the recording of a Fuji Television game show in Tokyo.

- Cable TV enters into service with eight channels on October 31.

- Commercial Radio launches "Ultimate Global Chinese Pop Chart" 「叱咤全球華語歌曲排行榜」, an indicator of the rising popularity of Mandapop.

1994

- Faye Wong releases *Random Thoughts* 《胡思亂想》, in which she uses—for the first time—her Chinese name "Fei Wang" 王菲 instead of the Hong Kong–styled "Ching-Man Wong" 王靖雯.

- Jacky Cheung is named the most popular singer in Asia at the US Billboard Music Awards.

- Hutchison Telecom rolls out a new large-scale advertising campaign with Leon Lai as the leading character. The title song "Thinking of You Every Day"〈那有一天不想你〉generates a new wave of Cantopop-commercial crossovers.

- Alan Tam holds concerts at the Hong Kong Stadium, reopened with an increased seating capacity of 40,000, from April 22 to 24. Owing to noise complaints, subsequent restrictions on noise levels render the venue unsuitable for concerts.

1995

- Commercial Radio initiates a campaign that only original songs can be aired on CR2 beginning March 21.

- The legendary Teresa Teng 鄧麗君 dies on May 8 from a severe asthma attack during her holiday in Chiang Mai.

- Leslie Cheung makes a comeback and releases the album *Beloved* 《寵愛》 on July 7.

- Faye Wong releases her last Cantopop (with the exception of one song in Mandarin) album, *Di-Dar*, in December, and thereafter she records mainly in her native Mandarin.

- The four major broadcasters jointly present four pop music awards: Best Album, Best Song, Outstanding Performance, and Media Grand Award.

1996

- Cass Phang 彭羚 reaches the apex of her career with two Most Popular Female Singer awards (TVB and CR2) won in January.

- In its October 14 issue, *Time* magazine dubs Faye Wong a songbird, joining "the chorus of women heard around the world."

- Leslie Cheung's androgynous style shines in the album *Red* 《紅》, released in November. "Grieving Man" 〈怨男〉, among others, showcases a man's unique beauty.

- Eason Chan 陳奕迅 releases his debut Cantopop album *Eason Chan* 《陳奕迅》.

1997

- Aaron Kwok becomes the first Chinese pop singer to sign with a global promotion project—Pepsi Cola.

- Jacky Cheung plays a leading role in Hong Kong's first modern musical, *Snow Wolf Lake* 《雪狼湖》, with over 100 performances around the world.

- Hong Kong is reverted to China on July 1.

- Andy Lau's Mandapop "Chinese" 〈中國人〉 is arguably the most remarkable composition to come out of the 1997 handover.

1998

- Leon Lai's Korean song "After Loving You" reaches top 10 on Korean pop charts, the first time a Hong Kong singer has managed to achieve this.

- PolyGram is acquired by Universal Music 環球唱片.

- Cantopop stars go global in transnational projects, such as Andy Lau's joining forces with saxophonist Kenny G in "You're My Woman" 〈妳是

我的女人〉and Sammi Cheng's collaboration with All 4 One in "I Cross My Heart."

- LMF (a.k.a. Lazy Mutha Fucka), a hip-hop group, forms by merging underground bands Anodize, Screw, and N.T., and local hip-hop star DJ Tommy.

- Cantopop sales drop from HK$1.853 billion in 1995 to HK$0.916 billion in 1998.

1999

- *Billboard* publishes an essay entitled "The Cantopop Drop" in its February 27 issue, advertising the fact that the golden days of Cantopop has passed.

- Leon Lai announces at his concert on December 12 that he will no longer accept music awards in Hong Kong.

- Aaron Kwok works with Janet Jackson, singing the Chinese version of the song written by Janet Jackson for Pepsi—"Ask for More" 〈渴望無限〉.

- The three remaining members of Beyond announce that they will stop working together after their December concert, signaling the end of a glorious era.

- Emperor Entertainment Group (EEG) 英皇娛樂 is established in September.

- The era of portable MP3s for music listening begins in Hong Kong.

2000

- Sammi Cheng's 鄭秀文 "Episode" 〈插曲〉wins the JSG Gold Song Gold Award (1999) on January 16, becoming the second female singer to receive this prize in the decade of the Four Heavenly Kings (the first was Sally Yeh in 1990).

- Kelly Chen 陳慧琳 is crowned a Heavenly Queen with the JSG Most Popular Female Singer Award (1999).

- Andy Lau enters the Guinness World Records for "Most Awards Won by a Cantopop Male Artist," with 292 awards throughout his singing career by April.

- Karen Mok 莫文蔚 wins the Most Popular Female Singer of the Year at the China Music Chart Awards.

- People Mountain People Sea 人山人海, a music production company established by Anthony Yiu-Ming Wong 黃耀明 with a team of artists and musicians on June 16, 1999, releases its first album, *Washing Machine Emergency Button* 《入洗衣機緊急掣》.

2001

- Eason Chan wins Commercial Radio's Ultimate Best Male Singer Gold Award. From 2001 to 2013, he has won this title a remarkable ten times.
- Miriam Yeung 楊千嬅 wins the JSG Gold Song Gold Award (2000) held on January 14 with "A Maiden's Prayer" 〈少女的祈禱〉, firmly establishing her status as a new Heavenly Queen.
- Joey Yung 容祖兒 turns into a Heavenly Queen with the tremendous success of albums such as *Solemn on Stage* 《隆重登場》.
- Charlene Choi 蔡卓妍 and Gillian Chung 鍾欣桐 form Twins in the summer.

2002

- Andy Hui 許志安 wins the JSG Most Popular Male Singer Award (2001) held on January 13, signaling the end of the Four Heavenly Kings decade.
- Hacken Lee 李克勤 holds five "comeback" concerts at the Hong Kong Coliseum in February to signal the (re)birth of a Cantopop King.
- Twins hold their first Hong Kong Coliseum concerts in September, and Charlene Choi becomes the youngest singer at 19 to hold a concert in the temple of Cantopop.
- Roman Tam dies on October 18 after an extended battle with liver cancer.

2003

- Hong Kong is badly hit by Severe Acute Respiratory Syndrome (SARS) from March to May.
- Leslie Cheung jumps to his death from the twenty-fourth floor of the Mandarin Oriental Hotel on April 1.
- James Wong obtains his PhD in May, with his thesis, "The Rise and Decline of Cantopop: A Study of Hong Kong Popular Music (1949–1997)" 《粵語流行曲的發展與興衰：香港流行音樂研究 1949–1997》 (in Chinese).
- Cancer robs the lyric master Richard Lam of his life on November 16.

- Cancer-stricken Anita Mui passes away on December 30.

- LMF disbands after the album *Finalazy* to strive for further developments in different fields.

2004

- Sam Hui stages a total of thirty-eight quickly sold-out "Keep on Smiling" comeback concerts at the Hong Kong Coliseum from May to August.

- James Wong dies of lung cancer on November 24.

- Gold Typhoon Group 金牌大風, incorporating Paco Wong's 黃柏高 Gold Label Entertainment in 2003, starts operating its digital music business in Greater China.

- Tat Ming Pair reunites to celebrate their twentieth anniversary, with four shows at the Hong Kong Coliseum in December.

2005

- The first edition of Entertainment Expo Hong Kong is held in March, with Hong Kong Music Fair being the key event for popular music.

- Candy Lo 盧巧音 releases a truly avant-garde concept album entitled *Evolution Theory* 《天演論》 in July, but her popularity fades after this.

- The comeback concerts phenomenon continues—Paula Tsui, Sally Yeh, Sandy Lam, and George Lam, among others, stage their comeback concerts at the Hong Kong Coliseum.

- A number of singer-songwriters come onto the scene, giving fresh but short-lived impetus to the industry.

2006

- According to figures of the Hong Kong Heritage Museum, record sales drop from HK$17 billion in 1997 to HK$0.56 billion in 2006.

- In February, Joey Yung, widely known as the Karaoke Queen, releases her album, *Ten Most Wanted*, in which she tries to broaden her music style.

- Denise Ho 何韻詩 is baptized into stardom with her first Hong Kong Coliseum concerts held in October.

- With an eye toward making new stars, EEG and TVB collaborate in the launch of the new Entertainment Channel 英皇娛樂台 on December 11 (which shuts down in December 2009).

2007

- Kay Tse 謝安琪 releases *The First Day* after signing with Cinepoly in January, bringing her fame from indie circles to the mainstream.

- The first local large-scale Cantopop exhibition "Riding a Melodic Tide: The Development of Cantopop in Hong Kong" is jointly held by the Leisure and Cultural Services Department, the Hong Kong Heritage Museum, Radio Television Hong Kong, and the School of Journalism and Communication at the Chinese University of Hong Kong from March to August.

2008

- Leo Ku 古巨基 wins the first of his JSG Most Popular Male Singer Awards (between 2008 and 2011).

- The album *Binary* released in July turns Kay Tse into a household name. Among other hits, "Wedding Card Street" 〈囍帖街〉 truly stands out as the song of the year.

- Major labels such as Universal Music, Gold Typhoon, and BMA Records formally absorb band music into their marketing plans (e.g., Universal Music's Mr. and Gold Typhoon's RubberBand).

2009

- Denise Ho decides to take a temporary leave from Hong Kong to tour in Taiwan and the Mainland to rekindle her music passion.

- TVB has a row with Hong Kong Recording Industry Alliance Limited (HKRIA) over copyright fees. Unable to resolve the dispute, TVB decides to ban singers in the four big companies—Universal, Warner, Sony, and EMI—from their programs.

- ATV and TVB launch the music talent programs "ATV-Asian Millionstar" 亞洲星光大道 and "The Voice" 超級巨聲 in July, respectively.

2010

- Hacken Lee becomes the only Cantopop singer to win music awards in four different decades—from the 1980s to the 2010s.

- In February, the local band Kolor launches their innovative project "Law of 14"—uploading a song onto the Internet for free listening every month on the 14th—which is an example of using new media to disseminate Cantopop.

2011

- Jacky Cheung's record-setting "1/2 Century Tour" runs from December 30, 2010 to December 29, 2011, with 105 live concerts in sixty-one cities around the world.

- The Seventh Entertainment Expo Hong Kong features the Asian Pop Music Festival in March.

- Digital Broadcasting Corporation Hong Kong 香港數碼電台 (DBC, formerly Wave Media Limited 雄濤廣播) begins to air in August.

2012

- Softhard 軟硬天師 and Grasshoppers 草蜢 stage twelve full-house shows at the Hong Kong Coliseum, a sign of the extension of the comeback phenomenon into the 2010s.

- Ivana Wong 王菀之 holds her debut "Water Lily" concerts at the Hong Kong Coliseum in October, making her one of the very few singer-songwriters to enter the Cantopop shrine.

2013

- At TVB's JSG Music Awards Presentation (2012) held on January 13, the Most Popular Male Singer in the Asia-Pacific Region Award goes to the Taiwanese group Lollipop 棒棒堂, the first time in twenty years that the title has been awarded to a non-Cantopop unit.

- The TVB-HKRIA dispute is settled in January, but damage has been done.

2014

- Hong Kong singers started going north to join Mainland hit reality shows and singing competitions after G.E.M. Tang's 鄧紫棋 success in Hunan Television's *I Am a Singer 2*.

- The song "Raise the Umbrella" 〈撐起雨傘〉, sung by Denise Ho, Anthony Yiu-Ming Wong, and other pop singers, becomes the anthem of the Umbrella Movement, which begins as the mass movement "Occupy Central With Love and Peace" to fight for genuine universal suffrage.

2015

- In the aftermath of the Umbrella Movement, singers such as Anthony Yiu-Ming Wong and Denise Ho, who have taken a high-profile stance in support of the movement, shift from the mainstream to the independent music scene.

Selected Bibliography

Abbas, Ackbar. *Hong Kong: Culture and the Politics of Disappearance*. Hong Kong: Hong Kong University Press, 1997.

Ashcroft, Bill, Gareth Griffiths, and Helen Tiffin. *Key Concepts in Post-Colonial Studies*. London: Routledge, 1998.

Baker, Hugh. "Life in the Cities: The Emergence of Hong Kong Man." *The China Quarterly* 95 (September 1983): 469–79.

Baranovitch, Nimrod. *China's New Voices: Popular Music, Ethnicity, Gender and Politics, 1978–1997*. Berkeley and Los Angeles: University of California Press, 2003.

Bennett, Tony, Colin Mercer, and Janet Woollacott, eds. *Popular Culture and Social Relations*. Milton Keynes: Open University Press, 1986.

Bhabha, Homi. *The Location of Culture*. New York and London: Routledge, 1994.

Brackett, David. *Interpreting Popular Music*. Berkeley, Los Angeles, and London: University of California Press, 2000.

Brown, Judith M., and Rosemary Foot, eds. *Hong Kong's Transitions, 1942–1997*. Basingstoke: Macmillan Press, 1997.

Campbell, Jonathan. *Red Rock: The Long, Strange March of Chinese Rock & Roll*. Hong Kong: Earnshaw Books, 2011.

Canclini, Néstor García. *Hybrid Cultures: Strategies for Entering and Leaving Modernity*. Minneapolis: University of Minneapolis Press, 1995.

Carroll, John. *A Concise History of Hong Kong*. Lanham: Rowman & Littlefield, 2007.

Caves, Richard. *Creative Industries: Contracts between Art and Commerce*. Cambridge: Harvard University Press, 2002.

Centre for Cultural Policy Research. *Baseline Study on Hong Kong's Creative Industries*. Hong Kong: Centre for Cultural Policy Research, the University of Hong Kong, 2003.

Chambers, Iain. *Urban Rhythms: Pop Music and Popular Culture*. London: Macmillan, 1985.

Chan, Sau-Yan 陳守仁, and Sai-Shing Yung 容世誠. "Hong Kong Cantopop in the 1950s and the 1960s" 〈五、六十年代香港的粵語流行曲〉 (in Chinese). *Wide Angle Monthly* (February 1990): 74–77.

Chan, Stephen C. K., ed. 陳清僑編. *The Practice of Affect: A Study of Hong Kong Popular Lyrics* 《情感的實踐：香港流行歌詞研究》 (in Chinese). Hong Kong: Oxford University Press, 1997.

Cheuk, Pak-Tong. *Hong Kong New Wave Cinema (1978–2000)*. Chicago: Intellect Books, 2008.

Choi, JungBong, and Roald Maliangkay, eds. *K-Pop: The International Rise of the Korean Music Industry*. Abingdon, Oxon: Routledge, 2015.

Chow, Rey. *Ethics after Idealism*. Bloomington: Indiana University Press, 1998.

———. *Not Like a Native Speaker: On Languaging as a Postcolonial Experience*. New York: Columbia University Press, 2014.

———. *Writing Diaspora: Tactics of Intervention in Contemporary Cultural Studies*. Indianapolis and Bloomington: Indiana University Press, 1993.

Chow, Yiu-Fai, and Jeroen de Kloet. *Sonic Multiplicities: Hong Kong Pop and the Global Circulation of Sound and Image*. Bristol and Chicago: Intellect, 2013.

Christenson, Peter G., and Donald F. Roberts. *It's Not Only Rock & Roll: Popular Music in the Lives of Adolescents*. Cresskill, NJ: Hampton Press, 1987.

Chu, Yiu-Wai 朱耀偉. *Age of Glory: A Study of Hong Kong Popular Bands/Groups 1985–1990* 《光輝歲月：香港流行樂隊／組合研究》 (in Chinese). Hong Kong: Infolink, 2000.

———. "Can Cantopop Industry Be Creative? The Transmission and Transformation of Hong Kong Popular Songs." In *Chinese Culture: Transmission and Transformation*, edited by Wang-Chi Wong, Yuen-Sang Leung, and Ping-Leung Law, 443–75. Hong Kong: Chinese University Press, 2009.

———. "Developing Local Popular Songs in Hong Kong: A Study of the 'All Cantonese Pop Music Station'." *Media International Australia Incorporating Culture & Policy* 105 (2002): 147–62.

———. "The Importance of Being Free: Fu©Kin Music as Alternative Pop Music Production." *Inter-Asia Cultural Studies* 12, no. 1 (2011): 62–76.

——— *Interpreting Popular Lyrics* 《詞中物：香港流行歌詞探賞》 (in Chinese). Hong Kong: Joint Publishing, 2007.

———. *Lost in Transition: Hong Kong Culture in the Age of China*. Albany: SUNY Press, 2013.

———. *Songs of Your Life: Talks on Hong Kong Cantopop* 《歲月如歌：詞話香港粵語流行曲》 (in Chinese). Hong Kong: Joint Publishing, 2009.

———. *A Study of Hong Kong Popular Lyrics: From the Mid 70s to the Mid 90s* 《香港流行歌詞研究：七十年代中期至九十年代中期》 (in Chinese). Hong Kong: Joint Publishing, 1998.

———. *A Study of the "Chinese Songs Campaign" in Hong Kong* 《音樂敢言：香港「中文歌運動」研究》 (in Chinese). Hong Kong: Infolink, 2001.

———. *A Study of the "Original Songs Campaign" in Hong Kong* 《音樂敢言之二：香港「原創歌運動」研究》 (in Chinese). Hong Kong: Bestever, 2004.

———. "The Transformation of Local Identity in Hong Kong Cantopop." *Perfect Beat: The Pacific Journal of Research into Contemporary Music and Popular Culture* 7, no. 4 (2006): 32–51.

Chu, Yiu-Wai, and Eve Leung. "Remapping Hong Kong Popular Music: Covers, Localisation and the Waning Hybridity of Cantopop." *Popular Music* 32, no. 1 (2013): 65–78.

Chu, Yiu-Wai, and Wai-Sze Leung 梁偉詩. *A Study of Post-1997 Cantopop Lyrics* 《後九七香港流行歌詞研究》 (in Chinese). Hong Kong: Enlighten & Fish, 2011.

Chu, Yiu-Wai, and Eva K. W. Man, eds. *Contemporary Asian Modernities: Transnationality, Interculturality and Hybridity*. Bern: Peter Lang, 2010.

Chun, Allen, Ned Rossiter, and Brian Shoesmith, eds. *Refashioning Pop Music in Asia: Cosmopolitan Flows, Political Tempos, and Aesthetic Industries*. London: Routledge, 2004.

Cooper, Lee. *Popular Music Perspectives: Ideas, Themes and Patterns in Contemporary Lyrics*. Bowling Green, OH: Bowling Green State University Popular Press, 1991.

Cultural Policy Studies Centre of the University of Hong Kong. *Baseline Study on Hong Kong's Creative Industries*. Hong Kong: Central Policy Unit, the Government of Hong Kong Special Administrative Region, 2003.

de Certeau, Michel. *The Practice of Everyday Life*. Berkeley, Los Angeles, London: University of California Press, 1984.

De Kloet, Jeroen. *China with a Cut: Globalisation, Urban Youth and Popular Music*. Amsterdam: Amsterdam University Press, 2010.

Eighth Hong Kong International Film Festival, The, ed. 第八屆香港國際電影節編. *A Study of Hong Kong Cinema in the Seventies*《七十年代香港電影研究》 (in Chinese). Hong Kong: Urban Council of Hong Kong, 1984.

Ferguson, Priscilla. "A Cultural Field in the Making: Gastronomy in 19th Century France." *American Journal of Sociology* 104, no. 3 (1998): 597–641.

Fiske, John. *Understanding Popular Culture*. London and New York: Routledge, 1991.

Fitzsimmons, Lorna, and John A. Lent, eds. *Asian Popular Culture in Transition*. New York: Routledge, 2013.

Frith, Simon. *Performing Rites: On the Value of Popular Music*. Cambridge: Harvard University Press, 1998.

———. *The Sociology of Rock*. London: Constable, 1978.

———. *Sound Effects: Youth, Leisure and the Politics of Rock 'n' Roll*. London: Pantheon, 1982.

Frith, Simon, Will Straw, and John Street, eds. *The Cambridge Companion to Pop and Rock*. Cambridge: Cambridge University Press, 2001.

Fu, Poshek, "The 1960s: Modernity, Youth Culture and Hong Kong Cantonese Cinema." In *The Cinema of Hong Kong: History, Arts, Identity*, edited by Poshek Fu and David Desser, 71–89. Cambridge: Cambridge University Press, 2000.

Fung, Anthony 馮應謙. "The Emerging (National) Popular Music Culture in China." *Inter-Asian Cultural Studies* 8, no. 3 (2007): 425–37.

———. *Hong Kong Popular Music Culture: A Reader in Cultural Studies*《香港流行音樂文化：文化研究讀本》 (in Chinese). Hong Kong: Wheatear, 2004.

———. *Riding a Melodic Tide: The Development of Cantopop in Hong Kong*《歌潮・汐韻・香港粵語流行曲的發展》 (in Chinese). Hong Kong: Subculture Press, 2009.

———. "Western Style, Chinese Pop: Jay Chou's Rap and Hip-Hop in China." *Asian Music* 39, no. 1 (2008): 69–90.

Fung, Anthony, and Michael Curtin. "The Anomalies of Being Faye (Wong): Gender Politics in Chinese Popular Music." *International Journal of Cultural Studies* 5, no. 3 (2002): 263–90.

Fung, Anthony, and Shen Si 沈思. *Melodic Memories: History of the Development of Hong Kong Music Industry*《悠揚・憶記：香港音樂工業發展史》 (in Chinese). Hong Kong: Subculture Press, 2012.

Fung, Lai-Chi 馮禮慈. *On the Small Path: The Steps of Hong Kong Alternative Music*《小路上：香港另類音樂的腳步》 (in Chinese). Hong Kong: Music Communication, 1996.

Funnell, Lisa. *Warrior Women: Gender, Race, and the Transnational Chinese Action Star*. Albany: SUNY Press, 2014.

Garafalo, Reebee, ed. *Rocking the Boat: Mass Music and Mass Movements*. Boston: South End, 1992.

Groenewegen, Jeroen. *Tongue: Making Sense of Underground Rock, Beijing 1997–2004*. New York: Lambert Academic Publishing, 2011.

Grossberg, Lawrence. *Dancing in Spite of Myself: Essays on Popular Culture*. Durham and London: Duke University Press, 1997.

———. *We Gotta Get out of This Place: Popular Conservatism and Postmodern Culture*. New York: Routledge, 1992.

Hebdige, Dick. *Subculture: The Meaning of Style*. London: Methuen, 1979.

Hesmondhalgh, David. *The Cultural Industries*. London: Sage, 2002.

———. *Why Music Matters*. Chichester: Wiley Blackwell, 2013.

Hesmondhalgh, David, and Keith Negus, eds. *Popular Music Studies*. London: Arnold, 2002.

Ho, Wai-Chung. "Between Globalisation and Localisation: A Study of Hong Kong Popular Music." *Popular Music* 22, no. 2 (2003): 143–57.

Holt, Fabian. *Genre in Popular Music*. Chicago and London: University of Chicago Press, 2007.

Hong Kong Heritage Museum. *Hong Kong's Popular Entertainment*. Hong Kong: Hong Kong Heritage Museum, 2006.

Hong Kong Policy Viewers. *Popular Culture under Hegemony: A Study of Hong Kong "Gold" Songs* 《霸權主義下的流行文化：剖析中文金曲的內容及意義研究》 (in Chinese). Hong Kong: Policy Viewers, 1994.

Jones, Andrew. *Like a Knife: Ideology and Genre in Contemporary Chinese Popular Music*. Ithaca: Cornell University East Asia Program, 1992.

———. *Yellow Music: Media Culture and Colonial Modernity in the Chinese Jazz Age*. Durham: Duke University Press, 2001.

Khun, Eng Kuah, and Gilles Guiheux, eds. *Social Movements in China and Hong Kong: The Expansion of Protest Space*. Amsterdam: Amsterdam University Press, 2009.

Kraidy, Marwan. *Hybridity, or the Cultural Logic of Globalization*. Philadelphia: Temple University Press, 2005.

Lau, Siu-Kai. *Hongkongese or Chinese: The Problem of Identity on the Eve of Resumption of Chinese Sovereignty over Hong Kong*. Hong Kong: Hong Kong Institute of Asia-Pacific Studies, the Chinese University of Hong Kong, 1997.

Lee, Gregory. *Troubadours, Trumpeters, Troubled Makers: Lyricism, Nationalism, and Hybridity in China and Its Others*. Durham: Duke University Press, 1996.

Lee, Joanna C. Y. "Cantopop Songs on Emigration from Hong Kong." *Yearbook for Traditional Music* 24 (1992): 14–23.

Lena, Jennifer. *Banding Together: How Communities Create Genres in Popular Music*. Princeton: Princeton University Press, 2012.

Leppert, Richard, and Susan McClary, eds. *Music and Society*. Cambridge: Cambridge University Press, 1987.

Leung, Helen Hok-Sze. *Undercurrents: Queer Culture and Postcolonial Hong Kong*. Vancouver and Toronto: UBC Press, 2008.

Leung, Ping-Kwan 梁秉鈞, ed. *Hong Kong Popular Culture* 《香港的流行文化》 (in Chinese). Hong Kong: Joint Publishing, 1993.

———. *Ye Si's 1950s: Essays on Hong Kong Literature and Culture* 《也斯的五〇年代：香港文學與文化論集》 (in Chinese). Hong Kong: Chung Hwa, 2013.

Leung, Wing-Fai. *Multimedia Stardom in Hong Kong: Image, Performance and Identity*. Abingdon, Oxon and New York: Routledge, 2015.

Liu, Ching-Chih 劉靖之. *History of Hong Kong Music* 《香港音樂史論》 (in Chinese). Hong Kong: Commercial Press, 2014.

Lo, Kwai-Cheung 羅貴祥, and Eva Man 文潔華, eds. *An Age of Hybridity: Cultural Identity, Gender, Everyday Life Practice and Hong Kong Cinema of the 1970s* 《雜嘜時代文化身份、性別、日常生活實踐與香港電影 1970s》 (in Chinese). Hong Kong: Oxford University Press, 2005.

Lo, Kwok Chim Jimmy 盧國沾. *Behind Lyrics* 《歌詞的背後》 (in Chinese). Hong Kong: Kwan Lam, 1988.

Lok, Fung 洛楓 (a.k.a. Natalia Sui-Hung Chan). *Butterfly of Forbidden Colors: The Artistic Image of Leslie Cheung* 《禁色的蝴蝶：張國榮的藝術形象》 (in Chinese). Hong Kong: Joint Publishing, 2008.

———. *Fin de Siècle City: Hong Kong Popular Culture* 《世紀末城市：香港的流行文化》 (in Chinese). Hong Kong: Oxford University Press, 1995.

Lui, Tai-Lok. *Hong Kong's 1970s* 《那似曾相識的七十年代》 (in Chinese). Hong Kong: Chung Hwa, 2012.

Ma, Eric Kit-Wai. *Culture, Politics and Television in Hong Kong*. London: Routledge, 1999.

———. "Emotional Energies and Subcultural Politics: Alternative Bands in Post-97 Hong Kong." *Inter-Asia Cultural Studies* 3, no. 2 (2002): 187–200.

Ma, Eric, ed. 馬傑偉編. *Selling LMF* 《出賣 LMF》 (in Chinese). Hong Kong: Ming Cheung, 2001.

Mathews, Gordon. "Heunggongyahn: On the Past, Present, and Future of Hong Kong Identity." *Bulletin of Concerned Asian Scholars* 29, no. 3 (July–September 1997): 10–11.

Mathews, Gordon, and Tai-Lok Lui, eds. *Consuming Hong Kong*. Hong Kong: Hong Kong University Press, 2001.

Mathews, Gordon, Eric Kit-Wai Ma, and Tai-Lok Lui. *Hong Kong, China: Learning to Belong to a Nation*. Abingdon and New York: Routledge, 2008.

Middleton, Richard. *Studying Popular Music*. Buckingham: Open University Press, 1990.

Mitchell, Tony. *Popular Music and Local Identity*. London: Leicester University Press, 1996.

Moskowitz, Marc. *Cries of Joy, Songs of Sorrow: Chinese Pop Music and Its Cultural Connotations*. Honolulu: University of Hawai'i Press, 2010.

Negus, Keith. *Music Genres and Corporate Cultures*. London and New York: Routledge, 1999.

———. *Popular Music in Theory: An Introduction*. Hanover and London: Wesleyan University Press, 1996.

Ng, Chun-Hung 吳俊雄. *Here and Now: Sam Hui* 《此時此處：許冠傑》 (in Chinese). Hong Kong: Enrich Publishing, 2007.

Ng, Ho 吳昊. *Talks on the History of Hong Kong Television* 《香港電視史話》 (in Chinese). Hong Kong: Subculture Press, 2003.

Ng, Janet. *Paradigm City: Space, Culture, and Capitalism in Hong Kong*. Albany: SUNY Press, 2009.

Niederhauser, Matthew. *Sound Kapital: Beijing's Music Underground*. New York: powerHouse Books, 2009.

Pennington, Martha. *Forces Shaping a Dual Code Society: An Interpretive Review of the Literature on Language Use and Language Attitudes in Hong Kong*. Hong Kong: City Polytechnic of Hong Kong, 1994.

Pieterse, Jan Nederveen. "Hybridity, So What? The Anti-Hybridity Backlash and the Riddles of Recognition." *Theory, Culture & Society* 18, nos. 2–3 (2001): 219–45.

Radio and Television of Hong Kong Ten Gold Songs Committee, ed. 香港電台十大金曲委員會編. *Reference Guide for Collectors of Hong Kong Cantopop Albums* 《香港粵語唱片收藏指南》. Hong Kong: Joint Publishing, 1998.

Research Institute for Hong Kong Policy. *The Hong Kong Culture and Arts Policy Review*. Hong Kong: Research Institute for Hong Kong Policy, 1998.

Robinson, Deanna, Elizabeth Buck, and Marlene Cuthbert. *Music at the Margins: Popular Music and Global Cultural Diversity*. Newbury Park, London, and Delhi: Sage, 1991.

Rojek, Chris. *Pop Music, Pop Culture*. Cambridge and Malden: Polity, 2011.

Shepherd, John, and Peter Wicke. *Music and Cultural Theory*. Cambridge: Polity, 1997.

Shin, Hyunjoon, Yoshitaka Môri, and Tunghung Ho, eds. "Special Issue: East Asian Popular Music and Its (Dis)contents." *Popular Music* 32, no. 1 (2013): 1–5.

Shuker, Roy. *Popular Music: The Key Concepts*. Second edition. Abingdon and New York: Routledge, 2005.

———. *Understanding Popular Music Culture*. Third edition. London and New York: Routledge, 2008.

Sinn, Elizabeth 冼玉儀, ed. *Hong Kong Culture and Society* 《香港文化與社會》 (in Chinese). Hong Kong: Centre of Asian Studies, the University of Hong Kong, 1995.

Siu, Helen, and Agnes Ku, eds. *Hong Kong Mobile: Making a Global Population*. Hong Kong: Hong Kong University Press, 2009.

Steen, Andreas. *Between Entertainment and Revolution: Gramophones, Records and the Beginning of the Shanghai Music Industry, 1878–1937* 《在娛樂與革命之間：留聲機唱片和上海音樂工業的初期，1878–1937》 (in Chinese). Shanghai: Shanghai Lexicographical Publishing House, 2015.

Tam, Alan 譚詠麟. *The 40th Anniversary of Alan Tam's Entertainment Career* 《譚詠麟走過的銀河歲月》 (in Chinese). Hong Kong: Joint Publishing, 2015.

Taylor, Timothy Dean. *Global Pop: World Music, World Markets*. New York and London: Routledge, 1997.

Turner, Matthew, and Irene Ngan, eds. *Hong Kong Sixties: Designing Identity*. Hong Kong: Hong Kong Arts Centre, 1995.

Wicke, Peter. *Rock Music: Culture, Aesthetics and Sociology*. Cambridge: Cambridge University Press, 1990.

Witzleben, Lawrence. "Cantopop and Mandapop in Pre-postcolonial Hong Kong: Identity Negotiation in the Performances of Anita Mui Yim-Fong." *Popular Music* 18, no. 2 (1999): 241–58.

Wong, Chi-Chung Elvin 黃志淙. *Flowing Melody* 《流聲》 (in Chinese). Hong Kong: Civil Affairs Bureau, 2007.

Wong, Chi-Wah 黃志華. *Early Hong Kong Cantopop* 《早期香港粵語流行曲》 (in Chinese). Hong Kong: Joint Publishing, 2000.

———. *Forgotten Treasures: The Chinese-Style Melodies in Hong Kong Popular Songs* 《被遺忘的瑰寶：香港流行曲裡的中國風格旋律》 (in Chinese). Hong Kong: Jim and Hall Publication, 2005.

———. *Forty Years of Cantopop* 《粵語流行曲四十年》 (in Chinese). Hong Kong: Joint Publishing, 1990.

———. *Hong Kong Lyricists and Lyric Talks* 《香港詞人詞話》 (in Chinese). Hong Kong: Joint Publishing, 2003.

———. *Lu Wen-Cheng, Cantonese Opera and Cantopop* 《呂文成與粵曲、粵語流行曲》 (in Chinese). Hong Kong: Joint Publishing, 2012.

———. *Master of Melodies and Lyrics: A Study of the Works of Wu Man Sam* 《曲詞雙絕：胡文森作品研究》 (in Chinese). Hong Kong: Joint Publishing, 2008.

———. *Pioneers: Popular Songs Composed by Cantonese Opera Writers* 《原創先鋒：粵曲人的流行曲調創作》 (in Chinese). Hong Kong: Joint Publishing, 2014.

———. *Selected Lyric Criticisms by Jimmy Lo* 《盧國沾詞評選》 (in Chinese). Hong Kong: Joint Publishing, 2015.

———. *Taking Music Seriously* 《正視音樂》 (in Chinese). Hong Kong: No Frills, 1996.

Wong, Chi-Wah, and Yiu-Wai Chu. *Eighty Talks on Hong Kong Popular Lyrics* 《香港歌詞八十談》 (in Chinese). Hong Kong: Infolink, 2011.

———. *Guided Interpretation of Hong Kong Popular Lyrics* 《香港流行歌詞導賞》 (in Chinese). Hong Kong: Infolink, 2009.

Wong, Chi-Wah, Yiu-Wai Chu, and Wai-Sze Leung. *The Way of Hong Kong Lyricists* 《詞家有道：香港16詞人訪談錄》 (in Chinese). Hong Kong: Infolink, 2010.

Wong, Chi-Wai 黃志華. "Hong Kong Cantopop Industry under the Domination of Transnational Music Companies" 《跨國唱片公司壟斷下的香港粵語流行樂壇》 (in Chinese). Hong Kong: MPhil thesis, the Chinese University of Hong Kong, 1991.

Wong, Jum-Sum 黃湛森 (a.k.a. James Wong). *Lyrics Writing of Cantopop* 《粵語流行曲的歌詞創作》 (in Chinese). Hong Kong: Centre for Literature and Translation Studies of Lingnan University, 1997.

———. "The Rise and Decline of Cantopop : A Study of Hong Kong Popular Music (1949–1997)" 〈粵語流行曲的發展與興衰：香港流行音樂研究 1949–1997〉 (in Chinese). Hong Kong: PhD thesis, the University of Hong Kong, 2003.

Wong, Kei-Chi 黃奇智. *History of Popular Songs* 《時代曲的流光歲月》 (in Chinese). Hong Kong: Joint Publishing, 2000.

———. *On Popular Songs* 《時代曲綜論》 (in Chinese). Hong Kong: School of Continuing Studies, the Chinese University of Hong Kong, 1979.

Yang, Hon-Lun Helan 楊漢倫. *Introduction to Cantonese Pop* 《粵語流行曲導論》 (in Chinese). Hong Kong: Education Bureau, 2009.

Yang, Hon-Lun, and Siu-Wah Yu 余少華. *Reading Cantonese Songs: The Voice of Hong Kong through Vicissitudes* 《粵語歌曲解讀：蛻變中的香港聲音》 (in Chinese). Hong Kong: Infolink, 2013.

Yau, Ching, ed. *As Normal As Possible: Negotiating Sexuality and Gender in Mainland China and Hong Kong*. Hong Kong: Hong Kong University Press, 2010.

Yau, Kinnia Shuk-Ting. *Japanese and Hong Kong Film Industries: Understanding the Origins of East Asian Film Networks*. New York: Routledge, 2010.

Yu, Audrey, and Olivia Khoo, eds. *Sinophone Cinemas*. New York: Palgrave Macmillan, 2014.

Yu, Siu-Wah 余少華. *Out of Chaos and Coincidence: Hong Kong Music Culture* 《樂在顛錯中：香港雅俗音樂文化》 (in Chinese). Hong Kong: Oxford University Press, 2001.

Yung, Sai-Shing 容世誠. *Sounds of Cantonese Tunes: Record Industry and the Art of Cantonese Songs 1903–1953* 《粵韻留聲：唱片工業與廣東曲藝 1903–1953》 (in Chinese). Hong Kong: Cosmos Books, 2006.

Index